NEW DIRECTIONS IN SOUTHERN HISTORY

SERIES EDITORS
Peter S. Carmichael, *West Virginia University*
Michele Gillespie, *Wake Forest University*
William A. Link, *University of Florida*

Bluecoats and Tar Heels:
Soldiers and Civilians in Reconstruction North Carolina
Mark L. Bradley

Becoming Bourgeois: Merchant Culture in the South, 1820–1865
Frank J. Byrne

Lum and Abner: Rural America and the Golden Age of Radio
Randal L. Hall

Entangled by White Supremacy:
Reform in World War I–era South Carolina
Janet G. Hudson

The View from the Ground: Experiences of Civil War Soldiers
edited by Aaron Sheehan-Dean

Southern Farmers and Their Stories:
Memory and Meaning in Oral History
Melissa Walker

The Lost State of Franklin

America's First Secession

Kevin T. Barksdale

THE UNIVERSITY PRESS OF KENTUCKY

Scholarly publisher for the Commonwealth,
serving Bellarmine University, Berea College, Centre
College of Kentucky, Eastern Kentucky University,
The Filson Historical Society, Georgetown College,
Kentucky Historical Society, Kentucky State University,
Morehead State University, Murray State University,
Northern Kentucky University, Transylvania University,
University of Kentucky, University of Louisville,
and Western Kentucky University.

Editorial and Sales Offices: The University Press of Kentucky
663 South Limestone Street, Lexington, Kentucky 40508-4008
www.kentuckypress.com

13 12 11 10 09   1 2 3 4 5

Library of Congress Cataloging-in-Publication Data

Barksdale, Kevin T., 1973–
The lost state of Franklin : America's first secession / Kevin T. Barksdale.
    p. cm. — (New directions in southern history)
Includes bibliographical references and index.
ISBN 978-0-8131-2521-3 (hardcover : alk. paper)
1. Franklin (State)—History. 2. Tennessee River Valley—History.
3. Social conflict—Tennessee River Valley—History. 4. Tennessee River
Valley—Social conditions. 5. Tennessee River Valley—Politics and
government. 6. Secession—Tennessee River Valley—History.
7. Secession—United States—Case studies. I. Title.
F436.B268 2008
976.8'03—dc22

                                            2008036154

This book is printed on acid-free recycled paper meeting
the requirements of the American National Standard
for Permanence in Paper for Printed Library Materials.

Manufactured in the United States of America.

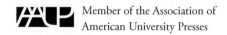
Member of the Association of
American University Presses

For Joseph Thompson Barksdale Sr.

Contents

Preface

I first became aware of the state of Franklin nearly a decade ago, while pursuing my master's degree at Western Carolina University in Cullowhee, North Carolina. Cryptic passing references often appeared in books, articles, and lectures, but the Franklin statehood movement remained obscured by the maddening complexity and confusion surrounding the event. Very few historians actually identified the underlying causes, participants, or results of the separatist movement, and it was nearly impossible to locate even a precise geographical definition of the boundaries of the "lost" state. Perhaps it was this cloud of obscurity that inspired my own fascination with the subject, but I gradually became more and more intrigued by the state of Franklin and the Franklinites. What was this long forgotten statehood movement? Why did it fail? Who were the leaders of the movement? These essential questions continued to spark my historical fascination and ultimately propelled this project forward.

By the time I arrived at West Virginia University in the fall of 2000 to pursue my doctoral degree, I had committed myself to writing my dissertation on the state of Franklin. As I began to study the history of America's early national period, I became transfixed by the political disquietude and socioeconomic turmoil precipitated by the American Revolution. The Revolutionary War unleashed a wave of bubbling social tensions previously submerged under the weight of British colonial rule and a decade of revolution. As politically marginalized and economically exploited groups of "new Americans" agitated for their share of the fruits of the American Revolution, postbellum America erupted in spasms of violence and political unrest. From Daniel Shay's rebelling Massachusetts yeoman farmers to trans-Appalachia's Whiskey Rebels, expressions of fierce backcountry localism and agrarian radicalism threatened to plunge America into its own Revolt of the Vendee.

Against this historical backdrop of political chaos and social unrest, the backcountry leaders of the Tennessee Valley initiated their effort to establish America's fourteenth state. As I gradually sifted through the materials relating to the state of Franklin, written primarily by admirers of both the movement and the state's only governor, John Sevier, I began to believe that the Tennessee Valley separatist movement emanated from the same ideological strains and reflected admirable goals similar to the other expressions of postrevolutionary frontier radicalism. I embraced the image of the Franklinites as noble adherents to the principles of the American Revolution and their movement as a grassroots expression of backcountry egalitarianism and passion for self-governance. Pennsylvanians had their Whiskey Rebels. North and South Carolinians had their Regulators. New Englanders had their Shaysites. So it seemed only natural for Tennesseans to have their Franklinites.

Of course, the deeper I delved into the primary source materials related to the state of Franklin, the less this romantic (and naïve) image of the movement and its leaders resembled historical reality. Many scholars who have chronicled the statehood movement refer to Franklin as the "lost state," and in many ways this project represents my effort to rediscover it and the statehood movement's far-reaching consequences for the new American Republic and Appalachia's Amerindian and Euroamerican residents.

As with many first historical monographs, this project began as my doctoral dissertation and could not have been completed without the support, encouragement, and compassion of a number of individuals, institutions, and organizations. My fascination with the Appalachian frontier began at Western Carolina University, where I had the pleasure of studying and working with several wonderful historians. They include Curtis W. Wood, H. Tyler Blethen, George Frizzell, and William L. Anderson. My time in the Cullowhee Valley remains one of the most magical periods of my life. I am also deeply indebted for the tremendous support I received from the faculty and my fellow graduate students at West Virginia University. They include Elizabeth A. Fones-Wolf, Mary Lou Lustig, A. Michal McMahon, Steven M. Zdatny, Tim Konhaus, Jennifer Egolf, and Elizabeth Oliver-Lee.

In many ways I am the product of these two universities, and this book represents not only my own struggle to become a historian, but also the struggles of the professors who worked so hard and gave so much to allow me the opportunity to participate in life's amazing historical conversation. I want to express my most heartfelt gratitude to Ronald L. Lewis, Ken Fones-Wolf, and Peter S. Carmichael for their inspiration and guidance on my quest to become a historian, and I am eternally grateful.

This project would not have been possible without the support of Marshall University and my friends and colleagues in the Department of History. I also want to thank East Tennessee State University archivist Ned L. Irwin for his gracious encouragement of this study and for compiling an exhaustive and invaluable bibliography related to the state of Franklin. Additionally, I want to express my thanks to the universities, organizations, and library/archival staffs that gave so freely of their time and resources to make this project possible. These include: West Virginia University (West Virginia Collection), Marshall University (Special Collections), East Tennessee State University (Archives of Appalachia), Western Carolina University (Special Collections), University of Tennessee (Special Collections and Archives), Tennessee State Library and Archives, University of North Carolina Manuscripts Department at the Wilson Library (Southern Historical Collection), North Carolina State Archives, Appalachian State University (W. L. Eury Appalachian Collection), East Tennessee Historical Society (McClung Historical Collection), and the Tipton-Haynes Historical Site.

I am fortunate to have the love and support of several wonderful families. I want to thank the Barksdale, Howell, Tjovaras, and McFerrin families for their kindness and encouragement. I also want to thank my "animal family" (Clyde, Otis, and Floyd) for their companionship and humor. Finally, to Kelli, this book is as much yours as it is mine. You have given me the confidence to see this project to its conclusion.

Doss Hill, West Virginia

The Lost State of Franklin

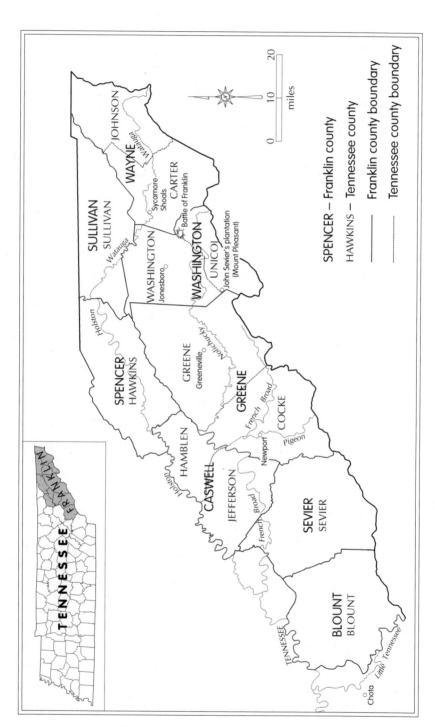

Boundaries and counties of historic Franklin and present-day Tennessee (map by Dick Gilbreath)

Introduction

Footstool of Liberty's Throne

Hero-Making versus Historiography

Yes, give me the land that hath legends and lays
That tell of the memories of long-vanished days.
Yes, give me the land that hath story and song
To tell of the strife of the right with the wrong;
Yes, give me the land with a grave in each spot
And names in the graves that shall not be forgot.
. . . .
And the graves of the dead, with the grass overgrown,
May yet form the footstool Of Liberty's throne.

—Father Abram J. Ryan,
　　from *Poems: Patriotic, Religious, Miscellaneous*

In the winter of 1784, an ambitious coalition of Tennessee Valley leading men and their small-holder supporters defiantly declared their independence from the state of North Carolina and formed the sovereign state of Franklin.[1] Over the next four years, the Franklinites crafted a backcountry bureaucracy aimed at defending their Tennessee Valley communities and their contested trans-Appalachian land claims, advancing their regional market economy and landholdings, eradicating the southwestern frontier's Native American inhabitants, and ultimately winning support for Franklin's admission into the union as America's fourteenth state. The Franklin statehood movement unleashed a cataclysmic wave of partisan violence and Indian warfare that left hundreds dead and the Tennessee Valley communities reeling from the devastation of political discord and backcountry bloodshed. The Franklin separatist movement resulted in the emergence of a tenacious faction of Anti-Franklinites, whose efforts to derail the statehood movement led to the polarization of the once unified trans-Appalachian communities. Despite the diplomatic efforts of the Franklinites, the statehood movement failed to garner political support from outside of the region and ultimately succumbed to external political pressure and intestine factionalism.

From its inception, the Franklin separatist movement evoked passionate responses from inside and outside of the Tennessee Valley, and the partisan tensions that emerged during the state's chaotic four-year existence persisted long after the movement's collapse and the passing of the participants in the Franklin affair. During the two hundred years of historical scrutiny, two diametrically opposed interpretations of the Franklin statehood movement and its leadership developed. After the state's violent disintegration in 1788, descendents and celebrants of the Franklinites recast the historical legacy and meaning of the trans-Appalachian separatist movement. Local historians, romance novelists, ambitious politicians, and regional business leaders defended the image of Franklin as a patriotic extension of the American Revolution and the Franklinites as virtuous adherents to the republican principles of self-determination and popular sovereignty. Throughout the twentieth century, historians repeatedly challenged this romanticized vision of Franklin's murky past and identified the often sordid maneuverings of the state's political leadership.

In an address delivered to the Historical Society of Washington County, Tennessee, in the early 1940s, the Honorable E. Munsey Slack described the state of Franklin as a "vision that was magnificent, a dream that illuminates history, a hope that stirs ambition and thrills men to this day!"[2] Slack's depiction of the Franklin separatist movement built upon the efforts of the Franklinites and their supporters to fashion an image that simultaneously connected their state to the glory and nobility of the American Revolution and distanced it from the economic motivations and internal factionalism tainting their statehood movement. In 1932, University of Virginia history professor Thomas Perkins Abernethy penned a scathing economic interpretation of the development of the Tennessee frontier, entitled *From Frontier to Plantation in Tennessee*. Against the backdrop of the Great Depression and the birth of "New Deal liberalism," Abernethy emphasized the central role land speculators played in the organization of Tennessee, and harshly condemned the consequences of their monopolization of land and corruption of regional politics on the unsuspecting yeoman farmers of the Tennessee Valley.[3] In his chapter on the state of Franklin, Abernethy argued that two powerful cabals of land speculators instigated the separatist movement in order to increase their personal landed wealth. As to the revolutionary sprit of the Franklinites, he stated, "There was nothing revolutionary in the minds of the men who had started out to establish this State of Franklin." Abernethy castigated previous Franklin defenders who "have heretofore treated the Franklin movement as a serious rebellion—the cry of the West for freedom."[4] Slack's laudation and Abernethy's condemnation reflected decades of misunderstanding, mythologizing, and distorting America's first postrevolutionary statehood effort in the trans-Allegheny frontier. These two divergent historical versions of Franklin evince the polarizing effect of the statehood movement on the residents and chroniclers of the Tennessee Valley. This study seeks to find Franklin's historical middle ground and reveal the complex, chaotic, and often tragic historical reality behind the backcountry movement to create America's first trans-Appalachian state.

The disparity between the popular perception and the historiography relating to the state of Franklin originated with the bitter political partisanship that fermented within the Tennessee Valley communities during the earliest days of the movement. The historical battle waged in print, oration, museum displays, and on granite memorials to recount and define the motivation and legacy of Franklin stands as a testament to the emotions the movement and its participants inspired in both its defenders and critics. Tennessee's first historians relied heavily on oral accounts offered by participants in the Franklin debacle in their efforts to record the early history of the state of Tennessee. In 1823, Tennessee judge John Haywood compiled the first historical account of the state of Franklin. During his judicial appointment in Tennessee, Haywood began to "collect the facts" for his history from the "remarkable men" who carved out East Tennessee. Haywood's book, *The Civil and Political History of Tennessee,* is one of the earliest and most important works on frontier Tennessee history and laid the historical groundwork for every student of Franklin.[5] Prominent Tennessee Valley historian and Franklinite descendent Dr. J. G. M. Ramsey relied heavily on the pioneering work of John Haywood in his own history of the Franklin movement. Ramsey's 1853 *The Annals of Tennessee* remains the definitive work on the early history of the state.[6] Dr. Ramsey's father, F. A. Ramsey, supported the Franklin movement, and his participation in the Franklin government occasionally led his son to dramatize the state's past. J. G. M. Ramsey concluded his account of the statehood movement with a forlorn "Vindication of Franklin." He assured his readers that "the action of the parties [participating in the Franklin affair] need not be ascribed to fickleness of purpose or bad faith, much less to disloyalty to their proper rules, or insubordination to regular government and law." Ramsey argued that the Franklinites seceded from North Carolina to "preserve quiet and order," and "their course was pacific and conservative . . . nothing destructive or revolutionary, much less belligerent, was intended or contemplated." Dr. Ramsey believed that "Every review of the conduct of both parties in the disaffected [Franklin] counties, from 1784 to 1788, reflects honour upon their patriotism, their moderation, their love of order, and their virtue."[7]

Haywood's and Ramsey's descriptions of the state of Franklin demonstrate similar historiographical characteristics, with both accounts relying upon suspect oral traditions offered by participants in the Franklin affair that negatively impacted historical accuracy. Additionally, both early histories ignored the significance of land speculation, the brutality of white on red violence, and the Franklin government's clandestine relationship with the nation of Spain. Despite the factual shortcomings of the accounts offered by Haywood and Ramsey, their scholarship inspired historical fascination into the obscure backcountry statehood movement and revived regional interest in the state of Franklin.

During the decades surrounding the Civil War, the state of Franklin largely faded into historical obscurity as American historians struggled to come to grips with the tragedy of war and the turmoil of reconstruction. In East Tennessee, survivors of the Civil War and localized "bushwhacker wars" confronted the horrors of postbellum life in their war-ravaged communities. The region's identification with radical abolitionism, vocal opposition to Tennessee's secession, and wartime unionism muddied the Tennessee Valley's Civil War legacy.[8] East Tennessee's historical reputation emerged tarnished from the carnage of the Civil War, and East Tennesseans found it difficult to draw upon the South's "Lost Cause" mythology to ease the pain of military defeat and the wrenching socioeconomic transformation of Reconstruction. They instead turned to two of the Tennessee Valley's defining moments, the revolutionary Battle of King's Mountain and the legacy of mountain separatism, to repair their region's historical image. The state of Franklin emerged from the Civil War and Reconstruction transformed.[9]

In the decades following the Civil War, the historiography and popular perception of the state of Franklin diverged. Historical scrutiny of the separatist movement intensified, and the simplistic and often romanticized nationalistic interpretations of historians like Haywood and Ramsey yielded to probing revisionism. As scholars deconstructed the events and meaning of Franklin, local East Tennesseans continued to reinvent and reinterpret the legacy of their "lost" state and its fallen heroes. On occasion the lines of historical scholarship and popular memory intersected, but more often, the two interpretive paths careened hopelessly in opposite directions.

More than any other Franklinite, the only governor of the state of Franklin, John Sevier, became the embodiment of the blossoming regional mythology surrounding the state. On January 7, 1873, East Tennessee resident William A. Henderson delivered a speech before the Board of Trade of the City of Knoxville. The lecture, entitled "Nolachucky Jack," offered attendees an aggrandized account of John Sevier's life. From his "distinguished services at [the revolutionary Battle of] King's Mountain" to his governorship of the state of Tennessee, Henderson lavished praise upon Sevier. He referred to the Franklin movement as a "little revolution," and argued that the "rebellion of Franklin" owed its very survival to the courage of John Sevier. Henderson's carefully crafted image portrayed Sevier as a friend to the Indian, fictively quoting one Cherokee treaty negotiator as saying, "Send us Nolachucky Jack; he is a good and great man, and will do us right." Henderson recounted another incident in which a young child and his father waited along a dusty roadside for "Nolachucky Jack" to pass. Apparently, Sevier's "legend" overshadowed his actual physical appearance, leaving the child disappointed that he "was only a man." According to Henderson's lecture, Sevier's heroic stature caused the supernatural death of the North Carolina judge responsible for issuing the warrant for the Franklin governor's arrest during the finals days of the statehood movement. Following his signing of the warrant for Sevier's arrest, Judge Spencer found himself "prostrated on a bed of sickness." After overcoming his mysterious illness, "he arose from his bed and seated himself under an oak in his yard, when his antagonist suddenly without warning, fiercely attacked him." Despite his "cries of help" and the rescue efforts of his family, Judge Spencer succumbed to injuries inflicted upon him by a "turkey gobbler." "The cause of the singular tragedy was referred by some to the red flannel worn at the time by the unfortunate victim, but many of the common people always stoutly maintained that it was because he had had John Sevier arrested!" William Henderson's exaggerated account of John Sevier's life represented a new phase in the burgeoning legend of John Sevier and the state of Franklin.[10]

In 1887, Sevier biographer James Roberts Gilmore published the second volume of his biography of John Sevier, entitled *John Sevier as a*

Commonwealth-Builder. Gilmore, best known for his Civil War stories and poems, advanced the "romantic" historical interpretation of the state of Franklin and the life of John Sevier.[11] He glowingly depicted Sevier as "the rear-guard of the Revolution and the guardian and defender of the newly planted civilization beyond the Alleghenies." Sevier valiantly "built up a great commonwealth in the very heart of the Western wilderness." The opposition leaders of the Franklin movement, John Tipton and Joseph Martin, are portrayed as Sevier's ruthless "enemies" who stopped at nothing to destroy the Franklin movement and its august leader. Gilmore harshly criticized Indian agent and land speculator Joseph Martin, labeling him "a treacherous friend" and "self-seeking demagogue." His descriptions of John Tipton are even more venomous, with Gilmore comparing Tipton to the biblical Prince of Darkness and Antichrist, "Belial."[12]

Gilmore's biography continued the antebellum historical feud between the Franklinites and Anti-Franklinites and created what one historian forgivingly labeled as the "Democratic" interpretation of the state of Franklin.[13] In Gilmore's hyperbolized version of Franklin, North Carolina's "indifference" and "parsimonious refusal of all appropriations" for the Tennessee Valley communities forced Sevier and the Franklinites to declare their independence. According to Gilmore, "North Carolina bade her over-mountain citizens look for security and protection, at the very time when they were in daily danger from the savage enemy." He mused, "With their parent state's refusal to protect their families, Can it be wondered at that, when tidings crossed the Alleghenies, it aroused a universal feeling of indignant consternation?" Gilmore caustically described the Tennessee Valley's principal Native American inhabitants, the Overhill Cherokee, as "savages" who refused to abide by lawfully concluded land treaties, and applauded the peace-seeking Franklinites who conducted assaults against the Native American communities only to protect their own families. He denounced a remarkable egalitarian frontier constitution, proposed for the state by a leading Tennessee Valley Presbyterian minister and defeated by Sevier and his fellow Franklinites, as a frame of government drafted by religious "zealots" and supported by an "intolerant minority." Gilmore also avoided acknowledging the Sevier family's role in a series of clandestine backcountry talks between Franklin and the nation of Spain, and accused John Tipton of "recklessly" instigating the climactic and tragic battle on his farm during the final days of the state of Franklin. In Gilmore's Shakespearean history of Franklin, Sevier gallantly led his fellow Tennessee Valley residents into a period of "unbroken prosperity," in which "Education had been fostered, law had been duly administered, and crime had been a thing almost unknown." Sevier defended the state of Franklin from "a swarm of warlike enemies," but alas, "The reign of peace and law and fraternal feeling was for a time to be interrupted by the machinations of a few reckless and ambitious men, who, with no power or influence of their own, were rendered potent for evil by the 'mother-State'" of North Carolina. James Roberts Gilmore created East Tennessee's own version of the "Lost Cause," and John Sevier's failed statehood movement became the forlorn "Lost State of Franklin."[14]

At the turn of the twentieth century, the first gaps emerged between the historical studies and the public's perception of the state of Franklin. As "Progressive" historians began to question and reshape our understanding of the past, the simplistic and nationalistic interpretations of the nineteenth century yielded to piercing historical revisionism. Influenced by the profound socioeconomic and political changes accompanying the opening decades of the twentieth century, the scholarship of Progressive historians "focused on the social [and economic] forces they believed drove history."[15] In 1905, President Theodore Roosevelt published his four-volume history of the American frontier, entitled *The Winning of the West*. His chapter on the state of Franklin offered one of the earliest unvarnished critiques of the movement and its supporters. Roosevelt described the Franklin movement as a "separatist" movement and downplayed its connection to the principles of the revolution. He acknowledged the "blunt truthfulness" and "real attitude of the Franklin people . . . towards the Indians," stating that the Franklinites "never swerved from their intention of seizing Indian lands . . . by force." He labeled the Franklinites as "freebooter[s]" and "pirates" who "lusted for the possessions of the Indian." Despite Roosevelt's Native American racism, he understood the tragedy that befell the southeastern Indian tribes when they found themselves "face to face" with a "masterful [race] of people, still in their barbarian prime." He believed that "the conquest and settlement by the whites of the Indian lands was necessary to the greatness of the race and to the well-being of civilized mankind. It was as ultimately beneficial as it was inevitable." "As to the morality or immorality" of these events, Roosevelt argued that "a conquest may be fraught either with evil or with good for mankind." He acknowledged that "Every such submersion or displacement of an inferior race, every such armed settlement or conquest by a superior race, means the infliction and suffering of hideous woe and misery." As to history's judgment of the Franklinites, Roosevelt stated, "All that can be asked is that they shall be judged as other wilderness conquerors, as other slayers and quellers of savage peoples are judged." Roosevelt's *Winning of the West* represented a watershed moment in the historiographical maturation of the state of Franklin and the "New History" being offered by Progressive historians.[16]

Despite the efforts of Progressive historians like Theodore Roosevelt to reinterpret the backcountry separatist movement, the mythology surrounding John Sevier and the "lost" state of Franklin continued to seep into the public's consciousness.[17] On March 11, 1910, Dr. William Edward Fitch delivered a speech to the New York Society of the Order of the Founders and Patriots of America at the Hotel Manhattan. The talk, entitled "The Origin, Rise, and Downfall of the State of Franklin, Under Her First and Only Governor, John Sevier," exemplified the popular perception of Franklin. Dr. Fitch described the Franklinites as "the fearless pioneers of the west, who had gone into the wilderness, had suffered incredible hardships, many of whom had been murdered by the savages, some had their wives and children massacred, and all had suffered in privation and property." John Sevier "stood guard over and protected the women and children of the State of Franklin," and "their absolute devotion to him . . . enabled him to conquer his greatly superior savage enemies." Fitch believed that Sevier "preferred peace to war" with the Indians, and that he made every effort to see that "the two races . . . live[d] together in perpetual amity."[18] Biblical imagery and language permeated Fitch's lecture. He described the Franklinites' unwavering devotion to independence and Sevier, conjecturing that "Had the destroying angel passed through the land, and destroyed the first born in every section, the feelings of the hardy frontiersmen would not have been more highly incensed." He closed his lengthy address with a rousing patriotic summary of the state of Franklin, describing the state as "the immediate offspring of the Revolution of the Regulators, culminating in the Battle of Alamance in 1771." In Fitch's fallacious history of "the little commonwealth of the State of Franklin," the Franklinites earned their "independence . . . before it was dreamed of elsewhere." Despite the fact that the state did not exist before the American Revolution, Fitch thought it necessary to reveal that "the British flag was never unfurled, and no British officer ever trod the soil" of Franklin. The Franklinites "paid tribute to no government on earth except their own," and their actions "set to the people of the new world the dangerous example of erecting themselves into a state, separate and distinct from, and independent of, the authority of the English Crown."

For Fitch, the Franklin separatist movement inspired America's Declaration of Independence and the Revolutionary War.[19]

The mythologizing and memorializing of the state of Franklin extended well beyond exalted speeches and lectures. On August 22, 1903, the Historical Society of Washington County held a public ceremony in Jonesboro (now Jonesborough) "to celebrate the founding, or organization, of the State of Franklin."[20] Fifteen years later, the Samuel Doak Chapter of the Daughters of the American Revolution unveiled a memorial to Franklin in the courthouse square of the former state capital of Greeneville. The marker commemorated "the courageous little commonwealth that repudiated the sovereignty of North Carolina, and for five years exercised statehood in defiance of North Carolina and the Continental Congress." The Dorian marble monument stood 6½ feet in height and 14½ feet in width, and included a bronzed "tablet inscribed" with the following:

1785–1788
To Commemorate the Capitol
of the
State of Franklin
and
To Honor
Governor John Sevier
and the Patriotic Pioneers
Who Followed Him in the
War of the Revolution
and Assisted in Establishing
in the Wilderness the
Foundation of
Law and Liberty.
Erected 1918
Through the Efforts of the
Samuel Doak Chapter
of the
Daughters of the American
Revolution
Morristown, Tennessee

Daughters of the American Revolution member Louise Wilson Reynolds penned a companion history of Franklin for the *Daughters of the American Revolution Magazine*. Reynolds recounted the "story of the brave little Franklin," whose history burned with "all the fire and romance which is usually attributed to fiction." She described John Sevier as "handsome, magnetic, and graceful in manner and form," one who dashingly "made his appearance on the page of frontier romance as a gallant admired by the belles in linsey." Reynolds believed that the Franklin Monument stood as a "deserving and too long neglected tribute to the fearless, liberty-loving patriots, the rugged pioneers of Tennessee."[21]

In 1924, amid the speeches, lectures, celebrations, and memorials, Tennessee historian and former justice of the Tennessee Supreme Court Samuel Cole Williams published the first book-length treatment of the state of Franklin. Williams's *History of the Lost State of Franklin* is a sweeping study of the Franklin statehood movement.[22] Williams understood the historical inaccuracies and ongoing public romanticization regarding Franklin, and he hoped his history would "extend the research, correct errors, and supplement the work of the earlier [Franklin] writers." Despite the effort of Judge Williams to correct the rampant fallacious mythology and historical inaccuracies surrounding the state of Franklin, the historical realities of the separatist movement remained obscured behind the blinding rays of patriotism and the deafening roar of local adulation.[23]

Following the 1932 publication of Thomas Perkins Abernethy's scathing revisionist history of Franklin, professional historians continued to reinterpret the state's past. In 1960, Tennessee historians Stanley J. Folmsbee, Robert E. Corlew, and Enoch L. Mitchell issued their seminal four-volume *History of Tennessee*. Their study of Tennessee reflected the social turbulence of the 1960s and the profound transformation of the historical discipline being ushered in by the emerging "New Left" historians. These New Left historians exploded the consensus historical interpretations of post–World War II America and explored the impact of societal conflict and the collision of countervailing forces on America's past. The three Tennessee history professors' treatment of the state of Franklin built upon the work of Progressive historians like Abernethy and Roosevelt and embraced their "accent on economic motives" behind the statehood movement.[24] The authors also pointed out the link between land speculation and the Franklin separatist movement, arguing that "Sevier assumed leadership" of the Franklin government "apparently in the hope that . . . [it] might be used as a means of reviving and advancing" a lucrative Tennessee River land deal.[25] Fifteen years after the publication of Folmsbee, Corlew, and Mitchell's book, the prolific Tennessee scholar Wilma Dykeman completed her bicentennial history of Tennessee. Dykeman's book, simply titled *Tennessee: A History,* offered another discerning interpretation of the Franklin movement. Dykeman criticized the "romanticization [of Franklin] by local writers," and asserted that the state stood as "an example of common public needs and desires shaped and used by powerful private interests allied with international ambitions." She believed that "money was a deep though often obscure motive behind the movement for the new state" and the "bloody skirmishes between Cherokees and Franklinites." Dykeman denounced the "land-hungry settlers" for initiating the Indian wars, and branded the execution of two peaceful Overhill Cherokee chiefs by a Franklinite as the "low point of Southern frontier history." As historians like Roosevelt, Abernethy, Folmsbee, Corlew, Mitchell, and Dykeman identified the economic motivations and grievous consequences of Tennessee Valley separatism, the myths and melodrama of earlier historical efforts largely disappeared from scholarly works on Franklin.[26]

Despite the biting historical revisionism offered by Franklin scholars throughout the twentieth century, the romantic historical interpretation of Franklin persisted. The pertinacious defense of Franklin's historical legacy by regional historical societies, local writers, the descendents of the Franklinites, and East Tennessee's political and economic leaders kept the mythology of Franklin alive.[27] Writers like Noel B. Gerson and Paul M. Fink continued to applaud Franklin "as a self-made state carved out of the wilderness almost overnight by ambitious, energetic frontiersmen who refused to be halted or even slowed by obstacles that would have forced the more cautious to wait, weigh risks and proceed slowly." Paul M. Fink, the most important twentieth-century collector of documents and artifacts relating to Franklin, wrote in a 1957 essay, "Such was the independence and individualism that characterized the founders of the State of Franklin, and sustained them in their valiant but temporarily fruitless efforts to enjoy self government—as a new state or as a separate nation."[28] In his 1968 history entitled *Franklin: America's Lost State,* Gerson proudly proclaimed that the Franklinites' "relentless drive . . . set in motion the forces that transformed an impenetrable wilderness into one of the most advanced and cultivated regions in the entire United States."[29]

As the state of Franklin entered its third century of historical interpretation and public celebration, its mythology and history continued to be at odds. The Progressive and "New Left" historians left little doubt that the Tennessee Valley separatist movement stood in sharp contrast to the distorted and often self-serving images being offered by the Franklinites' defenders, descendents, and admirers. The widening divide between professional historians and Franklin supporters continued to eerily parallel the eighteenth-century political partisanship that ultimately destroyed the state. Revisionist historians stepped into the role of the Tiptonites and modern Franklin loyalists continue to fill the part of Sevier and the rebellious Franklinites.

In sharp contrast to the previous historical dialectic separating Franklin's historiographical development and the regional evolution of popular perception, the statehood movement cannot be simply characterized as either a republican aftershock of radical idealism sparked by the American Revolution or a sinister plot forced upon the unsuspecting inhabitants of the Tennessee Valley by an edacious coterie of backcountry land speculators. The Franklin separatist movement emerged within the competitive and anarchic political and economic climate that materialized following the American Revolution on the rapidly developing trans-Appalachian borderlands. Under the strict limitations imposed by the Articles of Confederation on the powers of the national government, the United States proved incapable of governing, developing, or defending its western frontier. Faced with continued territorial threats posed by the British and Spanish, firmly ensconced in forts in the Northwest and Southwest respectively, and by Native American groups increasingly hostile to western expansion, the American government struggled to meet the demands of the nation's western settlers and to mediate the fierce competition for western land, political hegemony, and economic supremacy. This postrevolutionary political vacuum that emerged in the transmontane backcountry forced several state governments to engage in their own efforts at western governance, but geographical distances, political isolation, and powerful ideological forces presented enormous challenges to the effectiveness of these policies.[30] Across the new republic, disaffected factions initiated backcountry separatist movements aimed at creating new states, promoting economic growth, and securing local political autonomy. Throughout the final three decades of the eighteenth century, New Hampshirers (Vermonters), Virginians (Kentuckians), and North Carolinians (Franklinites) agitated for separation from their parent states and demanded control over their political and economic destiny. At its core, the Franklin separatist movement stood as a contest between two partisan ruling factions and their rank and file supporters to determine the economic and political future of the Tennessee Valley.[31]

Following the settlement of the Tennessee Valley, a diverse and competitive commercial economy blossomed within the communities of North Carolina's trans-Appalachian frontier. This specie-poor, land-dependent backcountry economy hungrily craved new territory and markets. Despite the financial rewards offered by the region's agrarian economy, mercantile interests, and available lands, the postrevolutionary economic malaise, inadequacies of regional trade and transportation arteries, marginalization by North Carolina's eastern political leadership, and the U.S. government's pacific Indian policies presented formidable obstacles to the expansion of the Tennessee Valley market economy. In the face of these limitations, an influential class of commercial farmers, merchants, and land speculators emerged within the valley communities and quickly secured control over the region's political economy. This ruling class utilized their regional influence, their shared wartime and frontier experiences, and their collective political and financial interests to secure the allegiance of their Tennessee Valley neighbors.[32]

Despite the existence of internal tensions provoked by fierce competition for landed wealth, control over the regional marketplace, and dominion over political and judicial positions of local and regional influence, the leaders and residents of the Tennessee Valley remained largely united immediately following the revolutionary and backcountry Indian wars. North Carolina's postbellum cession of its western lands (which included the Tennessee Valley) to the U.S. government disturbed the tenuous harmony among the valley residents and unleashed partisan forces that polarized the entire region. The 1784 Cession Act offered the Tennessee Valley's leading men the opportunity to pursue their own political and economic agenda unfettered by the policies of their parent state of North Carolina. The leadership of the Tennessee Valley quickly seized upon the political circumstance and initiated the Franklin statehood movement. Their decision forced valley residents to choose sides in the escalating separatist debate and opened up a widening gulf between the once unified Tennessee Valley inhabitants.

The Franklinites' efforts to expand their regional commercial economy and unrelenting pursuit of western lands inevitably brought them into direct conflict with the Native American groups who claimed much of the southwestern frontier. Franklin's political autonomy allowed the separatist leaders to carry out their long-delayed hawkish diplomatic and military campaign against the southeastern Indians that resulted in coerced land treaties, the intensification of backcountry savagery, and ill-fated alliances with the state of Georgia and the nation of Spain. The savvy political leadership and supporters of Franklin understood the interconnectedness of their land-based economy and diplomatic policies to the level of Indian warfare, but chose to accept the inherent dangers in exchange for opening new lands to white settlement. This tumultuous dynamic occurred across the rapidly expanding western frontier, and the state of Franklin simply represented another front in the conflict between Euroamerican expansion and Native American resistance. Franklin is not exceptional in this respect, but the ferocity and duration of the Indian wars in the Tennessee Valley made for one of the bloodiest periods in eighteenth-century America.

Over the course of four years, Franklin's leadership and small-holder supporters managed to fashion a functioning state government and court system, but failed to attract backing for their separatist movement from outside the region. Despite the overwhelming regional support for Franklin by the Tennessee Valley's yeoman farmers and merchants, the movement came under attack from the political leadership of eastern North Carolina, the U.S. government, and a determined minority faction within the Tennessee Valley. The inability of the Franklinites to amass support for their state within the halls of the North Carolina legislature or the U.S. Congress, North Carolina's divisive strategy for defeating the movement, and the hardening of partisan positions within the Tennessee Valley escalated the competition for control over the region's political and economic prospects. The polarization of the Tennessee Valley caused by the state of Franklin ultimately resulted in a bloody pitched battle between the two warring factions upon the snow-covered fields of Anti-Franklinite leader John Tipton's Washington County farm and the ruination of the Franklin separatist movement.

The state of Franklin remains a powerful symbol for many East Tennesseans, and its historical legacy is carefully preserved in the highway markers, business names, and stone monuments dotting the rolling hills of the Tennessee Valley. To East Tennesseans, Franklin and its charismatic governor, John Sevier, have come to represent rugged individualism, regional exceptionalism, and civic dignity. The purpose of this study is not to take this away from them, but to reevaluate the extraordinary history of their "lost" state. However one chooses to interpret the statehood movement, Franklin remains a complex and fascinating historical event. From their reckless assertion of independence to their undaunted diplomatic campaign to garner political and popular support for their movement, the Franklinites' attempt to establish a new state in the Tennessee Valley stands as a testament to boundless economic and political ambition. As one Franklin historian commented, "Perhaps the most prominent characteristic of the Franklinites was their relentless drive."[33] The state of Franklin's ruinous failure reminds us of the extraordinary and fragile nature of America's independence.

Chapter 1

Land of the Franks

The Backcountry Economy of
Upper East Tennessee

The state of Franklin emerged out of the shared desires of a powerful coalition of landed elite, yeoman farmers, and backcountry merchants to defend, expand, and dominate the Tennessee Valley's rapidly developing political economy. From the earliest permanent settlement of eastern Tennessee, a diverse, dynamic, and interconnected regional economy developed. Despite the potential financial rewards alluringly held out by commercial agriculture, mercantilism, and land sales, the region's full economic efficacy remained unrealized throughout the 1780s. Lack of support from the North Carolina state government for the improvement of the Tennessee Valley's infrastructure presented a formidable obstacle to economic advancement for the region's ruling and laboring classes. The perceived unresponsiveness of North Carolina's eastern political leaders to the demands made by backcountry farmers, stockmen, merchants, and land speculators for state funds for internal improvements ultimately served as one of the driving issues uniting many of the region's economic elite and small-holders behind the Franklin statehood movement. Both the frontier localism and internal factionalism that erupted in the Tennessee Valley during the Franklin movement found their origins in the fierce competition for control over the region's political and economic systems.

The state of Franklin began with a journey by a forty-eight-year-old Scots-Irish militia captain, planter, and long hunter named William Bean. Captain Bean and his wife, Lydia "Liddy" Russell, ascended the Great War Path, following the Appalachian Mountains southwest through the Shenandoah Valley of Virginia with their four children in tow, and settled in the upper Tennessee Valley, near the Watauga River. Bean is widely believed to have been the first white man to permanently settle in the Tennessee backcountry. Hundreds of families followed the Beans into the heart of the southwestern frontier to stake their claim to the rich resource-laden lands of the future state of Tennessee.[1]

In 1769, Bean built his mud-chinked log cabin at the mouth of Boone's Creek, a small tributary of the Watauga River he named for his friend and hunting companion Daniel Boone.[2] After a year spent busily improving land, cultivating crops, avoiding Indians, and giving birth to their fifth child, Russell, the first white child born to permanent settlers on the Tennessee frontier, the Bean family moved even deeper into the Tennessee interior.[3] The Beans finally settled along the banks of the lower Watauga River at the junction between two key frontier routes, the Old Catawba Road and the Great War Path. Bean constructed a four-room log cabin that served as the family's home and as a small inn for settlers, fur traders, and speculators who ventured into the Tennessee wilderness. The modest inn, known respectively as Bean's Crossroads, Bean's Cabin, or Bean's Station, soon grew to include a tavern and a small blacksmith shop.[4]

The settlement of Bean's Station and the rapid blossoming of a small community surrounding the homestead typified the early maturation of the Tennessee frontier. During a "long hunt," Captain Bean and Daniel Boone had camped above the future site of the Bean's Station settlement, and the weary hunters undoubtedly had made note of the abundance of water, land, game, nutrient-rich soils, and economic potential that lay at the foot of the Appalachian Mountains. Bean left his Pittsylvania County, Virginia, home and substantial landholdings to advance his family's economic fortunes. Despite the remoteness of Bean's Station, he managed to create a thriving and diverse business that served the needs of the newest settlers and entrepreneurs traveling the ancient Indian paths into the Great Valley of Tennessee. The same desires for land and prosperity that led Bean to ignore the threats posed by Indian massacres, harsh winters, and geographic and cultural isolation lured hundreds of frontier families into the southwestern frontier. The defense of these backcountry land claims and communities and the expansion of the region's multifarious economy compelled the descendents of the Tennessee Valley's first inhabitants to form the state of Franklin.[5]

After William Bean's pioneering effort in the Watauga Valley, several permanent settlements sprang up along the twisting banks of the Watauga, Tennessee, and Holston rivers. These upper Tennessee Valley communities included Carter's Valley, Shelby's Station, Sycamore Shoals, and the Nolichucky settlements.[6] Most of these early settlements developed similarly to

Bean's Station. Men with economic vision and a desire to benefit from a rapidly expanding frontier economy established these communities. John Carter, founder of Carter's Valley on the Holston River, was a Virginia merchant and trader who settled in the region sometime in 1772. He and his partner, Joseph Parker, watched a small community flourish around the backcountry store they erected to capitalize on the lucrative Cherokee fur trade and the influx of new frontier families.[7] The financial success of Carter's store led to its eventual looting by Cherokee Indians from the neighboring Overhill towns who bitterly complained that the store competed with their own fur trade.[8] In 1772, fifty-one-year-old Welshman Evan Shelby, a "hard-drinking Marylander," moved his family into the Watauga Valley and settled on a 1,946-acre tract of land he called Sapling Grove.[9] Shelby expanded his settlement, at the present-day site of the city of Bristol, Tennessee, by constructing a trading post and a small stockaded fort (appropriately named Fort Shelby) to protect his investment. Shelby's Station, also known as "North-of-Holston," became a critical trading post and rendezvous point for settlers venturing into the southwestern frontier.[10] Jacob Brown, an "itinerant trader" from South Carolina, and a small group of former North Carolina Regulators leased a tract of land from the Cherokee Indians and established the Nolichucky River settlements.[11] Brown opened a small store, a gunsmith shop, and a blacksmith shop on the north bank of the Nolichucky River to cater to Indian fur traders.[12] In the spring of 1770, James Robertson, an Orange County, North Carolina, farmer and participant in North Carolina's Regulator movement, erected a settlement on a piece of land he called Sycamore Shoals.[13] Robertson had fled into the Watauga Valley to escape the violence surrounding the Regulator movement. The Sycamore Shoals settlement quickly grew to include twenty families, most Robertson's own relatives.[14] Capitalism drove the first frontier settlers into the wilds of East Tennessee, and their successful businesses became the fiscal engines driving the economic development of the Tennessee Valley.[15]

Following the close of the American Revolution, the backcountry communities that would eventually comprise the future state of Franklin experienced tremendous demographic and economic growth. By 1784, population increases and the rapid expansion of the regional marketplace had transformed the underdeveloped Tennessee Valley frontier settlements. Historians Paul H. Bergeron, Stephen V. Ash, and Jeanette Keith described the "push-pull" effect responsible for this dramatic population explosion.

Either legal or financial difficulties "pushed" early Tennessee Valley frontier families out of their communities, or economic possibilities "pulled" them into the region.[16]

In May 1772, the Watauga settlers banded together and fashioned a quasi-frontier government they called the Watauga Association.[17] As the Tennessee Valley settlements continued to expand both economically and geographically, the backcountry residents realized the necessity of forming a frontier government in order to "manage land affairs and facilitate governance of the colony."[18] Under constant threat from the original Native American land claimants, mounting concern over the inadequacies of the local legal and political systems, and the looming revolutionary conflict, on July 5, 1776, the Watauga settlers sent a formal petition to the North Carolina General Assembly requesting to be annexed and organized into a frontier militia district or county.[19] In April 1777, North Carolina accepted their petition, temporarily established the Washington District, and appointed twenty-one justices of the peace to oversee political and legal matters within the region. Seven months later, the North Carolina Assembly formally recognized the Wataugans by creating Washington County and establishing a much-needed Court of Pleas and Quarter Sessions. Prior to the formation of the state of Franklin in 1784, administrative difficulties forced North Carolina to split off from Washington County the new counties of Sullivan (1779) and Greene (1783).[20] The counties of Washington, Greene, and Sullivan and the rapidly shrinking swath of Tennessee Valley land reserved for the Cherokee Indians eventually comprised the boundaries of Franklin.[21]

East Tennessee's frontier economy is best described as a complex mixture of semi-subsistence agriculture, early rural market capitalism, and expansive land speculation. The development of this mixed economy began with early frontier communities like Bean's Station and the other Watauga Valley settlements, but four critical factors collided to determine the future course of the Tennessee Valley's frontier economy: population growth, the abundance of natural resources and land, geography, and the tenuous economic climate resulting from the American Revolution. The rapid growth of East Tennessee's population dramatically impacted the region's economy. Utilizing the scarce census records available prior to the formation of the state of Tennessee in 1796, historians estimate the 1778 population of Washington County, at the time encompassing nearly all of the eventual state of Franklin, at roughly 2,500 residents.[22] This statistic reveals the tremendous regional growth in the six years following the settlement of the Watauga River Valley. The confusion presented by the division of Washington County into Washington, Sullivan, and Greene counties and the incomplete nature of early tax lists further complicate efforts to ascertain precise population statistics. A July 1, 1791, census conducted by the Southwest Territory's Governor William Blount established the population of the eastern section of the Southwest Territory at 36,043 residents, with approximately 29,000 of the settlers inhabiting the Tennessee Valley settlements.[23] Compiled tax lists for this same period show the population of a geographically diminished Washington County to be 5,862 persons.[24] Despite the ambiguities of these census and tax records, it is clear that the Tennessee Valley experienced a sustained period of population growth between 1772 and 1791. The increased population strained relations with the region's Native Americans and placed tremendous pressure on the Tennessee Valley's court system, economy, and frontier defenses.[25]

On May 28, 1788, the well-traveled Methodist bishop Francis Asbury recounted in his journal the challenges and conditions he found when piercing the Smoky Mountains and descending into the Great Valley of the Tennessee. Asbury wrote, "After getting our horses shod, we made a move for Holstein [Holston], and entered upon the mountains; the first of which I called steel, the second stone, and the third iron mountain: they are rough and difficult to climb." He also noted the "heavy rain" and "awful thunder and lightning" that plagued his journey into the Appalachian frontier. Asbury's journal entry concludes with a description of the "little dirty house where the filth might be taken up from the floor with a spade" that served as shelter for his traveling party.[26] Bishop Asbury's description of the Tennessee frontier inadvertently offered keen insight into Franklin's economy. The "rough and difficult" mountains made overland communication and trade enormously challenging and separated the Tennessee Valley settlers from their transmontane state government in Hillsboro, North Carolina.[27] The abundance of rainfall created excellent growing conditions for East Tennessee's backcountry farmers, and the steel, stone, and iron mountains Asbury identified reflected the tremendous untapped wealth contained in the mineral resources buried deep within the surrounding ranges.[28]

The Tennessee Valley's "dual economy" functioned as both a traditional subsistence-based "household economy" and as a peripheral commercial marketplace.[29] Most recent frontier scholars believe that America's preindustrial backcountry economies began as semicommercial and rapidly became "fully integrated in the world capitalist market system."[30] The notion of a pure subsistence "moral economy" in the southern mountains was a romanticized "invention of the industrial age."[31] The examination of early backcountry settlers in the Shenandoah Valley reveals the existence of "nascent commercialism" on Virginia's western frontier and the development of rural market capitalism immediately following the "pioneer phase" of settlement.[32] Across the southern Appalachian frontier, the presence of early land speculation, dense concentrations of wealth and land, slave labor, and the commodification of the region's natural resources provides ample evidence that the southwestern frontier fit into a "global capitalist paradigm."[33] The first settlers of eastern Tennessee embraced frontier market capitalism and positioned themselves to capitalize on the robust regional marketplace.[34]

Mercantile sales and hostelry emerged as two of the earliest businesses on the Tennessee frontier. Entrepreneurs like William Bean, Evan Shelby, John Carter, and Jacob Brown built inns, taverns, and a diverse array of shops to serve the needs of the expanding population and market demands. Small inns sprang up across the Tennessee Valley, and many of these businesses became hubs for commerce and the centers of community-building. In 1779, backcountry land surveyors laid out Tennessee's first town, Jonesboro (now Jonesborough), and sold the rustic town lots at a lottery for sixty dollars each. Within a few years, local businessmen developed two inns, a blacksmith shop, and a tavern in the frontier town. Jonesboro quickly became the "economic, political, and legal center of the region."[35] In the present-day town of Blountville, in Sullivan County, young William Deery purchased an old frontier trading post and expanded it to include an inn and public house. The financial success of the Old Deery Inn propelled the growth of Blountville, and the small frontier community eventually became an important stagecoach stop at the turn of the eighteenth century. Similarly, the town of Rogersville, on the banks of the Holston River, owes its early growth to the commercial success of town founder Joseph Rogers's frontier inn.[36]

Most of the early Tennessee Valley inns doubled as taverns or distilleries. Whiskey distillation, sales, and consumption remained fixtures in frontier America. As one historian commented, "a tavern host typically kept a tippling house for the sale of his own beverages."[37] Due to the geographic and transportation obstacles confronting frontier farmers, whiskey distillation served as a fiscally viable use of corn and other grains. The sale of whiskey at the various taverns and inns that dotted the Tennessee Valley frontier emerged as an important source of revenue and provided a close connection between the region's developing agrarian and mercantile economies.[38] Bishop Francis Asbury's complaints of the poor conditions at the inns in which he boarded during his mission into the Tennessee backcountry omitted descriptions of the local home brew most travelers imbibed to sooth the aches and pains of rigorous mountain travel. The county courts customarily fixed prices for distilled spirits. In the early 1780s, the Sullivan County Court set the prices of "good distilled rye whiskey at two shillings, six pence per gallon and good peach or apple brandy at three shillings per gallon." Some of the most prominent men in the region ran ordinary houses in the Tennessee backcountry. William Bean, William Deery, James Allison, Isaiah Hamilton, Richard Minton, and Valentine Sevier, the father of future state of Franklin governor John Sevier, all operated tippling houses. An inventory of Washington County estates illustrates the importance of whiskey distillation in the early East Tennessee economy. Men like Abraham Collet, Thomas Mitchell, and Thomas Dillard listed stills and vessels alongside their Bibles and cattle in their estates.[39] Captain Thomas Amis, one of the most successful early merchants in Tennessee, moved his family from Bladen County, North Carolina, and opened a small store and tavern in present-day Rogersville. Amis constructed his tavern and store "on a high piece of ground in sight of Big Creek" in what eventually became Hawkins County. He sold whiskey by the drink in his tavern and in bulk at his store.[40] Taverns also served as important meeting places in East Tennessee. The state of Franklin held its first senate meeting "in one of the rooms of the [Greeneville] town tavern." Even the presumably abstinent Bishop Asbury commented that during his stay at Thomas Amis's inn and tavern his host kept his guests "well-entertained."[41] These early tavern and inn owners made a significant contribution to the growth and development of the Tennessee Valley.[42]

Beyond public accommodations and grog shops, East Tennessee's early economy included a wide assortment of other businesses. Thomas Amis's store and tavern eventually grew to include a gristmill and forge, and most Tennessee Valley towns employed at least one blacksmith.[43] A search of the first tax lists for the region reveals trades such as silversmiths, weavers, fullers, stone masons, millers, and miners.[44] The mineral wealth of the "stone, steel, and iron mountains" of Tennessee's Unaka Mountain Range remained largely untouched until the early 1790s, but the presence of earlier forges in the Tennessee Valley proves that some mining occurred prior to 1790. In 1770, Moses Embree moved his family into the Tennessee Valley, "took up land, erected a cabin, and built a forge making iron." Embree's forge is typical of an early iron-making operation on the southern frontier. "Moses made iron on a limited scale getting his ore up on the top of the hill and on Jacob Knaff's farm." According to his descendents, the iron made in Moses's forge "was the first iron wrought in this section," and "the horses that went to [the Revolutionary War Battle of] King's Mountain were shod from iron made" at Embree's forge.[45] In 1784, Colonel James King also constructed an iron works in Sullivan County. Using twenty-five-ton flatboats, King incredibly shipped his iron nails, produced in an adjoining nail factory, to other Tennessee Valley settlements and to cities as far away as New Orleans.[46] Despite the small size of the furnaces, most producing less than five tons of iron a day, forges like the Embree family forge and King's Ironworks provided a vital economic link between the region and distant markets.[47]

Despite the region's rich mercantile diversity, agriculture and agriculture-related industries dominated the Franklin economy. The rich soils of the Tennessee Valley, "well-watered by the small streams issuing from the adjacent mountains," were ideal for crops, and the abundance of open land offered perfect conditions for raising cattle.[48] East Tennessee's temperate climate and ample precipitation added to the region's suitability for commercial farming. Corn, wheat, rye, oats, barley, and millet became staple crops in the early East Tennessee agrarian economy.[49] Regional farmers raised hogs, sheep, horses, and other cattle in the hardwood forests and cleared pastureland surrounding their farms and communities.[50]

Franklin farmers cultivated crops and raised livestock for household consumption as well as for local and regional markets. According to the Watauga Association of Genealogists, most of the farms in eastern Tennessee were "self-sufficient units," but the few extant store ledgers challenge this assertion.[51] Most farmers grew at least some corn due to its multiple uses in the Tennessee backcountry. A farmer who harvested a good crop of corn could sell it to taverns and distilleries for whiskey production, to ranchers for feed, or to millers to be ground into meal for sale on the local market. According to one historian, "Because it was easy to cultivate and matured quickly, corn became so ubiquitous and so central to people's lives that it could serve as a monetary standard and a form of currency."[52] Unquestionably, many Tennessee Valley farm families relied heavily on their own crops, orchards, livestock, and frontier ingenuity to survive in the wilderness, but the proliferation of stores and shops selling locally grown agricultural products reflected the connections between agriculture and commerce and the reliance on local markets for supplementation.[53]

Despite the climatic challenges that limited large-scale cultivation of cotton or tobacco, an adapted form of commercial agriculture and the use of slave labor emerged as early features of the Tennessee Valley frontier economy.[54] Many of the first Tennessee families that settled the region previously owned plantations and farms in North Carolina and Virginia, and the "topography of the land was well suited for plantation agriculture and the efficient use of slaves." It is estimated that approximately 10 percent of the early Watauga settlers owned slaves.[55] Prominent early East Tennesseans, such as William Bean, John Carter, and George Lumpkin, brought slaves into the region to farm large tracts of land. Franklin governor John Sevier brought seven slaves with him when he settled on the Nolichucky River. Tax records from Washington County list thirty-two slaveholders owning 102 "black poles" for 1779. In 1781, an incomplete tax assessment from the same county records seventy-two slaves for just the fifth district.[56]

Many early Washington County wills record slaves among the estates bequeathed to heirs. William Bean left his wife, Liddy, a "negro girl" named Grace, and Franklin militia captain John Fain willed his wife, Agnes, "the negro Punch."[57] A 1783 assessor return for Greene County, covering two of four county court–established tax districts, lists sixty-five slaves, and an unidentified tax record from the same year lists thirty-three "negroes." A July 4, 1787, census for Sullivan County, carved out of Washington County in 1779, lists "twenty-three Black male slaves and eighty female" among a total county population of 2,066 residents.[58] Due to lower tax rates, slave owners on the Tennessee frontier preferred to own either female or child slaves.[59] A Washington County tax assessment from 1787 records eighty-six slaveholders owning 223 slaves. In 1788, the final year of the state of Franklin's brief existence, it is believed that approximately 1,500 slaves worked in the Franklin counties. Although most East Tennessee slaveholders owned fewer than three slaves, some of the most prominent men in the region commanded as many as twenty. The growth of the Tennessee Valley population and expansion of commercial agriculture magnified the importance of slave labor in the regional market economy.[60]

Early court records and inventories of estates also provide evidence of a thriving Tennessee commercial cattle industry. Greene County court records list dozens of stock farmers registering their cattle marks and brands.

In the August 1783 Greene County court minutes, James Wilson noted his "poplar leaf" brand and Abraham Carter registered "a C ear mark [and a] crop of the right ear and a hole & slit in the left ear."[61] Washington County estate inventories list an array of livestock. The 1781 estate of John Bond recorded "four head of horses, nine head of cattle, four head of sheep, seventeen head of hogs, and sixteen pigs."[62] Additionally, many of the region's landed elite, including Evan Shelby and John Carter, also maintained substantial herds of commercial cattle.[63] Cattle drives north through the Shenandoah Valley of Virginia became a fixture in frontier Tennessee, with most Tennessee Valley residents keeping "one or two milk cows" and raising "the rest of the cattle as beef for local and regional markets."[64] East Tennessee's commercial livestock industry also included hogs, sheep, and horses, and the long livestock drives and drovers' stands provided a constant market for both tavern and inn owners as well as for commercial farmers. Despite the inadequacies of transportation routes across the region, the livestock trade "connected upper East Tennessee to markets extending far beyond the Appalachian region."[65]

The Tennessee Valley's backcountry economy was amazingly diverse, tightly amalgamated to local and regional markets, and perpetually expanding. Despite the success of the region's economy, Tennessee's frontier entrepreneurs confronted two major obstacles to their region's continued economic growth: geographic isolation and the economic crisis following the American Revolution. The debate over the level of cultural, political, and economic isolation in the southern mountains remains a thirty-year fixture in Appalachian scholarship, but the Tennessee Valley settlers avoided economic isolation by cultivating close fiscal connections to local and regional markets and to each other. Despite their Herculean trade efforts, geographic distances from the centers of commerce and the region's treacherous mountain topography created enormous difficulties for Tennessee Valley residents during the region's frontier stage.

These shared economic challenges and the growing chorus of demands for state-funded internal improvements united Tennessee Valley residents across class lines. In South Carolina's developing backcountry, the "expensive, time-consuming, and often hazardous" effort to transport local products to coastal markets forged connections between the backcountry planter elite and the yeoman farmers.[66] In the Tennessee Valley, the landed commercial elite maintained a shared interest with the region's small farmers and merchants in the construction and maintenance of roads and the establishment and efficient functioning of county courts. These appeals for internal improvements and feelings of eastern political marginalization transcended socioeconomic lines and became a galvanizing force that allowed the Tennessee Valley's economic elite to win political support from many of the region's small-holders for the Franklin statehood movement.[67]

The Unaka, Smoky, and Blue Ridge mountain ranges separated the Tennessee Valley from the thriving markets in eastern North Carolina and along the Atlantic seaboard. These formidable obstacles made trans-Allegheny travel, trade, and communication extremely difficult and forced most early travelers to enter and exit the region from the north or south. Pioneering mountain merchants on the eastern slope of the Allegheny Mountains maintained close southern market connections to South Carolina, Georgia, and eastern North Carolina. The challenges of trading across the highest mountains in the east forced most Tennessee Valley merchants and commercial farmers to rely almost exclusively on markets in Virginia, Georgia, South Carolina, and the blossoming southwestern frontier. Those who did venture into upper East Tennessee from the east traversed rugged transmontane passes, such as the Unicoi Trail and the Catawba Trail, and struggled through treacherous mountain gaps, such as Boone's Gap and Saluda Gap. The Tennessee Valley itself is thirty to fifty miles wide and connects to the much larger Shenandoah Valley of Virginia. These two valleys provided the perfect corridor for traveling into upper East Tennessee from the north, and most of the early traces, or trails, utilized the valleys' gentle slopes. The Tennessee Valley's northern and western commercial orientation fiscally and politically separated the region's landed elite and small-holders from their state government in Hillsboro, and eventually fostered a shared sense of alienation and abandonment among them.[68]

Much like many of the other frontier roads in Appalachia, eastern Tennessee's earliest transportation system utilized well-worn Indian paths, most likely first carved out by buffalo or other large mammals thousands of years earlier, as the primary corridors to connect the region.[69] Prior to the settlement of the region, traders, hunters, missionaries, and explorers traveled along the Native American hunting and trading paths that traversed the area. In 1673, two Virginians, James Needham and Gabriel Arthur, undertook an expedition into the Tennessee Valley and attempted to establish trade contacts with the Overhill Cherokee communities.[70] Men like Needham and Arthur crossed into the Tennessee frontier following Indian paths like the Occaneechi Path, the Great War Path, and the Great Buffalo

Trail to trade English goods for furs and pelts with the native populace. These backcountry entrepreneurs became some of the first Europeans to witness the grandeur of the Great Valley of Tennessee and to confront the challenges the region posed to frontier commerce.[71]

The first road construction undertaken by Euroamericans in eastern Tennessee corresponded with the military preparations surrounding the French and Indian War, and most of these early war traces connected British forts, such as Fort Loudon and Fort Robinson. The English laboriously built these military roads to defend their Indian allies and economic interests from the French.[72] Europeans, including Colonel William Byrd III of Virginia's Great Road or Island Road, carved out dozens of traces to transport wagonloads of supplies to the soldiers occupying these remote backcountry forts. The British used many of these military roads to wage war against the French-allied Cherokee towns, and eventually, these routes developed into critical arteries connecting the Tennessee Valley settlements to the north and east.[73]

In 1775, "thirty axe-men" managed by Daniel Boone improved a small stretch of the Great Indian War Path, subsequently given the name Boone's Wilderness Trail, Boone's Trace, or simply the Wilderness Road. The Wilderness Road snaked through the northern section of the Tennessee River Valley and eventually terminated two hundred grueling miles later in Virginia's Kentucky territory. The road became one of the primary routes for thousands of frontier families settling East and Middle Tennessee, as well as the Kentucky country.[74] Boone's road also fed the rapidly expanding East Tennessee economy, and dozens of businesses sprang up along the rugged route. From 1775 to 1795, the Watauga communities received a constant stream of wayfarers navigating Boone's Wilderness Road. "At the supply stations from Bristol to Long Island, the many thousands of travelers to the West stopped to visit with neighbors and friends, gather supplies, repair their guns, fill their packs, and push off into the wilderness in large companies with armed guards."[75] The embryonic communities of the upper Tennessee Valley supplied the settlements in the Cumberland District (Middle Tennessee) and the distant Kentucky frontier.[76]

Following the completion of the Wilderness Road, skilled axe men carved out dozens of smaller traces across eastern Tennessee. Most of these early roads connected East Tennessee towns and communities to one another and to the region's principal transportation arteries. Roads became the first public works projects in the region. During the American Revolution, the town of Jonesboro constructed roads that "linked the town" to settlements along the Watauga, Nolichucky, and Holston rivers. The area's economic elite often convinced local courts to build roads to their property or privately funded roads linking their own farms and businesses to these feeder outlets. Prominent men such as James Stuart, Robert Young, Charles Robertson, John Sevier, and John Tipton "marked off" roads to ensure the success of their commercial ventures.[77] The existence of these early roads not only promoted the fiscal links between eastern Tennessee and regional markets, but also connected the region's economic elite and yeoman farmers to each other. Despite the growth of trade and transportation routes throughout the 1780s, "the difficulties encountered establishing, maintaining, and using this limited set of roads argues for a powerful sense of remoteness." The shared belief among both wealthy landholders and small farmers that North Carolina had failed to adequately improve their region's trade and transportation network emerged as one of the earliest and most persuasive arguments for the Franklin separatist movement. Additionally, the central role local courts and county political offices played in allocating funds for road construction projects meant that controlling these backcountry institutions gained increasing significance to the Tennessee Valley's emerging economic elite.[78]

Perhaps more than any other single factor, the economic consequences of the American Revolution shaped the Tennessee Valley's economic landscape. The financial cost of America's rebellion exacerbated an already calamitous national specie shortage and caused a disastrous disruption of the Tennessee Valley's agrarian economy. This turbulent economic climate proved to be the ideal condition for the emergence of a land- and natural resource–based economy dominated by local landed elites who doggedly speculated in land and unyieldingly controlled regional politics.

Following the revolution, the economy of the new American Republic experienced a dramatic deflation in the value of both state and federal currencies and the precipitous loss of the infinitely more stable British pound. Additionally, mounting debt, the loss of the lucrative trade with England, the fiscal inadequacies of the Articles of Confederation, and the destruction of the American merchant fleet and urban centers further exacerbated the postrevolutionary financial disaster.[79] The frontier economy of the Tennessee Valley never relied heavily on paper money for business transactions. Instead, most local merchants and farmers utilized a combination of barter, trade, and cash payments. During the short-lived existence of the state of

Franklin, the cash-starved Franklin government enacted a Legal Tender Act that paid its civil officials with animal pelts. The 1785 legislation provided the governor of Franklin one thousand deer skins annually, the chief justice and attorney general five hundred deer skins annually, the secretary of state four hundred and fifty otter skins annually, the county clerks three hundred beaver skins annually, and the members of the Franklin Assembly three raccoon skins per session.[80] The economic crisis accompanying the American Revolution simply sapped an already cash-poor region of specie and forced a greater reliance on traditional modes of exchange.[81]

By 1782, the state of North Carolina stood on the precipice of financial collapse. In order to repay foreign creditors, militiamen, and the federal government, the state issued certificates or promissory notes to creditors and as payment to her revolutionary soldiers. When the notes became virtually worthless in a few short months, the results proved to be disastrous. In order to repay the revolutionary promissory notes, North Carolina sold off huge swaths of its western territory, including some of the land that eventually became the state of Tennessee. The sale of North Carolina's western territory initiated further state-sanctioned land speculation in the Tennessee Valley, but the commercial investment in territory began much earlier for the region's economic elite.[82]

Speculators settled, developed, and controlled frontier East Tennessee. Whether they speculated in land, slaves, natural resources, or commercial markets, the region's earliest settlers sought to cash in on the untapped and unclaimed (Cherokee, Creek, and Chickasaw tribes aside) lands of the Tennessee Valley. In a region as specie poor as East Tennessee, slaves and land became the most stable mediums of exchange, and those who owned thousands of acres controlled the region's political and economic fortunes.[83]

Land speculation and surveying emerged as two of the earliest and most lucrative business ventures in the Tennessee Valley.[84] The earliest negotiations for land cessions occurred between the first Watauga settlers, who were in fact squatters, and the Overhill Cherokee Indians. In October 1770, the British Superintendent of Indian Affairs for the Southern District, Captain John Stuart, negotiated the Treaty of Lochaber in South Carolina with the Cherokee, which ceded a large "triangle of land" in the upper Holston Valley to the British. The Wataugans held no official deeds for their settlements, but they hoped that the Treaty of Lochaber legitimized their squatters' rights. The treaty eventually inspired a second wave of backcountry emigration.[85] Despite being forbidden by the British government and the Proclamation Line of 1763 to purchase land from the Native Americans, the Wataugans remained determined to secure legal rights to the Watauga settlements.[86] In 1773, Wataugans James Robertson and John Bean negotiated a ten-year lease for land in the Tennessee Valley for five to six thousand dollars worth of "merchandise and trade goods, plus some muskets and household articles." Prominent Wataugans John Carter, Andrew Greer, and William Bean financed the lease agreement, and James Robertson's cousin, Charles, served as the trustee of the lease. Charles Robertson (Robinson) established an "informal land office" that collected payments from Watauga settlers and registered land claims. The success of the land lease deal granted temporary possession of the Watauga land, and many settlers believed that the lease agreement ensured future permanent ownership of their land claims.[87]

On March 17, 1775, Richard Henderson, a former North Carolina judge and successful land speculator, secured 20 million acres from the Cherokee for two thousand English pounds and ten thousand pounds worth of trade goods. Henderson's land firm, the Transylvania Company, utilized the turmoil surrounding the American Revolution to secure an enormous tract of land that encompassed the entire Cumberland Valley in Middle Tennessee and the southern section of the Kentucky territory. The Henderson Purchase, the largest private land purchase in American history to that date, paved the way for the settlement of Kentucky and Middle Tennessee and set an important precedent for the Watauga settlers in attendance during the treaty negotiations at Sycamore Shoals.[88] Just two days after the Henderson Purchase, the Watauga settlers convinced the Cherokee to sell the land they previously leased for two thousand pounds. With the Watauga Purchase, Tennessee's earliest inhabitants finally secured two thousand square miles of land along the Watauga, Holston, and Great Conaway (now New) rivers. These two monumental Cherokee land deals allowed Jacob Brown to purchase two large tracts encompassing the Nolichucky settlements and John Carter to acquire the land surrounding his Carter's Valley settlements. Despite dubious land claims and underhanded Indian treaties, these earlier land transactions between the future Franklinites and the region's aboriginal land claimants precipitated a disputatious wave of speculation that eventually consumed the entire region.[89]

On April 1, less than a month after the Watauga Purchase, the Wataugans opened a land office at the home of John Carter. Charles Robertson (trustee), James Smith (land office clerk), and William Bailey Smith (surveyor) oversaw the administration of the land office. The land office allowed the valley speculators to use the proceeds of the land sales to repay the financiers of the Watauga Purchase, to reserve the choicest parcels of land for the Watauga settlement's economic elite, and to "dispose of the remainder for the good of the community." Over the next few months, several of the more prominent Wataugans, including John Sevier, John Carter, William Bean, Jonathan Tipton, James Robertson, and Robert Lucas, purchased large acreages. Despite the accumulation of landed wealth by the Tennessee Valley's economic elite, individual farming families managed to purchase most of the land in two-hundred- to four-hundred-acre patents. By facilitating the acquisition of land for many of the region's small farmers, the Tennessee Valley's ruling class tied their own interests to that of the regional small-holders. These economic connections served as the first and perhaps strongest bonds uniting backcountry residents across class lines.[90]

These initial land sales served as the first step in the economic stratification of frontier Tennessee, but also tied the region's landed elite to the region's smaller landholders. Challenges to these land claims from the British Empire, North Carolina, the U.S. government, and the region's Native Americans threatened both large and small landholders alike. Shared concerns over the preservation of land claims led both groups to demand the construction of county courts and land offices in order to register and protect their land claims. These same collective interests allowed the Tennessee Valley's ruling class to secure the support of the region's lower class in the Franklin independence movement.[91]

The American Revolution and corresponding Indian wars accelerated the distribution of land in East Tennessee. Campaigns against the British-allied Cherokee tribe brought thousands of militiamen into the Tennessee country, and many of these soldiers purchased land in the region. The continued threat of Cherokee and Tory attacks in the southern mountains, anguished pleas by the mountaineers for protection, and the desire to defend their landholdings led to the eventual annexation of the Watauga settlements by the state of North Carolina. The creation of the Watauga District in 1776 and the subsequent formation of Washington County in 1777 legitimized earlier land purchases, as North Carolina recognized "the loyalty of the West to the Patriot cause."[92]

The U.S. Continental Congress offered the first federal land grants on the Tennessee frontier immediately after declaring independence from Brit-

ain. Congress lacked the specie to raise an army, so they utilized land boun-
ties to recruit and pay Continental soldiers. Revolutionary leaders like
Thomas Jefferson believed that offering America's western lands to yeoman
soldiers ensured the settlement of western lands and the spread of Republican ideals.[93] The 1780 and 1782 land bounty acts guaranteed enlistees
backcountry acreage, based on military rank, in military districts previously reserved for recruitment purposes. Because land speculators, valley
settlers, and the Overhill Cherokee claimed the bulk of the available lands
in East Tennessee, most of the military land grants issued in what eventually became the state of Tennessee were in the Cumberland District of
Middle Tennessee (Davidson County). Due to the complicated and costly
nature of obtaining a title to the military land claims, many of these grants
ended up in the hands of land speculators, including a number of prominent Franklinites. Land speculators "had both the money and political
connections to acquire good land in the military districts," and to "manage
the complications and costs" associated with obtaining a title to the land.[94]
These "land-jobbers" used their political and economic leverage, and some-
times fraud, bribery, and corruption, to amass enormous tracts of land in
Tennessee.[95]

Postrevolutionary land speculation in the Tennessee Valley demanded
further land cessions by the Cherokee Nation, who claimed vast tracts of
land in the lower Tennessee Valley, and the acquiescence of the North
Carolina government to the interests of powerful regional land speculators.
In 1783, a group of influential and politically connected land speculators,
led by William Blount, "pushed" the "Land Grab Act" through the North
Carolina legislature. The act "offered for sale at a price of ten pounds per
hundred acres all unappropriated land in the Tennessee country, with the
exception of military counties and the Cherokee Reservation east of the
Tennessee River and south of the French Broad and Big Pigeon."[96] This
often-overlooked piece of legislation reinvigorated land speculation in eastern Tennessee. The desire for land became so ravenous that the small land
office opened by the state from October 20, 1783, to May 25, 1784, sold
nearly 4 million acres of land. This period of wild speculation "created the
foundations for large fortunes" for several prominent Tennessee Valley entrepreneurs and smaller homesteads for thousands of backcountry yeoman.
The preservation of these land claims played a central role in the Franklin
independence movement for both groups.[97] Over the course of Franklin's
brief existence, securing access to the rapidly shrinking aboriginal territo-

rial claims remained an important priority in the Franklinites' political and economic agenda.[98]

By the opening of the first session of the Franklin Assembly in August 1784, the frontier communities of eastern Tennessee had matured into a hierarchical society dominated by an entrenched economic and political elite. The leaders of the state of Franklin consolidated their political and economic power by drawing upon their entrepreneurial spirit, military prowess, and most importantly their vast land holdings. These men utilized their control of the complex and advancing backcountry economy to determine the Tennessee Valley's political course for the next decade, but they did so with the support of a large segment of the region's small-holders. Commercial connections, land sales, feelings of political marginalization, and a shared interest in the development of the regional economy and the preservation of land claims connected the landed elite to the yeoman mountaineer. As the opening phase of the Franklin separatist movement dawned, the Tennessee Valley landed gentry increasingly relied on the unyielding support of the region's small-holders.

Chapter 2

Acts of Designing Men

Community, Conflict, and Control

Following the conclusion of the American Revolution, the newly created national and state governments found themselves heavily indebted to foreign and domestic creditors and on the cusp of a financial catastrophe. Many political leaders believed that the most promising and expedient solution to America's postrevolutionary economic crisis lay in the sale of the "uninhabited" western lands claimed by several expansive and powerful states and combative Native American groups. Beginning in 1780, the Confederation Congress began lobbying state leaders from New York, Virginia, Georgia, and North Carolina to cede their western territory to the federal government. Congress hoped to sell the land and use the proceeds to stall the mounting national debt. New York agreed to cede her lands in 1780 and Virginia followed suit in 1781, but political leaders in North Carolina remained bitterly divided on the subject.[1] During the April 1784 session of the North Carolina General Assembly, the financially embattled state finally agreed to surrender her western lands to the national government. The state relinquished "all lands west of the Appalachian mountain watershed," including the counties of Washington, Greene, Sullivan, and Davidson (in Middle Tennessee), in order to "hasten the extinguishment of the debts" incurred during the American Revolution and to avoid paying a potential "continental land tax" being considered in Congress.[2] This first Cession Act proved to be the spark that ignited the combustible fumes of backcountry resentment, fear, and separatism lingering in the Tennessee Valley. The supporters of western independence waited less than six months after the passage of this act to declare their political sovereignty.[3]

The Franklin statehood movement drove a divisive wedge through the once united Tennessee Valley communities and forced the region's emerging economic elite, mountain farmers, and backcountry merchants to choose sides during the tumult surrounding the separatist affair. Tennessee frontier settlers faced crucial decisions regarding their partisan loyalties, and these choices ultimately determined the future political course of the state of Franklin and the trans-Appalachian frontier. The determination to either support or oppose the Franklin statehood movement was undoubtedly an agonizing choice for Tennessee Valley residents, and these decisions were not concluded haphazardly. A careful examination of the leaders and supporters of both factions during the Franklin affair reveals the multiplicity of factors that combined to determine personal and familial loyalties. Although cultural factors undoubtedly influenced backcountry partisanship during the events surrounding Franklin, frontier fidelity transcended ethnic, religious, and class lines. Partisan loyalties were closely tied to the influence of the region's leading men, their shared wartime and frontier experiences, and their collective economic and political interests. Both factions understood the relationship between controlling political offices (sheriff and surveyor) and county courts (judge and justice of the peace) and assuring future economic prosperity, and the leaders of trans-Appalachia's first economic ruling class were well aware of the dire consequences if they failed.[4]

The vast majority of first families settling the upper Tennessee Valley migrated to the region from Virginia and North Carolina. Pioneering settlers like William Bean and John Carter emigrated from the Shenandoah Valley and tidewater region of Virginia. Frontier entrepreneurs like Jacob White and Nashville founder James Robertson came from eastern North Carolina. Many prominent Franklin families, including the Sevier, Cocke, Carter, Campbell, Cage, Christian, Martin, Donelson, and Looney families, once called the Old Dominion home.[5] Several of the most important families in early Tennessee history, including the White, Hutchings, and Love families, embarked from North Carolina counties east of the Allegheny Mountains. Not all influential pioneer Tennesseans migrated from North Carolina and Virginia. Powerful regional opponents of Franklin like Evan Shelby and John Tipton arrived in eastern Tennessee from Maryland, and several other eminent Tennessee Valley families relocated from Pennsylvania and South Carolina.[6]

For a region long considered predominantly Scots-Irish, the ethnic composition of frontier East Tennessee is surprisingly heterogeneous. The vast majority of the earliest inhabitants of the region traced their roots back to the British Isles. In a survey conducted of the roughly 31,913 residents of the Tennessee country in 1790, approximately 83.1 percent were English, 11.2 percent were Scots-Irish, and 2.3 percent were Irish. The study concluded that "From these percentages it is evident that Tennessee was considerably ahead of the United States in the number of its citizens who traced their ancestry back to the British Isles." Despite being less than 12 percent of the total population of Tennessee, many scholars continue to argue that the Ulster-Scots comprised the largest ethnic group of first families in Tennessee, meaning families who arrived before Tennessee was granted statehood in 1796.[7] The story of the politically and religiously oppressed Ulster-Scots and their flight to America is entrenched in the history of the Appalachian region, but it often obscures East Tennessee's cultural diversity and the contributions made by these disparate ethnic groups.[8]

In addition to the ethnically dominant Anglo-Saxon strains, the 1790 ethnic survey included Germans, Welsh, Dutch, Swiss, Alsatians, Africans, and French Huguenots.[9] Many of the region's leading frontier families traced their ancestry back to these minority ethnic groups. The Sevier, Vincent, and Amis families emigrated from France with groups of Huguenots who fled religious persecution and traveled among the Protestant congregations of William Penn.[10] Eminent Welsh families like the Shelby, Conway, Evans, and Williams families also called Tennessee home in the late eighteenth century. The ethnic diversity of the Tennessee Valley contributed to the development of the region's distinct political and social culture.[11]

The men at the epicenter of the state of Franklin controversy are representative of the region's multiethnic composition. Franklin's only governor, John Sevier, descended from French Huguenots from the village of Xavier, who fled France after 1685 when Louis XIV revoked the Edict of Nantes and began imprisoning the Protestant minority.[12] William Cocke, Franklin's emissary to the American Congress, and Landon Carter, Speaker of Franklin's first senate, traced their ancestry to England.[13] The families of James White, founder of Knoxville and "early speaker" in the Franklin Senate, and Gilbert Christian, Speaker of the Franklin Senate in 1786, emigrated from Ulster.[14] The descendents of Presbyterian minister Samuel Doak, the Franklinites' spiritual and educational advisor, migrated from Ireland, and the well-traveled mercenary George Elholm, adjutant general of the Franklin militia, came to America at the beginning of the Revolutionary War from the Duchy of Holstein in Denmark.[15] Even the opponents of the Franklin movement, usually referred to as Tiptonites after their leader John Tipton, came from diverse ethnic backgrounds. Colonel John Tipton's family claimed its origins in Scotland, and Evan Shelby, probably the most politically influential opponent of Franklin, was of Welsh descent. Both leading Franklinites and Tiptonites and their rank and file supporters clearly exhibited the Tennessee Valley's ethnic variance, and therefore ethnic identity does little to explain the motives behind the hardening of partisan loyalties during the events surrounding the Franklin struggle.[16]

The region's cultural diversity did lead to the growth of several socially and politically influential religious denominations in the Tennessee backcountry. By 1784, ministers representing no less than five denominations proselytized in upper East Tennessee, including Presbyterians, Baptists, Methodists, Moravians, and Quakers. These leaders and their churches played critical roles in the political, educational, and cultural development of the Tennessee Valley and the state of Franklin. From the earliest exploration of the region, organized religion helped to transform the Tennessee Valley. Early frontier explorers like Daniel Boone and Nathan Gist were "traditionally Baptists," and ordained ministers often accompanied groups of would-be settlers into the backcountry. In 1758, Presbyterian missionaries from the Society for Managing the Mission and Schools traveled into the future state of Tennessee to propagate the gospel among the Overhill Cherokee. Led by such ministers as John Martin and William Richardson, these Presbyterian missionaries became the "first ministers to preach the gospel in the Tennessee country."[17] In 1761, North Carolina Baptist preacher Jonathan Mulkey accompanied a party of explorers venturing into the region. Mulkey eventually settled in Carter's Valley in 1775, where he came under attack by a group of Cherokee Indians less than a year later. Presbyterian missionaries constructed Taylor's Meeting House in 1773, and the small log building became the first structure used for religious instruction in the Tennessee backcountry. Circuit riders from various denominations often catechized from the log cabin, and also used the rustic structure as a fort and a school.[18]

The Watauga residents organized the two earliest permanent churches in the region during the American Revolution, Sinking Creek Baptist Church and Buffalo Ridge Baptist Church. The Reverend Matthew Talbott, from Bedford County, Virginia, established Sinking Creek Baptist Church (originally called Watauga River Church) sometime between 1775 and 1783. Talbott, an early Watauga landowner, constructed the church on a small tributary of the Watauga River in what is now Carter County, Tennessee.[19] The first extant records from the church date back to July 5, 1785, and include a plea to an unknown "Virginia [Baptist] Association" to end "the [unspecified] divisions between us."[20] Remarkably, the church is still in existence and is now considered the "oldest church in Tennessee occupying its original location and foundation." Tidence Lane founded Buffalo Ridge Baptist Church between 1778 and 1779, considered by most state historians to be Tennessee's first church. Reverend Lane migrated from Sandy Creek, North Carolina, to Watauga in 1776, and constructed his church atop Buffalo Ridge in Washington County. The founding of these two frontier churches initiated a dramatic proliferation of Baptist churches across the Tennessee Valley.[21]

Presbyterians soon followed these early Baptist churches onto the Tennessee frontier. In 1780, Presbyterian minister Samuel Doak organized Salem Church near Jonesboro, and soon after, Samuel Houston and Hezekiah Balch, Presbyterian ministers from Mecklenburg County, North Carolina, joined Doak in the Tennessee Valley.[22] These Presbyterian leaders played important roles in the development of the state of Franklin and used their pulpits for catechizing and politicking. The blending of god and politics ultimately fostered divisions within the Tennessee Valley and the Franklin movement, but the contributions of these Presbyterian ministers led to the creation of an exceptional frame of government and the establishment of the Tennessee Valley's first educational institutions.[23]

Reserving the in-depth discussion of the debate over the Franklin Constitution and the role played by Presbyterian ministers in the Franklin movement for a later chapter, it is important to note the relationship between the Tennessee Valley's first schools and the efforts of Presbyterian ministers in the backcountry. The "pioneering Presbyterian ministers" of East Tennessee "brought with them the traditional Scottish practice of founding a school beside each church."[24] In 1780, Samuel Doak erected the first school west of the Appalachian Mountains beside his Salem Church. Doak's Martin Academy, named after North Carolina governor Alexander Martin, eventually received an official charter from the North Carolina Assembly in 1783. In 1785, the Franklin government supported the academy, often called "Doak's Log College" by local residents, and in 1795 the school became Washington College.[25]

During the early formative months of the state of Franklin, education emerged as a politically divisive issue. East Tennessee's influential Presbyterian ministers led the effort to construct public schools and to utilize tax revenue to finance the construction and administration of these institutions. During the 1785 debates surrounding the drafting and ratification of the Franklin Constitution, the Reverend Samuel Houston, a Washington

County Presbyterian minister, coauthored a radical constitution (ultimately rejected by the Franklinites) that included provisions for building and financing schools in the state. According to section thirty-two of this document, "All kinds of useful learning shall be encouraged by this commonwealth." The constitution called for the construction of "one University" and "a Grammar School" for each county, and the employment of "a [school] master or masters of approved morals and abilities." Reverend Houston proposed paying for these educational improvements through an endowment funded through the collection of taxes on land purchases and surveys and the sale of indigo, flour, and tobacco.[26] Reverend Houston's effort to establish a state university and public school system in 1785 is remarkable considering that the state of Tennessee made no attempt to create a tax-supported public school system until the middle of the nineteenth century.[27]

Although the constitutional debates surrounding the public school efforts did not survive, most Tennessee historians believe that the Presbyterian minister Hezekiah Balch led the effort to abandon the progressive Franklin Constitution. Section forty-one of the compromise constitution provided for a drastically scaled-back version of Houston's original proposal. The alternative constitution provided for "a [public] school or schools" and "one or more universities" to be established by the [Franklin] legislature for the "convenient instruction of youth," and for the teachers' salaries to be "paid by the public, as may enable them to instruct at low prices."[28] The new constitution failed to provide the same levels of financial support or urgency for the construction of public schools and universities. The controversy surrounding public school and university funding in the state of Franklin became one of numerous contentious issues that fractured the Tennessee Valley communities following the American Revolution.[29]

Supporters of Franklin's public school initiative argued that education would have a civilizing effect on the Tennessee backcountry and curtail crime and moral indiscretions.[30] According to Episcopal minister Charles Woodmason, whose missionary work led him to visit the Carolina backcountry, the educationally deficient southern frontier was rampant with "Lewd, impudent, abandon'd Prostitutes, Gamblers, Gamesters of all Sorts—Horse Thieves, Cattle Steelers, Hog Steelers—Branders and Markers, Hunters going naked as Indians. Women hardly more so. All in a Manner useless to Society, but very pernicious in propagating Vice, Beggary, and Theft." An examination of the surviving East Tennessee county and court records from the years surrounding the state of Franklin reveals a very different community than the one described by Reverend Woodmason in 1768. Residents of the Tennessee Valley were both highly literate and largely law abiding. The images of rough and tumble frontier communities in the Tennessee Valley do not hold up under scrutiny.[31]

From the earliest settlement, the Tennessee Valley residents concentrated their efforts on maintaining law and order and protecting private property. As the Tennessee Valley communities and regional economy advanced, the emerging economic ruling class quickly determined that control over the county courts and judicial offices were the key to securing back-country hegemony. According to one historian, the earliest residents of Washington County "lived, administered their laws, established courts and laid their penalties upon evil-doers according to the legal system of their parent States." Tennessee Valley settlers held the first court in the region on February 23, 1778, at the home of Charles Robertson. The lack of a permanent courthouse forced the Washington County residents to hold court in several private homes.[32] Despite this limitation, the earliest court records reveal a community concerned with crime and punishment. At the second court meeting, local leaders appointed Valentine Sevier Jr. (brother of the clerk of the court, John Sevier) sheriff of Washington County. During the August 27, 1778, meeting, the frontier court ordered its tax collectors for the several districts in the county to collect "sums" for the construction of a "court house, prison, & stocks." These early court sessions provided the leadership of Washington County with an opportunity to establish tax rates, pay officials, fix prices on essential items, and, most importantly, sell and purchase landed property.[33]

A survey of the Washington County court records from 1777 through 1789 shows the preponderance of early cases to be breach of contract suits and land fraud cases. A typical example of a breach of contract case occurred on March 15, 1789, with a suit brought by Andrew Grier against Mark Mitchell. According to court records, Mitchell "made a certain promissory note . . . to pay unto the said Andrew . . . one-hundred and eight pounds Virginia money" for an undisclosed amount of land. Grier stated that Mitchell intended "to deceive" him and refused to "pay him the said sum of money." In a region so heavily reliant upon land for credit, exchange, investment, and growth, it is not surprising that cases involving land disputes most frequently appear in court records. As the region's landed elite and yeoman small-holders increasingly expanded their land holdings and external scrutiny of these controversial land claims intensified, the importance of establishing ascendancy over county courts and judicial offices dramatically increased. During the state of Franklin's existence, competition for Tennessee Valley courts and court positions became fierce, emerging as another critical factor shaping partisan loyalties within the backcountry rank and file.[34]

Several court cases dealing with relatively minor criminal offenses, usually theft of livestock or slander suits, also dot the early Washington County court records. In a July 29, 1781, case, William Deal accused Marshall Higdon of "having taken [several horses] in a clandestine manner." The August 18, 1789, case of *Henry Colback v. William Blevins* involved accusations of "scandalous and defamatory" speech. According to court records, Blevins sullied Colback's "good name" when he accused him of "stealing John Gorsach's Bridle." Colback defended himself by stating that he "was good and honest and always kept himself free and clear from theft." In addition to larceny and slander cases, several Tennessee Valley women initiated cases against men for fathering illegitimate children. In a December 28, 1779, case, Jane Odell stood before the court and accused Absalom Booring of "begetting [her] said child." John Tipton and Henry Nelson, the two Washington County justices of the peace, ordered Booring arrested and brought before the court to "answer these charges." Booring ultimately paid a small fine for having "carnal knowledge of her body." These nonviolent cases abound in the Washington County court records.[35]

Despite the relative peacefulness within the communities themselves, East Tennessee remained a dangerous and violent region throughout the eighteenth century. Native American attacks, revolutionary warfare, frontier Toryism, and bitter partisanship surrounding the state of Franklin fostered a lingering sense of fear and acrimony within the Tennessee Valley. The military efforts to confront these threats elevated several of the Tennessee Valley's economic elite into positions of unrivaled backcountry authority. As these leading men commanded backcountry farmers-turned-militiamen in deadly pitched battles with British forces and terrifying irregular warfare against regional Indians, their political influence among the Tennessee Valley's residents solidified. Shared Revolutionary War experiences and the prolonged threat posed by the Cherokee and Creek Indians to their communities further united the Tennessee Valley's ruling class and yeoman farmers. The growing influence of East Tennessee's leading men and the wartime strengthening of their bonds with mountain farmers and merchants played a critical role in the coalescence of support for the Franklin statehood movement.[36]

A detailed analysis of the relationship between the regional Native American tribes and white East Tennesseans is contained in later chapters, but it is critical to briefly mention that violent clashes between frontier whites and the southeastern tribes remained a powerful permanent feature of the region until the early nineteenth century. From the struggle between the British and the French-allied Cherokee warriors at Fort Loudon during the French and Indian War to the extremely bloody Cherokee and Creek wars following the collapse of the state of Franklin, the constant threat of Native American violence served as a salient political and economic issue that united Tennessee Valley residents across socioeconomic lines. Communal cohesion among Tennessee Valley inhabitants remained largely intact until the rancorous Franklin political debates severed these bonds.[37]

Most of the leading Tennessee Valley men served in some military capacity, and several of their forebearers participated in the agrarian radicalism of the North and South Carolina Regulator movements. Prior to the American Revolution, the South Carolina Regulators demanded that local government officials halt the roving bands of thieves, bandits, and criminals terrorizing their backcountry agrarian communities. South Carolina backcountry settlers and a "fledgling" group of slaveholding planter elite banded together to form extra-governmental police units, calling themselves Regulators, to end the anarchic situation and to defend their families and property. The Palmetto State Regulators also demanded the establishment of much-needed courts, the construction of jails, and the strengthening of the woefully inadequate backcountry legal system.[38] In North Carolina, backcountry settlers, also calling themselves Regulators, sought to end governmental and fiscal corruption by their local and state government officials, unscrupulous creditors, and land speculators. The North Carolina Regulators formed a quasi-military force that challenged North Carolina governor William Tryon and the state's political and economic leadership. On May 16, 1771, Governor Tryon and several thousand well-trained colonial troops crushed the backcountry insurgency at the bloody Battle of Alamance Creek, and many of the surviving supporters of the movement fled the region. The Regulator movement is often hailed as the "first battle of the American Revolution," and several scholars maintain that many supporters of the movement immigrated into the Tennessee Valley to escape retaliation for their actions and to find "freedom."[39] Other historians challenge the assertion that "the colonization of the trans-Appalachian region" occurred as a "result of the Regulator trouble," arguing that the earliest settlers of the region "were seeking land rather than freedom" when they settled in the Tennessee Valley. Historians disagree over the significance of the Regulator movement in the settlement of the trans-Appalachian frontier, but it is clear that at least a few former supporters and leaders of the movement, including Jacob Brown and James Robertson, settled in the upper Tennessee Valley. Additionally, it is worth noting that many of the grievances and goals of both Carolina Regulator movements and the supporters of the Franklin movement were remarkably analogous, including demands for courts, land offices, enhanced political influence, internal improvements, and improved frontier defenses. Despite these similarities, there is little evidence to prove any direct connection between the ideologies of backcountry regulation and trans-Appalachian separatism.[40]

The internal threat posed by local Tories and British-allied Indians, combined with the participation of many of the residents in the combat surrounding the American Revolution, altered the socioeconomic dynamics within the Tennessee Valley and forged a strong bond between the region's emerging ruling class and yeoman soldiers. The American Revolution became the economic and political springboard for many of the region's leading men, and the events that occurred in the rolling hills of the North Carolina piedmont transformed a ragtag group of backwoods farmers and merchants into the "Rearguard of the Revolution." The involvement of Tennessee Valley settlers in the Revolutionary War fostered the rank and file loyalty and radical separatism defining the state of Franklin movement, as well as the political allegiance to North Carolina underlying the ideology of the Anti-Franklinites.[41]

Prior to 1780, the American Revolution seemed like a distant event for most residents of the upper Tennessee Valley. The only significant manifestations of revolutionary violence in the region came in the form of increased numbers of Overhill Cherokee attacks on white settlements and the arrest, prosecution, and execution of backcountry Tories. Trade relations and continued land encroachment by American colonists ensured the British support from the Overhill Cherokee, and the intensification of Indian raids on American settlements created a highly volatile situation in the backcountry communities.[42] In response to the threat of Cherokee violence, the Tennessee Valley settlers organized several revolutionary committees of safety, bolstered their frontier defenses and armaments, and expanded the ranks of their militia companies. The American Revolution opened an epoch of warfare between the Overhill Cherokee and Tennessee Valley settlers that lasted for several decades.[43]

Second only to the Cherokee, the danger posed by Tennessee Tories loomed as the greatest internal revolutionary threat to the valley settlements. Exact statistics regarding the level of loyalist support in the Tennessee backcountry remain obscure, but Tennessee Valley settlers unquestionably believed Toryism to be a grave threat to their communities.[44] Backcountry leaders and militia companies targeted known pockets of loyalists, forcing them to take loyalty oaths to the United States, to flee the region, or to languish in local jails. East Tennesseans targeted "nests of Tories" on the Nolichucky River and in the Watauga settlements, capturing roughly seventy suspected loyalists.[45] Adding to the challenges confronting Patriot supporters in the Tennessee backcountry, many eastern Tories fled across the trans-Appalachian frontier to escape prosecution in the east. By 1780, tales of Tory conspiracies and sabotage spread across upper East Tennessee. According to one John Sevier biographer, in the fall of 1779, Sarah Hawkins Sevier, John Sevier's first wife, helped to foil a plot to assassinate Colonel Sevier by a "noted and infamous Tory" named Jacob Dykes. Dykes's wife divulged the plan to Sarah Sevier "after receiving favors [a quart of meal and a slice of meat] from the [Sevier] family."[46]

In response to the elevated threat of Tory violence, the Tennesseans formed two companies comprised of thirty "dragoons" to "patrol the whole country," and to "capture and punish with death all suspected persons." These patrols succeeded in capturing several high-profile Tory leaders, including Isam Yearley and Captain Grimes.[47] Many of the captured Tories faced their American accusers in the Washington County court. On February 23, 1778, an unidentified Tory was "imprisoned during the [remainder] of the present war with Britain, and the sheriff take the whole of his estate into custody." In another case, a loyalist identified as "J.H." received a sentence of one year in prison "in order to prevent further and future practices of [a] pernicious nature."[48] A patrol unit led by Robert Sevier captured and executed several Tories, including two loyalists accused of conspiring to assassinate John Sevier. In all, the Washington County court tried fourteen cases of high treason from 1778 to 1783.[49] Tories like Dykes, Halley, Jesse Green, and John Gibson did not have the luxury of a court trial. Valley militiamen hanged these men for their loyalty to the British cause. In 1850, the son of Franklin judge David Campbell recounted the backcountry execution of a Tory named Hopkins. After a two-mile chase up the Holston River, David Campbell and a small party of frontier militiamen cornered the desperate Hopkins. Upon being confronted by his pursuers, Hopkins plunged his horse off a twenty-foot bluff into the Holston River. David Campbell managed to throw Hopkins from his horse and wrestle him to the ground. During the violent struggle, Hopkins, "the strongest man," nearly drowned Campbell before "Edmiston and several others" rushed to his aid. With their assistance, Hopkins "was subdued and taken to the bank" of the Holston River. David Campbell's son described what happened next: "Some of the company knew him, and knew some of his acts of felony—all knew his desperate character. . . . The company held a consultation & decided that they would hang him and did so forthwith by sticking his neck into the fork of a leaning sycamore which bent over the river."[50] The arrests, prosecutions, and executions of local Tories galvanized the largely pro-American Tennesseans and stoked the flames of backcountry patriotism.[51]

The Tennessee Valley's first external participation in the American Revolution occurred early in 1780 when the British launched the southern offensive of their struggling American campaign. After British general John Burgoyne's stunning defeat at the Battle of Saratoga in upstate New York in October 1777, King George III and his military planners decided to move the war from the mid-Atlantic region to the southern colonies.[52] This shift brought the main British thrust to the doorstep of the Tennessee Valley residents. During Britain's 1780 winter assault on Charleston, South Carolina, North Carolina general Henry Rutherford sent a request to the residents of his state to dispatch their militia units "for the defense of their sister state [South Carolina]." On March 19, 1780, the militia officers of Washington County, including John Sevier, Jonathan Tipton, Robert Sevier, Landon Carter, John McNabb, Godfrey Isbell, Joseph Wilson, and William Trimble, met "in order to raise one hundred men, agreeable to the command of the Honorable Brigadier Rutherford, to send aid to South Carolina." The city of Charleston fell to the British on May 12, 1780, but the militiamen of Washington County remained committed to Rutherford's call.[53] In Sullivan County, Colonel Isaac Shelby recruited volunteers to fill the ranks of the Sullivan County militia. Despite the failure to save Charleston and British victories in South Carolina at Waxhaw, Ninety-Six, and Camden, Sevier and Shelby succeeded in raising roughly four hundred militiamen for the mission into South Carolina. The willingness of the

Valley settlers to volunteer for a losing southern effort and to leave their homes and families largely unprotected from the Cherokee Indians demonstrates their level of commitment to the American cause and growing trust in the Tennessee Valley's military leadership.[54]

Led by Colonel Isaac Shelby, the Tennessee volunteers saw their first revolutionary action during the assault on Fort Anderson at the Battle of Thicketty Creek. Fort Anderson, a small fort in the piedmont of South Carolina, housed both British soldiers and a large contingent of South Carolina Tories. On July 30, 1780, Colonel Shelby dispatched William Cocke, whose diplomatic skills would be relied upon heavily during the Franklin affair, to demand the surrender of Fort Anderson. The British commander of the fort, Captain Moore, eventually agreed to surrender the post, and the Washington County militia captured ninety-three loyalists, two hundred and fifty weapons, and one British sergeant-major. Following their victory in South Carolina, the East Tennesseans engaged the British and their regional loyalists at skirmishes near Cedar Spring and Musgrove Mill. These encounters served as a prelude to the defining revolutionary moment for East Tennessee, the Battle of King's Mountain.[55]

In May 1780, British general Charles Cornwallis established his southern military headquarters at Camden, South Carolina. From Camden, Cornwallis and Major Patrick Ferguson drew upon the recent British military successes and waning southern support for the American cause to recruit local loyalists. By the fall of 1780, the ranks of Major Ferguson's 71st Regiment Highlanders had swollen with the addition of Tories drawn from across the Carolinas. After sending a request to loyal North Carolinians to join the British cause, Ferguson, nicknamed "Bull Dog" for his tenacity in battle, menacingly paraded his regiment across the Carolina frontier, capturing Patriots and recruiting additional Tories. Ferguson's backcountry campaign created confusion within the Tennessee Valley communities.[56] Hundreds of "refugee" American supporters fled across the Allegheny Mountains seeking shelter among the East Tennesseans. One of these refugees, Samuel Philips, carried a message from Major Ferguson threatening to "march his own men over the mountains, hang their leaders, and lay the country to waste with fire and sword."[57]

The danger posed by Ferguson's forces strengthened the resolve of the valley residents. Led by Colonel John Sevier (Washington County), Colonel Isaac Shelby (Sullivan County), Charles and Joseph McDowell (Burke County, North Carolina), Andrew Hampton (Rutherford County, North

Carolina), and William and Arthur Campbell (Washington County, Virginia), a combined force of Tennessee Valley, North Carolina, and Virginia troops met on September 25, 1780, at Sycamore Shoals on the Watauga River. The next day, the assemblage of roughly one thousand militiamen commenced their march toward the fateful conflict atop King's Mountain. Before they departed, the Reverend Samuel Doak treated the volunteer militia force to a passionate sermon. Mixing spirituality and patriotism, Doak urged the soldiers to "Go forth then in the strength of your manhood to the aid of your brethren, the defense of your liberty and the protection of your homes. And may the God of justice be with you and give you victory."[58]

After a grueling ten-day march across the Appalachian Mountains, on the evening of October 6, 1780, the expanded force of fifteen hundred men made contact with Major Ferguson's loyalist regiment in the foothills bordering the two Carolinas. The next day, the militia forces surrounded the British troops taking a defensive position atop King's Mountain. Sevier's Washington County militiamen formed a column on the right flank, and Shelby's Sullivan County troops joined the Virginia forces to form a column in the center. Aided by North Carolina troops commanded by colonels Charles and Joseph McDowell and Benjamin Cleveland, the Tennessee Valley men launched a withering attack on Ferguson's forces. Utilizing guerilla warfare tactics honed during their irregular encounters with the southeastern Indians, the Patriot militia engaged the Loyalist forces for a little more than an hour. As the black powder smoke cleared from atop King's Mountain, the Tennesseans found themselves victorious. The American troops succeeded in capturing 716 and killing 225 British loyalists, including Major Patrick Ferguson. American forces suffered only twenty-eight dead and sixty-two wounded militiamen. The continued threat of Cherokee attacks against their communities did not allow the triumphant East Tennesseans to bask in their momentous victory, and soon after the battle's conclusion, Sevier and Shelby led their troops back across the rugged southern mountains to a heroic welcome in the Great Valley of the Tennessee.[59]

The Battle of King's Mountain and the mythology surrounding the men who fought there created a sense of civic pride and solidarity among East Tennesseans. The leaders of the assault on Ferguson's forces parlayed their exploits into further political and economic hegemony in the rapidly expanding Tennessee frontier. The relationship between political and fiscal power and the battle some historians refer to as "the turning point of the

American Revolution" is unmistakable. An examination of the militia leaders during the expedition reveals that most of the Tennessee Valley's able-bodied leading men served in leadership capacities during the battle. This connection extended into the postrevolutionary Franklin movement, where men like John Sevier, Landon Carter, and William Cocke all held prominent positions both in the revolutionary militia and the Franklin government. Even the opponents of Franklin, men like Jonathan Tipton and Isaac Shelby, served as colonels in the King's Mountain volunteer militias and held positions of power in the North Carolina government. There is no discernable difference between the percentages of King's Mountain participants among the rank and file supporters or opponents of the Franklin statehood movement, and it appears that postrevolutionary developments on the Tennessee frontier played a much more critical role in determining state loyalties during the Franklin debacle. Each side drew heavily upon the rhetoric and ideology of the revolution and their experiences, both real and romanticized, during the Battle of King's Mountain to win local, regional, and national support for their causes. The influence wielded by these leading men played an important role in securing support from the backcountry rank and file during the partisanship surrounding the Franklin movement.[60]

Participants on both sides of the state of Franklin controversy came from comparably mixed ethnic and religious backgrounds, and also shared similar experiences with localized Indian violence and revolutionary combat. These factors created deep personal connections between East Tennessee's emerging economic elite and yeoman mountaineers, and therefore fail to explain the development of bitter regional factionalism surrounding the state of Franklin movement. In fact, the communities, leadership, and residents of the Tennessee Valley emerged from the American Revolution more united than at any other time in the region's brief history.

At its core, backcountry partisanship was rooted in the cutthroat postrevolutionary competition between two factions of the Tennessee Valley's economic elite for control over the enormously lucrative regional economy. Land speculation and ownership served as the primary method for accumulating wealth and influence in the Tennessee Valley's mixed economy, and control over local, county, and state political and judicial offices stood as the most effective means of securing and ensuring regional hegemony. Within this economic and political framework, regional support for the Franklin movement is intimately connected to the efforts of both wealthy and "middling" mountaineers alike to expand personal land holdings, defend land claims, and remove any barriers to financial success.

A brief examination of the postrevolutionary Tennessee Valley ruling class reveals a significant concentration of wealth among a relatively small number of families. During the state of Franklin's brief existence, John Sevier served as the embattled state's only governor. As one might expect, Sevier and his family maintained extensive land holdings in the Tennessee Valley. "Nolachucky Jack," as the soldiers who served under him lovingly referred to him, owned roughly 84,000 acres of land spread out in several counties and military districts. Sevier's brother Valentine claimed approximately 900 acres in Washington County. Landon Carter, Franklin's Speaker of the Senate and secretary of state, claimed more than 31,000 acres in the Tennessee Valley. The state of Franklin's most prominent attorney and skilled diplomat, William Cocke, owned 11,000 acres of land, and Alexander Outlaw, sheriff of Greene County and one of Franklin's primary Cherokee negotiators, claimed nearly 19,000 acres. In all, the leadership of the state of Franklin maintained a disproportionately high level of land holdings, averaging approximately 6,600 acres, in a region where most residents owned only a few hundred acres. In a time when property ownership became essential to fully participating in the embryonic American Republic, the leaders of the state of Franklin movement utilized their substantial land holdings to control the socioeconomic dynamics and political destiny of an entire region.[61]

Franklinites were not the only regional leaders with high concentrations of landed wealth. The Anti-Franklinites, or Tiptonites, also owned large swaths of land in the Tennessee Valley, but these acreages did not compare to the significant tracts controlled by the Franklinite leaders. John Tipton, leader of the efforts to derail the Franklin movement, claimed approximately 2,750 acres of land, and North Carolina congressman Thomas Hutchings, a loyalist during the Franklin affair, owned roughly 4,360 acres in East Tennessee. Evan Shelby, perhaps the most politically powerful opponent of Franklin, maintained the largest landholdings, roughly 6,000 acres of fertile bottomland. In sharp contrast to the Franklinites, the Tiptonite's leadership claimed an average of 2,600 acres. These figures lead to the conclusion that political influence in postrevolutionary East Tennessee corresponded to regional land holdings.[62]

Despite the high concentration of landed wealth among the leading families of both Franklinite and Tiptonite factions, most Tennessee Valley residents managed to acquire smaller tracts of land. External threats from North Carolina and the national government and internal threats from Native Americans and local competitors united yeoman small-holders and mountain elites in their effort to defend their land claims and economic interests. As the Tennessee Valley population expanded and the postrevolutionary uncertainty in the trans-Appalachian frontier escalated, competition for control over the region's economic and political future rent the once united backcountry communities. The bonds forged by revolutionary combat, the loyalist presence, and the Native American threat were shattered as two competing political coalitions emerged. Leaders of both the Tiptonites and the Franklinites maintained disparate visions for the political and economic future of the Tennessee Valley, and support and opposition for Franklin's statehood became the platform upon which these ruling men promoted their agenda and galvanized local support.[63]

The inhabitants of the Tennessee Valley remained largely united throughout the American Revolution, but the Franklin separatist movement transformed these backcountry communities. The strong communal connections, built upon cultural, economic, and martial bonds, were catastrophically strained by the postrevolutionary struggle for control over the trans-Appalachian frontier. It was this fight for political and economic supremacy between two groups of backcountry leading men that forced the region's small farmers and merchants to choose sides during the political chaos surrounding the state of Franklin. The resulting partisanship would be disastrous for the inhabitants of the Tennessee Valley, and ultimately doomed the state of Franklin.

Chapter 3

Agreeable to a Republican Government

The Rise of Backcountry Partisanship, 1784–1785

The residents and communities of the Tennessee Valley emerged out of the violence and chaos of the American Revolution largely united. The economic expansion, eastern political marginalization, and backcountry wartime experiences of the previous decades muted any potential underlying tensions fostered by commercial and political competition. However, the postwar materialization of a determined separatist movement within these same backcountry communities led to the polarization of the region's ruling and laboring classes. From the debate over the passage and meaning of North Carolina's 1784 Cession Act to the public dispute over the ratification of the state of Franklin's egalitarian frame of government, gaping fissures appeared among the trans-Allegheny's leading men and their rank and file supporters. These men knew that their political and economic fortunes were at stake, and the Franklin statehood movement represented a fundamental divergence of opinion over the policy decisions that best served the collective fiscal and political interests of the region's inhabitants. Partisan supporters of the Franklin separatist movement believed that an independent Tennessee Valley would allow them to expand and enhance the region's economy by (a) removing the political barriers blocking a more aggressive Native American policy, (b) allowing for the utilization of regional taxes for internal improvements, and (c) permitting the backcountry ruling class to wield greater political influence than under the governance of the state of North Carolina.

As the residents of the Tennessee Valley struggled to make sense of the postrevolutionary political decisions emanating from their state capital at Hillsboro, a small contingent of regional frontier leaders met on December 14, 1784, at Washington County's rustic log courthouse in Jonesboro to address the tenuous situation the communities of the upper Tennessee Valley found themselves in after the passage of the Cession Act a few months prior. This diverse group, comprising the region's economic, military, political, and religious leadership, confronted the political ambiguities created by the actions of the North Carolina Assembly. During this meeting of the as yet unnamed Franklin Assembly, the delegates debated declaring the Tennessee Valley counties of Washington, Sullivan, and Greene independent from the state of North Carolina.[1] One attendee rose in front of the assemblage and impassionedly drew upon the legacy of the American Revolution to attempt to inspire and unify the delegates. The future Franklinite pulled from his coat pocket a copy of the Declaration of Independence and began to "show that a number of the reasons which induced their separation from England . . . applied to the [Tennessee Valley] counties."[2] In what became the first of many contentious decisions made by the increasingly fractured leadership of the Tennessee Valley, a majority of the members of the convention fatefully cast their vote to adopt the state of Franklin's declaration of independence.[3]

The events of that winter day simultaneously obscured the political and economic realities underlying the North Carolina Cession Act and illuminated the dawning of the regional factionalism that steadily divided the Tennessee Valley communities and ultimately destroyed the state of Franklin. The Franklin separatist movement never stood as a unified political movement to secure the independence of the westernmost section of North Carolina in order to protect and defend the communities of the Tennessee Valley. From its conception in the mind of Washington County, Virginia, resident Arthur Campbell, to its collapse in the fall of 1788, economic motivations, partisan divisions provoking communal discord, and the suppression of backcountry democratization characterized the movement. Upon closer scrutiny, the "noble beginnings" and enlightened revolutionary political agenda propagated by the leadership and supporters of the movement melt away and reveal essentially a conservative movement rejecting social, political, and economic innovation in exchange for the preservation of landed property, political hegemony, and the backcountry status quo. The leadership of Franklin quashed the efforts of more progressive elements within the Tennessee Valley to bring about meaningful political and social change within the region, thus further dividing the region's inhabitants. An examination of the struggle over the Franklin Constitution and the inner workings of the Franklin government from 1784 to the end of 1785 exposes the movement's fiscal motivations, political conservatism, and divisive impact on the Tennessee Valley.

The Franklin separatist movement originated in neighboring Washington County, Virginia.[4] Colonel Arthur Campbell of Royal Oak called Washington County, just across the heavily disputed northern border separating Virginia and North Carolina, home. In addition to his geographical proximity, Colonel Campbell also maintained close military, economic, and personal ties to the Tennessee Valley. During Virginia governor Lord Dunmore's 1774 Ohio Valley campaign against the Shawnee and their Native American allies, Major Arthur Campbell fought alongside several prominent Tennessee Valley leading men and future Franklin supporters, including Evan Shelby, Anthony Bledsoe, William Cocke, Samuel Newell, John Carter, and Gilbert Christian. During the American Revolution, Campbell also served with Evan Shelby and William Campbell (his cousin) as lieutenant of the 70th Regiment of the Washington County militia. Although he "missed" the Battle of King's Mountain in order to protect Washington County from local British loyalists, Campbell's Virginia militiamen rendezvoused with the Tennessee Valley's Overmountain Men at Sycamore Shoals in 1780.[5] The Washington County militia triumphed alongside Sevier's and Shelby's troops at King's Mountain, and also joined in the joint Virginia–North Carolina campaigns against the Overhill and Chickamauga Cherokee Indians that followed the defeat of the British forces.[6] In addition to serving during Dunmore's War and the American Revolution with several of the Tennessee Valley's leading men, Colonel Campbell was also related to several influential Franklinites, including his brother David Campbell, who served as Franklin's "chief judge."[7] Campbell's connections to the region also included extensive landholdings in Sullivan County, North Carolina, where the Virginia resident owned approximately 1,240 acres along the Holston River.[8] Campbell's important ties to the Tennessee Valley gave him tremendous political influence among the Tennessee Valley inhabitants and a great personal stake in the region's economic fortunes.[9]

In January 1782, Colonel Campbell became aware that the state of Virginia had recently passed a resolution expressing willingness to cede her western territory to the U.S. Confederation Congress. Despite mounting criticisms that he was "mainly interested in private aggrandizement," Colonel Campbell used his political and economic clout within southwest Vir-

ginia to win support for a new western state.[10] In a scene foreshadowing the
Franklin movement, Campbell argued that the ineptitude of the Virginia
state government in dealing with the Cherokee tribe and the shared economic interests of the western residents made the creation of a new state the
obvious decision.[11]

In April 1782, Campbell circulated a proposal among his fellow Washington County residents to gauge the level of support for a new state.
Campbell's proposal received popular support from many Washington
County residents, and his vision of a new western state rapidly gained mo-
mentum.[12] By the summer of 1782, the boundaries of Campbell's independent state carved out of southwestern Virginia grew to include portions of
western North Carolina, including the Tennessee Valley settlements, and
Virginia's newly developing Kentucky territory. He began contacting Tennessee Valley leaders to garner support for his statehood effort, and it was
within these correspondences that Campbell and future Franklin leaders
John Sevier, William Christian, William Cocke, and David Campbell formulated the plan and principles for a popularly supported trans-Appalachian
statehood movement. The exchanges between the members of the Tennessee
Valley ruling class and the Washington County, Virginia, militia colonel
reveal the strategy utilized by both parties to win support for their independence movements. In a series of legal depositions taken between 1785 and
1786 during the state of Virginia's prosecution of Arthur Campbell for "mal-
practices and misconduct in his Office of a Justice of the Peace," it was divulged that Campbell defiantly implored his fellow westerners to refuse to
pay Virginia's public taxes or to elect citizens to Virginia's General Assembly.
Additionally, Campbell's accusers leveled accusations of treason, stating that
he "openly and secretly, [attempted] to induce the Inhabitants of Washington County to Separate from this [Virginia] Commonwealth."[13] Campbell's
communications with the Franklinites exposed his resentment toward Virginia for not using more forceful tactics to halt Cherokee Indian violence,
for failing to utilize state taxes for desperately needed internal improvements
in the region, and for denying the western leaders political influence within
their state government in Richmond. These arguments supporting separation led to regional partisan divisions and failed to receive broad and sustained support in southwest Virginia, but resonated among Campbell's
neighbors in Washington County, North Carolina.[14]

The rationale offered by Arthur Campbell for independence reemerged
during the turmoil surrounding the controversial North Carolina Cession

Act of 1784. The North Carolina cession debate polarized North Carolina's political leadership. Supporters of the Cession Act argued that by passing the legislation North Carolina could diminish much of its enormous revolutionary debt and aid the struggling federal government in "defraying the expenses of the late war."[15] Opponents of the act believed that it was not in the interest of North Carolina to cede its vacant land to Congress because of the growing number of taxpayers moving into the region and the unwillingness of state leaders to abandon their Tennessee Valley constituency. These patriotic and nationalistic arguments masked the ulterior motives of many of the partisans on both sides of the debate.[16]

In reality, the cession debate centered on the struggle to control North Carolina's valuable western lands. Many of the leaders of the future Franklin statehood movement doggedly lobbied the North Carolina Assembly to pass the Cession Act. These same delegates in turn used the eventual passage of the Cession Act to justify their political separation, arguing that their December 1784 declaration of independence came as a reluctantly forced response to the abandonment of their communities by their parent state. In truth, most of the economic leadership of the Tennessee Valley supported the Cession Act of 1784 and hoped to capitalize on the postrevolutionary political confusion and fiscal crisis plaguing North Carolina and the federal government to secure political and economic control over their own communities and, more importantly, the vast swath of unclaimed and valuable western lands.[17] Powerful regional land speculators and local ruling elites, including Stockley Donelson (surveyor for the Franklin government), Charles Robertson (Speaker of the Franklin Senate), Joshua Gist (Franklin judge and member of the constitutional convention), and David Looney (justice of the peace under Franklin), voted for the passage of the Cession Act. The issue of cession divided the residents of the Tennessee Valley, but despite the controversy surrounding the legislation across the state, in an unusual collaborative effort, the Tennessee Valley leaders supporting the territorial cession joined with members of North Carolina's eastern economic elite to secure passage of the act in April 1784.[18] Eastern supporters of the act defended their decisions by arguing that the Tennessee Valley residents' perpetual war with the regional Native American tribes was unnecessary and exceedingly costly, and several outspoken members of the North Carolina Assembly branded "the inhabitants of the Western Country" as "the scourings of the Earth" and "fugitives from Justice."[19]

The passage of the Cession Act of 1784 awakened the separatist sentiments planted into the political consciousness of the inhabitants of the Tennessee Valley by Arthur Campbell. According to one critic of Tennessee Valley separatism, "The whole history of the State of Franklin grew out of the miscarriage of the plans of the land speculators."[20] Regional supporters of the Cession Act believed that passage of the legislation would open up land the state of North Carolina previously reserved for the Cherokee by allowing for the renegotiation of land treaties and the intensification of localized warfare against the embattled tribe. Other proponents of the act believed that "congressional ownership of the western land would raise land prices," and since "one of the provisions of the Carolina [land] cession was the guarantee of all land entries already made," many large land owners outside and inside the region stood to financially benefit from the legislation.[21] The Cession Act indeed removed several of the political obstacles to expanding the Tennessee Valley's economy and furthering regional land speculation by allowing the land-hungry residents to intensify their genocidal campaign against the Cherokee Nation. The passage of the Cession Act may have polarized the Tennessee Valley's political leadership, but it also allowed the leaders of the Franklin movement to galvanize a large portion of the backcountry populace under the banners of self-defense, political alienation, economic prosperity, and popular sovereignty.[22]

During their first convention, held on August 23 and 24, 1784, the leadership of the Tennessee Valley met at the Jonesboro log courthouse to address the political uncertainty created by the passage of the Cession Act. The forty delegates to the August meeting agreed to form an association, similar to the Watauga Association; to maintain law and order; and to defend themselves from the "tomahawk of the savages."[23] The assemblage elected John Sevier president and Landon Carter clerk of the convention, and the body also formed a committee to "take under consideration the state of affairs" within the region. Finally, the group agreed to petition North Carolina for "countenance" regarding the possibility of forming a separate government and drafting a state constitution. Before adjourning on August 24, the valley delegates agreed to hold a second convention the following month and reappraise the situation.[24]

As news of the August convention traveled across the Appalachian Mountains, North Carolina's eastern political leaders became furious at the actions of the Jonesboro delegates. Many of North Carolina's congressional leaders believed that the residents of the Tennessee Valley willfully violated the provision of the Cession Act requiring that the ceded lands "be deemed a common fund, for the benefit of all existing and future States of the Union."[25] The Cession Act also mandated congressional consent before a new state could be created out of the ceded lands. For simply contemplating the possibility of forming a separate state, opponents of the Cession Act leveled accusations of treason against the Tennessee Valley leaders. The Cession Act emerged as a divisive political issue in the 1784 state elections, and eastern congressional leaders recently opposing the legislation again attacked the act in the fall session of the North Carolina Assembly. At the October 22 session held in Newbern, North Carolina, oppositional state congressional leaders forced a vote on repealing the Cession Act, arguing that the act failed to adequately compensate the state of North Carolina for her territorial donation and did not provide reimbursement for the money the state spent on backcountry Indian diplomacy and warfare. Under considerable protest, in late October North Carolina's congressional leadership passed an act to repeal the Cession Act by a vote of thirty-seven to twenty-two in the House of Commons, and nineteen to eleven in the state senate. North Carolina defiantly reclaimed her western territory and thrust the Tennessee Valley separatists into a partisan political firestorm that eventually engulfed the entire region.[26]

It was during the third convening of Tennessee Valley leaders that the first signs of bitter internal factionalism emerged. The forty-three delegates met again at the Jonesboro courthouse on December 14 and quickly realized that the repeal of the Cession Act divided them over the issue of forming "a distinct state, independent of North Carolina."[27] The delegates supporting the creation of a separate state argued that, by ceding their western territory, North Carolina left the Tennessee Valley communities exposed to attacks by regional Indian tribes. Proponents of statehood also charged the state of North Carolina with unfairly raising taxes in their region and failing to use the tax revenue to improve their communities and regional economic infrastructure. In a report presented by William Cocke to the assembled Tennessee Valley leaders, the supporters of statehood further defended their case for separation. The report stated that the creation of an independent state would encourage people to settle the region, "which would strengthen us, improve agriculture, perfect manufacturers, encourage literature and everything truly laudable." The report went on to assert that a self-governing state offered solutions to the regional shortage of specie and allowed regional taxes to be used to improve the local situation.[28] After a short prayer offered by the Reverend Samuel Houston, twenty-eight delegates agreed with the committee's report and voted "yea" on statehood, including the Reverend Houston, Gilbert Christian, William Cocke, and Valentine Sevier. No one at the convention pointed out the hypocrisy of Charles Robertson, Stockley Donelson, and Joshua Gist, leading Tennessee Valley men who had openly supported territorial cession a few months earlier but now were using the passage of the Cession Act to justify their affirmative vote for an independent state.[29]

Initially, John Sevier, the future governor of the state of Franklin, led the regional opposition against forming a new state. The North Carolina Assembly had recently appointed Sevier brigadier general of the newly formed militia of the District of Washington, and the expansion of the regional militia into a full brigade, coupled with the repeal of the Cession Act, apparently resolved his concerns regarding the region's vulnerability to Indian attacks and political abandonment. Just prior to the opening of the December convention, Sevier conceded, "The grievances which the people complained are redressed, and my recommendation to them is that they proceed no farther in their design to separate from North Carolina."[30] Sevier's popularity among his Tennessee Valley neighbors necessitated that the proponents of statehood secure his support for their movement. The separatist leaders charged William Cocke with this difficult task, and the future Franklin diplomat conducted "an interview with him and [temporarily] erased" his resistance to the statehood effort. Sevier eventually voted in favor of a separate state, and Colonel John Tipton, David Looney, and Daniel Kennedy led the "nays" during the contentious vote. After a vote of twenty-eight to fifteen, a delegate rose and "declared the three western counties independent of North Carolina."[31] The elected assemblage of Tennessee Valley community leaders, now calling themselves the "Assembly at Frankland," agreed to reconvene early in 1785 to discuss "public sentiment" regarding their actions and the ratification of a Franklin constitution. The December vote signaled the birth of the state of Franklin as well as the beginning of a unrelenting resistance to the statehood movement. From the ashes of political defeat, John Tipton erected a powerful anti-statehood movement seeking to destroy the state of Franklin and elevate himself and his supporters into positions of political dominance.[32]

As a new year opened, the residents of the Tennessee Valley found themselves embroiled in a controversy threatening to tear apart their backcountry communities. The first months of 1785 initiated a new round of political contentiousness among North Carolina, her regional loyalists, and

the Franklinites. The internal divisions within the region and the vulnerability of the Franklin movement itself left the embryonic state with an uncertain future. Many of the members of the Franklin Assembly continued
to maintain reservations regarding the constitutionality and benefits of
declaring their independence. In a letter dated January 2, 1785, John Sevier
shared his lingering concerns with Colonel Daniel Kennedy of Greene
County. Sevier reasserted that North Carolina's repeal of the Cession Act
and bolstering of the regional militia strength "satisfy the people with the
old state" and made the creation of "a new state" unnecessary.[33] Sevier also
sent an "official address to the people of Greene County" cautioning them
to "decline all further action in respect to a new government."[34] Despite
Sevier's warnings, the wheels of statehood continued to grind forward.[35]

In March 1785, the elected delegates from the three Tennessee Valley
counties comprising the state of Franklin reconvened at the Jonesboro courthouse. It was during this first official meeting of the Franklin Assembly that
the supporters of statehood learned the full extent of North Carolina's resistance to the state of Franklin. During the spring meeting, the Franklin legislature elected John Sevier, finally convinced of the necessity and
advantages of statehood, to be Franklin's first governor. The assembly proceeded to elect David Campbell judge of Franklin's Superior Court, Joshua
Gist and John Anderson as assistant judges, Landon Carter as Speaker of the
Senate, Thomas Talbot as clerk of the senate, William Cage as Speaker of
the House of Commons, and Thomas Chapman as clerk of the House of
Commons.[36] Franklin's first elected political leadership wielded enormous
economic power within the region and maintained in excess of 131,000
acres in Tennessee Valley land claims.[37] With thousands of acres of landed
wealth at stake, it comes as little surprise that the first legislation passed by
the Franklin Assembly established "the legal claims of persons claiming
property under the laws of North Carolina, in the same manner as if the
State of Franklin had never formed itself into a distinct and separate State."[38]
The legislature went on to pass a number of additional pieces of legislation
on March 31, of which two more were concerned with defending landed
property. The other acts dealt with taxation and additional economic policies, the election and compensation of government and judicial officials, the
creation of four new counties (Wayne, Spencer, Caswell, and Sevier), the
establishment of a state militia, the procurement "of a great seal for the
State," and finally, "an act for the promotion of learning."[39]

In addition to the election of legislative leaders and the passage of numerous individual pieces of legislation, the Franklinites also elected "state officers," court officials, and military personnel. Those appointed to important positions within the Franklin state government included: Landon Carter, secretary of state; William Cage, treasurer; Stockley Donelson, surveyor-general; Daniel Kennedy and William Cocke, brigadier generals of the state militia; and William Cocke, "Commissioner of Franklin" to Congress. James Sevier (Washington County), John Rhea (Sullivan County), Daniel Kennedy (Greene County), Thomas Henderson (Spencer County), Joseph Hamilton (Caswell County), and Samuel Weir (Sevier County) comprised the state's judicial leadership. These men also commanded significant economic influence within the Tennessee Valley and laid claim to hundreds of thousands of acres across the trans-Allegheny frontier. From these positions of political power, the leading Franklinites finally secured control over the Tennessee Valley's political and economic future.[40]

The Tennessee Valley's landholding elites were not the only interested parties present at the March Franklin Assembly. By February, North Carolina governor Alexander Martin had grown increasingly concerned regarding the actions of the Franklinites. Governor Martin dispatched Major Samuel Henderson, brother of Judge Richard Henderson, to travel to the Tennessee Valley and apprise him of whether the Franklin movement drew its support from "a few leading men" or "whether it be the sense of a large majority of the people that the State be dismembered at this crisis."[41] Henderson carried with him a letter from Martin addressed to Brigadier General John Sevier, which the governor read before the Franklin Assembly. The exact content of that letter did not survive for scrutiny, but judging by the hasty response of the Franklinites, the letter unquestionably challenged their declaration of statehood, and demanded a full disclosure of reasons behind their actions. The frenetic excitement surrounding the creation of the Franklin government gave way to the defense of political sovereignty.[42]

On March 22, William Cage and Landon Carter crafted a response to Governor Martin's inquiry. In a carefully worded defense of the independence movement, the Franklinites argued that the passage of the Cession Act and the "unjust reproaches" of the North Carolina legislature "convinced [us] it was the Sense of the [North Carolina] Genl. Assembly to get rid of" the Tennessee Valley communities. According to Cage and Carter, the state of Franklin emerged out of necessity in order to "obtain the best terms" possible from the federal government and to defend themselves from the "frequent murders committed by the Indians." Additionally, the two

Franklinites argued that both the North Carolina Constitution and the U.S. Confederation Congress "encourage" and "consent" to the formation of new states in the west. The letter concluded by stating, "We unanimously agree that our lives, Liberties, and Property Can be more secure & our happiness Much better propagated by our separation, & Consequently that it is our duty and inalienable right to form ourselves into a New Independent State."[43] A personal letter from John Sevier to Governor Martin accompanied the legal and constitutional defense composed by Carter and Cage and endorsed by the legislature of the state of Franklin. Sevier's correspondence purported to convey the true sentiments of the rank and file supporters of the Franklin movement, stating, "The people of the Country Consider themselves Illy Treated, first being ceded without their consent, Secondly by repealing the act in the same measure," and that the failure of North Carolina to compensate the Indians for lands previously purchased have made "an Indian War [likely] This Summer." Both letters attempted to appease Governor Martin by stressing that the Franklinites considered themselves to be "friends" of North Carolina and by "begging" Martin to allow the state of Franklin to exist without interference. These appeals ultimately fell upon deaf ears, as Governor Martin, North Carolina's political leadership, and Franklin's regional opponents launched their efforts to dissolve the new state.[44]

On April 25, Governor Martin responded to the Tennessee Valley separatists with a calculated and threatening public manifesto. The proclamation challenged the arguments for statehood presented by the Franklinites in their March letters and asserted that "a considerable number, if not a majority" of the "leaders of the present revolt," actually voted for the Cession "Act they now deem impolitic, and pretend to reprobate, which in all probability would not have passed but through their influence and assiduity." The governor also stated that the North Carolina Assembly repealed the Cession Act because of the "uneasiness and discontent" it caused the Tennessee Valley residents. Additionally, by expanding the Washington County militia district and establishing a court in Washington County, Martin believed that the state government removed "the only general inconvenience and grievance they [Tennessee Valley residents] labour under." Martin's manifesto systematically refuted the arguments put forth by the Franklinites for separation, asserting that "restless ambition and a lawless thirst of power" are behind the movement and that the citizens of the Tennessee Valley "have been seduced from their Allegiance" through "specious pretences and the Acts of designing Men." Martin demanded that the Franklinites "return to their allegiance and duty, and forebear paying any obedience to any self-created power and authority unknown to the Constitution of the State, and not sanctioned by the Legislature." Martin reminded the Franklin supporters that "far less causes have deluged States and Kingdoms with blood," and that the actions of the Franklinites could set a precedent for other groups to engage in "dangerous and unwarranted procedures" that may ultimately topple the new American Republic.[45]

The foreboding declaration circulated widely among the Tennessee Valley residents, and the two distinct responses offered to Martin's manifesto illustrate the passionate communal dichotomy emerging within the region. The Franklinites' counter manifesto accused Governor Martin of attempting to "create sedition and stir up insurrection among the good citizens of this State, thinking thereby to destroy that peace and tranquility that so greatly abounds among the peaceful citizens of the new happy country." The Franklinites argued that North Carolina's "own acts . . . invited us to the separation," and that the creation of the state of Franklin "saved the State [of North Carolina] from impending [financial] ruin."[46] The response from John Tipton and his Anti-Franklin supporters further polarized the Tennessee Valley and forced the Franklinites to attach a warning to their counter-manifesto demanding that all Tennessee Valley residents obey the laws of the new state. In a May 13 letter to Governor Martin, Tipton pledged his obedience to North Carolina and to Martin's "commands." Tipton informed his "Excellency" Governor Martin of his willingness to "continue to discountenance the lawless proceedings of my neighbors."[47] These two divergent reactions to Martin's pleas for the abandonment of the statehood movement highlighted the expanding partisan rift emerging within the Tennessee Valley communities. The relatively sparse regional population and intimate communal connections ensured that the frontier communities could not escape the impending political fallout.[48]

In the spring of 1785, the growing tensions between the Franklin government and its parent state gradually subsided with the election of Richard Caswell to the North Carolina governorship. Governor Caswell maintained close personal and economic ties to the Tennessee Valley, and he and Franklin governor John Sevier remained both intimate friends and business partners. Prior to the Franklin movement, Sevier, Caswell, William Blount, Griffith Rutherford, John Donelson, and Joseph Martin formed a land company to purchase the Muscle Shoals territory on the Tennessee River. The fertile Muscle Shoals bottomlands, at the "bent" of the Tennessee River in present-day Alabama, offered a tremendous economic windfall for land speculators and farmers able to secure its purchase from the various Native American claimants.[49] The governors of Franklin and North Carolina did not limit their joint speculation to the Muscle Shoals land deal. In a bizarre business arrangement, newly elected North Carolina governor Richard Caswell and the governor of the rebellious state of Franklin actually speculated in land together during the Franklin affair. According to North Carolina land grant records, Sevier and Caswell purchased a two-hundred-acre plot of land in Greene County. The two partners applied for the grant on June 7, 1784, and received the grant on November 15, 1787. In addition to Governor Caswell's business dealings with John Sevier, Caswell also owned 5,480 acres of land in Sullivan, Greene, and Washington counties.[50] Governor Caswell maintained a substantial economic stake in the avoidance of partisan bloodshed in the Tennessee Valley. In a letter dated May 14, 1785, Sevier informed Governor Caswell of the accusations leveled by former Governor Martin and reiterated that the leadership of Franklin "will not be intimidated" into abandoning their plans.[51] Both Sevier's letter and Caswell's June 17 response reflected a more civilized tone. Caswell assured Sevier that he did not intend to pursue a policy of confrontation and, in fact, hoped to delay action against the Franklin government until after he consulted with the North Carolina Assembly.[52] The animosity between the two states further abated when John Sevier assured Richard Caswell that the Franklinites "wish to do nothing that will be inconsistent with the honor and interest of each party." Sevier closed his May correspondence by extending his government's "hearty and kind wishes" to "the parent state."[53] As one Franklin supporter jubilantly exclaimed, "We have now the most friendly assurances from North Carolina, since Governor Martin's administration has expired."[54] These amicable exchanges marked an amazing de-escalation of the friction between the governorships of the two sides but failed to calm the rising tension between partisans inside the Tennessee Valley.[55]

During the closing months of 1785, backcountry separatism finally bore fruit when the Franklin government entered into its first treaty negotiations with the Cherokee tribe. On June 10, a small delegation of Franklinites, including John Sevier, Joseph Hardin, Luke Boyer, Ebenezer Alexander, Joshua Gist, and Alexander Outlaw, traveled to the mouth of

Dumplin Creek to purchase "all the lands lying and being on the South side of Holeson [*sic*] and French Broad Rivers, as far South as the ridge that divide the Waters of Little River from the Waters of Tenesee [*sic*]" from the Overhill Cherokee. The parlay conducted at Dumplin Creek represented a new phase in frontier negotiations with the Cherokee. The Franklin negotiators invited only a fraction of the Cherokee's leadership, eschewing native leaders resistant to land cessions, and demanded that the tribe relinquish a huge swath of their remaining lower Tennessee Valley lands.[56] The Treaty of Dumplin Creek added an enormous tract of land to Franklin's state boundaries, provided new territory for the expansion of the regional economy, opened up new speculative opportunities for the landed elite, and encouraged hundreds of new families to settle in the Tennessee Valley. Despite leading to the escalation of warfare between the white inhabitants of the Tennessee Valley and the Cherokee, Franklin's political leaders hailed the treaty as a major political and economic triumph. The treaty negotiations at Dumplin Creek and the resulting backcountry warfare repudiated the conciliatory postrevolutionary Indian policies of both North Carolina and the Confederation Congress. The Native American inhabitants of the Tennessee Valley no longer stood as an impediment to the economic, territorial, and political ambitions of the region's landed elite and small-holders.[57]

Despite the success of the Treaty of Dumplin Creek, the leaders of the Franklin movement failed to secure approval from the U.S. Congress for their state's admittance into the confederation of states. On May 16, Franklin's emissary to Congress, William Cocke, traveled to New York and presented Franklin's case for statehood before that esteemed body. In a memorial presented to the Confederation Congress, Cocke reiterated the reasons behind the statehood movement and formally requested "Congress to accept the offered [North Carolina] cession and to receive us into the federal union."[58] On May 20, a congressional committee took under consideration "whether Congress had, or had not a right to Accept the cession, & whether it was not still binding upon the State, notwithstanding the repealing Act." The committee issued their opinion the very same day, accepting "the cession of western territory made by North Carolina."[59] According to North Carolina congressman Richard Dobbs Spaight, who was absent from the deliberations and adamantly opposed to Congress upholding the Cession Act, "Contrary to the established rule, the report was taken up, and Acted on, the same day [May 20] without allowing any time for consideration or giving any notice to the member from the State."[60] Even without the participation of North Carolina's state representative, the statehood report failed to garner the necessary two-thirds majority required by the Articles of Confederation to win Franklin congressional consent. New Jersey, Rhode Island, Connecticut, New York, New Hampshire, Pennsylvania, and Georgia voted for recognizing Franklin; Maryland and Virginia voted against recognizing Franklin; and South Carolina split its vote on the issue.[61] Despite being denied congressional recognition by a single vote, William Cocke and his fellow Franklinites believed they faired well in New York. Virginia governor Patrick Henry wrote to Thomas Jefferson that "The new Society sent Wm. Cocke to Congress to solicit [sic] Admission into the Union. His Mission was fruitless, tho' he said the contrary as I am told."[62] Congress accepted their argument against the repeal of the Cession Act, and a number of powerful states, including New York and Pennsylvania, openly supported their statehood movement. The savvy Cocke remained in New York for several weeks attempting to increase support for Franklin, but the effort to secure congressional approval for America's fourteenth state remained stalled for the immediate future.[63]

Against the backdrop of the Indian negotiations at Dumplin Creek and Cocke's failed effort to secure congressional approval for his state, the Franklin legislature officially met for a second time at the log courthouse in Jonesboro. During this brief August session, the Franklinites discussed the daunting task of drafting a permanent Franklin constitution. The delegates resolved to meet at the Greeneville Presbyterian Church, in the new Franklin capital of Greeneville, "on the second Monday in November . . . for the express purpose of adopting the then existing frame of government or altering it as the people see proper."[64] The November constitutional debate irreparably fractured the Franklin movement and further widened the breach between Franklin's supporters and her opponents. The constitution controversy also revealed the extent to which Franklin's leadership would go to ensure their political worldview at the expense of an expanded backcountry electorate.[65]

Prior to the November constitutional convention, the state of Franklin existed under a slightly modified version of North Carolina's state constitution. At the December 1784 meeting of the future Franklin Assembly, the delegates had agreed to accept a temporary constitution modeled on that of their parent state and to reconvene within a year to adopt a permanent frame of government. According to the Franklinites, they "patronized her [North Carolina] constitution and laws" in order to "influence Congress to precipitate our reception into the federal union."[66] The sixty-four delegates to the constitutional convention represented both the political and economic leadership of the Tennessee Valley, but the region's Presbyterian religious leaders led the heated clash over the ratification of the document.[67]

On November 14, the first day of the constitutional convention, the Reverend Samuel Houston, minister of the Providence Presbyterian Church, read before the Franklinites for the first time a radically democratic frame of government. Houston's former teacher the Reverend William Graham, head of Liberty Hall Academy (now Washington and Lee University) in Lexington, Virginia, and Virginia separatist Arthur Campbell aided Houston in composing the extraordinary document.[68] The constitution, entitled *A Declaration of Rights and a Constitution, made by the representatives of the freemen of Frankland,* blended the visionary democratic principles of Campbell with the Presbyterian morality of Graham to create one of the most unique frames of government ever conceived. The authors of the Houston-Graham Constitution divided the document into two sections, *A Declaration of Rights* and *The Constitution or Form of Government.* The Declaration of Rights closely resembled the state of North Carolina's 1776 Declaration of Rights, with the first clause powerfully asserting the concept of popular sovereignty. The document also listed twenty-four civil liberties, including the right to be treated fairly before the law, the freedom of the press, the right to bear arms, the right to assembly, and the freedom "to worship Almighty God, according to the dictates of their own consciences." The constitutional section offered sweeping changes to the North Carolina Constitution and greatly expanded the electorate in the Tennessee Valley. The Houston-Graham Constitution "limited the power of the [political] officials and provided for a wide participation in the government" by calling for a unicameral legislature and population-based political representation, and allowing "Every free male inhabitant of this State . . . a vote in electing all officers chosen by the people, in the county where he resides." The document restricted the influence of the region's entrenched political leadership by forcing representatives to reside in the county which they represented, limiting the terms of elected officials, allowing for direct popular elections of most state officials and militia officers, and publishing "all Bills of a public and general nature . . . for the consideration of the people, before they are read in the General Assembly for the last time." In addition to these political elements, the constitution also encouraged "learning" by erecting one regional university "near the center of the state" and allocating land and tax revenues for the construction of "a Grammar School" in each county. Interspersed among these democratic ideals, the Presbyterian architects of the constitution inserted several unusual religiously oriented political restrictions, including denying citizens "of an immoral character, or guilty of such flagrant enormities as drunkenness, gaming, profane swearing, lewdness, or Sabbath breaking" from holding political offices, and restricting political access to citizens who deny the Judeo-Christian god, heaven and hell, the Old and New Testaments, or the Christian Trinity. The proposed Franklin Constitution also established several secular limitations on political participation, including prohibiting ministers, lawyers, and doctors from serving in the Franklin Assembly, and placing property qualifications on members of the House of Representatives.[69]

The Houston-Graham Constitution's melding of Enlightenment principles and the Protestant Reformation generated an enormous amount of controversy among the convention attendees. After completing his reading of the constitution, the Reverend Houston moved the assembly to vote on ratifying the document. In response, assembly members opposed to the Houston-Graham Constitution asked that the Presbyterian minister Hezekiah Balch be allowed to address the convention. Despite not being a member of the Franklin Assembly, the Reverend Balch "animadverted severely upon the manuscript constitution."[70] Those in attendance did not record the nature of Balch's criticisms, but his arguments appear to have been effective. In a vote of twenty-four to nineteen, opponents of the Houston-Graham Constitution defeated the proposed frame of government. Governor John Sevier immediately moved to formally ratify the modified North Carolina Constitution. Despite the efforts of the Reverend Houston and his supporters to replace the North Carolina Constitution, the Franklin Assembly voted to accept Sevier's constitution as the permanent frame of government for the state of Franklin. The rejection of the Houston-Graham Constitution by the leadership of Franklin reflected their desire to dominate Tennessee Valley politics by containing the democratic impulses unleashed by the American Revolution. By defeating passage of the radical frame of government and ratifying North Carolina's less egalitarian document, the faction of the Tennessee Valley's landed elite comprising the leadership of Franklin ensured their economic and political hegemony.[71]

The ratification of the amended North Carolina Constitution initiated a fiery "pamphlet war" between partisans on both sides of the issue. Despite residing in a region devoid of printing presses, supporters of both frames of

government blanketed the Tennessee Valley with political tractates pro-
claiming their positions on the constitutional debate. A group supporting
the Houston-Graham Constitution, calling themselves the Franklin
Commonwealth Society, published two pamphlets defending the rejected
constitution. The two pamphlets were entitled "Principles of Republican
Government by a Citizen of Frankland" and "Essay on Government by a
Citizen of Frankland."[72] A third William Graham–penned pamphlet, entitled "An Address to the Inhabitants of Frankland State," sharply criticized
the federal government, members of the clergy, and opponents of the
Houston-Graham Constitution. Graham's pamphlet evoked such ire among
leading Franklinites that "the [Washington County] court directed the
sheriff to burn it," and "an effigy of Graham was [also] burned."[73] Supporters of the new Franklin Constitution countered by publishing their own
pamphlets and utilizing legal and physical intimidation to curtail dissension. Eventually Hezekiah Balch "brought charges against [William] Graham before the predicatory of the Presbyterian Church" in Philadelphia,
and the Philadelphia Presbytery ultimately censored Graham.[74]

The Greeneville constitutional convention "brought about a sharp
conflict . . . between the advocates of political equality and the partisans of
privileges for a few." On one side, the group led by Arthur Campbell and
Presbyterian ministers Samuel Houston and William Graham advocated a
frame of government based on a union between democratic principles and
moralistic religiosity. On the other side, the group led by the Reverend
Hezekiah Balch, John Sevier, and William Cocke hoped to mitigate radical
changes in the Franklin government and Tennessee Valley politics by ratifying the existing modified North Carolina Constitution.[75] John Sevier
and supporters of the modified North Carolina Constitution hoped to
maintain control over the political and economic fortunes of the Tennessee
Valley by blocking the democratization of regional politics. The interconnectedness of political and landed power and the challenges the proposed
radical "clerical" constitution presented to Sevier and his supporters threatened to dilute the regional hegemony of Franklin's leading men. The leaders
of Franklin who orchestrated the effort to defeat the Houston-Graham
Constitution did so to ensure that they could determine who served in influential political, judicial, and military positions within the Tennessee
Valley.[76]

The stormy debate over the Franklin Constitution highlights the internal discord among the early supporters of statehood. An examination of the

nineteen convention members who dissented from the ratification of the modified North Carolina Constitution reveals that men holding high-level positions within both the Franklin government and the opposition contingent supported the Houston-Graham Constitution. The nineteen members of the Franklin state government opposing the adopted constitution included David Campbell, David Looney, and Samuel Newell. The rejection of the Houston-Graham Constitution expanded the ranks of the Anti-Franklinites by attracting several prominent Tennessee Valley residents to their cause. Several of these men initially supported statehood, but the debates within the Franklin constitutional convention ultimately led to their defection. After expressing their opposition to the modified North Carolina Constitution, Robert Love, James Stuart, Peter Parkinson, and George Maxwell joined John and Joseph Tipton in their effort to destroy the state of Franklin. The controversy surrounding the Franklin Constitution exacerbated the lingering hostilities between the Tiptonites and the Franklinites, and the rejection of the far more democratic plan of government expressed in the Houston-Graham Constitution alienated several of the new state's most ardent supporters.[77]

During the final days of 1785, the residents of the upper Tennessee Valley found themselves in an increasingly precarious position. Their state government remained in political limbo after failing to secure recognition from the federal government. The Tennessee Valley communities, once united behind shared political and economic interests, the American Revolution, and perpetual Indian warfare, found themselves torn between two bitter factions competing for control over their region's political and economic fate. The passage of an act by the North Carolina Assembly in November that offered "to put into oblivion" the actions of the residents of Washington, Greene, and Sullivan counties promoting "an independent government" further threatened the fragile loyalties of Tennessee Valley supporters of statehood.[78] Despite these challenges, the leadership of the state of Franklin remained confident in the success of their movement and believed that the concerns over internal and external resistance to Franklin paled in comparison to the potential financial and political rewards independence offered the Tennessee Valley's ruling class.

Chapter 4

Strange Spectacle of Two Empires

Statesmanship, Speculation, and the Dimming Fortunes of Separatism

As the year 1786 dawned, the residents of the Tennessee Valley found themselves embroiled in a bitter partisan contest to determine the political future of their increasingly divided communities. During the previous two years, competition between two ruling backcountry factions polarized trans-Appalachian North Carolina. The contentious interregional debates over the constitutionality of the Franklin statehood movement and the Franklin Constitution exasperated antagonisms between supporters and opponents of statehood and political democratization. From January 1786 until the winter of 1787, defenders and enemies of the state of Franklin intensified their partisan efforts within the Tennessee Valley. The debilitating failure of William Cocke's congressional lobbying effort, the escalation of opposition to statehood from a swelling minority faction within the Tennessee Valley, and North Carolina's increasingly deft political leadership ensured an uncertain and perilous future for the Franklinites. Franklin's leadership attempted to divert political ruin by launching an intense public relations campaign to attract support from influential state and national political figures. In conjunction with this propaganda blitz, the Franklinites continued their efforts to expand their state's boundaries and their personal landholdings by reengaging in further speculative land ventures at Muscle Shoals on the "Great Bend" of the Tennessee River. The Muscle Shoals land scheme eventually drew the Franklinites into an aborted military coalition with the state of Georgia against the unfortunate landholding Upper Creek tribe.

As the Franklinites escalated their efforts to defend their political and economic interests, opponents of Tennessee Valley separatism redoubled their campaign to derail the statehood movement and secure control over the region's political and judicial offices. Under the direction of Governor

Richard Caswell, North Carolina's savvy political leadership initiated an effective "divide and conquer" political strategy within the region that sought to exploit preexisting communal divisions and erode internal support for Franklin. With the backing of John Tipton's Anti-Franklinite supporters, this "divide and conquer" strategy combined the lure of economic and political concessions with the extension of a parallel North Carolina state bureaucracy into the region to intensify internal opposition to the state of Franklin. For roughly two years, the residents of the Tennessee Valley "were presented with the strange spectacle of two empires exercising at one and the same time over one and the same people." The violent political and economic repercussions and communal discord resulting from the uproarious competition over the Tennessee Valley's principal organs of government sowed the seeds of Franklin's violent demise.[1]

The emergence of North Carolina's strategic détente with the Franklin government can be traced to the relationship between North Carolina governor Richard Caswell and the embattled state's political leadership. Governor Caswell's very public friendship with Franklin governor John Sevier, extensive regional landholdings, and his own western speculative desires undoubtedly influenced his strategy for dealing with the rebellious Franklinites. In a letter dated July 12, 1786, to Governor Sevier, Caswell acknowledged the strangely amicable relationship between himself and the rebellious Franklin leader. Governor Caswell lamented the fact that his position as "chief executive" of a state that refused to "recognize the State of Franklin" made it "impolitic & inconsistent with my Station to carry on a correspondence with you under that Character whatever my private sentiments may be," but assured his longtime friend that "it always did and will give me pleasure to Correspond with you and that it is my intention to do so either in public or private life, at all convenient opportunities."[2] In striking contrast to the animus that characterized former North Carolina governor Alexander Martin's policies toward the Franklinites, the Caswell administration's "divide and conquer" strategy sought to peel off partisan support from within the region and topple the Franklin government with as little loss of life and disruption to the land-based regional economy as possible. The Caswell administration's new diplomatic tactics proved to be both tremendously effective and tragically deadly.[3]

In an act passed at their November 1785 session, the North Carolina legislature attempted to further fragment the residents of the Tennessee Valley by introducing legislation offering to pardon Franklinites for their previous rebellious actions contingent upon the return of their political allegiance to their parent state. The "act of pardon" served as the first diplomatic salvo in Governor Richard Caswell's political strategy for restoring the valuable Tennessee Valley territory and the residents' political loyalties to North Carolina without initiating civil war.[4] The November legislation also directed backcountry loyalists to organize regional elections to select representatives to the North Carolina legislature from Washington, Sullivan, and Greene counties and to appoint regional civil, judicial, and military officials. In essence, the North Carolina Assembly asserted that the "governmental posts held by individuals who were still in rebellion" must be filled with state loyalists.[5] The Caswell administration hoped to further divide the Franklin movement by "building on the dissension that the Tipton [Anti-Franklinite] camp was generating."[6] The 1786 regional elections confirmed the existence of a growing internal opposition to the state of Franklin and offered Anti-Franklinites their first opportunity to effectively express political dissent. The existence of dual state mechanisms within the Franklin communities added to the growing confusion and hostilities within the region. The results of holding the North Carolina–governed elections in Franklin paid significant political dividends for the Caswell administration and the Tiptonites.[7]

In response to North Carolina's election demands, on July 19, 1786, acting Washington County sheriff George Mitchell hesitantly announced that "there will be an election held the Third Friday in August next, at John Rennoe's near the Sycamore Shoals to choose members to represent Washington county in the General Assembly of North Carolina."[8] The Franklinites rallied their own regional supporters and began preparations to hold separate elections for the North Carolina Assembly on the very same day. The Franklinites intended to demonstrate the level of regional support for their independence movement by electing their own officials to the legislative assembly of the state from which they had recently rebelled.[9] The Franklinites believed that the election of two representatives to the North Carolina Assembly might convince North Carolina legislators to agree to support Franklin's statehood bid in the upcoming November state legislative session. The August elections revealed the rising intensity of partisanship engulfing the Tennessee Valley communities and the importance both factions placed upon controlling the region's political and judicial bureaucracy.[10]

Throughout the summer of 1786, partisans from both sides prepared to hold the contentious elections in the Franklin counties. As political campaigning intensified, the two opposing parties riotously rallied under the banners of "new state" and "old state" men.[11] By the opening of the August elections, both groups managed to secure substantial political backing for their candidates, but the surging level of regional support behind the Anti-Franklinite (old state) faction illustrated the growing opposition to the statehood movement within the Tennessee Valley. The results of the August elections came as little surprise to the region's voters, since both sides erected their own polling stations and calculated their own election returns. The Franklinites held their elections in Jonesboro and unanimously elected Landon Carter and Thomas Chapman to serve as Franklin's representatives to the North Carolina legislature. Despite accusations of voter intimidation by local Franklinites, old state supporters managed to hold their own elections at the home of John Rennoe on Sinking Creek in Sycamore Shoals. The Tiptonite faction predictably elected John Tipton as senator and cast their votes for two outspoken critics of the state of Franklin, James Stuart (Stewart) and Richard White, to serve as representatives to the North Carolina House of Commons.[12] "Without violence and in an orderly manner," both sides managed to conduct elections in the state of Franklin. The ramifications of these two elections ultimately proved to be far from "orderly" or nonviolent.[13]

An examination of the results of the August 1786 elections demonstrates the growing sectional fragmentation of political support within the Tennessee Valley and the importance of "neighborhood affiliations" in determining partisan loyalties.[14] Although hard polling numbers are scarce, there is a distinct voting pattern in the Franklin counties. In the counties in which the two leading figures of the political clash resided, John Tipton in Washington County and John Sevier in Sullivan County, local residents tended to lend their political support to their neighbors. In Sullivan County, support for John Sevier and the "new state" movement remained strong. According to the returns made by polling inspectors, all 254 votes went to the two Franklinite candidates. In Washington County, an area in which "disaffection to the Franklin government began to manifest itself," citizens cast all 179 ballots for Tipton's old state candidates. The overwhelming support given to three old state men in Washington County proved to be another "ill-omen to the future fortunes of Franklin."[15]

The August legislative elections served as just the beginning of North Carolina's effort to weaken the Franklin movement by exacerbating the growing antagonisms within the Tennessee Valley. As support for Franklin began to diminish, old state loyalists commenced electing and appointing civil, judicial, and military officials to influential posts within the region. New state supporters quickly countered these efforts by electing Franklinites to many of these same positions. In Washington County, Tiptonite forces appointed Jonathan Pugh "North Carolina sheriff," and in Sullivan County Franklin supporters commissioned Andrew Caldwell sheriff.[16] The erection of competing state bureaucracies quickly involved the region's judicial system, as both sides appointed their own judges and clerks and organized parallel court systems. The Franklinites appointed John Sevier's son James to be Washington County court clerk, and the Tiptonites selected Thomas Gourley as their clerk of court. As lecturer William A. Henderson described in his 1873 speech to Knoxville, Tennessee's Board of Trade, "Each county had a Franklin sheriff and a North Carolina sheriff, two sets of legislators were running at the same time, two courts held their sessions as regularly as the other side would let them."[17]

The existence of competing legislative and judicial systems predictably led to clashes between the opposing Tennessee Valley factions. The regional court systems became the battleground in which proponents on each side of the Franklin issue waged disruptive campaigns in order to cement their control over the region's judicial system. In the competing Washington County courts, John Tipton held sessions "under the authority of North Carolina" at Buffalo, and James Sevier presided over the Franklin court just ten miles away in the town of Jonesboro. The distance separating these two courts failed to prevent violent confrontations from occurring throughout 1786 and into 1787. According to one Tennessee historian, "As the processes of these courts frequently required the sheriffs to pass within the jurisdiction of each other to execute them [state laws], a recounter [sic] was sure to take place. Hence it was necessary to appoint the stoutest men in the country to the office of sheriff."[18] One such encounter occurred in late 1786, when John Tipton and fifty armed men burst into James Sevier's Jonesboro courtroom and removed court papers from the court clerk and threw the "justices out the doors." The Franklinites responded by invading John Tipton's courtroom in Buffalo, reclaiming the Franklin court documents, stealing North Carolina court papers from court clerk Thomas Gourley, and turning "the court out of doors." The courtroom violence eventually involved the two leading political figures in the Tennessee Valley. The only direct physical confrontation between John Sevier and John

Tipton occurred in the Jonesboro courthouse.[19] A verbal altercation between the two former Revolutionary War soldiers eventually escalated into violence, "when Sevier, no longer able to bear the provocations which were given to him, struck Tipton with a cane. Instantly the latter began to annoy him with his hands clinched. Each exchanged blows for some time in the same way with great violence and in convulsions of rage." Eventually those present at the courthouse brawl managed to separate the two combatants, but incidents like this one became commonplace—so routine, in fact, that one Franklin chronicler quipped, "families took lessons in pugilism from each other at public meetings."[20] These disturbing episodes increasingly forced Tennessee Valley residents to choose political camps in this escalating affair.[21]

The presence of two independent civil and judicial systems in the Tennessee Valley led to confusion among the region's inhabitants in the most fundamental areas of everyday life. Beginning in late 1786, it became necessary for residents of the Franklin counties to be married in both court systems in order to ensure the legality of their nuptials in the future. According to one writer, "When some Franklinite would win or steal some North Carolina maid, it is said that, if the lady was at all political and self-willed, the ceremony had to be performed under both governments, from which we may conclude that it was not unusual to find a man who had been twice married, but had never had but one wife."[22] In addition to the matrimonial befuddlement caused by the competing court systems, residents of the Tennessee Valley also confronted the fiscal dilemma of choosing which state government should receive their tax contributions. Most citizens resolved this quandary by "choosing to pay neither" state's taxes, but "citizens who elected to deal exclusively with one side risked the wrath of the other."[23] In an April 9, 1787, letter to his state's namesake, Benjamin Franklin, Governor Sevier conveyed his anger toward the bureaucratic anarchy gripping the region. Sevier stated, "They [North Carolina] have, contrary to the interest of the people in two of the counties, to wit, Washington and Sullivan, by their acts removed the former places of holding courts to certain places convenient to the disaffected [Tiptonites], as we conceive, in order that they might have a pretext to prevaricate upon."[24]

Amid the political chaos unleashed by North Carolina's "divide and conquer" strategy, in October 1786 the Franklin Assembly convened once again at the rustic Greeneville capital building. The deteriorating political situation within the region, a potentially lucrative land deal, and a proposed joint invasion of Creek territory with the state of Georgia dominated the legislative session. During the meeting, the Franklinites appointed two of their most eloquent and experienced spokesmen, William Cocke and David Campbell, to attend the upcoming November session of the North Carolina Assembly. Franklin's leadership charged the envoys with the unenviable task of convincing the North Carolinians to relinquish their challenge to Franklin's statehood. Once again, the Franklinites placed their state's political destiny in the hands of their most skilled orator, William Cocke.[25]

As the November legislative session approached, Governor Sevier dispatched a letter to Governor Caswell intended to again persuade his gubernatorial counterpart of the justness of the Franklin separatist movement. Sevier's letter is a masterful attempt at diplomacy and reflects the continued amicable relationship between the two governors and business partners. Sevier informed Caswell of the Franklin legislature's appointment of "Some Commissioners to Wait on the parent State" to "cheerfully Consent to the separation as they once before did" with the Cession Act of 1784. The Franklin governor also assured Caswell that "It gives us inexpressible Concern to think that any disputes should Arise between Us." Sevier reminded Caswell that the Franklin statehood movement resulted from an "Act of your Assembly" and the Tennessee Valley's political leadership never expected the "Cession Act would be Repealed, otherwise Matters might Not have been Carried to the length they are."[26] He affirmed that the Franklinites did "not Wish to separate from you on any Other terms but those that may be perfectly Consistent with the Honour and interest of each party." Sevier concluded his appeal with one final plea for separation. Sevier writes, "there is no Set of people Can think more highly of your Government than those who Want separation, and they only wish it to answer There better Conveniency, and tho' want to be separated in Government, wish to be united in friendship."[27] Sevier's correspondence succeeded in convincing Governor Caswell to reconsider the Franklin movement, but Franklin delegates William Cocke and David Campbell faced a much more difficult challenge in swaying the unyielding representatives of the North Carolina legislature.

The November session of the North Carolina legislature held in Fayetteville provided yet another opportunity for the Franklinites to present their case for separation and to garner backing from within their parent state for the movement. Attendees of the fall meeting witnessed the effort by the Franklinites to redefine and expand the reasons for their disunion from North Carolina.[28] During the Cession Act debates of 1784, the Franklinites asserted that North Carolina's abandonment of the Tennessee Valley communities forced their separation from the parent state. Sevier reiterated this idea in an October 28, 1786, letter sent to Governor Caswell, but the same letter also contained several new arguments promoting separation. Sevier contended that Tennessee Valley's "Trade and Commerce is Altogether Carried on With other States," and the "five to eight hundred Miles" separating the trans-Appalachian communities from the center of North Carolina political power prevented his neighbors from enjoying "the [same] blessings of Civil Government as their Neighbors who live East, South, or any other point."[29]

At the Fayetteville convention, William Cocke presented Franklin's case to the distinguished and skeptical body. In what one delegate sarcastically described as "pathetic," Cocke "depicted the miseries of his distressed countrymen," and implored the representatives to support Franklin's effort to create an independent state.[30] Cocke's principal argument for Franklin's political sovereignty focused on the necessity of collecting state taxes to maintain a militia force for the defense of their communities from the threats posed by the region's aboriginal "savages." Cocke maintained that neither the state of North Carolina nor the federal government "had any interest in their safety." Cocke again contended that the creation of Franklin occurred out of necessity, and he bluntly asked the delegates, "What were the people of the ceded territory to do to avoid the blow of the uplifted tomahawk?" The gifted barrister reflected, "Immediate and pressing necessity called for the powers to concentrate the scanty means they possessed of saving themselves from destruction. A cruel and insidious foe was at their doors. Delay was but another name for death." Cocke concluded his lengthy address with an eloquent appeal to "let us remain as we are, and support ourselves by our own exertions; if otherwise, let the means for the continuance of our connection be supplied with the degree of liberality which will demonstrate seriousness on the one hand and secure affection on the other."[31]

In a letter to Governor Caswell dispatched by the gravely ill Franklin judge David Campbell, the Franklinite urged the North Carolina governor to support "the ratification of our independence." Campbell offered essentially identical reasons for Franklin's separation from North Carolina. He wrote, "If we set out wrong, or were too hasty in our separation, this country is not altogether to blame, your state pointed out the line of conduct, which we adopted; we really thought you in earnest when you ceded us to Congress." Campbell also addressed the Native American conflict that threatened the Tennessee Valley settlements and astutely concluded, "Our laws and government must include these people [the Cherokee] or they will become dangerous." Remarkably, Campbell closed his correspondence by claiming, "Nature has separated us; do not oppose her in her work; by acquiescing you will bless us, and do yourself no injury, because you lose nothing but people who are a clog on your government, and to whom you cannot do equal justice by reason of their detached situation." The Franklinites combined economic concerns, political marginalization, geographic isolation, and the looming threat of Native American violence with the earlier abandonment claim to create a persuasive justification for independence. Unfortunately for the new state supporters, these arguments fell upon deaf ears in the Fayetteville assembly.[32]

The North Carolina Assembly clearly failed to see urgency in the Franklin issue, with both the senate and House of Commons waiting three weeks to even address the Franklinites' petitions for statehood. In a stinging report, the North Carolina Senate stated that "the Legislature of North Carolina cannot accede to a separation at this period." While empathizing with the "sense of suffering of those people [Tennessee Valley residents] during the anarchy which has long prevailed among them," the distinguished legislative body deflected the Franklinites' arguments for separation. Responding to the Franklinites' abandonment claims, the senate charged "that some designing persons in that Country have so far deluded many of the citizens as to make them wish a separation under an Idea that they, by the act of cession passed in June 1784, were forever secured from this Government and its protection, and would be an emancipation from slavery." In sharp contrast to the Franklinites' accusations of political marginalization, the North Carolina senators argued that the Tennessee Valley's political leadership "were equal partakers with the rest of the State in the mild influence of its Constitution and Laws and were equally represented in its Councils."[33] The senators also openly condemned Franklin's leadership, blaming them for the "recent anarchy" and characterizing the recent policies of the Franklin Assembly as "highly reprehensible."[34]

The North Carolina Senate also included an offer of reconciliation with its firm rebuke of the Franklin movement. Undoubtedly influenced by the Caswell administration's détente, the senate attempted to strengthen support for North Carolina in the Franklin counties by again passing "an act of oblivion, so as to conciliate and quiet the minds of those who may have, through Blindness or passion" supported the state of Franklin. In addition to extending a full pardon to the Franklinites for a second time, the senate offered to "release" the Tennessee Valley residents "from the payment of taxes which have become due for the years 1784 and 1785." The representatives concluded that the Tennessee Valley inhabitants "enjoyed none of the benefits of [the North Carolina] government" during those years; therefore "they ought not in Justice to be taxed with its burthens." The senate closed its December report by further extending a diplomatic olive branch. In a generous concession eventually supported by Governor Caswell, the senate stated, "altho' a separation is at this time impracticable, yet whenever wealth and numbers of the Citizens on the western waters so much increase as to make the same necessary, that then we are free to say a separation may take place upon friendly and reciprocal terms and under certain Compacts and Stipulations." The senate accepted the report and forwarded the document to the House of Commons, where on December 15 its members "concurred." The report diminished any hope among the Franklinites that North Carolina could be convinced to agree to their separation, and over the next several weeks the North Carolina government continued its effective "divide and conquer" strategy.[35]

The North Carolina Assembly next turned its attention to the recent violence surrounding the Tennessee Valley's judicial system. In an attempt to prevent a repeat of these events and to strengthen the position of Franklin opponents, both the senate and the House of Commons passed acts removing "the place of holding Courts in the County of Sullivan." In a clear swipe at Franklin governor John Sevier and the Sullivan County Franklinites, the North Carolina Assembly attempted to destroy the principal court used by the Franklin government. The assembly also targeted the Franklin court at Jonesboro in Washington County by passing a bill that restructured the county courts and appointed "Commissioners to fix on the most convenient place for holding" the new court. In a final effort to assert their authority in the rebellious Franklin counties by controlling the Tennessee Valley judicial system, both the house and senate agreed to a resolution "to prevent doubts as to the right of Sovereignty and Jurisdiction in and over the Counties of Washington, Sullivan, & Greene." The failed diplomatic efforts of Sevier, Cocke, and Campbell and a North Carolina Assembly determined to maintain political dominion over the Tennessee Valley forced the Franklinites to look elsewhere to preserve and expand support for their statehood movement.[36]

In response to the defeat of their bid to secure acquiescence for their movement from within the North Carolina Assembly, the Franklinites initiated a remarkable propaganda campaign aimed at earning the approval for their separation from influential state and national leaders. In June 1786, leading Franklinites opened a line of communication between themselves and their state's namesake, Benjamin Franklin. In addition to their nomenclatural tribute, the Franklinites hoped to align themselves with one of America's most celebrated and respected citizens. In two separate letters, the Franklinites subtly requested Franklin's support for their statehood effort. In an April 1787 communication, Governor Sevier informed Franklin of the state's failed efforts within the North Carolina Assembly and the rapidly deteriorating situation in the Tennessee Valley caused by the competing state bureaucracies. Sevier then revealed the true intentions of his correspondence, beseeching Franklin to "give us your approbation," "write on the subject," and offer "any advice, instruction, or encouragement, you may think we shall deserve."[37] The aged revolutionary leader never responded to Sevier's requests, and apparently the Franklinites ultimately failed to win Franklin's political endorsement.

The events unfolding in the Tennessee Valley drew the attention of other prominent Americans, including Patrick Henry, James Monroe, Richard Henry Lee, Alexander Hamilton, George Washington, and Thomas Jefferson. Unfortunately for the Franklinites, most of these figures opposed their efforts, or at least the manner in which their movement was being carried out. In a letter mailed from Paris, Thomas Jefferson, now serving as America's minister to France, described his feelings regarding the state of Franklin to George Washington. Jefferson wrote of his "increased anxieties" caused by the "late example of the state of Franklin," and warned Washington that these separatist tendencies could spread to Virginia.[38] In a letter to Virginia congressman Richard Henry Lee, Jefferson again described his displeasure with the actions of the Franklinites, stating, "I am anxious to hear what is done with the states of Vermont and Franklin. I think that the former is the only innovation . . . which ought to be admitted. If Congress are [sic] not firm on that head, our states will crumble to atoms by the spirit of establishing every little canton into a separate state."[39] The inability of the Franklinites to convince one of the United States' most vocal proponents of western expansion and the creation of new western states exemplifies the enormous challenges facing their diplomatic effort.[40] Even Jefferson's fiercest political foe, Alexander Hamilton, offered a trenchant criticism of the state of Franklin. In his essay *Federalist #6,* Hamilton utilized the "revolt of a part of the State of North Carolina" as proof for the necessity of a strong federal government. Hamilton warned against "those who endeavour to lull asleep our apprehensions of discord and hostility between the States."[41] Had the Franklinites managed to secure the support of at least one of these prominent Americans, then perhaps their efforts to win approval within the halls of the U.S. government and the North Carolina Assembly might have been more successful.[42]

Despite waning support within the Tennessee Valley and public condemnation from political leaders across the United States, the resilient Franklinites managed to form a brief alliance with the state of Georgia. The two states formed their accord upon a shared political and economic objective, securing the coveted bottomlands stretching from the great bend of the Tennessee River to the North Carolina border, an area collectively known as Muscle Shoals.[43] Land speculation at Muscle Shoals commenced two years prior to the formation of the state of Franklin. In 1783, a group of prominent North Carolinians, including William Blount, Richard Caswell, John Donelson, Joseph Martin, and John Sevier, formed the Muscle Shoals Company in order to raise venture capital to purchase the valuable property from the Native American claimants. The investors hoped to convince the aboriginal tribes, which included at various times the Creek, Chickasaw, and Cherokee, to peacefully relinquish their lands so that the speculators might profit from land sales to would-be settlers and the resulting market opportunities. The Muscle Shoals land "was valuable for farming purposes and for trade with both the neighboring Indian tribes and the growing white settlements in the Mississippi Valley."[44] Before separatist sentiments plunged the region into chaos, North Carolina congressman and prominent land speculator William Blount and his business partners secured a controversial claim to the Muscle Shoals land from the Chickasaw claimants for roughly $5,000 in trade goods and lobbied the Georgia legislature to consider establishing a new county, to be named Houston, out of the Muscle Shoals acquisition. The original Muscle Shoals Company dissolved during the inception of the Franklin movement, but the former investors in the aborted venture, many of whom joined the Franklin government, did not relinquish their desire to profit from speculating in Native American land.[45]

The Muscle Shoals land scheme inevitably became intertwined with the state of Franklin's "expansionist plans." The valuable lands on the "Bent of the Tennessee River" and the Native Americans who remained the principal obstacle to the success of the lucrative land deal cemented the bond between the state of Georgia and the Franklinites.[46] The Muscle Shoals connections between these two governments are multifold. First, after a 1782 survey of the territory, surveyors determined that the Muscle Shoals district, originally thought to be within North Carolina's borders, lay within the territorial bounds of Georgia. Additionally, a number of influential Georgians, described by William Blount as having "a great Thirst for Tennessee Lands," served as members on the original Muscle Shoals Company commission.[47] The links between the Tennessee River land deal and the Franklin government are also readily apparent, with John Sevier, Valentine Sevier, Anthony Bledsoe, and John Donelson (father of Franklin's chief surveyor Stockley Donelson) all serving in leadership capacities in the original Muscle Shoals Company. The political and economic leadership of Georgia and Franklin believed that the Muscle Shoals district could remedy their states' mounting fiscal problems, encourage frontier settlement, and increase their own personal fortunes. Both governments also conveniently subscribed to similar policies for expanding their states' borders, including the use of violence and intimidation to force the Native American populace to acquiesce to land cessions.[48]

In 1786, hostilities between the state of Georgia and the Upper Creek tribe, led by mixed-blood Alexander McGillivray, erupted and again plunged the Muscle Shoals land deal into question. The designs of land speculators and the westward expansion of white settlements by Georgians onto Creek lands in the Mississippi River Valley forced McGillivray to raise "the red hatchet" of war.[49] An unidentified Virginian who maintained contact with the Creek chief described to an associate McGillivray's intention to use "his utmost exertions to engage the Creek Indians in a War not only with Georgia but with the Western parts of Virginia and No. Carolina." Additionally, he believed McGillivray's "object is to make war as hot as possible at first, which will induce overtures for peace, and make the United States be glad to grant advantageous terms, such as to acknowledge the independence and sovereignty of the Creek nation, and admit them as a member of the federal Union."[50] The Creek War ultimately drew the political leadership of Franklin and Georgia into an alliance because Georgia lacked the financial and military resources to mount a successful assault on the Creeks, and the Franklinites lacked any legal territorial claims to the Muscle Shoals lands and desperately needed a way to bolster support among the Tennessee Valley's small-holders. Additionally, McGillivray's Creek forces allied with Dragging Canoe's Chickamauga Cherokee to drive white settlers from the Cumberland District in Middle Tennessee and the southern communities of Franklin.[51] In exchange for Georgia's political support for the Franklin movement and the cession of Muscle Shoals land to the Franklinites, the leadership of the state of Franklin agreed to join the Georgians in their war with the Creeks.[52] One politically astute North Carolinian offered his view of the events unfolding on the Tennessee River, bluntly declaring, "If I were to venture a conjecture, the good of the commonwealth is not at the bottom, but the views of a few crafty land-jobbers, whom you know, who are aiming at purchasing the great bend of the Tenasee [sic] from the Indians, and if not successful that way, to contrive a quarrel, and drive the natives out by force."[53]

Throughout 1785 and 1786, the leadership of Franklin and Georgia, many former partners in the original 1783 land company, continued to correspond regarding the future of Muscle Shoals. Under the direction of the recently formed Bend of the Tennessee Company, the Franklin government briefly attempted to operate a land office to parcel out the Muscle Shoals lands before eventually being driven out of the region by the Creeks.[54] The efforts to settle the "Great Bend of the Tennessee" intensified during the spring of 1786. North Carolina governor Richard Caswell clearly understood the concerns of the Creek Nation and expressed his empathy in a letter to Creek leader Alexander McGillivray. Caswell assured McGillivray that the North Carolina Assembly "expressed a concern that any citizens of this State should have given your people any just cause of Complaint by their encroachments upon the Hunting grounds of the Creek Nation." The governor reassured the Creek chief that "nothing shall be done under the authority of the State respecting your people but what shall be strictly Consistent with the Ties of Friendship."[55]

Amid the intensification of Creek warfare and Caswell's efforts to avoid further bloodshed, Georgia governor Edward Telfair and the Franklinites initiated preparations to rend the Muscle Shoals lands. Colonel Anthony Bledsoe described the resulting Creek reaction in a May 12, 1786, letter to

Governor Caswell. The Franklinite reported that John Taylor, "the half breed that we sent to the Cherokees," informed him that "there is one hundred and fifty Creeks coming against this Country to lay waste, and in all probability anything in the future will be done in the name of the Creeks." Bledsoe then requested that Caswell "write to the Governor of Georgia on the subject."[56] Governor Caswell also articulated his concern over the mounting frontier tensions caused by the disputed Muscle Shoals land in a July 1786 letter to John Sevier. Caswell expressed his pleasure "respecting the conduct of the [Muscle Shoals] Commissioners & the business transaction regarding the Tenesa [sic] Lands" and stated that he "was very glad the attempt for settling them was not made, or rather no Attempt was made to Survey the Lands."[57]

Despite the "land-jobbers" and the state of Georgia's willingness to delay the survey and settlement of the Muscle Shoals lands, Alexander McGillivray and his Creek followers continued their effort to drive whites from their lands. In another letter to Governor Caswell, Alexander Outlaw, a representative to the Franklin legislature, described Creek attacks on frontier settlers that left several Indians and whites dead on the banks of the Holston River. Despite Caswell's rising alarm regarding the future of the Muscle Shoals land scheme, he remained "hampered by [his] obligations to North Carolina" and could not "render" any meaningful support for the efforts against the Creeks.[58]

Continued resistance to white encroachment by the Upper Creeks hastened the opening of discussions for a joint campaign against the tribe by the states of Georgia and Franklin. In a May 14, 1786, letter to Georgia's Governor Telfair, John Sevier warned, "The success of the Muscle Shoals enterprise, greatly depends on the number [of troops] that will go down to that place. A small force will not be adequate to the risk and danger that is encountered, and the people here [Franklin] will not venture to so dangerous a place with a few."[59] Governor Telfair dispatched Major Caesar Augustus Christian George Elholm to serve as arbiter for the proposed alliance. Elholm emigrated from the Duchy of Holstein (present-day northern Germany) during the American Revolution and fought alongside Georgia troops at the siege of Savannah and along the banks of the Ogeechee River.[60] His service to the state of Georgia during the revolution "so ingratiated himself with [newly elected Georgia] Governor [George] Mathews and the Legislature, that he was received by the Executive Council with marks of honor [and] was invited to a seat in their meetings."[61] After the war, the state of Georgia commissioned Elholm adjutant general of the Georgia militia. During the war, Elholm also served under South Carolina general Francis Marion and probably first met future Franklin governor John Sevier during the southern campaign of 1780–1781. Sevier and Elholm's camaraderie made him the obvious choice to broker a military alliance between Georgia and Franklin against McGillivray's Creeks. Elholm spent much of 1785 and 1786 in the Tennessee Valley hammering out the logistics with the Franklinites.[62] By the outbreak of the Creek War in the spring of 1786, the leadership of Franklin considered George Elholm one of their own, and during one of his trips back to report to Governor Mathews, the battle-tested veteran reciprocated his admiration for the Franklinites by lifting a toast wishing "Success to the State of Franklin, his Excellency John Sevier, and her virtuous citizens."[63]

By the fall of 1786, Georgia and the Tennessee Valley Franklinites succeeded in finalizing the details of their military alliance. In a resolution passed on October 13, 1786, the Franklin legislature agreed to aid the state of Georgia in its war against the Creeks. The resolution stated that "the Creeks had declared war against the white people, and had committed several murders on the frontier of late." As a consequence of Creek aggression, Governor Telfair "sent a Peace Talk to the nation of Indians," and the Upper Creeks responded by informing the Georgia governor that "they intended to make vigorous assaults on the white people, as soon as they [Creeks] gather corn." The Franklinites expressed their willingness to join Georgia's "vigorous campaign against the Indians," planned to commence "by the first of November next."[64] The resolution also pledged "one-fourth of the militia of each [Franklin] county . . . to march on horse to the frontiers of this state [Georgia]." Alexander Outlaw reiterated the arrangement to Richard Caswell. Outlaw explained that "The Georgians are now carrying on a Campaign against the Creeks and have sent for our Assistance." Outlaw informed Caswell that he expected "that the [Franklin] Men will March from here against the Creeks" and suggested that the North Carolina "Assembly should take our local Situation under consideration and pass a separation Act on such conditions as will do justice to us all and make the purchase from the Indians."[65]

In September 1786, Major Elholm returned to Georgia carrying the Franklin legislature's "sealed instructions" relating their intent to provide Georgia "one thousand rifleman and two hundred cavalry" in their impending war with McGillivray's Creeks.[66] Sevier also sent Governor Telfair a personal note informing him that the Creek attack may need to be "pro-crastinated" in order to give the Franklin army adequate time to muster.[67] As 1786 drew to a close, both states hurriedly made preparations for the impending assault on the Upper Creeks.

As the military commanders of Georgia and Franklin continued to or-ganize their troops, the economic and political leadership of both states drew increasingly cordial in their diplomatic relations. In an extract from the Georgia Executive Council minutes recorded by Secretary J. Meriweather, the governing body declared that they "entertain a high Sense of the friend-ly relations of the People of Franklin, and at the same time feel every Dispo-sition to Continue the Correspondence between the Honorable John Sevier and his State."[68] For the struggling Franklinites, the military alliance with the Georgians offered desperately needed support for their faltering state-hood movement. In a letter sent to Governor Mathews, Governor Sevier bemoaned the continued resistance to their independence being offered by the state of North Carolina. Sevier then included an impassioned appeal for further support for his state. He informed the Georgia governor that the Franklinites "remember the bloody engagements, we have fought together [during the revolution] against the common enemy, the friendly, kindly, and mutual supports afforded between the State of Georgia and the people of this country." He entreated Mathews and his state's government to "afford the State of Franklin, such of your countenance, in promoting the interest of our infant republic, and reconciling matters between us and the parent state, in such a manner as you in your magnanimity and justice, may think most expedient and the nature of our case deserve."[69] By their willingness to ally with the Franklinites, the state of Georgia helped to legitimize the state of Franklin. Undoubtedly, the Franklinites hoped that the precedent set by Georgia's recognition of their state might influence the actions of other states and, more importantly, the U.S. government.[70]

As preparations continued throughout the opening months of 1787, letters of encouragement from prominent Georgians reached the Tennessee Valley. In February 1787, General Elijah Clark dispatched a letter from Augusta, Georgia, to his compatriot and fellow revolutionary soldier John Sevier containing much-needed words of reassurance. Clark assured Sevier of his "ardent friendship" and pledged the "approbation of all our citizens, and their well wishes for your prosperity." He acknowledged the shared "benefit the friendship of yourself and the people of your state will be to Georgia" and implored Sevier and his fellow Franklinites to "Open a land

Office as speedily as possible" to sell the Muscle Shoals lands and to "never [re]join North-Carolina more." Clark concluded his correspondence by predicting that, under the Franklin government, the residents of the Tennessee Valley "will prosper as a people."[71] In another exchange with Governor Sevier, Clark again pledged his support for Franklin and reiterated his disapprobation with the ongoing policies of the North Carolina government. Clark expressed his indignation over the inability to "peaceably" establish the state of Franklin and the prolonged "unhappy contention . . . with the State of North-Carolina." Clark vowed to defend Franklin if North Carolina "thinks of reducing you by force of arms," and again expressed his belief that "it is the received opinion of the sensible part of every rank in Georgia, that you will, and ought to be, as independent as the other states in the Union."[72] Another Georgian, described as a "gentleman of distinction and character," also professed his support for the fledgling state. He assured Governor Sevier that the "different opinions of a number of the greatest politicians in our state respecting yours . . . [is] that it will support itself without a doubt; and from what I understand, would give every assistance in their power." The show of allegiance emanating from Georgia cast a much needed ray of hope across the Tennessee Valley for the Franklinites.[73]

The proposed joint military campaign against the Creeks also provided the Sevier administration with a diversion for the Tennessee Valley residents from the escalating political factionalism within their own communities. In what eventually became a recurring strategy, the leadership of the state of Franklin utilized Indian warfare to distract the region's inhabitants from the political turmoil and Indian policies threatening their homes and families. According to one Tennessee historian, "The only chance of preserving the integrity of his [Sevier's] government, was that the projected campaign would silence the clamour of the malcontents, and restore harmony and concert to the distracted members of his little republic." In a region galvanized by revolutionary and frontier combat, Nolachucky Jack sought to unify his constituency once again under the glory of his battle flag. Despite Sevier's martial designs, the Creek campaign never came to fruition.[74]

In October 1787, Alexander McGillivray and his Creek followers broadened their insurgency against the white settlements on the Holston River. Washington County, Virginia, resident Arthur Campbell described the deteriorating situation to Virginia governor Edmund Randolph. Campbell warned Governor Randolph that "a large body of Creek Indians had crossed the Hiwasee river, and was in full march against the Holstien In-habitants." Campbell went on to describe a six-hour engagement between Georgia militiamen led by General Elijah Clark against a force of "500 Creeks." Campbell also alerted Randolph to a threat posed by the Creeks to the "Settlements on the French Broad [River]."[75] The increasingly bleak circumstances surrounding the conflict with the Creek tribe, a series of failed peace negotiations, and numerous logistical delays in the joint cam-paign placed increasing pressure on the financially unstable Georgia trea-sury. By the close of 1787, the state's finances had become "more and more disordered" and "munitions supply more and more depleted." The state of Georgia "had a war on her hands without the means to wage it."[76]

During the opening months of 1788, newly elected Georgia governor George Handley was forced to open formal diplomatic negotiations with the Upper Creeks. In conjunction with his state's ratification of the U.S. Constitution, Governor Handley agreed to pursue the federal government's fiscally pragmatic policy of peacefully negotiating with the Native Ameri-can tribes.[77] Distracted by plans by Franklin surveyor Landon Carter to "make as many surveys as possible" of the Muscle Shoals territory, John Sevier remained totally unaware of the treaty negotiations.[78] In a February 19, 1788, correspondence, Governor Handley finally delivered the disap-pointing news to Sevier. Handley informed the Franklin leader that the U.S. "Congress, agreeable to their act of the 26th of October, ordered one Commissioner to be appointed from each of the states, North-Carolina, South-Carolina, and Georgia, to hold a treaty with the Indians, and we now only suspend our operations till the determinations are known."[79] The tremendous political and financial rewards held out by the planned military alliance dissolved and again delayed the acquisition and development of the Muscle Shoals territory.[80]

The collapse of the Muscle Shoals speculative venture and the aborted coalition with the state of Georgia added to the bitter disappointment cre-ated by the Franklinites' ineffectual diplomatic efforts in the North Caro-lina Assembly and among some of the United States' most influential statesmen. By the end of 1787, the majority of Franklin's political leadership began to realize that their state's days were numbered. The communal dis-order fueled by North Carolina's "divide and conquer" political strategy and the mercurial rise of a strident opposition faction within the Tennessee Valley forecasted the mayhem that clouded the final months of the malig-nant state of Franklin.

Chapter 5

Where the Fire of Peace Is Always Kept Burning

Land, Diplomacy, and the Tragedy of the Tennessee Valley's Principal People

On June 8, 1787, Cherokee chief King Fisher (Kingfisher) delivered an emotional "talk" to U.S. Indian Agent Joseph Martin. The aging King Fisher pleaded with Martin to "move these people [Franklin settlers] off our lands" so that "our people have room to live and hunt." The Cherokee chief implored him to see to these "matters so that our young seed may grow up in peace," and the "few of us left" might keep "the land we live on." King Fisher's conversation with Joseph Martin encapsulated the tragedy of the previous twenty-five years of Euroamerican-Indian relations in the Tennessee Valley.[1]

The defining elements of the Euroamerican Indian policy are all present in the chief's "talk." First, the primary goal of Euroamerican Indian policies centered on the unrelenting pursuit of coveted Indian land. Second, the tactics utilized by whites to acquire Indian territory involved some combination of extralegal white encroachment, the creation of paternalistic relationships through treaties and trade relations, and the uncompromising use of violence and physical intimidation. King Fisher's appeal also reveals the complex diplomatic strategy utilized by the southeastern tribes in their efforts to avoid bloodshed and preserve what was left of their way of life. These frontier dynamics existed from the beginning of permanent white settlement in the Tennessee Valley, and continued largely unabated until the Tennessee Valley's white settlers reduced the regional tribes and their land holdings to insignificant levels at the close of the eighteenth century. The leadership of the state of Franklin and their Native American policies fit onto this tragic continuum, but their ferocity and unquenchable thirst for land dramatically escalated regional violence in the Tennessee Valley.

The potential land speculation opportunities and the rapidly advancing regional population and economy fueled the desire to expand Franklin's geographical boundaries and natural resource–based market economy. The leaders of the Franklin government believed that these determined regional Indian tribes and North Carolina and the Confederation Congress's Native American diplomatic agenda served as the primary obstacles to the Tennessee Valley's socioeconomic growth and stabilization. The trans-Appalachian separatist movement freed the leaders of Franklin from the diplomatic shackles placed upon them by their parent state and allowed them to pursue one of the most draconian Native American policies of the eighteenth century.[2] An examination of the relationship between leaders and supporters of Franklin and the Tennessee Valley's principal tribe, the Overhill Cherokee, reveals the tragic consequences of the abandonment of conciliatory diplomacy and the intensification of postrevolutionary Indian warfare. Despite the remarkable diplomatic efforts engaged in by the Cherokee, the Franklin Indian policy, aimed at securing Indian land through dubious treaties, undermining armistice attempts, and engaging in perpetual bloody warfare, plunged the Tennessee Valley into decades of turmoil.

The earliest interaction between the Tennessee Valley's first inhabitants and the Spanish adventurers who first journeyed into the region appeared to be congenial. In the summer of 1540, Spanish conquistador Hernando de Soto and a group of approximately six hundred treasure-seeking Spanish soldiers traveled north from Florida, crossed the Blue Ridge Mountains at Swannanoa Gap, and followed the French Broad River into the Great Valley of the Tennessee. De Soto and his men became the first-known Europeans to traverse the daunting Appalachian Mountains and make contact with the region's native peoples.[3] De Soto briefly visited several Indian towns on the Little Tennessee and French Broad rivers before departing southward toward present-day Alabama. After a short visit by another Spanish explorer, Juan Pardo, in 1567, the Native Americans living in the Tennessee River Valley did not encounter another white traveler until the second half of the seventeenth century.[4] One can only imagine the misconceptions and mythology that emerged during the 150-year absence of whites among the Amerindian people. Despite the relatively peaceful beginnings of Euroamerican-Indian relations, the Spanish explorers' demands for food, women, and information on potential riches foreshadowed the pending tensions between the two cultures, one rooted in capitalist expansion, the other in cultural and territorial preservation.

During the century-and-a-half absence of Europeans, the once expansive and powerful Mississippian Culture chiefdoms splintered, and smaller tribal bands quickly filled the vacuum.[5] In the upper Tennessee Valley, the Overhill Cherokee emerged as the dominant tribal group. The Cherokee, or "principal people," rapidly extended their political, economic, and cultural influence throughout the Southeast. They maintained a matrilineal, clan-based society, devoid of notions of private property and the accumulation of land or wealth. The Cherokee's "communal subsistence" economy, utilizing a combination of agriculture, hunting, and gathering, required vast amounts of land to provide for the populace.[6] The Cherokee people lived in a relatively peaceful community, where a system of privileged retaliation mitigated intertribal warfare, and the existence of powerful war chiefs in each town ensured a strong cohesive military preparedness.[7] The socialist utopias often used by some historians to depict pre-contact Indian societies did not exist. Throughout the seventeenth and early eighteenth centuries, the Overhill Cherokee forced the remaining Indian tribes out of the region and rapidly cemented their control over the Tennessee Valley. By the time of the second arrival of whites in the region, the Cherokee population numbered roughly ten thousand to twelve thousand people.[8]

Prior to permanent white settlement in the Tennessee Valley, most contact between Europeans and the Cherokee involved trade and Protestant missionary efforts. During the late seventeenth and eighteenth centuries, white traders ventured into the Tennessee River Valley to trade with the Overhill Cherokee. In July 1673, British trader James Needham and his teenage indentured servant, Gabriel Arthur, traveled from Fort Henry on the Appomattox River into the Tennessee frontier in an effort to open direct trade with the interior tribes.[9] Needham and Arthur made contact with the Overhill Cherokee at the town of Chota on the Little Tennessee River, but despite their efforts, geographical distance and Cherokee suspicions derailed their attempts to secure permanent trade relations with the Overhill Cherokee. Large-scale trade between the two groups did not materialize for several more decades.[10]

By the opening of the eighteenth century, entrepreneurs from the Carolinas, Virginia, and Georgia finally established commercial relations with the Overhill Cherokee. These backcountry businessmen traveled great distances to trade inexpensive British goods, such as guns, hatchets, farm implements, and other metal wares, for the furs and pelts of whitetail deer and smaller game animals. The demands for furs in Europe created an enormous market for animal pelts, and Cherokee hunters supplied this growing global commercial market. The fur trade resulted in tremendous socioeconomic consequences for the Cherokee tribe. Prior to the fur trade, Cherokee hunters maintained a sacred relationship with their prey and treated any animal harvested with respect and a deep sense of appreciation. The Cherokee took great pains to utilize the entire animal, including meat, bones, pelt, internal organs, and bodily fluids. As profits replaced necessity, the European fur trade destroyed the spirituality of the hunt. The fur trade also increased intertribal conflicts by stretching the available hunting lands, depleting animal stocks, and introducing cutthroat capitalist competition into the Native American communities.[11]

The fur trade drew the Cherokee into a disastrous dependent relationship with the Europeans.[12] The Tennessee Valley's Native American communities became reliant upon European trade goods for survival, and these financial relationships quickly became military alliances as European nations competed for control over North America and its rapidly emerging colonial economy.[13] By the opening of the French and Indian War in 1756, the Cherokee found themselves faced with a critical decision. The tribe maintained significant trade relations with both the French and the British, and both nations sought to draw the tribe into a military coalition. The English constructed Fort Loudon in the Tennessee Valley to bolster Cherokee support for their war effort. Despite the efforts of the British in the region, the Cherokee's lucrative economic relationship with the French and often acrimonious business dealings with the English convinced the majority of them to side with their French "fathers" during the conflict.[14] From the opening of hostilities in the area in 1758 until the signing of the Treaty of Holston on November 19, 1761, Cherokee warriors fought ferociously against British troops and their Native American allies.[15] Amid a ruinous smallpox epidemic and against insurmountable odds, the Tennessee Valley's principal people assaulted English forts, plundered British towns, and fought pitched battles with well-trained and heavily armed British regulars. As the fighting subsided in the so-called Cherokee War, both warring parties faced the consequences of battle. Fort Loudon lay in ruins, and several important Cherokee towns no longer existed. The human casualties proved to be staggering, as hundreds of Cherokee and British combatants sacrificed their lives for European imperialism.[16]

The end of the French and Indian War signaled a new phase in Cherokee-Euroamerican relations and inadvertently paved the way for the first white settlements in the Tennessee Valley. In November 1763, the Cherokee Nation attended a large peace conference, held in Augusta, Georgia, in which they agreed to "a treaty of mutual peace and friendship." The British used the Treaty of Augusta as part of a larger strategy to resuscitate the war-torn Indian trade network.[17] Also in the fall of 1763, the British created an artificial geographical barrier separating eastern white settlements from the rapidly retreating Native American communities of the trans-Appalachian frontier. The Proclamation Line of 1763 demarked an imaginary boundary running along the crest of the Appalachian Mountain chain that served as a dividing line for the two seemingly incompatible societies. The proclamation prohibited white settlement and land speculation west of the Appalachian Mountains and created a border between the two generally hostile peoples.[18] In reality, the Proclamation Line of 1763 only briefly appeased the Native Americans, as illegal white encroachment by British colonists increased significantly with the conclusion of Indian hostilities at Augusta. The Overhill Cherokee left the Augusta meeting convinced of the security of their Tennessee Valley homes and hunting grounds, but the years between the conclusion of the French and Indian War and the American Revolution witnessed the steady advance of Anglo-American settlements.[19]

The period between the closing of the French and Indian War in 1763 and the development of the Watauga settlements in the 1770s is often called the decade of the Long Hunter. During the 1760s, hunters from across the Southeast traveled into the Tennessee frontier to hunt the region's plentiful wildlife. Men like Daniel Boone, William Bean, Samuel Callaway, Henry Scaggins, and Elisha Walden spent months (thus the moniker long hunter) tracking deer, bear, and buffalo across the Tennessee Valley. Many of these long hunters returned to their communities with descriptions of the region's abundant wildlife, unclaimed arable lands, and economic potential. These frontier accounts inspired the first permanent white settlement of the region. The long hunters became the first whites to ignore the Proclamation Line of 1763, but soon itinerant traders and devout Protestant missionaries followed in their footsteps.[20]

It comes as little surprise that the resumption of Cherokee hostilities coincided with the development of the Watauga settlements. The illusion of royal protection from white encroachment quickly faded away as British Indian agents and colonial entrepreneurs pressured the Cherokee to voluntarily cede their lands. Treaties conducted at Hard Labor in 1768 and

Lochaber in 1770 forced the Cherokee to relinquish huge sections of their land to British Indian agents and land speculators.[21] According to Cherokee historian James Mooney, "While these transactions were called treaties, they were really forced upon the native proprietors, who resisted in each turn and finally signed only under protest and on most solemn assurances that no further demands would be made."[22] Even in these early negotiations with British officials, the Cherokee demonstrated the remarkable ability to engage in tense diplomatic negotiations. As hundreds of white settlers illegally poured into their lands and "guns ratted all over the Holston hills," the Cherokee attempted to mitigate the inevitable loss of land by simultaneously appealing to the British Crown and negotiating with frontier entrepreneurs.[23] Unfortunately, the Cherokee's desire and ability to defend their land could not withstand the march of Euroamerican expansion. Diplomacy turned into despondency, and negotiations gave way to violent resistance.[24]

The settlement of the upper Tennessee Valley exacted a steep price from both the Overhill Cherokee and the Watauga settlers. Early settlers like William Bean, James Robertson, Jacob Brown, and John Carter erected illegal communities on territory claimed by the Cherokee and protected by the Proclamation Line of 1763. The Wataugans' total disregard for tribal sovereignty and British authority stoked the coals of smoldering Cherokee resentment. In addition, the gradual replacement of the Indian fur trade with a land- and natural resource–driven market economy further eroded the relationship between the Tennessee Valley's white squatters and the Overhill Cherokee. Isolated incidents of Cherokee aggression occurred sporadically in the buildup to the American Revolution, but epidemic diseases and casualties incurred during the French and Indian War depleted the Overhill Cherokee population and prevented the tribe from successfully repelling the white squatters.[25] The Cherokee instead chose to continue to utilize diplomatic negotiations and incremental territorial concessions to appease the Wataugans. This delaying tactic culminated in a series of massive land sales, including the purchase of huge tracts of land by frontier speculators like Richard Henderson, Jacob Brown, and John Carter. The Tennessee Valley settlers became increasingly aware of the Overhill Cherokee's growing anger over continued white encroachment and the abandonment of mutually beneficial business arrangements.[26] The Wataugans created the quasi-governmental frontier organization known as the Watauga Association to unite the disparate Tennessee Valley communities together against the Cherokee and to defend their "illegal" land claims.[27] The preservation of these land claims eventually drew the Watauga settlers into a bloody war against the Cherokee and convinced the Tennessee Valley's principal people to ally with the British during most of the American Revolution.

By the end of 1774, powerful land speculators controlled hundreds of thousands of acres of Cherokee land in the Tennessee Valley, and much of the tribe's leadership began to question the policy of white appeasement. Cherokee leaders like Dragging Canoe criticized large white land purchases and agitated for armed conflict in a desperate effort to preserve their hunting grounds.[28] Dragging Canoe informed a British Indian agent that the Cherokee "were almost surrounded by White People, that they had but a small spot of ground left for them to stand upon and that it seemed to be the Intention of the White People to destroy them from being a people."[29] The previous decades of conciliation, trade and military relations, strategic acculturation, and racial intermixing created deep divisions among the Cherokee. Indian leaders like Atakullakulla (Little Carpenter) and Oconostota hoped to continue to utilize diplomacy to preserve their tribal sovereignty, but internal pressures for war against the white squatters continued to mount.[30] As the first shots of America's war for independence rang out across the rolling hills of Massachusetts, the Cherokee began their own struggle for tribal sovereignty in the Tennessee River Valley.[31]

According to one Cherokee historian, "The outbreak of the Revolutionary War was viewed as a godsend by the leading warriors of the Cherokee nation. It seemed to give them the opportunity to correct the mistakes they had made in the years from 1769 to 1775."[32] The growing disillusionment among the Cherokee over the failure of peaceful diplomacy and incremental land cessions to halt white encroachment created the ideal opportunity for the British to convince the tribe to join their cause. The Cherokee's disastrous decision to cast their lot with the soundly defeated French during the French and Indian War did little to deter their willingness to again ally with another European nation to protect their interests. The Cherokee's leaders believed in the inevitability of a British victory over the rebelling American colonists, and more importantly over the Tennessee Valley squatters. The desperate tribe trusted that British military success equated to the removal of the white trespassers from their Tennessee Valley hunting grounds.[33]

In 1776, the Cherokee "plunged the upper Tennessee frontier into a racial conflict that . . . resulted in an overwhelming defeat of the tribesmen."[34] Cherokee chief Dragging Canoe led the Overhill Cherokee during the second Cherokee War. The Cherokee's plan for the 1776 invasion of East Tennessee called for approximately seven hundred Cherokee warriors to form three separate divisions to attack the scattered white settlements in the Tennessee Valley's recently established Washington District. The first group of three hundred Cherokee warriors, led by Cherokee chief Old Abraham of Chilhowe, hoped to lay waste to the Nolichucky and Watauga settlements. The plan also called for a Cherokee chief identified only as the Raven to take a small detachment and destroy the Carter's Valley settlement. The remaining Indians, led by Dragging Canoe, targeted the southernmost settlements at Long Island.[35] The three-pronged attack might have succeeded in its goal of the total obliteration of the Tennessee Valley settlements if not for the actions of the Cherokee's "Beloved Woman," Nancy Ward. Using white traders as go-betweens, Ward warned the valley settlers of the impending attack and undoubtedly saved hundreds of Wataugans.[36]

During the months that followed, the Tennessee Valley militiamen repelled the Cherokee warriors at the Battle of Island Flats and the assault on Fort Watauga. As Cherokee forces retreated, a retaliatory force of several thousand Virginia, North Carolina, and Georgia militiamen, led by Colonel William Christian, invaded the Cherokee territory. As the Anglo-American forces surrounded several Cherokee towns, many of the tribe's leaders met to weigh the options presented to them by Colonel Christian.[37] When faced with the decision to either "treat or be destroyed," most of the tribe's leaders wisely supported negotiating with Colonel Christian, but a small vocal faction, led by Dragging Canoe, refused to submit.[38] As Dragging Canoe and his supporters secretly escaped to Chickamauga Creek (near present-day Chattanooga, Tennessee), the remaining chiefs sent word to Colonel Christian that they were prepared to negotiate a peace treaty.

On July 20, 1777, several months after the Cherokee War's conclusion, Cherokee leaders met with Nathaniel Gist, an emissary dispatched by George Washington, at Long Island to negotiate the terms of the treaty.[39] The subsequent Great (Long) Island Treaty required the Cherokee to remain neutral during the remainder of the revolution and to return white prisoners and stolen livestock to the Tennessee Valley settlers. The Great Island Treaty also demanded that the Cherokee cede millions of acres, "everything east of the Blue ridge [Mountains]," to their white conquerors. The Cherokee War left hundreds dead on both sides and several critical towns, settlements, and forts destroyed.[40] The brief and bloody conflict also increased the ranks of Dragging Canoe's Chickamauga Cherokee, an increasingly desperate, determined, and violent Cherokee splinter group now calling themselves the Ani-Yunwiya ("the real people").[41]

The signing of the Great Island Treaty of 1777 failed to curtail Cherokee violence on either side of the Appalachian Mountains. Cherokee warriors from Dragging Canoe's Chickamauga Cherokee continued to conduct raids on the upper Tennessee Valley settlements, and Cherokee tribal leaders from the Middle and Lower towns escalated their war efforts against Americans in South Carolina and Georgia. The Great Island Treaty further fractured the Cherokee Nation, which was never really politically unified to begin with, and rendered the more moderate elements within the tribe ineffectual. The controversial terms of the Great Island Treaty and the resulting polarization of the Cherokee Nation ensured that "the Cherokee War had not ended but only begun."[42]

In the Tennessee Valley, tensions between the Cherokee and the white squatters continued to mount, and another cycle of backcountry violence seemed inevitable. British Indian agents supplied the Cherokee tribe with weapons and pressured their warriors to attack valley settlers.[43] Dragging Canoe's Chickamauga Cherokee terrorized the Tennessee Valley settlements, and in April 1779 Colonel Evan Shelby retaliated with a raid on the group's forces at Chickamauga Creek. By using boats to launch a stealthy attack, Shelby's force of six hundred militiamen caught Dragging Canoe's soldiers by surprise. The Chickamauga Cherokee fled their homes and Shelby's forces torched all twelve of the group's towns.[44] The final revolutionary conflict between the trans-Appalachian Cherokee and the Tennessee Valley militiamen occurred shortly after the militia force's resounding victory at the Battle of King's Mountain in 1780. The combined forces of John Sevier's Washington County, North Carolina, militiamen and Arthur Campbell's Washington County, Virginia, militiamen swooped down on the Overhill Cherokee. The raid on the Cherokee towns proved to be catastrophic for the tribe. John Sevier's youngest son, James, only sixteen at the time, described the engagement. After pursuing a small group of Overhill Cherokee for ten miles, Sevier and his party found a large body of Indians "prepared for battle." After the two sides exchanged fire, "the Indians broke for a cane-brake" in an effort to "save themselves" from the Franklin militia's withering assault. "Thirty or more [Cherokee], however were run into the open pine wood, [and] killed." According to James Sevier, "this last battle was fought & so many Indians killed," but "not a single white [man was killed], & but one slightly wounded."[45] The frontier militia forces destroyed all but two of the Cherokee towns in the Tennessee Valley and burned their yet to be harvested cornfields. The Cherokee "once again gambled [by siding with a European nation] and lost." The ultimate defeat of the British in the American Revolution left the Cherokee Nation "abandoned to their worst enemies."[46]

The conclusion of the American Revolution did not halt frontier violence between the Tennessee Valley settlers and the Cherokee. White encroachment continued and many of the Cherokee remained steadfast in their efforts to protect their territory. The persistence of violence on North Carolina's western edges resulted in tremendous financial expenditures for the fiscally struggling state. The postrevolutionary financial crisis coupled with the expenses of Indian warfare further exacerbated the region's dire economic situation. The state of North Carolina reevaluated their postrevolutionary Indian policies and began to rely more heavily on cost-efficient diplomacy rather than cost-intensive armed conflict. The Tennessee Valley's leadership viewed the return to Cherokee appeasement as a huge mistake. Despite the reservations of western settlers, North Carolina restored diplomatic relations with the Overhill Cherokee, and for a brief period following the revolution it appeared as though further frontier violence might be avoided. These hopes quickly vanished as the political and economic leadership of the Tennessee Valley began to clamor for independence and vocally criticized North Carolina's conciliatory Indian policies.

The beginning of the political conflict between North Carolina and the future Franklinites occurred immediately after the destruction of the Overhill Cherokee towns in 1780. The defeat of the Cherokee initiated a new wave of white encroachment in the Tennessee Valley. By 1781, white squatters extended their western settlements to "within a day's walk" of many of the Overhill Cherokee's most important towns. The Cherokee's leadership pleaded with North Carolina governor Alexander Martin to "have all your people moved off our land."[47] In a correspondence between Governor Martin and Overhill Cherokee chief Old Tassel, the desperate Cherokee informed the governor, "Your people from Nolichucky are daily pushing us out of our lands. We have no place to hunt on. Your people built houses within a day's walk of our towns. We don't want to quarrel."[48] North Carolina's eastern leadership did not "want to quarrel" either. In 1783, the state began to make concessions to the Cherokee, including the establishment of a new boundary line against white settlements. Despite the efforts of eastern North Carolinians to curtail frontier violence, Tennessee Valley settlers continued to press southward and westward. The region's militia units engaged in dozens of raids on Cherokee towns throughout 1783 and continued to argue in the North Carolina Assembly that the state needed to increase military expenditures for the safety and security of their western frontier. The two divergent strategies to deal with the Overhill Cherokee created palpable tensions between the state's eastern and western leaders.[49]

With the passage of the 1784 Cession Act, the North Carolina legislature decided to rid itself of its Indian problem. The nearly bankrupt state hoped to repay its revolutionary debt to the federal government while removing itself from the impossible task of balancing the interests of the Cherokee and the Tennessee Valley settlers. North Carolina governor Alexander Martin wrote to the Cherokee in 1784 "that the Great Council of thirteen American States [the Continental Congress], at Philadelphia should transact all affairs belonging to the Red People." The Land Cession Act of 1784 provided the political opening for the Tennessee Valley's frontier leadership to enact their new Cherokee policies. A future Franklinite outlined the objectives of the new policy as "the disposal of the Indian country," and to "fix the limits of the new State [Franklin], and appropriate the lands, as a fund, to the support of our own government." The Franklinites rejected the ideology of Indian appeasement and initiated a new strategy that combined the threat and focused use of violence with increasingly corrupt Indian negotiations. The Cession Act supplied the rationale for the trans-Appalachian statehood movement, and the birth of the state of Franklin provided the political freedom to radically transform Euroamerican-Cherokee relations on the Tennessee frontier.[50]

In 1785, the newly established Franklin government wasted little time in initiating their new Indian policy and expanding their backcountry settlements. By passing the Cession Act, North Carolina ceded much of her influence over frontier Indian diplomacy to the federal government, and the Confederation Congress initially proved unable or unwilling to intervene in the Tennessee Valley. North Carolina and Virginia Indian agent Joseph Martin wrote several letters to Virginia governor Patrick Henry regarding the fulminant situation. Martin warned Governor Henry that "Gov. [Alexander] Martin Tells me he is well informed that the Greatest part of the Cherokee and Creek Indians are for war, occasioned by the State of Franklyn [sic] passing an Act to Extend their Boundery [sic] within Twenty [miles] of Chota without Holding any Treaty with them." Martin also communicated to Henry that the North Carolina governor "has Declined holding any Treaty with the Indians, as the people [Franklinites] over the mountains has separated themselves from North Carolina."[51] In another exchange, Joseph Martin attempted to persuade Governor Henry that it was imperative for him to "insist upon the observance of a strict neutrality towards the citizens of Virginia" in the impending Indian war. Martin advised the Virginia leader to "give very particular attention to the subject" of Franklinite "encroachment . . . on Cherokee Lands," and if he found the trespass "likely to terminate in hostilities" that could "reach our [Virginia] settlements," the Indian agent recommended that Governor Henry "communicate to the Indians in somewhat specific manner a solemn assurance that the State of Virginia is not a party, ordering or assisting in the encroachment on their territory."[52]

Despite the efforts to prevent further bloodshed on the southwestern frontier, the leaders of the state of Franklin remained free to pursue their own Indian stratagem unimpeded by the federal government, Virginia, or North Carolina, and unencumbered by revolutionary financial obligations or unwanted outside influences. The Franklin Indian policy served as one aspect of a larger strategy aimed at organizing the Tennessee Valley's scattered communities into a unified state and then creating a public domain out of the unimproved and unclaimed territory to finance the nation's fourteenth state. In addition to the internal partisanship surrounding the separatist movement, the Franklin political strategy faced another serious hurdle. The Overhill Cherokee maintained claims to the only remaining substantial tracts of unsettled land in the region, and the embattled tribe did not intend to make any further land cessions. To the Tennessee Valley's ruling class, the Overhill Cherokee represented the single greatest obstacle to their efforts to consolidate the Tennessee frontier, strengthen the region's land- and resource-dependent economy, and maintain their political and economic hegemony.[53]

On May 31, 1785, the Franklinites negotiated their first formal treaty with the Overhill Cherokee. The two sides held the diplomatic discussions, ironically called "a Treaty of Amity and Friendship," at the mouth of Dumplin Creek and the French Broad River (in present-day Jefferson County, Tennessee). Alexander Outlaw, Joseph Hardin, Luke Boyer, Joshua Gist, Ebenezer Alexander, and John Sevier represented the state of Franklin, while Anchoo (Ancoo), chief of Chota; Abraham of Chilhowe (Chelhowa); the Bard, head warrior of the Valley towns; the Sturgion of Tallassee; the

Leach from Settico; and the Big Man Killer from Tallassee represented the Cherokee.[54] The Franklinites dispatched their most skillful negotiators and most experienced Indian fighters, including their governor, their Speaker of the House of Commons, an assistant judge, and a militia captain. Many of the most influential and circumspect Cherokee chiefs did not attend the meeting, including Old Tassel, Dragging Canoe, and Hanging Maw.[55] The Franklinites chose not to invite Cherokee leaders possibly resistant to further land cessions. The absence of the principal Cherokee chiefs imbued the Treaty of Dumplin Creek with a sense of illegitimacy and offered the Franklinites an unmistakable advantage in the treaty negotiations.[56]

The Treaty of Dumplin Creek provides an archetypal example of the state of Franklin's Indian diplomacy in application. First, the Dumplin Creek treaty served two purposes, to force the tribe to formally recognize illegal land claims previously made by white squatters and to secure further territorial concessions. One Franklinite paternalistically stated that the treaty negotiations aimed "to incorporate them [Cherokee], and make them useful citizens."[57] Governor Sevier argued that previous white "settlements, even if unjustly made, were nevertheless made and could not be unmade." Sevier pressured the Cherokee delegation to accept the inevitability of relinquishing land already settled by whites in the Tennessee Valley. Sevier also attempted to shift the blame for white encroachment away from the state of Franklin by stating, "I am takeing [sic] every measure in my power to prevent Encroachments on the Indians' Land. This, however, is a difficult Task, because North Carolina actually sold the Land up To these [Cherokee] Towns."[58] The Franklinites also hoped to further extend their state's land holdings in an effort to boost the state treasury and free up land for speculators within the Franklin government. The treaty eventually agreed to by the Cherokee delegation provided the tribe with clothing and trade goods for "all lands lying and being on the South side of the Holeson [sic] and French Broad Rivers, as far South as the ridge that divide the Waters of the Little River from the Waters of the Tenessee." Not surprisingly, the land deal proved to be extremely lucrative for the Franklinites. For an amount of "reasonable and liberal compensation," the state of Franklin secured thousands of acres of valuable Tennessee Valley bottomland. A word in the final sentence of the treaty reveals the true nature of the Dumplin Creek land deal: "bargain."[59]

The second characteristic of the Franklin Indian strategy demonstrated by the Treaty of Dumplin Creek is the selective assemblage of Cherokee leaders by the Franklinites. By excluding Cherokee leaders possibly hesitant to sign away huge swaths of land for very little compensation, the Franklinites assured their negotiators highly agreeable treaty delegations and lucrative diplomatic arrangements. This strategy did not go unnoticed by the Cherokee chiefs excluded from Dumplin Creek. In a "talk" delivered by Old Tassel, the Cherokee chief recounted his version of the Dumplin Creek Treaty. Old Tassel and the principal leaders of the Cherokee Nation did not attend the gathering "on the French Broad [Dumplin Creek]" organized by the Franklinites, but instead waited to parlay with representatives of the "great men of the thirteen states" at Hopewell, South Carolina, scheduled for later that same year. Despite the absence of the Cherokee "head men" and the fact that the "young men" representing the Cherokee tribe informed the attendees that "they had no authority to treat about lands," the Franklin negotiators made a series of territorial demands. The Franklinites "wanted [the Cherokee to cede] the land on the Little [Tennessee] River" and to allow the white families already settled there to "remain . . . till the head men of their nation were consulted on it." The "young" Cherokee negotiators agreed to allow the Tennessee Valley squatters to remain "living on the lands," but the Franklin government took the temporary concession to be permanent. Old Tassel described the events that followed the treaty negotiations: "Since then we are told that they claim all lands on the waters of Little River, and have appointed men among themselves to settle the disputes on our lands [establishment of Franklin land office], and call it their ground."[60] Old Tassel's letter also reveals a third element of the Franklin Indian policy, the misrepresentation or manipulation of the terms of treaties. Despite the verbal commitment to delay officially sanctioning land claims until the principal Cherokee chiefs could be consulted, the Franklinites proceeded to validate squatter claims and initiate the legal mechanisms for the sale of the Cherokee territory. The ruthless focus on securing land, strategically selecting Native American leaders for treaty negotiations, and the prevaricating of the agreed-upon diplomatic terms characterized the Treaty of Dumplin Creek and all future Franklin-Amerindian negotiations.[61]

Nationalist historians argued that America's native peoples failed to grasp the nature of Euroamerican diplomacy, the concept of property ownership, and the dynamics of frontier capitalism. To these scholars, this fundamental misunderstanding of the European socioeconomic mind-set led to the tragic consequences that cost the American Indians their homeland, culture, and lives. The diplomatic strategy utilized by the Overhill Cherokee during the Franklin movement refutes these misconceptions. The Tennessee Valley's "people of the sacred fire" engaged in a series of treaty negotiations with the federal government, the state of North Carolina, and the state of Franklin. The tribe sought to curtail the loss of their lands through formal diplomatic channels and resorted to violence only out of desperation.

The first effort to halt the advance of Franklin settlers occurred prior to the dubious treaty negotiations at Dumplin Creek. During the Cession Act controversy, the Overhill Cherokee petitioned both the state of North Carolina and the Continental Congress to intervene in the situation unfolding in the Tennessee Valley. North Carolina agreed to meet with an Indian delegation at the end of 1784 to discuss the details of a new treaty, but the territorial cession prevented the meeting from occurring. With the repeal of the Cession Act, North Carolina once again agreed to meet with the native leaders of the tribe. Because of the absence of a public domain in the Tennessee Valley, the federal government initially held little interest in intervening on behalf of the Cherokee and "did not do as it was doing at that very time in the Northwest, that is, build garrisons, supply troops, and remove squatters."[62] Despite the reluctance of Congress to directly intercede in the conflict, the federal government did agree to provide frontier diplomats to aid the southern states in treaty negotiations with the southeastern tribes. As the situation quickly deteriorated on the Tennessee frontier, congressionally appointed Indian agents and North Carolina negotiators agreed to meet the Cherokee leadership at Hopewell, South Carolina.[63]

The Cherokee and American diplomats conducted the Treaty of Hopewell without consulting or including the Franklin government or the Chickamauga Cherokee.[64] From November 18–29, 1785, Benjamin Hawkins, Joseph Martin, Andrew Pickens, and Lachlan McIntosh, the congressionally appointed Indian commissioners, engaged the Cherokee in a series of talks. The negotiations proved to be strikingly different from those held between the Franklinites and the Cherokee at Dumplin Creek.[65] First, the Hopewell negotiations included all of the tribe's principal chiefs and more than a thousand representatives from various Cherokee towns.[66] Second, the participants in the meetings considered the diplomatic agendas of both parties, and negotiators held the maintenance of peace as being equally as important as the protection of land claims. Third, the Treaty of Hopewell also included a provision that provided the Cherokee Nation the authority to "punish" any white settler who settled illegally on tribal lands. Finally, the results of the Treaty of Hopewell proved to be mutually beneficial for both parties. As one historian stated, "The treaty held at Hopewell . . . is an admirable example of how generous a government can be with Indians when lands in question do not belong to that government." The extension of Cherokee justice into the lives of Americans created a backlash against the Treaty of Hopewell among many North Carolinians as well as Franklinites.[67]

Whatever the motivations behind the equity displayed by the federal government at Hopewell, the treaty came as a much-needed diplomatic success for the Cherokee Nation. In exchange for recognizing the U.S. government as "sovereign of all our land," the tribe secured the restoration of the territory forfeited after the signing of the Great Island Treaty in June 1777.[68] The American representatives also agreed to disavow Franklin's Treaty of Dumplin Creek. As important as the reclamation of their Tennessee Valley lands, the Treaty of Hopewell convinced the Cherokee that the members of the U.S. Continental Congress might be sympathetic to their cause. This perceived alliance instilled the tribe's leadership with the confidence to continue to resist both the advance of the Franklin squatters and the use of political and military pressure by the new state for further land cessions. The Franklinites reacted quite differently to the news of the South Carolina negotiations. Congress's willingness to make concessions to the Cherokee and to exclude the rebellious state's leadership from the treaty negotiations strengthened the resolve of the Franklinites to defend their statehood effort. The land returned to the tribe by the Treaty of Hopewell also meant that several of the state of Franklin's most significant towns and communities, including the new capital of Greeneville, now rested in Cherokee territory. The treaty signed at Hopewell proved to be a watershed moment for the Tennessee frontier that simultaneously rekindled the Overhill Cherokee's hope that the American government intended to remove the white squatters from their lands and strengthened the Franklinites' resolve to expand their state's geographical boundaries and defend the land claims of their citizens.[69]

The negotiations at Hopewell signaled the beginning of an unusual political dynamic on the Tennessee frontier: the existence of two competing Indian policies. The state of North Carolina completely ignored the land cessions contained in the Treaty of Dumplin Creek, and the Franklinites responded by refusing to recognize the terms of the Treaty of Hopewell. The Cherokee Nation faced the uncertainty of two state political systems conducting discrete Native American diplomacy. The confusion caused by the divergent diplomatic efforts quickly spread among the valley residents, as both states continued to maintain separate judicial, political, and military infrastructures. For the Cherokee, the escalation of political tensions between North Carolina's Tennessee Valley loyalists and rebellious Franklinites and the persistence of white encroachment on their hunting grounds forecasted the resumption of frontier violence.[70]

The year 1786 opened with a renewed determination by both the Franklinites and the Overhill Cherokee to defend their homes. Franklin's chief judge, David Campbell, clarified his state's position in a November 30, 1786, letter to North Carolina governor Richard Caswell. Judge Campbell apprised Caswell of the "many families settled within nine Miles of the Cherokee Nation," and warned him of the "consequence of those emigrations." Campbell implored the governor to extend "Our laws & Government" to the Indians "or they will become dangerous." The Franklinite reminded Governor Caswell that "all [of] America [has] extended their back Settlements in opposition to Laws & proclamations" of their states and that "It is in vain to say they must be restrained" from further encroachments. He closed by predicting that the "Indians are now become more pusilanimous [sic], and consequently will be more & more incroached [sic] upon," and demanding that "They must, they will be circumscribed."[71] Cherokee chief Old Tassel echoed the determination expressed by Judge Campbell in a talk delivered to Joseph Martin on April 10, 1786. Old Tassel warned Martin, "Some of my young men have lately come from the Western Tribes of Indians and they tell me they are preparing for War and they will most certainly strike on your Frontiers this Spring and Summer." In a remarkable display of compassion, the aging chief expressed sorrow "that your people are suffered to Come in our Country making disputes," and assured Martin that the Cherokee "want to live in peace with our friends, the White people, and will never Quarrel with them if we can help it." He pleaded with him to "take pity on us and do us Justice and keep your people from us, only such as you point out to trade with us, which we shall take great care of." Old Tassel expressed his concern that his supporters will "be blamed if" more militant factions of the Cherokee who "have gone out do any Mischeif [sic]." He assured Martin that "we did everything we could to stop them," but "We have been waiting a long time to see the people moved off our lands on the South side of the French Broad river, but they still come nearer."[72] Despite the previous territorial cessions and diplomatic concessions agreed to by the Overhill Cherokee, the unwillingness of the state of Franklin to halt the advance of its citizens ensured the rekindling of hostilities in the Tennessee Valley.[73]

The resurgence of backcountry bloodshed commenced in the spring of 1786 with a series of Cherokee raids against white western settlements. Led by mixed-blood chief John Watts, Chickamauga Cherokee forces, roughly one thousand strong, attacked settlements near present-day Knoxville. The tribe specifically targeted the Beaver Creek home of Mr. Briam due to its location only a few miles from the Cherokee town of Chota. The attack served as a warning against future encroachment on the north side of the Holston River.[74] The Indian attacks terrorized the Tennessee Valley settlers and forced frontier whites to hastily organize a volunteer militia force to retaliate against the Overhill Cherokee. Led by Governor Sevier, 150 mounted Franklinites amassed at Houston's Station to conduct their invasion of the Cherokee towns. After crossing the Tennessee River, the Franklin militia forces attacked the Hiawassee Overhill towns, burning three villages and killing fifteen Cherokee.[75] The destruction of the Overhill Cherokee towns resulted in a brief pause in combat, and both parties used the lull in fighting to prepare for future confrontations. Joseph Martin described the uneasiness gripping the Tennessee Valley during the late spring of 1786, warning Governor Caswell that "the accounts from the Cherokee Country are somewhat alarming." He recounted the violence of the previous months and cautioned the governor that the Cherokee recently warned the Franklinites that "they did not wish for war but if the white people wanted war it was what they would get."[76]

As spring gave way to summer, Dragging Canoe's Chickamauga Cherokee continued their attacks on the region's white settlements, killing "two [white] traders . . . on their way to the Chickasaws from Cumberland." Joseph Martin warned Governor Caswell that he feared that "Draggon [sic] Canoe's" Chickamauga followers might "join the Creeks" in an "open war" against white settlers. Ellis Haslin, considered "one of the principal Traders in the Cherokee Country," described to Martin a foreboding encounter with "a party of Creeks & Chickamawgahs [sic] on their way to [attack the] Cumberland" settlements. Haslin made an attempt to "turn them back . . . but they would not go back."[77] The leaders of Franklin did not distinguish the Overhill Cherokee from the Chickamauga Cherokee and therefore often unfairly retaliated against towns that "all seemed very Friendly."[78] The threat posed by the Chickamauga Cherokee convinced the Franklinites to conduct a preemptive strike against the Cherokee Upper towns. On May 12, 1786, Franklin militia colonel Anthony Bledsoe informed Governor Caswell of the deteriorating situation in the Tennessee backcountry. Upon his "return from [the North Carolina state capital] New Bern," Bledsoe found the Tennessee Valley's "peaceable situation . . . disturbed by the Indians stealing Horses" and "murdering and wounding" white settlers. Bledsoe responded to these attacks by ordering "look outs in different parts of the Country" and expanding the ranks of the militia. Bledsoe warned Caswell that "Our Country being a frontier alround [sic] and in all appearances likely to be invaded on every quarter, and driven to stations and fortifications leaving their property exposed to the savage, to the destruction of this Infant Country." The exasperated Franklinite admitted to the governor that "we seem to be at a loss to know with Certainty by what hand we suffer in particular."[79] Colonel Bledsoe concluded his correspondence by "loudly calling [North Carolina] for assistance" and looking to Governor Caswell "to revenge her Blood." Bledsoe then requested "permission" to lead a raid "against some small Town[s] of the Chickamawgahs [sic]."[80]

Governor Caswell reluctantly approved Colonel Bledsoe's request for a raid on the Cherokee communities, and in August 1786 a group of two hundred Franklin militiamen, led by William Cocke and Alexander Outlaw, marched into the Overhill Cherokee territory. After destroying an Overhill town, the Franklinites forced the tribe into treaty negotiations.[81] Amid the threat posed by the invading Franklinites against their homes and families, the Overhill Cherokee leaders, led by Old Tassel and Hanging Maw, met with Outlaw and Cocke at Chota Ford from July 31 to August 3. During the talks, the Franklin negotiators accused the Overhill Cherokee of murdering "our young men," stealing horses, robbing, and most importantly, abandoning the land agreements contained in the Treaty of Dumplin Creek. Old Tassel defended his tribesmen by stating, "The men that did the Murder is bad men and no warriors is gone, and I can't tell you where they are gone. They live in Coytoy at the Mouth of the Holston. This is all I have to say; they have done the murder." The Franklinites argued that the Cherokee must relinquish all of the land "on the North side of the Tennessee and Holston [rivers]" because North Carolina "has sold us all the Country."[82] In reality, North Carolina never sold the Franklinites any land, and many of the state's political leaders actively sought to destroy the embryonic state. The savvy Overhill chief Old Tassel called the Franklinites' bluff, stating, "I will tell you about the land. What you say concerning the

and traders. In reality, the isolated incidents occurring in the Tennessee Valley after the Treaty of Coyatee simply continued the hostile relationship between the region's Native American and white residents.

Despite the continued failure of backcountry negotiations to secure the removal of white squatters from their hunting grounds, the Cherokee maintained their commitment to diplomacy. The year 1787 not only witnessed the drafting of a new U.S. Constitution, but also the reengagement of the federal government and the state of North Carolina in southeastern Indian affairs. In July, newly elected North Carolina governor Samuel Johnston issued a "Proclamation forbidding any of the Citizens of the State [Franklin/North Carolina] from entering on the Indian Territory without the Order of the Commanding Officer of that Quarter." Johnston also instructed Joseph Martin "to use his utmost efforts, to restrain the people in his [southern] District from further outrages & by every means in his power to conciliate the minds of the Indians and to act altogether on the defensive."[86] Notwithstanding the federal government's inability to enforce the territorial agreements spelled out in the Treaty of Hopewell, the Cherokee still held onto their belief that further frontier bloodshed could be avoided by using diplomatic channels and direct pleas to prominent American political figures. Cherokee chiefs continued to correspond with state and federal leaders and meet with various Indian agents to secure their territorial boundaries. At a March 24, 1787, meeting at the Overhill Cherokee town of Chota, Hanging Maw described the tribe's frustration with the U.S. government to Indian agent Joseph Martin. Hanging Maw expressed his disappointment with the U.S. Congress's inability to enforce the provisions of the Treaty of Hopewell. He lamented, "We have several Treaties with the Americans, when Bounds was always fixt [sic] and fair promises always made that the white People should not come over. But we always find that after a treaty they settle much faster than before." Hanging Maw continued, "when we Treated with Congress [at Hopewell] we made no doubt that we should have Justice." The Cherokee chief described the advice his followers received from "People a great way off" that implored the Cherokee Nation not to "set still till all our Lands is Settled" or to allow "the Americans . . . to deceive us." Hanging Maw concluded his talk by imploring Joseph Martin to use his influence and "take pity on us and have their people moved off our Lands."[87]

Hanging Maw's argument that treaties intensified white settlement proved to be prophetic. Following the signing of the Treaty of Coyatee, the state of Franklin and her citizens intensified the settlement and sale of territory in the Tennessee Valley. At the September 1787 meeting of the Franklin legislature held in Greeneville, the Franklinites opened a land office for the purpose of selling the territory claimed from the Overhill Cherokee at Dumplin Creek and Coyatee. The Franklin legislature provided for land purchases to be transacted using both scarce specie and abundant animal pelts. The land office quickly began to sell land in the Tennessee Valley both within and outside the two treaty boundaries.[88] Joseph Martin described the chaotic situation to recently retired North Carolina governor Richard Caswell. After arriving at the town of Chota, Martin "found the Indians in greater confusion [*sic*] than I had ever seen them before." "Colonel John Logan's Expedition" and the "daily Incroachments [*sic*] of the Franklinists on their Lands" created an air of desperation among the Overhill Cherokee. Martin expressed horror upon discovering that the Franklinites "opened a land office for Every Acre of Land that the Legislature of North Carolina Ceded to them [Franklinites] North of the Tennessee [River], which includes Several of their [Cherokee] Principal cornfields and part of the beloved Town, Chota and the whole Town of Niol, and Now Settling on the Banks of the River."[89] Colonel Evan Shelby, a staunch opponent of the state of Franklin, joined Martin in condemning the actions of the Franklin government. Shelby also recounted that the Franklin government "Opened an Office for the Lands from French Broad River to Tinnise [*sic*] River, being the Lands Reserved to the Indians By the General Assembly of No. Carolina to them and their heirs for Ever." According to Shelby's intelligence, the Franklinites "are Forceably [*sic*] Takeing possession of the Same, and Setling [*sic*] in View of their Towns." He warned that these actions "Cannot faile [*sic*] bringing On the Resentment of the Indians, and Involve us in A War with them, which Your Frontiers must share in its dreadful Consequences."[90] The state of Franklin's land policies also drew the criticism of one of America's most respected statesmen, Benjamin Franklin. Franklin condemned the Franklinites' "encroachments" in a letter to William Cocke, calling them "unjustifiable" and unnecessary. He believed that the Cherokee "usually give very good [land] bargains; and in one year's war with them you may suffer a loss of property and be put to an expense vastly exceeding in value what would have contented them perfectly in fairly buying the lands they can spare." Franklin expressed sympathy for the Cherokee Nation as the "No. Carolinians on one side, and the people of your State [Franklin] on the other, encroach upon them daily."

He also warned that the Franklinites' continued breach "of a solemn treaty [Hopewell]" could one day "bring upon themselves an Indian war [in which] they will not be supported by" the U.S. government.[91] Even the state of Franklin's political leadership realized the anger created among the Cherokee by the opening of the Franklin land office. Franklin militia colonel Anthony Bledsoe acknowledged to Governor Caswell that the "opening [of] a land office from the French Broad to the Tennessee River . . . gives a general disgust to the Indians, and I judge gives them cause to harass the Cumberland settlements [in Middle Tennessee]."[92] The opening of the Franklin land office and the hostile stance taken toward the Overhill Cherokee by the government and citizens of Franklin all but ensured another full-scale Cherokee war. As one concerned Virginia resident stated, "Should these ill advised people [Franklin residents] force them [Indians] into a War, we shall have all the Southern Indians against us."[93]

Amid the diplomatic maneuvering with members of Congress and the state governments of Virginia, Georgia, and North Carolina, the Cherokee Nation prepared for the impending frontier clash. One historian described the military buildup as "a Cherokee movement that in 1788 was to bring into the field a great conquering Cherokee army organized to sweep every settler from south of the French Broad."[94] In the spring of 1788, the Cherokee commenced hostilities and began incursions into the Franklin communities. Surry County, North Carolina, resident Mark Armstrong wrote to North Carolina governor Samuel Johnston that the Cherokee "have killed several persons and taken some prisoners. Whilst I staid in Hawkins County [in the state of Franklin], four men were killed & scalped."[95] Joseph Martin also grimly apprised Virginia governor Edmund Randolph of the situation on the Tennessee frontier. In his correspondence, Martin enclosed "copies of letters showing the alarmed state of the frontiers of Washington, Russel [sic] and Hawkins Counties, and indeed throughout the whole Western N. Carolina and what had been known as Franklin, on account of the incursions of the Savages." Across the Tennessee Valley, Martin found that "the inhabitants are ready to leave the country."[96]

The situation in the Tennessee Valley continued to spiral out of control, and the struggling Franklin government proved incapable of either offering protection to their citizens or pacifying the enraged Cherokee. The failure of the Franklinites to secure formal recognition from the U.S. Congress, the loss of national and regional support for the statehood movement, and North Carolina's strategy of conducting its affairs within Franklin's ever-expanding borders continued to steadily derail the state of Franklin. In a letter dated April 12, 1788, North Carolina's Governor Johnston warned that "Should the people in that part of the Country wantonly involve themselves in an Indian War without real necessity, but with a view to harass [*sic*] and drive them from their settlements I cannot promise them any assistance from this side of the Mountain." By the opening of the 1788 Cherokee hostilities, America's would-be fourteenth state stood on the verge of collapse and faced the likelihood of a unilateral Indian engagement.[97]

As the mounting turmoil engulfed the state of Franklin, in May 1788 a Cherokee named Slim Tom murdered eleven members of a Tennessee Valley family residing nine miles from Chota on the Little Tennessee River.[98] The Kirk family massacre proved to be the spark that once again triggered open warfare between the Franklinites and the Cherokee. The Kirk family incident and subsequent Franklinite response illustrated the barbarity perpetrated by both sides during the struggle for control of the Tennessee Valley. The sole surviving member of the Kirk family, John Kirk, described the massacre to Chickamauga Cherokee chief John Watts in a letter dated October 17, 1788. Kirk wrote, "For days and months the Cherokee Indians, big and little, women and children, have been fed and treated kindly by my mother." According to Kirk, during a period "When all was at peace with the Tennessee towns," a Cherokee named Slim Tom, "with a party of Sattigo [Citico] and other Cherokee Indians," fell upon the Kirk family and "murdered my mother, brothers and sisters in cold blood." As the Kirk children played "about them as friends," "the bloody tomahawk" mutilated their "smiling faces." Kirk signed his correspondence "John Kirk, Jun. Captain of the Bloody Rangers."[99] The Franklinites predictably responded to the Kirk murders by sending out the Franklin militia, under the command of John Sevier, to retaliate against the Overhill and Chickamauga Cherokee. Sevier and approximately 150 soldiers departed from the appropriately named Hunter's Station, on a small tributary of the Holston River, on June 1, 1788, with "outrage rankling in their heart."[100] Despite the lack of evidence proving Overhill Cherokee involvement in the Kirk family massacre, the Franklin militia force once again targeted the Cherokee's Hiawassee Overhill towns. Sullivan County Tiptonite Thomas Hutchings claimed that "Colonel Sevier, contrary to the Council of Officers in June [2], fell on Kiewkah on Hiawassa, and, is said, killed about 20 Indians."[101] Sevier then burned the Cherokee town and marched his forces deeper into the Overhill Cherokee Nation. Sevier's campaign against the Overhill Cherokee led to the destruction of several important Cherokee towns and a tremendous loss of life for the embattled tribe.[102]

After destroying many of the Cherokee valley settlements, John Sevier turned his attention to the destruction of the largely peaceful Overhill town of Chilhowe, unfortunately the hometown of Slim Tom. At Chilhowe, Sevier's forces surrounded the Cherokee community and the home of the town's beloved chief Old Abraham. At the time of the occupation, Old Abraham happened to be in council with chief Old Tassel. The two Cherokee chiefs most dedicated to mutual peace received an invitation from the Franklinites to meet them at their encampment across the Little Tennessee River. Under a white flag of truce, Old Abraham and Old Tassel, men described as "remarkable for their good Offices & Fidelity," gathered in Sevier's tent.[103] According to Thomas Hutchings, "Abram's [Abraham] son ferried them [the Cherokee party] over, and swam their horses—this done, they [John Kirk and James Hubbard] fell on the Indians, killed the Tassel, Hanging Man [sic], Old Abram, his son, Tassell's [sic] brother, and Hanging-Man's [sic] brother, and took in Abram's wife and daughter—brought in 14 Scalps—altogether a scene of cruelty."[104] According to first-hand accounts of the tragic events of that summer day, John Sevier was "nearly a Quarter of a Mile from the Place" during the "braining" of the unarmed Cherokee, but the militia commander's absence did not shield him from criticism.[105] The Continental Congress offered several resolutions condemning the act, and many of Sevier's contemporaries blamed him for the actions of the troops in his command. According to one Franklin historian, "the [Kirk] incident devalued Sevier's reputation with President Washington, who wanted to keep peace with the frontier Indians," and "the president called Sevier an Indian murderer."[106] Thomas Hutchings warned that Sevier's conduct would "leave an evil tendency, in so much as it may involve us in a war."[107] Charles Thomson, secretary of the Continental Congress, suggested to North Carolina's Governor Johnston that "Hostilities alleged to have been committed by John Sevier & others into which you are earnestly requested to cause enquiry to be made & if found true to take measures to have the perpetrators thereof apprehended & punished."[108] Governor Johnston responded to the Continental Congress's demand for justice by "issuing a warrant for apprehending them [Sevier and party]."[109] The Washington County District Court ultimately found Sevier innocent of the charges brought against him relating to the murders, but the damage to the Overhill Cherokee could not be undone.[110]

The tragic consequences of the barbarous acts of that June day extended far beyond the cold-blooded execution of two beloved Cherokee chiefs and their families. The reverberations from the deaths of Old Tassel and Old Abraham sparked a wave of terror and fear that swept across the Cherokee and white communities in the Tennessee Valley. Governor Johnston hoped that the arrest of John Sevier and several Franklin militiamen might "conciliate the Indians & restrain the Whites from Committing Outrages." In an open letter to the Cherokee Nation, Johnston promised that if "any of them [Franklinites] have injured you without sufficient cause to take them up and send them to us that they may receive Correction & punishment."[111] Colonel George Maxwell of Sullivan County believed that "Sevier's conduct, so exasperated the Indians that the whole body of them is now at war with us."[112] Hugh Williamson, North Carolina delegate to the Continental Congress, described the far-reaching ramifications of the murders in a September 6, 1788, letter to Governor Johnston. Williamson believed that "the conduct of Mr. Sevier was . . . fatal" to the ongoing efforts of South Carolina, Virginia, and Georgia to conclude a "Treaty [that] is now pending with the Southern Indians [Creeks]." He expressed his concern that the murders of Old Tassel and Old Abraham might ignite "a general Indian War," and entreated that the "delegates from these States earnestly request that preventative measures may be taken."[113] Despite the efforts by the Continental Congress and several southern state governments to conciliate the Cherokee Nation, the actions of Sevier and his fellow Franklinites ensured the continuation of backcountry warfare.

By murdering the two Cherokee chiefs most dedicated to maintaining a harmonious coexistence between the Indian and white Tennessee Valley residents, the Franklinites destroyed any hope for peaceful relations with the Overhill Cherokee and inadvertently united the Cherokee behind a larger war effort. Richard Winn informed Governor Johnston that "the said Cherokee Chiefs have given Notice, they mean to spill Blood."[114] No longer could the frontier whites rely on the peaceful intervention of Cherokee chiefs like Old Tassel and Old Abraham on their behalf. Now the efforts of Cherokee resistance groups, such as Dragging Canoe's Chickamauga Cherokee, became the accepted course of action for all Cherokee tribesmen.[115] The state of Franklin leadership's uncompromising pursuit of land at any and all costs, use of corrupt diplomatic practices, and campaign to undermine the treaty efforts of North Carolina, Virginia, Georgia, South Carolina, and the U.S. government caused the bloodiest Indian war ever fought in the Tennessee Valley. John Sevier's son, James Sevier, described this period as "the hottest Indian war I ever witnessed."[116] After the state of Franklin's demise, North Carolina's Governor Johnston inherited the Cherokee war, which he characterized as "horrid Murders & Massacres."[117] This conflict raged for several years until the Overhill Cherokee and their many tribal allies finally agreed to sign a treaty ending the bitter hostilities. Long after the collapse of Sevier's state of Franklin, on July 2, 1791, the Cherokee signed the Treaty of Holston (in present-day Knoxville), effectively ending the three-year Cherokee war initiated by the Franklinites.[118]

At their motivational core, the leaders and supporters of Franklin believed that their statehood movement would remove the political obstacles impeding the development of their backcountry communities and economy. An independent state bureaucracy offered the Tennessee Valley's ruling class the opportunity to control state and local political and judicial positions, expand and command the rapidly developing trans-Appalachian economy, and implement their own Native American policy. The impact of the blending of the ideologies of backcountry separatism and Indian racism was most acutely experienced by the Overhill Cherokee. As the Franklin government replaced conciliatory diplomacy with their relentless policy of forced land cessions and violence, the Native American communities of the Tennessee Valley found themselves threatened as never before.

Chapter 6

Death in All Its Various and Frightful Shapes

The Last Days of the State of Franklin

After nearly two years of political lobbying, the leaders of the state of Franklin had failed to garner approval from the U.S. Congress, the North Carolina legislature, or a single influential national political figure for their statehood movement. Throughout 1787, the residents of the Tennessee Valley continued to suffer against the backdrop of the heightening Cherokee and Creek resistance movements, the disruption to their communities caused by two competing state bureaucracies, and the increasingly treacherous local factionalism threatening their homes, families, and businesses. The state of North Carolina maintained its conciliatory strategy aimed at nonviolently defeating the Franklin separatist movement by driving a political wedge between the residents of the Great Valley of the Tennessee. Considerable risks accompanied North Carolina's divisive political maneuverings, and as early as May 1787, Governor Caswell warned the embittered residents of "the Counties of Sullivan, Greene, Washington, and Hawkins" that if they failed to "evince the necessity of Mutual Friendship and the Ties of Brotherly love" between themselves, "the Blood of some of your dearest and worthiest Citizens may have been spilt and your Country laid to waste in an unnatural and Cruel Civil War."[1] Caswell's prophetic admonishment captured the social and political chaos rending the Tennessee Valley communities. The Caswell administration's growing alarm over the potential outbreak of civil war mounted as a result of the further escalation of partisan political strife within the region.

In an effort to avoid the outbreak of a partisan civil war within the Tennessee Valley, the state of North Carolina initiated a series of backcountry negotiations throughout the first half of 1787, between herself and the leadership of Franklin. Initially these high-level meetings held out the possibility of a peaceful compromise, but the eventual failure of the negotiators to secure a substantive and lasting agreement between the two states and their Tennessee Valley proponents resulted in further hostilities. Tensions between the Franklinites and Tiptonites intensified as the leaders and supporters of Franklin scrambled to preserve their statehood movement. The contentious 1787 state elections held in the Tennessee Valley and the ongoing struggle to control local political and judicial offices resulted in violent clashes between partisans. As news reached the Tennessee Valley of the existence of a new U.S. Constitution containing language unfavorable to the future of the state of Franklin, many rank and file supporters of statehood abandoned the movement and returned their political loyalties to North Carolina. The dwindling local support for Franklin and the federal government's rebuke placed the remaining Franklinites in an increasingly desperate position. Despite the inevitable fall of the state of Franklin, Tennessee Valley partisans remained determined to assert their local hegemony and to defeat their political adversaries. During the final months of the state of Franklin, the communities of the Tennessee Valley erupted into a violent partisan clash that left several Tennessee Valley residents dead, the region in complete bedlam, and the state of Franklin in smoldering ruins.[2]

At the opening of 1787, Governor Caswell chose to expand his effort to bring about a harmonious conclusion to the Franklin separatist movement by dispatching several strategic correspondences with his son Winston into the Tennessee Valley. In late February 1787, the first of these letters arrived in the hands of the still recovering Franklin judge David Campbell. Caswell assured Campbell that Franklin's independence may eventually be secured "if those can be brought to agree among themselves and make a General application to the Legislature hereafter, returning to the former Government and agreeing to certain reasonable stipulations."[3] Winston Caswell also carried a letter from his father to Governor Sevier in which the North Carolina leader recounted his assembly's fateful decision during the previous November session. Caswell regrettably reported that "the Assembly, from representation of persons among yourselves [specifically Senator John Tipton], was induced to believe that it was proper for the people to return to subjection to the laws and Government of North Carolina." Caswell clearly understood the perilous situation unfolding on the Tennessee frontier and included a plea for calmer heads to prevail among the region's partisan leaders. Caswell appealed, "In the mean Time, the most Friendly intercourse between the Citizens on the Eastern & Western Waters is strongly Recommended." The North Carolina governor concluded his com-

be divided among his friends, and a wooden sword to the most deserving of them."[8]

By the start of spring, a number of partisan leaders on both sides of the Franklin issue had grown increasingly eager to resolve the statehood affair through diplomacy and to avoid the resulting "Effusion of Blood."[9] On March 20, two delegations, led by Franklin governor John Sevier and his aging friend and Anti-Franklinite General Evan Shelby, rendezvoused at the home of Samuel Smith in Sullivan County in a bid to forestall the impending warfare between the region's two opposing factions.[10] General Shelby described the situation to Governor Caswell in a report written the day after the parlay. He detailed the intensifying "Animosity arising from difference of opinions in Government among" the residents of the Tennessee Valley and related to the governor that "Many people are firmly attached to North Carolina, Others are as Obstinate against it." Shelby "hoped that time and reflection will restore them friendly to North Carolina" and that the March meeting with Sevier would "quiet the minds of the People and Preserve the Peace and tranquility till something better could be done."[11]

The conference proved to be one of the few examples of backcountry diplomacy that, at least briefly, offered the possibility of a peaceful resolution to the Franklin conflict. The two principal articles agreed upon addressed the violence and confusion destroying the region's judicial system and emptying their states' treasuries. In an effort to end the months of courtroom violence, the negotiators agreed to limit the types of cases and decisions adjudicated in the competing "Courts of Justice." Both sides agreed to avoid trying partisans on either side of the conflict for criminal offenses. By limiting the kinds of court cases being seen in the Tennessee Valley to "the trial of Criminals, the proving of Wills, deeds, bills of sales, and such like Conveyances," negotiators hoped to avoid further judicial hostilities. The second article acceded to by the two diplomatic contingents allowed "the Inhabitants residing within the said disputed Territory . . . to pay their Public Taxes to either the State of North Carolina or the State of Franklin." This unusual decision allowed the competing state bureaucracies to function independently without fear of having their constituencies' tax contributions diverted to the opposing government. The agreement concluded with one final concession to the Franklinites, in which the delegations recommended that Franklin's case for separation be considered for a third time "at the Next Annual Meeting of the [North Carolina] General Assembly."[12]

The Shelby-Sevier negotiations provided few cogent solutions to ebb the partisan rancor imperiling the Tennessee Valley communities, and the articles agreed upon during the March meeting may have actually exacerbated regional hostilities. According to one Franklin historian, Governor Sevier's willingness to sign a "truce" with the North Carolina government divided Franklin's leadership and led to "the decline of the morale of numerous followers."[13] Less than two months after signing the truce, General Evan Shelby informed Governor Caswell that "the People of Franklin have not assented to the agreement which was entered into with their Governor for the preservation of peace and good order in this Country." The futile effort to bridge partisan grievances further dissevered the region's inhabitants and rendered lame the brief accord signed in Sullivan County.[14]

During the months following the conference held between Shelby and Sevier, the Tennessee Valley continued to be savagely torn apart by political infighting. Colonel Anthony Bledsoe described the circumstances to Governor Caswell. "Politics in this part of the country run high, you hear in almost every collection of people frequent declarations for North Carolina, and others in the manner for the State of Franklin; I have seen it in much warmth." In response to Governor Caswell's request to "know how the Laws and a Return to the Old Government Set on the minds of the people" of the Tennessee Valley, Colonel Thomas Hutchings offered this optimistic analysis, "I find in the County of Green [sic] the People are much Divided, in the other three Counties [Washington, Sullivan, and Hawkins] about two thirds much pleased with the Laws and a Return to the Old Government."[15] Just a week earlier, Franklin judge David Campbell recorded this conflicting assessment of the political leanings of his fellow Tennessee Valley residents: "You must not conclude that we are altogether unanimous but I do assure you [Caswell] a very Great Majority, perhaps Nineteen twentieths, seem determined to Preserve [Franklin] at all hazards." Although impossible to verify, these statements regarding the distribution of political loyalties in the Tennessee Valley reflected the escalating political dissension within the state of Franklin.[16]

In the face of increasing internal opposition and the damaging impact of North Carolina's divide-and-conquer political tactics, the leaders of Franklin remained unflinching in their effort to secure their political sovereignty. In a fiery letter addressed to Governor Caswell, David Campbell offered a sharp criticism of the effects of North Carolina's conciliatory strategy. Judge Campbell stated, "I also blame the Law which passed in your

Assembly to enable the People here to hold partial Elections [to the North Carolina Assembly]; if it was intended to divide us and set us to measure one another, it was well concerted; but an ill planned Scheme, if intended for the good of all." The vocal Franklinite also included his own judgment regarding the treacherous political landscape of the Tennessee Valley, informing the North Carolina governor that "The People here . . . dread the Idea of Reversion" back to North Carolina. He derided North Carolina's ongoing policies toward the Franklin government, asking, "if No. Carolina is in earnest about granting them a Separation why not permit them to go on as they have begun and not involve them in inextricable difficulties by undoing the work of two or three years Past?" Judge Campbell also mocked Caswell's efforts to restore the loyalties of the Tennessee Valley separatists, informing the governor that "many who were formerly lukewarm are now flaming patriots for Franklin; those who were real Franklinites are now Burning with enthusiastic zeal." The increasingly rabid Franklinites publicly denounced their former government, accusing North Carolina of treating the Tennessee Valley like "a step Dame" and abandoning them as a "sacrifice . . . to the Indian Savages."[17] Campbell warned the North Carolina government that "The Sword of Justice and vengeance will I believe, be shortly drawn against those of this country who attempt to overturn and violate the Laws and Government of Franklin, and God only knows what will be the event."[18]

In an April 6, 1787, exchange with Governor Caswell, John Sevier also conveyed his belief in the Franklinites' indomitability. Sevier expressed his disillusionment over the North Carolina Assembly's continued refusal to agree "to the separation on Honourable Principles & Stipulations." He lamented recently missed opportunities to reunite "us upon such terms as might have been lasting & friendly," and confidently informed Caswell that "We shall continue to Act as Independent and would rather Suffer death in all its Various and frightful shapes than Conform to any thing that is disgraceful."[19] Caswell's response to Sevier's letter reiterated his support for Franklin's political sovereignty, stating, "You may rely upon it that my sentiments are clearly in favor of a separation." Caswell's correspondence warned against "the violences of the passions of some men among you," and repeated his call for "unanimity among the Tennessee Valley residents." The forewarnings offered to Governor Caswell by two of the most influential Franklinites reflected the heightening animus developing between the Tennessee Valley factions.[20]

During the spring of 1787, the leading opponents of the state of Franklin intensified their efforts to topple the Sevier government. On April 27, General Evan Shelby met with several Anti-Franklin leaders, including Thomas Hutchings, George Maxwell, and John Tipton, at his home in Sullivan County. The Tiptonites convinced General Shelby to appeal to the government of North Carolina for a surge in their support for the Franklin opposition. Responding to the Tiptonite request, General Shelby penned a letter to the North Carolina Assembly requesting "immediate assistance" in their escalating struggle with the Franklin government. Shelby described the political climate in the Tennessee Valley as "truly alarming," and warned that "it is beyond a doubt with me that Hostilities will in a short time Commence" between the two partisan factions. He warned that North Carolina must abandon its "lenient and Conciliatory Measures" toward the Franklinites in order to avoid "an effusion of Blood." Shelby appealed for North Carolina to dispatch "one thousand troops" to confront the Franklin militia and predicted that a large show of force "might have a good effect" and induce the separatist government to "immediately give Way." He warned that the "consequences" of failing to oppose the Franklinites or to offer only "a faint and feeble resistance" "might be very fatal and would tend to devastation, ruin, and distress."[21] In addition to what was ostensibly a plea for military intervention by the North Carolina militia, Evan Shelby included a request for "a quantity of Ammunition" and an alliance with the state of Virginia to crush the Franklin movement. In response to the creation of a Franklinite army to "Oppose the Operation of the Laws of North Carolina" just weeks earlier, the Tiptonites hoped to raise their own militia force to "put an end to the present unhappy Disturbance."[22] Throughout the spring of 1787, the Tennessee Valley communities increasingly resembled armed camps, as both sides prepared for the predicted outbreak of civil war.[23]

In May 1787, the Franklinites held a constitutional convention in Greeneville to formally ratify the Franklin Constitution drafted in November 1785. The delegates voted to accept the Franklin Constitution, and the once controversial document became the frame of government for the embattled state. William Cocke used the constitutional convention as a platform upon which to convince the Franklinites to organize another round of state elections parallel to the North Carolina Assembly. Governor Caswell and the North Carolina Assembly's willingness to consider an independent state at a later date convinced Cocke "that some individuals of the said Assembly now warmly express themselves in favor of separation." Cocke believed that if the Franklinites elected new representatives to the North Carolina Assembly, it "would enable us [Franklinites] to send members to negotiate a separation, and thus we could easily obtain our wish without trouble or hazard." Even Governor Caswell assumed that the North Carolina Assembly might be willing to concede Franklin's independence at the November 1787 legislative session.[24]

Cocke's seemingly benign electoral motion set off a furious debate among the Franklin leaders. A vocal group of militant Franklinites, largely drawn from the newly formed southern Franklin counties of Caswell, Sevier, and Blount, openly opposed Cocke's motion to hold North Carolina elections. Opponents of the elections offered varying arguments against Cocke's political assertions. Colonel Samuel Wear (Weir) claimed that the uncertainty of the plan "required the greatest deliberation and more time for consideration," so "he would therefore vote against" opening the polls. Although one of the newest Franklinites, Colonel George Elholm forcefully asserted his disdain for the parallel elections. In a stinging soliloquy, Elholm denounced the proposed elections, stating that "to take seats merely as pretended friends of North Carolina, was inconsistent with the character of a people whose bravery in the field [of battle during the American Revolution] had changed the gloomiest aspects to that of the most pleasing." Elholm implored the delegates to "not sit like old women in council when their rights and privileges were in question." The former Georgian also reminded those supporting the elections that North Carolina refused to recognize the 1786 representatives elected by the Franklinites and that the parent state's assembly might choose to do so again. General Daniel Kennedy introduced another compelling argument against holding the controversial elections. Kennedy contended that by holding the elections, the Franklinites de facto denied the political sovereignty of their own state. George Elholm concurred, stating that "if we suffered any of our friends to represent us in the Assembly of North Carolina, by choice of our citizens under any pretence whatever, we had in fact made void the cession act [1784] on our part, and of course reverted insensibly [back] to [the] North Carolina government."[25]

Although Governor Sevier failed to directly address the issue of holding a new round of elections, he did offer a rare public oratory defending Franklin's independence. Sevier denounced the repeal of the Cession Act of 1784 by North Carolina and declared "the independency of Franklin" to exist "in full force undeniably." The Franklin governor reminded the delegates of their March passage of a bill directing the Franklin Assembly to "make use of hostility" if necessary to "prevent elections within the limits of the State of Franklin [being held] under the authority of North Carolina." Sevier warned that holding the elections "would bring the friends of independency under the rigors of that act." Colonel George Doherty, Major Samuel Newell, and Colonel Samuel Barton added their voices to the growing chorus of opposition to the Cocke measure. Despite the efforts of Colonel William Cage, Colonel Thomas Amis, and others, General Cocke regretfully withdrew his motion to hold elections to the North Carolina Assembly in the state of Franklin for a second time. In its place, the Franklin delegates agreed to appoint another delegation to attend the upcoming November session of the North Carolina Assembly in order "to negotiate peace with the State of North Carolina consistent with the honor of, and with justice to, those two States as independent of each other." The heated debate surrounding the 1787 elections confirmed the effectiveness of North Carolina's divisive political tactics, and the growing rupture continued to widen within the Franklinite ranks.[26]

Shortly after the conclusion of the May constitutional convention, an "open letter" from Governor Caswell circulated through the Franklin communities exhorting the inhabitants to consider "the dreadful consequences which must ensue in case of the shedding of blood among yourselves." Caswell's letter implored the Franklinites to desist in opposing "the due operation and execution of the laws of the State [of North Carolina], menacing and threatening [North Carolina loyalists] . . . with violence," and committing "outrages . . . on the good citizens of the said counties." Caswell's petition "entreat[ed]" the Tennessee Valley partisans to "lay aside your party disputes" because they are a "very great disadvantage to your public as well as private concerns." Caswell's plea to end the caustic political factionalism, in order to prevent "private interests from suffering," appealed directly to the financial motivations of both Tennessee Valley rival groups. In Caswell's last public address as governor, the "friendly and pacific" leader made one final effort to avoid "the dreadful calamities and consequences of civil war." His efforts again proved fruitless, as the two cabals continued to move closer toward an explosive showdown.[27]

At the end of June, John Sevier and North Carolina's political leadership tried for a second time to fashion an accord to deflect the outbreak of civil war in the Tennessee Valley. In a July 6, 1787, letter to General Daniel

Kennedy, Sevier recounted his second meeting with the North Carolina delegation. During the Franklin governor's June 27 meeting with representatives of the "Old State party," Sevier "found them much more compliable than I could have expected." The attendees agreed to convene for a third time in Jonesboro on the last day of July, and Sevier remained optimistic about the future meeting, writing, "I flatter myself something for the good of the public may be effected."[28] Although it is unclear whether the meeting planned for July 31 actually took place, the June 27 conference served as one of the final efforts by the leadership of both states to craft an agreement. By the end of summer, the opening bands of the forecasted partisan tempest swept across the Tennessee Valley communities.[29]

During the months leading up to the ensanguined fall of the Franklin government, the fragile coalition of Tennessee Valley Franklinites began to disintegrate. Despite the failure to prevent the outbreak of frontier violence, North Carolina's divisive political tactics did manage to fracture the Tennessee separatist movement and to lure key regional figures back into the folds of the North Carolina government. This coercive process dated back to 1785, when several Tennessee Valley political leaders once open to the idea of forming a new state out of North Carolina's 1784 territorial cession, including John Tipton, James Stuart, and Richard White, reversed their political loyalties and emerged as outspoken opponents of the state of Franklin.[30]

Over the next two years, additional Franklinites reverted their political allegiances back to their former state. The commissioning of Franklin loyalists to influential posts within the North Carolina state government proved to be one of the most effective reversionary tactics utilized by the Caswell administration. From the election of senators to the appointment of county sheriffs, prominent Franklinites continued to accept lucrative and prominent civil, judicial, and military commissions from the North Carolina government. In February 1787, Governor Caswell offered Franklin's chief judge, David Campbell, an appointment as "Judge of the Washington district."[31] The ultimate insult to the Franklin government came in the fall of 1787, when, at the behest of Evan Shelby, North Carolina offered John Sevier a commission as brigadier general of the Washington District. The allure of a guaranteed state salary and regional prestige undoubtedly influenced some Franklinite decisions, and the continued abandonment of the fated Franklin government aggravated the festering regional hostilities.[32]

The "failure of the [diplomatic] conferences" between Sevier and the North Carolina commissioners and the "discord and strife" accompanying the August North Carolina Assembly elections forced the Franklinites to "hurriedly [fall] back on [William] Cocke's [election] strategy which had been discussed and discarded in May."[33] For a second time, Franklin candidates competed with North Carolina candidates in state elections, but the 1787 elections witnessed both state's candidates appearing on the same ballot. According to one Franklin historian, the Franklinites "put up their own candidates to oppose 'old state' men in their elections!" The 1786 legislative balloting occurred in a relatively peaceful and organized manner, but the results of the August 1787 elections nearly incited the valley residents to war. The 1787 polling results and the violence surrounding the elections illustrated the irreconcilable divisions within the Tennessee Valley. The southern Franklin counties of Blount, Sevier, and Caswell reaffirmed their allegiance to the Franklin government by overwhelmingly electing Franklinites to represent their interests at the upcoming North Carolina legislative session.[34]

The elections held in the northern Franklin counties of Washington, Sullivan, Greene, and Hawkins proved far more contentious. Although no hard polling numbers survive, the political factionalism in these hotly contested counties unquestionably led to the election of two sets of representatives. The threat of polling station violence in Hawkins County (called Spencer County by the Franklinites) led North Carolina county sheriff John Hunt to declare that only Tennessee Valley inhabitants making tax contributions to North Carolina could cast their votes.[35] This decision drew the ire of William Cocke and a group of Greene County Franklinites. According to the only available account of what transpired that summer day, "when about three votes were taken, Col. [William] Cocke appeared with a number of men, some of whom were from Greene County." Sheriff Hunt "had [received] undoubted information that these men had come part of the way armed, in consequence of which he [John Hunt] was apprehensive a riot would ensue."[36] One determined Hawkins County voter declared "that if the people were all ot [sic] his mind he would have his vote or a blow and he did not care which he gave first."[37] The threat of violence forced Sheriff Hunt to shut down the polling station, and a few days later the Franklinites declared their own candidate, Stockley Donelson, the victor.[38] Despite the Franklinites' triumphant declaration, three Hawkins County "inspectors of the polls" "jointly granted to Mr. [Thomas] Amis [the North

Carolina candidate] a Certificate specifying that he was duly elected on said third Friday & Saturday in August." The confusion surrounding the Hawkins County elections forced the North Carolina Assembly to announce "that neither of the parties is entitled to a seat" at the state legislative session.[39] As the North Carolina government contemplated the bewildering election results, the acrimony surrounding the 1787 legislative elections further pushed the Tennessee Valley toward civil strife.[40]

The 1787 legislative elections proved to be the spark igniting the partisan fumes of civil discord. In July 1787, an altercation between two Washington County sheriffs nearly led to a pitched battle between the Tiptonites and Franklinites. Jonathan Pugh, the North Carolina sheriff, described the incident in a sworn deposition delivered to James Stuart on September 20, 1787. Pugh recounted that "on [the] thirty-first day of July last he" arrested James Sevier in the town of Jonesboro for failure to pay taxes. Sheriff Pugh demanded that Sevier provide financial "security for his appearance at [the] next court" session, "which he refused to do." James Sevier then informed Pugh that "he despised the deponent's authority, and that he would not pay obedience to the laws of North Carolina."[41] The fracas escalated after Andrew Caldwell, the Franklin sheriff of Washington County, confronted Pugh and "violently struck and abused the deponent." Sheriff Caldwell's threat to arrest Pugh forced the North Carolina loyalist to flee Jonesboro. Caldwell pursued Pugh and eventually "put him in prison and shut the door."[42]

The commotion in Jonesboro quickly drew the attention of Governor Sevier, who confronted Pugh about having the audacity to serve a North Carolina writ in the state of Franklin to his son. Sevier declared that he "paid no obedience to the laws of North Carolina" and that he "despised her authority." A few weeks later, John Tipton and a group of armed men traveled to Jonesboro to "redress" the "quarrel" between the two Washington County sheriffs.[43] The Tiptonites succeeded in confiscating county records from the Jonesboro courthouse, but never found Sheriff Caldwell. The unexpected Tiptonite foray inexplicably "produced a rapid [but faulty] report" among the Franklin supporters "that they had made a prisoner of his Excellency" John Sevier. The erroneous report "caused two hundred men to repair immediately to the house of Col. Tipton, before they became sensible of the mistake."[44] Governor Sevier narrowly prevented the Tiptonites from becoming a "sacrifice to [the] Franks," but the incident further fanned the flames of partisanship.[45]

During the final months of 1787, the Franklin independence movement suffered several devastating political blows. Concurrent with the conclusion of the September U.S. Constitutional Convention, meeting in Philadelphia, the Franklin government gathered for the last time to discuss the logistics of their military alliance with the state of Georgia against the Upper Creeks and to select another set of diplomats to attend the upcoming session of the North Carolina Assembly. To make matters worse, several prominent members of the Franklin government "had accepted office under North Carolina" and others "had failed to meet their colleagues" at the most recent session of the "Legislature of Franklin." According to one Franklin historian, the Franklin government "manifested a strong tendency to dismemberment."[46]

Amid the political dissension plaguing the meeting, Governor Sevier managed to secure financing for the proposed joint expedition with Georgia. The delegates appointed Landon Carter and David Campbell to serve as commissioners to lobby the November session of the North Carolina Assembly to reconsider Franklin's independence. The remaining Franklinite leadership predictably passed another act to open a land office to issue grants for territory previously secured from the Cherokee by the treaties of Dumplin Creek and Coyatee.[47]

As the Franklin government continued to crumble, the Franklinites received word that the delegates to the U.S. Constitutional Convention had finally completed their difficult task of crafting a new frame of government for the young American Republic. On Monday, September 17, the president of the convention, George Washington, transmitted a copy of the newly drafted U.S. Constitution to all thirteen state governments for "assent and ratification." Washington attached a personal correspondence to the documents, describing the importance of the redrawn frame of government, the inevitability of resistance from some states, and the necessity of at least nine states quickly ratifying the constitution. Washington closed his letter to the state assemblies by assuring America's political leadership that the new constitution will "promote the lasting welfare of that Country so dear to us all, and secure her freedom and happiness."[48] As copies of Washington's letter and the new constitution spread among the Tennessee Valley communities, the reeling Franklin supporters anticipated a decision on the admittance of new states into the federal union. In a constitution designed to defend America's sovereignty, Article IV, section 3, effectively destroyed the

Franklin independence movement by codifying that "new States may be admitted by the Congress into this Union; but no new State shall be formed or erected within the Jurisdiction of any other State; nor any State be formed by the Junction of two or more States, or Parts of States, without the Consent of the Legislatures of the States concerned as well as of the Congress."[49] As one Tennessee historian stated, "Any hope that had remained for Federal intervention was now gone."[50] After years of unsuccessfully lobbying the federal government to support their independence movement, the only prospect for the state of Franklin's improbable survival now lay with the North Carolina Assembly.[51]

In November, the North Carolina Assembly convened for their fall session. Rabid Anti-Franklinites overwhelmingly represented the Tennessee Valley inhabitants at the convention, including Robert Allison, George Maxwell, and James Stuart in the House of Commons, and John Tipton and Joseph Martin in the senate. Only David Campbell, whose political loyalty wavered, appeared on the membership rosters for the Franklinites.[52] During the lengthy sessions, the representatives made several critical decisions regarding the Franklin counties, including passing an act to reconsider the ceding of her "Western lands" to the federal government, commissioning regional military officers, and reexamining a bill "declaring what crimes and practices shall be deemed Treason . . . for quieting the tumults and disorders in the Western parts of this State."[53]

Late in the legislative session, the North Carolina Senate also considered a "Petition of the inhabitants of the Western Country," circulated by Franklin supporters after the adjournment of the final Franklin Assembly.[54] In a desperate final plea for North Carolina to "graciously . . . consent to a Separation," the commissioners carried with them a petition signed by roughly 450 Tennessee Valley residents. The frontier document reiterated many of the same arguments for separation, including the passage and subsequent controversial repeal of the Cession Act of 1784, the guarantee of statehood contained in the North Carolina Constitution, the geographical "remoteness" of the region from the seat of state government, and the inadequate distribution of funds for the promotion of internal improvements and the defense of their communities against the regional Indian tribes.[55] The senate chose not to take any action regarding the petition or any subsequent appeals by the Franklin attendees. As the North Carolina government continued its conciliatory policy toward the Franklinites by again extending pardons for "the offences and misconduct of certain persons in the Counties of Washington, Sullivan, Greene, and Hawkins," the likelihood of Franklin's independence evaporated all together.[56]

By the end of 1787, the repeated failure of diplomatic appeals to both the federal and North Carolina governments, the fragmentation of Franklin's political leadership, and the collapse of regional support among the rank and file dismantled the statehood movement, but deep-seated partisan hatred persisted in the burned-out hull of America's aborted fourteenth state. Franklinite descendent J. G. M. Ramsey described the scene. "Vestige after vestige of Franklin was obliterated; its judiciary gone; its legislature reduced to a skeleton; its council effete, defunct, powerless; its military disorganized, if not discordant, and its masses confused and distracted, with no concert, and unanimity among themselves."[57] In the northern Franklin counties of Hawkins and Sullivan, former Franklinites grudgingly accepted the defeat of the Franklin movement. Surry County resident Mark Armstrong informed newly elected North Carolina governor Samuel Johnston that "the unhappy division which has for some time past subsisted between the people of the Old State & New State of Franklin . . . [seemed] to be done away and [a] reconciliation [had] taken place."[58] In neighboring Washington and Sullivan counties, the resumption of peaceful relations failed to materialize, as partisan tensions continued to flare.[59] John Sevier never wavered in his belief in the salvation of his government through its doomed alliance with the state of Georgia and support from powerful Americans. Governor Sevier optimistically informed General Daniel Kennedy in January 1788 that "I find our friends very warm and steady—much more than heretofore." Over the coming months, partisans in Washington County pushed the Tennessee Valley to the brink of civil war.[60]

It came as little surprise that a dispute involving state jurisdiction and private property initiated the outbreak of bloodshed between the Tennessee Valley partisans. The "fieri facias" commenced after Colonel John Tipton, serving as colonel and clerk of court for Washington County, ordered Sheriff Jonathan Pugh to execute a seizure of John Sevier's property to satisfy unpaid taxes to the state of North Carolina.[61] Revenge served as Tipton's true motivation for ordering the raid on Sevier's Washington County plantation, and the collection of back taxes simply offered him the justification to order the search and seizure.[62] Sheriff Pugh traveled to the Sevier farm at Plum Grove and confiscated several of Sevier's slaves and livestock as payment for the delinquent tax contributions. In a fateful decision, John Tipton ordered Pugh to deliver Sevier's property to his home on Sinking Creek "for safe-keeping."[63]

Governor Sevier received word of the loss of his slaves while drilling the militia forces of the southern Franklin counties, whose rabid support for Franklin remained unwavering, for a spring assault on Dragging Canoe's Chickamauga Cherokee. Sevier ordered the Franklin troops to march to Tipton's farm to reclaim their governor's property and defend their state's sovereignty. In a sworn deposition taken August 20, 1788, several Tiptonites recounted the events of that winter morning. "On the 27th of February last John Sevier Marched within sight of the house of the said John Tipton, Esqr. With a party of men to the amount of One Hundred or upwards with a drum beating colours flying In Military Parade and in a Hostile manner."[64] By the early afternoon of February 27, Franklin governor John Sevier and a force of roughly 150 Franklin troops surrounded the Tipton home and made preparations to arrest John Tipton.[65]

As the Tipton family and approximately forty-five loyalists found themselves surrounded by Franklin troops, the ominous predictions of bloodshed appeared to be at hand. Within hours of the beginning of the siege, John Sevier dispatched Colonel Henry Conway with a flag of truce and a letter demanding immediate capitulation from the Tiptonites.[66] General Sevier's dispatch "requested" that John Tipton "and the party in his house surrender themselves to the discretion of the people of Franklin within thirty minutes from the arrival of the flag of truce."[67] The Tiptonites stubbornly refused to surrender, and Colonel Conway returned to the Franklinites' military encampment with only a "verbal answer" to Sevier's "daring insult."[68] Tipton retorted that "he begged no favours, and if Sevier would surrender himself and leaders, they should have the benefit of North Carolina Laws." Over the next several hours, Conway tauntingly paraded his detachment of Franklin troops across John Tipton's snow-covered fields before taking their positions "near to the [Tipton] spring and still house."[69] The Tiptonites managed to get word to their supporters of the ongoing encirclement, and a small detachment of Washington County troops, under the command of Captain Peter Parkinson, quickly rushed to the aid of the Tiptonites. As the sun dipped below Sinking Creek canyon, both factions prepared for the ensuing assault.[70]

The hostilities, which historians later dubbed the Battle of Franklin, "commenced" early that evening with "the firing on Captain Parkinson's company." As Parkinson's small detachment of troops approached the Tipton farm, the "Governor's whole body [of troops] opened fire."[71] The Franklinites managed to take five of Captain Parkinson's troops prisoner, shoot three horses from under their riders, and force the Washington County rescuers to retreat. The exchange of fire caused panic among the Tiptonites, and under cover of darkness, two women fled the Tipton home attempting to escape with their lives. As the two women emerged from the besieged farmhouse, Henry Conway's troops opened fire on the unsuspecting escapees. One of the women, Rachel Devinsly, "received a ball through her shoulder," but apparently lived to recount her tale. Despite withering gunfire from both sides, the first day of the Battle of Franklin ended without a single human fatality.[72]

As the sun rose on the second day of the standoff (February 28), two Tiptonites succeeded in eluding Franklinite sentries and securing additional Sullivan County reinforcements for the beleaguered old state loyalists. Apprized of the Sullivan County troop mobilization by Franklin supporter William Cox, Governor Sevier attempted to block their passage by guarding every available route to the Tipton farm.[73] As approximately forty Franklin militiamen, under the command of Captain Joseph Hardin and John Sevier Jr., "started for the [Dungan's Mill] ford to dispute the passage of the Sullivan men," the Franklinites sent another flag of truce to John Tipton and his supporters.[74] Although Tipton described this offer as "more mild in nature," he recounted in a deposition taken several months after the incident that he again refused to surrender and informed the Franklinites that "all I wanted was a submission to the laws of North Carolina, and if they would acquiesce with this proposal I would disband my troops here and countermand the march of the troops from Sullivan."[75] The Franklinite troops rejected Tipton's ultimatum and his offer to recall the Sullivan County force being raised by George Maxwell and John Pemberton. Governor Sevier's inexplicable absence from the Franklinites' military command post forced his soldiers to reply without their commander. The Franklin men informed John Tipton that Captain Parkinson's troops "were easy about" defeated, and "as for the troops on their march to join [him], they could countermand their march themselves."[76] As reports of Sullivan County troop movements continued to filter into the Franklinites, both factions drew closer to the precipice of war.[77]

While a thick blanket of snow fell across the Tennessee Valley, the Sullivan County troops continued "to move undiscovered and unmolested" toward the Tipton farm. "On the morning of the 29th, before daylight,

[John Tipton] received information that Colonel Maxwell, with the approximately [180] troops from Sullivan County, and a number from [Washington] county, had collected in a body at Mr. Dungan's, about six miles from" the Tipton homestead.[78] From the opposite direction (from the east side of the Tipton house), Governor Sevier's two sons, John and James, led a second reconnaissance expedition comprising thirty men toward Dungan's Mill Ford to intercept the Sullivan County troops. After traveling only three hundred yards, the Franklin men came under fire from the Sullivan County militiamen. As minié balls "rattled the fences" surrounding the Tipton farm, the Sevier brothers, "at full gallop," led their scouting party in a desperate retreat.[79] As the small unit of Franklin scouts fled blindly through the driving snowstorm, they undoubtedly heard the opening volleys fired by their troops against the Tipton home ring out across the Tennessee Valley. The Battle of Franklin was finally at hand.[80]

The sudden reverberations from the Sullivan County troops' guns caught the Franklinites by surprise. Despite the continued warnings of advancing Tiptonite troops, "Sevier thought himself very secure, and was very sure he should take Tipton and his men." Governor Sevier's overconfidence proved his undoing. A witness to the events of February 29 described what transpired: "a great body of Sullivan men attacked him [Sevier] with heavy firing, and rushed among them, took a number of prisoners, arms, saddles, and dispersed the whole of the Franklinites." As the Sullivan County forces engaged the Franklinites, John Tipton and the remainder of the barricaded Tiptonites "sailed out [of the farmhouse] and drove them [Franklinites] from their ground without much resistance."[81] The two-pronged attack overwhelmed the Franklinites, and "forced the Governor to retreat without his boots."[82] As the partisans continued to exchange volleys, both sides suffered casualties. Franklinite John Smith sustained a fatal shot to the thigh, and Henry Polley and Gasper Fant each received a devastating wound, to a leg and arm, respectively. As Sevier's forces hastily retreated from the battlefield, the Franklinites' delaying fire led to the deaths of Washington County sheriff Jonathan Pugh and John Webb of Sullivan County, as well as the wounding of Captain William Delancy and John Allison.[83] As Sevier's troops suffered "total defeat" at the hands of the old state men, their governor deserted them and absconded himself "15 miles from [Tipton's] home," beaten and "barefooted."[84]

As John Sevier and his Franklinite forces retreated from Sinking Creek, the scouting party led by John and James Sevier finally penetrated the curtain of snow to belatedly enter the fight. In their confusion, the Franklinites apparently fired upon their own troops, but fortunately missed their intended targets. Following the friendly fire incident, the scouting party continued toward the firefight. As the Franklinite forces rode "up to the camp [with] Col. Sevier's flag still flying, they did not suspect the sudden & complete change in affairs that had taken place during their brief absence." As they approached the Tipton home, "A volley of guns arrested them and some few, amazed & wondering were pulled from their horses & called in to surrender, among them, James & John Sevier [Jr.] & their cousin John Sevier."[85] In a stunning reversal of fortune, the Tiptonites routed the Franklinites and captured the sons and nephew of Franklin governor John Sevier. As word of the crushing defeat of his forces and the apprehension of his family members reached the Franklin governor, John Sevier reluctantly sent a verbal communiqué to John Tipton "asking [for] his life [and that] of his parties," and agreeing to "Submit to the Laws of the State" of North Carolina. The Tiptonites accepted the Franklinites' terms of surrender and "Colonel [George] Maxwell sent him [Sevier] a flag giving him and his party to the 11th [of March] to submit to the laws of North Carolina."[86] In the meantime, John Tipton "determined to hang both" of Sevier's sons, but "Apprised of the rash step which he intended to take, the young [Sevier] men sent for Mr. Thomas Love and others of Tipton's party" to intervene on their behalf. After Love and others "urged their arguments so effectively," John Tipton agreed to "restore [the Sevier brothers] to their liberty."[87] The release of the Sevier brothers and the capitulation of Governor Sevier ended the Battle of Franklin, but the legal and political fallout from the three bloody days of fighting remained.[88]

The Franklinites' humiliating defeat on the snow-cloaked fields of the Tipton farm destroyed lingering support for their statehood movement in Washington and Sullivan counties, but the southern Franklin counties continued to defend Sevier and the importance of statehood. The diminishing support in the upper Tennessee Valley counties became painfully apparent to the Franklinites during a failed bid to retaliate against John Tipton in early March. Thomas Hutchings described the events in a letter to Brigadier General Joseph Martin. "Captain [William] Cocke issued his general orders to Thomas Henderson to raise a militia of their party to march against Colonel Tipton. They had so little success that I presume they are much dispirited. Every one of their captains, I believe, refused. They cannot make a party of any consequence."[89] On March 1, 1788, John

Sevier's term as governor of the state of Franklin expired, but he continued to attract the loyalty and admiration of the majority of the Tennessee Valley's southernmost inhabitants.[90] In early March, Sevier finally sent his response to John Tipton and George Maxwell's "flag of truce dated 29th February 1788." Sevier maintained that he "did not fully comprehend" the terms of surrender, and assured his opponents that the Franklin "council, equally now as heretofore, to be amendable to the laws of the Union for our conduct." He also expressed his desire that the Tiptonites "will be answerable to the same laws for your proceedings, and actuated by principles of humanity and discretion of the people, and honor of both parties." Sevier's letter surprisingly did not reveal any hint of defeat, and the former Franklin leader even included a defiant request for the "return of property that fell into [Tiptonite] hands."[91] A day after the March 11 deadline for Sevier and his fellow Franklinites to submit to the laws of North Carolina, John Tipton and George Maxwell informed Arthur Campbell that the Franklinites "never Came in to Comply with the Terms" and "that he [Sevier] is trying to Raise another party." The Tiptonites requested "a few volunteers to quell the Insurrection" and "save [the region] from future bloodshed."[92] In another exchange with General Martin, Tipton reiterated his concern over the likelihood of future "private injuries if not murders," but also insisted that the "violators of the [North Carolina] law should be brought to justice, especially those who have so flagrantly transgressed."[93] The political and judicial uncertainties surrounding the Franklinites forced John Sevier to hide among his southern supporters.[94]

Before any of the leaders of the separatist movement could be "brought to justice," John Sevier fell back upon his highly effective diversionary tactic of launching Indian warfare to deflect any civil or criminal retribution and to bolster his regional support. Joseph Martin clearly understood Sevier's potent blending of racial identity and patriotism to resuscitate the Franklin movement. In a March 24 exchange with North Carolina governor Samuel Johnston, Martin warned that "Sevier had gone towards the French Broad River since the 10th instant; that Colonel Canaday [sic], with several others, had gone the same way to carry on an expedition against the Cherokee Indians, which I am well assured wishes to be at peace." Martin expressed his disbelief that "Sevier and his party are embodying under the color of an Indian expedition to amuse us," believing instead that the Franklinites' "object is to make another attack on the citizens of this State [Tiptonites]."[95] Governor Johnston suspected the Franklinites of "wantonly involving themselves in an Indian War without any real necessity," and charged Joseph Martin with the daunting task of "cultivating a good understanding with the [Cherokee] Indians & preventing by all means any Hostilities or Insults committed on them by Citizens of this State."[96] As John Tipton and Samuel Johnston prepared to indict John Sevier for treason, the former Franklin governor launched his spring campaign against the Chickamauga Cherokee.[97]

The months surrounding his defeat at the Battle of Franklin proved disastrous for "Nolachucky Jack" and the Franklin statehood movement. The recent resignation of Franklin sympathizer and Sevier compatriot Richard Caswell from the governorship and his replacement by the unsympathetic Samuel Johnston threatened any hope for an amicable reunification of the two states. Despite Sevier's overtures of peace, Governor Johnston refused to negotiate with the Franklinites and openly called for the prosecution of the state of Franklin's political leadership. In an April exchange with Beaufort County, North Carolina, congressman John Gray Blount, Governor Johnston described his frustration over what he saw as the continued failure of North Carolina's conciliatory policies toward the Franklinites. He described the "dangerous Riots in which some blood has been spilt and two men killed by Rioters under the Command of Sevier." Johnston also expressed his "hope the [North Carolina] Assembly at their next meeting [in November] will either use means effectually to enforce the Execution of the laws in the Country or leave them to Govern themselves." He warned that a continuance of North Carolina's current strategy "may in time be attended with very bad influence on the Conduct of the Citizens in other parts of the State."[98] Johnston branded the Franklinites "outlaws and vagrants," and promised to "exert the whole power of [the North Carolina] Government to bring to Condign punishment all such [persons] as shall presume to violate the laws and disturb the peace of the State."

John Sevier continued to defend his actions during the Franklin movement, blaming North Carolina for causing "all of these disturbances," and reiterating that he was involuntarily "drafted into the Franklin measures by the people of this country."[99] In addition to the installation of a dogged Franklin opponent in the North Carolina governor's seat, John Sevier also became embroiled in the controversy surrounding John Kirk's retaliatory execution of the peaceful Cherokee delegation led by Old Abraham and Old Tassel. Governor Johnston and many of North Carolina's political leaders blamed John Sevier for the slaughter of the two peace chiefs and their families by bloodthirsty Franklinite soldiers.[100] In a July 1788 address to the Cherokee Nation, Johnston expressed regret for the murders and promised the tribe that "if any of them [Franklinites] have injured you without sufficient cause to take them up and send them to us that they may receive Correction & punishment." The secretary of the U.S. Congress, Charles Thomson, expressed Congress's support for punishing the "perpetrators" of the murders. He informed Johnston that if the charges against "John Sevier & others" are "found true," then the state of North Carolina should "take measures to have the perpetrators thereof apprehended & punished." As the Chickamauga campaign raged in the Tennessee backcountry and southern Franklinites refused to bow to the authority of the North Carolina government, Governor Johnston finally issued his long-awaited warrant for the arrest of John Sevier for treason.[101]

In July 1788, North Carolina governor Samuel Johnston wrote to the former chief judge of the state of Franklin, David Campbell, regarding John Sevier's prosecution. Johnston believed that "John Sevier, who styles himself Captain General of the State of Franklin, has been guilty of High Treason in levying troops to oppose the Laws and Government of this State, and has with an armed force put to death several good Citizens." Governor Johnston gave his consent for Judge Campbell to "issue a warrant to apprehend the said John Sevier, and in case he cannot be sufficiently secured for Tryal [sic] in the District of Washington, order him to be committed to the Public Gaol [sic] for the District of Hillsborough." Johnston also ordered "the Commanding Officer of Washington District [Joseph Martin] to furnish sufficient Guard to assist the Sheriff in the Execution of his duty" and if necessary, to carry out the arrest and prosecution "in secrecy and dispatch in order that it may succeed in such manner as to restore peace & tranquility to that part of the State."[102] After months of pressure applied by John Tipton and Sevier's determined political enemies, the leader of the state of Franklin finally faced the stark reality of being executed for treason.[103]

Despite Governor Johnston's issuance of an arrest warrant and his guarantee of a militia force sufficient to capture the wildly popular former Franklin governor, Judge Campbell refused to carry out the apprehension of John Sevier. Although Campbell remained silent regarding his reasons for letting Sevier remain free, several Franklin historians assert that Campbell's friendship with the fugitive prevented him from executing the arrest.[104] Campbell's decision and Sevier's prolonged absence from the region delayed the inevitable legal showdown between John Tipton, Samuel Johnston, and John Sevier. Sevier remained in the Tennessee backcountry throughout much of the spring and summer of 1788, before eventually returning to his home in early October. According to several sources, Sevier "openly" visited public places in Jonesboro, and defiantly continued to conduct business with the region's economic elite. Astoundingly, Sevier, who undoubtedly knew of the warrant for his arrest, initiated clashes with his political and economic opponents.[105] The day before his arrest, the former Franklin governor instigated an altercation outside of a Jonesboro store. According to court depositions taken by Justice of the Peace William Cox at the end of October 1788, David Deaderick testified that he and former Washington County sheriff Andrew Caldwell "were peacefully sitting in his shed adjoining his store house . . . when [his] boy informed him that [John] Sevier was at his door." Upon opening the door, Deaderick "was surprised to see a number of men [ten or twelve] on horseback . . . [with] John Sevier, Senr., at their head." Sevier commanded that Deaderick stop "whistling" and demanded "Whiskey or Rum." Deaderick replied, "as to whistling, he hoped he might do as he pleased, but whiskey or Rum he had none." Sevier then became belligerent and stated that he "was informed [that] he had [liquor] & they wanted it & would pay money for it." Upon being told that "he was informed wrong," Sevier asked Deaderick if "[Andrew] Caldwell was with him." Caldwell "came to the door & Sevier asked him nearly the same respecting Liquor, who also informed him he had none." Sevier then flew into a rage and "began to abuse this place, then its inhabitants without distinction." Deaderick and Caldwell confronted Sevier, asking him "if he aimed that discourse or abuse at" them. Sevier answered, "Yes, at you or anybody else," and then called Deaderick "a son of a Bitch." Deaderick replied, "[that Sevier] was a dead son of a Bitch, and stepped close to Sevier, who immediately drew out his pistol, or pistols."[106]

As Sevier and Deaderick prepared to square off, Andrew Caldwell stepped between the two men to prevent the escalation of the altercation. Caldwell's efforts at diplomacy proved futile, as Deaderick, armed with his own pistol, charged into the street after Sevier. As the dispute intensified, "Caldwell and Sevier began to quarrel; in the Course of which the former desired Sevier to pay what he owed him. He replied he owed him nothing. Caldwell said he was damned eternal liar. Sevier swore by God he would shoot him & rais'd [sic] his pistol. It went off, and wounded a certain Richard Collier."[107] After accidentally wounding an innocent bystander, John Sevier and his party quickly fled the scene of the crime. Sevier's betrayal of former Franklin sheriff Andrew Caldwell and involvement in the Jonesboro shooting provided his opponents with a fortuitous opportunity to exact their revenge.[108]

After the altercation in Jonesboro, John Sevier attempted to avoid capture by hiding at the home of Jacob Brown's widow. Caldwell immediately informed John Tipton of Sevier's involvement in the shooting. At approximately "2 o'clock, after midnight [on October 10], Colo. Tipton, Adw. Caldwell & several others [eight to ten men] came to the deponents store [Deaderick] when he joined them and persued [sic] Sevier whom they overtook & Apprehended about day light [the] next morning."[109] After apprehending his hated rival, John Tipton madly waved his pistol in the prisoner's face and threatened to hang him before he could stand trial. The Sevier family's friendship with influential Washington County resident Colonel Robert Love saved John Sevier from execution, but the former Franklinite's connections to powerful North Carolinians could not prevent his transfer to the Morganton jail. Despite his appeal to be incarcerated in Jonesboro in order to stay near his family and friends, John Tipton insisted that Sevier be held at the Burke County jail in order to avoid potential rescue attempts by Franklin loyalists. As Sevier began his long march of shame over the southern mountains, John Tipton triumphantly paraded the Franklin leader in shackles in front of the home of the widow of Jonathan Pugh. After several days of difficult winter travel, Sevier's armed escort delivered the former Franklin governor to the Morganton jail to await trial.[110]

The arrival of one of North Carolina's most celebrated and infamous sons drew the immediate attention of Sevier's Burke County supporters. Fortunately for the former Franklin governor, the sheriff of Burke County, William Morrison, served with Sevier at the Battle of King's Mountain, and upon his compatriot's arrival at the jail "he knocked the irons from his hands & told him to go where he pleased."[111] As Sevier awaited arraignment in Morganton, Charles and Joseph McDowell, two brothers who also fought alongside Sevier during the American Revolution, posted his bail.[112] Shortly after being freed, Sevier rendezvoused with a small group of friends and family who traveled to Burke County to secure his release. The group of rescuers found Sevier in a local tavern enjoying a drink with Major Joseph McDowell. Sevier's would-be liberators "told him frankly [that] they had come for him & he must go."[113] Sevier confidently remained in Morganton several more hours before preparing to depart. Contrary to several fanciful accounts describing his gallant escape from the custody of his Morganton jailers, "Sevier [simply] ordered his horse & [they] all started off [toward Washington County] before noon, in the most public & open manner."[114]

The ease by which John Sevier "escaped" from Burke County demonstrated his steadfast support among the inhabitants of western and central North Carolina, but the former Franklin separatist still faced ferocious opposition within the North Carolina government. A few days after returning to his Tennessee Valley home, Sevier began the daunting process of restoring his political influence within his former government and defending his actions during the Franklin affair. On October 30, 1788, Sevier sent an address to the North Carolina General Assembly describing his reasons for jumping bail in Burke County and, more importantly, justifying his decisions as the governor of the state of Franklin. As to his flight from justice, Sevier argued that he could not receive a fair trial "borne off, out of District, at a distance from his friends & neighbors who can only be the best Judges of his innocence or Guilt." He informed the delegates that his arrest, extradition, and incarceration "not only deprive[d] a man of His liberty, but treated him with wanton cruelty and savage insults before Trial, or any evidence of the breach of the Laws adduced." As to his scheduled trial, Sevier asked the legislators, "Is it not obvious to you, that the rigid prosecutions now carried on is more to gratify the ambition and malice of an obscure and worthless individual [referring to John Tipton], than to appease the Justice of the State?"[115]

Sevier defended his participation in the Franklin independence movement, and reminded the North Carolina Assembly that he and his fellow Franklinites "were all [recently] employed and deeply engaged" in throwing "off the British yoke of slavery and tyranny . . . at the expense of their blood and loss of their dearest relations." Sevier deflected personal responsibility for the chaos and tragedy surrounding the Franklin movement by reiterating his initial reluctance to join the statehood effort, and insisting that "the people [of the Tennessee Valley] wish[ed] for separation." Despite his recent prosecution by the state of North Carolina and public rebuke by Governor Samuel Johnston, Sevier contended that he always maintained his loyalty to his former government and wished only that North Carolina "flourish and become great." As the North Carolina Assembly opened their November session, John Sevier nervously awaited his legal and political fate.[116]

As the November meeting got under way, delegates again debated pardoning former Franklinites for "the offenses and misconduct" carried out during the separatist movement. As the act of pardon easily passed in the senate and the House of Commons, a group of John Sevier's political rivals introduced a "Bill to repeal part" of the act of clemency in order to exclude him from the general pardon. The delegates formed a special committee to consider the proposal, and on November 30, "on examining sundry papers and hearing oral Testimony," the committee offered their final decision.[117] The committee's chairmen, John Rhea, declared that, "John Sevier, Esquire, together with sundry other persons in the said Counties [of Washington, Sullivan, Greene, and Hawkins], did in the years 1785, 1786 and 1787, . . . subvert the peace & good order of Government of the State of North Carolina." Despite the fact the committee found that Sevier's "conduct was in many particulars highly reprehensible," they believed that he "ought to be placed in the same situation" as "all the citizens" who "have been pardoned and consigned to oblivion."[118] Despite the protests of John Tipton and several other Franklin opponents, the state of North Carolina pardoned John Sevier.[119]

John Sevier's congressional exoneration ended his legal difficulties, and the vindicated former rebel quickly joined many of his fellow Franklinite leaders in reestablishing his political standing in the Tennessee Valley. After publicly swearing his loyalty to the laws of North Carolina in February 1789, the residents of Greene County elected John Sevier to the North Carolina Senate. The North Carolina Senate appointed the former rebel leader to the state committee that eventually ratified the U.S. Constitution, as well as electing Sevier to be the brigadier general of the District of Washington.[120] Miraculously, the former governor of the state of Franklin rose from the ashes of his still smoldering state and perched himself high atop North Carolina's political mountaintop.

The violence surrounding the 1787 Tennessee Valley elections, the bloodshed that occurred on John Tipton's Washington County farm, and the Jonesboro shooting became the tragic consequences of the intensification of partisanship surrounding the state of Franklin. The deadly conclusion of the Franklin statehood movement resulted from the prolonged fervent struggle between two rival factions of the region's ruling class to determine the political and economic destiny of the trans-Appalachian frontier. North Carolina's remarkably effective divide-and-conquer diplomatic strategy, combined with the repeated repudiation of the principles of backcountry separatism from both outside and inside the Tennessee Valley, led to the loss of local support for statehood and ultimately the tumultuous collapse of Franklin. As former Franklinites attempted to forget the

Chapter 7

Vassals del Rey de España

The Franklin-Spanish Conspiracy, 1786–1789

During the chaotic months separating John Sevier's defeat at the Battle of Franklin and his arrest for treason by John Tipton, former North Carolina congressman Dr. James White secretly visited the former Franklin governor at his Washington County plantation at Plum Grove.[1] During their clandestine meeting, Dr. White revealed a "shadowy scheme" that tantalizingly held out the possibilities of simultaneously resurrecting backcountry separatism and reviving the elusive Muscle Shoals land deal.[2] The events that unfolded between July 1788 and April 1789 involved the government of Spain, a small group of powerful land speculators, prominent Franklinites, and the communities of "Lesser Franklin."[3] To the leaders and remaining supporters of the Franklin statehood movement, the Spanish conspiracy stood as their last opportunity to preserve their political and economic hegemony, to pressure North Carolina and the U.S. government into acceding to Franklin's admittance into the union, to eliminate the ongoing Native American threat, and to advance their collective fiscal and political interests. The sordid details of the "Spanish Intrigue" reveal a conspiracy that threatened to fracture the southwestern frontier in order to reconstruct the shattered remains of Franklin and advance the political and financial fortunes of a cabal of influential Tennessee Valley leading men.[4]

The genesis of the Spanish Intrigue in the Tennessee Valley originated with the 1783 speculative efforts of William Blount's Muscle Shoals Company and the postrevolutionary alliance forged between the southeastern Indian tribes and the nation of Spain.[5] The southern aboriginal tribes, the Spanish government, and America's eastern political leadership desperately sought to halt America's westward expansion at the southern Appalachian Mountains.[6] As America's frontier communities extended beyond the southern mountains, many of the once divided southeastern tribes united against the white squatters and their state governments. The vast majority of the postrevolutionary Indian wars fought in the Appalachian backcountry resulted from white encroachment on Indian lands.[7]

On the Tennessee frontier, two Native American resistance leaders, Dragging Canoe, leader of the Chickamauga Cherokee, and Alexander McGillivray, leader of the Upper Creeks, engaged in guerilla warfare in a futile effort to end the western advance of Anglo-America.[8] Spain also hoped to halt the United States' territorial growth to protect their diminished North American colonies in Florida and the Mississippi River Valley.[9] In a strategic plan to preserve their colonial possessions, the Spanish government provided material aid and logistical support to the Chickamauga Cherokee and the Upper Creeks. In 1784, Alexander McGillivray negotiated the Treaty of Pensacola with Spanish emissaries in Florida. Through their surrogate, the Pensacola, Florida, trade firm Panton, Leslie, and Company, Spain agreed to secretly provide weapons and ammunition to the Creeks to finance their continued struggle against white expansion.[10] During the state of Franklin's infancy, the growing cost of prolonged Indian warfare, mounting casualties, and Spanish interference prevented the states of Georgia, South Carolina, North Carolina, and Franklin each from laying claim to the Muscle Shoals land. Despite these hurdles, the Franklin leadership refused to surrender their dream of securing and developing the increasingly profitable bend of the Tennessee River.[11]

In the summer of 1786, James White met privately with Spanish Minister (Charge d'Affairs) Don Diego de Gardoqui at his home in New York City.[12] Dr. White was born into a prominent Philadelphia Catholic family and received his education at Jesuit College in French Flanders. Upon earning his medical degree from the University of Edinburgh in Scotland, White returned to the American colonies, practiced medicine outside of Philadelphia, and eventually served as a "Doctor Physick" to the Continental Army during the American Revolution. In 1783, he purchased a sizeable tract of land in eastern North Carolina and moved to Chatham County (near the current city of Fayetteville). White was elected to serve as Chatham County's representative to the 1784 North Carolina House of Commons and as one of North Carolina's six representatives to the 1785–1787 U.S. Congress. At the time of his meeting with Gardoqui, he also held the influential post of U.S. Superintendent of Indian Affairs for the Southern District and owned substantial tracts of trans-Appalachian land in both Greene County in the state of Franklin and Davidson County in North Carolina's rapidly expanding Cumberland District.[13] White's close personal and business connections to numerous Tennessee Valley leaders and his familiarity with the challenges confronting potential backcountry land speculation led him to Gardoqui's home at the Kennedy House at #1 Broadway. During the August 26 meeting, White described the escalating tensions between Spain and the United States over the commercial use of the Mississippi River. White informed Gardoqui that he "realized that you are going to win what the United States never expected to cede to Spain, which is the Navigation of the Mississippi," and that the "Southern States . . . will never agree" to the concession. White predicted that "as soon as they [southern political leaders] learn of the Cession, they will consider themselves abandoned by the Confederation and will act independently."[14] The North Carolinian believed that "This situation offer[ed] Spain the most favorable opportunity to win them forever." White asserted that if the Spanish government kept the Mississippi River open to the southern states and eased trade restrictions, then "His Catholic Majesty [Carlos III] will acquire their eternal goodwill and they, as an Independent State, will draw closer to His Majesty." White told Gardoqui that he planned to return to his home along the Cumberland River (Middle Tennessee) to "sound out the minds of [regional] leaders," and promised to report back by February of the following year. The stunned Gardoqui "replied with very polite words [but] without committing himself" to such a dangerous scheme.[15]

White's eagerness to ink a deal between the political leadership of the southwestern frontier and the Spanish government drove him to expedite his political reconnaissance mission. White returned to Gardoqui's New York home four months early and related to the Spanish official that "the fears of the [southern] States had increased greatly" over the Mississippi River deal.[16] In reality, White's characterization of southern sentiment applied primarily to the western frontier communities of Virginia and North Carolina, and he probably exaggerated the scope of his knowledge regarding the regional reaction to the commercial controversy to convince Gardoqui to risk opening backcountry talks. During the October 4 meeting, White failed to name any specific frontier communities or willing participants, but he did assure Gardoqui that "the new [western] settlements are much inclined to separate from the United States upon the least apparent pretext and the matter of the surrender of the navigation of the Mississippi was so important that it would cause them to give themselves up, or at least ally with the English or the Spaniards." White warned Gardoqui not to forgo the opportunity to unite the "two Nations," "because a contrary action would cause the loss of a Bulwark the power and strength of which the world in general has no conception." White's arguments proved extremely persuasive, and he offered to visit Spain's Mississippi Valley plantations following his return trip to his Nashville home. Gardoqui approvingly provided him with four letters requesting that White "be treated as one of my friends, and as a person of honor and esteem, and that he should be granted every assistance" by Spanish officials.[17] After two months of lobbying, Dr. White had succeeded in securing the Spanish government's consent to initiate the backcountry coup.[18]

Amid the ongoing negotiations between Gardoqui and U.S. Secretary of State John Jay over the future navigation of the Mississippi River and the Franklinites' struggle to secure independence, the secret channels of communication remained open between Spain and the Tennessee Valley. However, over the next eighteen months, correspondence between Spain and the southwestern frontier slowed. Spain's continued support of the aboriginal resistance movements strained relations with the East Tennessee separatists. Reports from the Tennessee frontier emerged accusing Spain of aiding and abetting the southeastern Indian tribes in their struggles against the white encroachers.[19] In January 1788, James Robertson and Anthony Bledsoe, two Cumberland leaders, informed North Carolina governor Samuel Johnston that "Indians have killed Seven of the Inhabitants [of Davidson and Sumner counties]." Robertson and Bledsoe accurately believed the "Invaders to be the Creek Nation who are at this time Allies to the King of Spain." They pleaded with Governor Johnston to intervene on their behalf in order to "prevent the further effusions of Blood." The men suggested that Johnston appeal to Gardoqui to prevent "their [the Creeks'] further Acts of Savage Barbarity," and if the "Minister of Spain . . . [does] not think proper so to do," then U.S. Superintendent of Indian Affairs James White would "be of Service."[20]

Governor Johnston quickly responded to Robertson and Bledsoe's request and agreed to present their concerns "before the Council of State at their first meeting." Johnston also sent copies of their January 4 letter to the "Delegates in [the United States] Congress to make sure use of them as may be proper." He assured the two men that "Congress will no doubt apply to the Resident from the Court of Spain [Gardoqui] for an Explanation of the Conduct of Col. McGilvery [sic]." On April 18, Gardoqui dispatched a formal denial of his nation's involvement in the "Cruelty of the Savages" on the "Frontiers of North Carolina." The Spanish minister protested, "Your

Excellency [King Carlos III] may give full assurances to the contrary that
the Spanish Government entertain such sentiments of good will and Amity
to the United States, that it would rather sedulously prevent than encourage
any outrages upon their Citizens."[21] Shortly after receiving the King of
Spain's denial, Governor Johnston received a letter from Dr. James White
reassuring him that the "the Catholic King is relaxing in its policy" toward
territorial disputes on the southern frontier. In an amazing effort at deception, James White, a former U.S. congressman representing the state of
North Carolina, effectively misled his governor regarding Spanish designs
on the United States' southeastern frontier. In addition to his own ongoing
efforts to promote Spain's acquisition of North Carolina's transmontane
territory, White was also aware of Spain's support for McGillivray's Creek
insurgency.[22]

Despite contradictory reports emanating from the western frontier, on
May 8, 1788, Governor Johnston accepted Gardoqui's protest of innocence.
He informed the Spanish minister that he "had confidently entertained
that the Citizens of our Western Frontiers were not well informed when
they attributed the Cruelties experienced by the savages to the interference
or connivance of the subjects of his Catholic Majesty." Amazingly, Johnston
agreed "to inform the citizens on the Western Frontiers" of the King of
Spain's growing concern over the "abhorrent" attacks by the Spanish-aligned
Creeks, and to "promote & conciliate sentiments of Good will and amity in
the minds of the Citizens . . . towards their neighbors the Subjects of his
Catholic Majesty." Governor Johnston also sent a letter to James White
expressing his willingness to publicly accept Spain's denial and assuring
him that "it has been my wish to Cede that Country [North Carolina's
western frontier] to Congress yet as that measure [1784 Cession Act] was
afterwards done away I shall do everything in my power to save the Interest
of that people." Johnston and the political leadership of North Carolina
remained dangerously unaware of the treachery being devised by Dr. James
White.[23]

The first appearance of the state of Franklin in Spanish communications occurred on September 25, 1787, in a confidential communiqué between New Orleans governor Estevan Miro and Minister of the Indies Don
Antonio Valdes. Miro included a map of the settlements "West of the Appalachian Mountains" with his letter to Valdes. The map's key listed "a
Republic with the Name State of Franklin," and also included brief accounts of the state's failed bid for admittance into the union and continuing

struggle to "preserve their independence." The inclusion of Franklin in the Spanish survey of western settlements demonstrates the Spanish government's growing interest in the embattled state. A few weeks later, Gardoqui described the ongoing "revolt" in "the new County of Franklin" to the governor of Cuba, Don Josef (Joseph) de Ezpeleta. The Spanish ambassador believed that the Franklinites might be persuaded to join Spain if a commercial route could be established connecting the Tennessee Valley to the Mississippi River. Although optimistic regarding a future alliance between Spain and Franklin, efforts to construct a viable trade route faced considerable geographical challenges from the "rugged mountains" and five hundred miles of "swampy lands" separating Franklin's farmers from Spain's Mississippi Valley settlements.[24]

The first direct communication between Franklin and Spain appeared in the spring of 1788. The Franklinites' repeated failure to win approval for their independence and waning regional support for the statehood movement created the perfect political atmosphere for the efforts to lure the Tennessee Valley communities into Spain's sphere of influence. Apprised of John Sevier's debilitating defeat by opponents of the statehood movement at the Battle of Franklin in February, Spain and James White both hoped to capitalize on the dimming fortunes of the Franklinites. In April 1788, White returned to Gardoqui's Manhattan home "encouraged" by recent reports out of Franklin and "enthusiastic" about the future success of their scheme. After toasting each other's health, White and Gardoqui mapped out the details of a secret compact between Franklin's political leadership and the government of Spain. White offered to "go to the state of Franklin" and attempt to gauge the level of support for a Franklin-Spanish alliance. If the Franklinites embraced his overtures, White planned to travel from the Tennessee Valley to either Natchez or New Orleans to put the plan into motion. Gardoqui described the plot to Spain's secretary of state, Conde de Floridablanca. The Spanish diplomat disclosed to Floridablanca the existence of "secret reports from some of those settlements [Franklin, Cumberland, and Kentucky] whose principal inhabitants have received favorably the idea ('of turning to us')." He believed that "it would be impossible to oblige this people by force, but . . . would be easy to win them by Tact and generosity, leaving them their customs, religion, and laws, on the supposition that in time they will be imperceptibly drawn to ours." Gardoqui also claimed to be in possession of additional "secret information" confirming that "the District of Frankland" was "ripe" for an alliance, and he proposed "sending Don Jaime [James White] there to promote it." Gardoqui expressed his concerns over "trusting [his nation's] affairs to foreigners [meaning James White]," and he remained cognizant of the diplomatic "consequences" if the United States discovered Spain's "consideration" of the "complicated and dangerous business."[25] Gardoqui included a group of petitions from unnamed Franklinites expressing their support for the Spanish alliance, and the minister proposed rewarding these future allies with "large tracts of land, powerful interests, and other brilliant advantages."[26] Following their meeting, James White embarked for the crumbling state of Franklin with a Spanish passport and three hundred pesos in hand.[27]

White arrived in the Tennessee backcountry during the darkest days of the state of Franklin. During White's brief visit to the Tennessee Valley, North Carolina's Governor Johnston issued an arrest warrant for John Sevier, and Franklin's southern communities confronted the daily horrors of Chickamauga Cherokee and Upper Creek attacks. The state's economy suffered a terrible blow with the recent abandonment of a joint military campaign with the state of Georgia and the resulting derailment of the most recent plans to acquire the elusive Muscle Shoals territory. As one Franklin historian commented, "In these circumstances Sevier proved responsive to White's overtures."[28] Neither participant recorded what transpired during their summer discussions, but clearly the two frontier leaders recognized their shared interests. On September 12, 1788, John Sevier drafted two letters to Gardoqui and entrusted their delivery to his son James.[29] Sevier's two correspondences disclosed specific details regarding the Franklin-Spanish alliance. In the first communiqué, Sevier expressed his desire to extend Franklin's settlements to "the Tenesee [sic] River or near the Mussell [sic] Shoals." The former Franklin governor "solicited" Gardoqui's "interposition" with Spain's Indian allies in order "to keep the peace" during Franklin's territorial expansion. After more than four years of failure, Sevier hoped to utilize Spain's influence to finally conclude the Muscle Shoals land deal and to bolster Franklin's contentious Indian policy.[30]

In the second of the two letters, Sevier reported to Gardoqui that "the people of this country with respect to the future of an alliance, and commercial connection with you are very sanguine and that we are unanimously determined on the event." The secrecy of the frontier plot makes it impossible to verify the true level of support among the Franklinites for the Spanish alliance, but Sevier did offer the Spanish minister several compelling reasons motivating his fellow Franklinites. Sevier lashed out at the state of North Carolina, decrying "the embarrassment we labour under in respect to the parent state, who make use of every stratagem, to obstruct the growth, and welfare of this country." Sevier warned Gardoqui that "there will not be a more favorable time than the present to carry in to effect the plan on foot," and implored Spain's highest-ranking American diplomat "to make every speedy and necessary preparation for defense; should any rupture take place." Sevier asked Gardoqui to consider "the advantages" of a Spanish-Franklin "connection," and then made several requests of the Spanish government, including "a few thousand pounds" to alleviate the "great scarcity of specie in this country," "military supplies," and Spanish passports.[31] In exchange for their sworn allegiance to the Spanish king, the political and economic leadership of Franklin hoped to advance their personal economic fortunes and defend their political autonomy.[32]

As James Sevier departed the Tennessee Valley to deliver his father's communications to Don Diego de Gardoqui, Franklin supporters in the southern Tennessee Valley communities struggled to keep alive their hopes for independence. Sevier arrived at Gardoqui's New York residence on the same day John Tipton, leader of the Anti-Franklinites, apprehended his father for high treason.[33] Unaware of the arrest, James Sevier presented his father's two letters to Gardoqui. Just a week before this meeting, Gardoqui informed Governor Miro of the escalating danger surrounding the ongoing Franklin conspiracy. The Spanish diplomat warned that even James White "no longer consider[ed] it safe nor proper to remain in this country." White's mounting fear that his role in the scheme might be discovered forced him to assume several aliases (Don Jaime and Jacques Dubois), and Gardoqui's concerns over being implicated in the plot led him to distance himself from the conspiracy. Gardoqui instructed James Sevier to travel to New Orleans and contact Governor Miro for future "aid and protection."[34] Gardoqui also dispatched James White to the Spanish territory to mediate the clandestine negotiations. After receiving several Spanish passports and travel money, Sevier left for New Orleans unaware of the ever-increasing importance of his mission.[35]

Over the final two months of 1788, the governments of Georgia, Virginia, and South Carolina renewed efforts to establish peaceful relations with the southeastern Indian tribes. At Governor Johnston's behest, North Carolina joined the other southern states in their ongoing negotiations with the Creeks and Chickamauga Cherokee. Despite publicly criticizing the 1785 Treaty of Hopewell upholding Cherokee land claims, the Johnston "out of the power of the Militia Officers to Assist us." The petition also con-veyed their mounting apprehension over the impact ongoing diplomatic negotiations with the regional Indian tribes would have on their homes. In an effort to legitimize their land claims, the Greene County citizens requested that the North Carolina Assembly carve a new county out of the southern communities of Greene County, establish a local courthouse and "Administration of Justice," and most critically, erect a land office to legally register their land claims. The petition revealed a grudging abandonment of independence by Franklin's remaining supporters, and placed even greater importance on John Sevier's negotiations with Spain.[39]

Despite the enterprising efforts of James White, Don Diego de Gardoqui, and the Sevier family, the Spanish conspiracy began to collapse toward the end of 1788. Rising Spanish suspicions, glaring cultural incongruities, and a rapidly shifting political climate made the relationship between Spain and Franklin untenable. The Spanish Intrigue never progressed far enough for the two parties to work out the complex logistics of a Franklin-Spanish alliance, but Spain's designs for the incorporation of Virginia's Kentucky frontier offers a glimpse into the possible inner workings of such a plan. In addition to courting the political leadership of Franklin and Cumberland, Spain also conspired with Brigadier General James Wilkinson to consolidate Virginia's rapidly developing Kentucky settlements into their North American colonies. The Spanish Intrigue in Kentucky advanced much further than either the Franklin or Cumberland schemes.[40] In August 1787, Wilkinson traveled to New Orleans, where he presented a memorial to Governor Miro laying out a proposal for the union of the Kentucky communities and Spain. Wilkinson's exasperation over the U.S. government's inability to acquire navigation rights to the Mississippi River from Spain primarily motivated his seeking an alliance. Tobacco had become the principal cash crop in Kentucky's frontier economy, and the navigation of the Mississippi River offered the most viable commercial route to regional markets. In order to compete with Virginia's powerful eastern planters, Wilkinson needed access to the Mississippi River and to new markets in Spain's Louisiana Territory. Wilkinson offered "two propositions" as to how Spain might acquire the Kentucky territory. The first involved the King of Spain's "receiving the inhabitants of the Kentucky region as subjects" and then "taking them under his protection." Wilkinson's second proposal attempted to draw Kentucky and Spain together culturally through emigration and intermixing.[41] The Spanish government viewed the Kentucky intrigue as an opportunity to expand Spain's North American land holdings and to further distance the Spanish colonies from the land-hungry American government.[42]

Planning for the Spanish conspiracy in Franklin and Kentucky would have been very similar. In a letter dated September 25, 1787, Governor Miro and Intendant-General of Florida Martin Navarro described the details of the Kentucky plot to Spanish Minister Don Antonio Valdes. Miro and Navarro's "instructions" on what to do if Wilkinson's "predictions" came "true" offered an extensive list of legal, political, economic, and cultural directives. They first considered the potential religious conflicts that could emerge when joining Catholic Spain with the overwhelmingly Protestant Kentuckians.[43] During Gardoqui's initial contact with future Franklin conspirator James White, the Spanish minister reassured Spain's secretary of state of White's trustworthiness by describing him as "a Catholic" who "has never used [his Catholicism] to serve his ends, nor for anything else."[44] In the initial negotiations with Wilkinson, Spain insisted that the Kentuckians "permit Churches served by Irish catholic priests, without the exercise of any other Religion being permitted." The Spanish government attached a conversionary mission to what ostensibly stood as a territorial annexation. Spanish officials agreed to allow the Kentuckians to privately "exercise their present religion," but ultimately hoped that the frontier Protestants could be "converted by [the] persuasion and good example" of frontier Catholics. The chance of a mass Catholic conversion of the overwhelmingly Protestant communities scattered across the southeastern frontier seems extremely unlikely.[45]

Despite concerns over religious pluralism, the Wilkinson plot remained fundamentally a scheme born out of mutual economic and political necessity. In their consultation with Valdes, Miro and Navarro addressed the fiscal aspects of a Spanish-Kentucky compact. These considerations included: the sale of Kentucky tobacco, trade tariffs and duties, and future trade relations with the United States and Britain. If Kentucky became part of Spain, then the region's commercial farmers faced the prospect of a "six percent" export tax, an "import duty," and a potential trade embargo from the United States and Britain. For Kentucky's commercial tobacco farmers, access to the Mississippi River and Spain's global agricultural markets eclipsed these meager economic concessions. The Spanish officials weighed the financial rewards of the Kentucky conspiracy against the potential political and military repercussions they faced from the United States. Miro and Navarro determined that "it would be obligatory and necessary to place detachments [of Spanish troops] at the principal points of these new dominions . . . in order to watch out for any attempt the United States might begin, to impede the introduction of commerce, and to settle difference among the inhabitants."[46] In addition to stationing soldiers in Kentucky's backcountry communities, the Spanish officials concluded that there needed to be "Justices of the Peace" to enforce Spanish law. In essence, Miro and Navarro believed that Spanish Kentucky must be governed by Spanish appointees and defended by Spanish troops.[47]

The circumstances surrounding the proposed Franklin-Spanish alliance differed slightly from Wilkinson's Kentucky scheme, but Spain's diplomatic "blueprint" for governing Franklin presumably would have contained many of the same elements. Perhaps the most revealing description of the proposed inner workings of the Spanish conspiracy in Franklin is contained in an exchange between Josef de Ezpeleta and Don Antonio Valdes. After meeting with James White in Havana in the winter of 1788, Cuba's Governor Ezpeleta recounted recent developments occurring on "the Western side of the Allegheny Mountains and the Appalachians." Ezpeleta informed Valdes that "more than two hundred thousand inhabitants settled in the Territories of Kentucky, Cumberland, and Franklin . . . [are] awaiting whatever fortune they might expect from [the United States] Congress." He believed the westerners felt "cramped now by this dependency" upon congressional support and this led them to their decision "to live under a separate Government" and to consider making "alliances of another kind."[48] Ezpeleta then described intimate details about the potential Franklin-Spanish pact. Briefed by White, Ezpeleta explained the political and economic benefits offered by the backcountry compact for both Franklin and Spain. The Franklinites stood to profit financially from their partnership with the Spanish government. A Franklin-Spanish commercial relationship offered the Franklinites unfettered access to Spain's ports, markets, shipping, and most importantly the Mississippi River. Franklin's land speculators also potentially gained "an increase in their territory" after Spain halted Native American resistance to the expansion of white settlements across the Tennessee backcountry. Spanish interests also potentially benefited from a proposed merger with the Franklinites. The Tennessee Valley settlers' military experience would make them ideal Spanish soldiers, and if an agreement could be concluded between their government and Spain, King Carlos III expected the Franklinites "to defend the King's territory against any attack by another Power." Ezpeleta elaborated on the other possible Spanish advantages, which included: developing "commerce that will greatly increase the Merchant Marine," providing manpower for Spain's "Royal Navy," and creating "a secure barrier against the unjust attempts of the United States" to annex Spanish territory. Ezpeleta envisioned the Franklinite "Vassals" pledging "an oath of fidelity" to Spain and being "employed in the service of the King like real Spaniards."[49] Ezpeleta reiterated James White's assertion that the Spanish government needed to "promptly" move forward with the necessary arrangements for the secret alliance.[50]

Even as Ezpeleta, Gardoqui, Sevier, and White encouraged the Spanish government to "place [the Franklinites] under the protection of the King," rumblings of discontent could be heard from both sides.[51] In an October 30, 1788, address to North Carolina's General Assembly, John Sevier attempted to curry favor and remove treasonous suspicion by warning the representatives of the "formidable and inveterate enemies watching to take advantage of our divisions."[52] Sevier's reference to foreign threats is remarkable in light of his ongoing negotiations with Spain and probably reflected his growing doubts about the wisdom of a deal with the Spanish king. The increased urgency of James White's appeals to Spanish officials also confirmed the cooling of support for a Franklin-Spanish alliance within the Tennessee Valley. From the start, Spain's political leadership worried about a possible deal with the Franklinites. As early as September 1787, Estevan Miro cautioned his government that the Tennessee Valley settlement's expanding population and military power posed a threat to Spain's Louisiana Territory. Miro also warned that denying these frontiersmen access to the Mississippi River could provoke a war that might ultimately cost Spain all of the North American territories and Mexico. Miro strongly advised allying with the western settlers before they are "driven back into the arms" of the U.S. government.[53]

By the end of 1788, the growing chorus of suspicious Spanish voices threatened to derail the conspiracy in Franklin. James White attempted to calm the Spanish government's growing hesitancy over continuing the ongoing Franklin negotiations. On December 24, 1788, White argued that "the policy of the Spanish Government" should be aimed at "attracting" the Franklinites "as friends [rather] than taking precautions against them as enemies." White promoted the trade benefits of the alliance, as well as the strategic advantages of "using these people as a barrier" against American

aggression and territorial encroachment. He also reminded Governor Ezpeleta that Spain's diplomatic delays allowed the Tennessee Valley settlements to "take on more formidable proportions," and pose an even greater
threat to Spain's North American colonies. White offered Spain's political
leaders his optimistic vision of an alliance with the Franklinites. He believed that "Spain now has in her hands the power to assure herself of this
Country [Franklin] by peaceful and humane methods. Then its inhabitants will be a Source of advantage instead of dangerous and turbulent
neighbors." If the Franklinites remained "United to the American Republics, they may be especially suspicious," but if they could be "Separated"
from the United States, their alliance offered the Spanish Empire numerous advantages. Dr. White echoed Governor Ezpeleta's contention that a
Franklin-Spanish alliance would "keep them [Tennessee Valley residents]
from Mercantile rivalries [with Spain], stimulate . . . an increase of Sailors
for the Royal Navy," and expand maritime trade of "Tobacco, Hemp, iron,
Food, and other bulky articles" from Spain's "Ports on the Mississippi
[River]."[54] White concluded his defense of the Franklin plan by recom-
mending that the Spanish government move slowly with the efforts to
convert and acculturate the Tennessee Valley residents. White queried, "As
to internal policy, Will it not be best to indulge them by granting them the
continuance of their manners, Customs, and Prejudices that habit makes
the Love?" White understood the disastrous consequences of forcing cultural uniformity on the Franklinites, and he argued that, "With time, if
other customs are considered necessary, they can be substituted for these."
White's attempts to prevent future cultural and religious disharmony revealed one of the fundamental obstacles preventing a Franklin-Spanish
union: cultural intolerance.[55]

Back on the Tennessee frontier, the rupture between the remaining
southern separatists and the state of North Carolina gradually began to
close. Most of Franklin's former political leaders accepted the inevitability
of reunion and returned their political allegiance to North Carolina.[56] Only
in Greene County did significant support for statehood remain. On January 12, 1789, sixteen Greene County residents met at the courthouse to
once again address the Indian attacks and ongoing treaty negotiations en-
dangering their settlements. The group never mentioned the state of Franklin nor Spain during the conference, but the attendees overwhelmingly
supported the creation of a new state west of the Appalachian Mountains.
The frontier leaders castigated the state of North Carolina for failing to

bolster western defenses and for appointing the much maligned Indian agent Joseph Martin as a member of the North Carolina delegation negotiating with the southeastern tribes.[57] The Greene County men adopted fifteen articles primarily aimed at strengthening their frontier defenses and defending their land claims. The representatives also reaffirmed their allegiance to John Sevier, electing him to "keep the command of the inhabitants on the frontiers" and conduct all future "talks with the Indians." The frontier leaders concluded their meeting by calling on Washington and Sullivan counties to join their "Voluntary plan of Safety."[58] Clearly John Sevier's overtures to the Spanish government failed to stop Spain's Indian allies from attacking white settlements south of the French Broad River, and just two days prior to the Greene County conference, Sevier and "the arms of Franklin" confronted a "combined force of Creeks and Cherokees" at Flint Creek. In the shockingly bloody Battle of Flint Creek, the frontier militiamen slaughtered the Native Americans, leaving 145 dead and countless others mortally wounded. In what historians have dubbed "The Last Battle of Franklin," Sevier struck a crippling blow to the Indian resistance movement.[59] Despite their defeat at Flint Creek, determined members of the Cherokee and Creek tribes continued their attacks on western settlements. The persistence of Indian violence and a growing awareness of cultural disparities further diminished the likelihood of a Franklin-Spanish alliance.

In February 1789, John Sevier became the last in a long line of former Franklin leaders to pledge his fealty to the laws of North Carolina. Despite the rapidly changing political dynamics of the Tennessee Valley and the recent death of Spain's King Carlos III, James White remained convinced that a backcountry compact could still be concluded. During the spring of 1789, White delivered several letters to unnamed Tennessee Valley "leading men," stipulating that they must swear an "oath of allegiance to the [new] King . . . if it was their wish to come under the protection of Spain." White's April 18 correspondence to Governor Miro expressed his growing impatience over Spain's measured approach to frontier negotiations. White again urged Miro to offer the Franklinites "refuge under the King's protection" before it was too late.[60] In response to White's appeals, Miro issued a statement to the Tennessee Valley "Westerners" that expressed Spain's desire to "favor and protect" them. The April 20 memorandum promoted James Wilkinson's recently proposed strategy for uniting Kentucky and Spain through emigration and cultural intermixing. Miro extended an invitation to the Tennessee Valley residents to settle in the Louisiana Territory on land

and company's Spanish collusion contend that the backcountry affair stemmed from the insatiable desire of influential land speculators, such as William Blount, Richard Caswell, and John Sevier, to secure control of the valuable Muscle Shoals bottomland for personal financial gain.[65] In truth, Sevier and the leadership of Franklin hoped to benefit both politically and financially from the Spanish collusion. The Franklin statehood movement grew out of the eagerness of the Tennessee Valley's ruling class to cement their control over the region's political and economic future. They truly believed that the backcountry conspiracy stood as their last opportunity to preserve their statehood movement and their regional hegemony. Regardless of the rationale, the Spanish Intrigue remains the final arresting chapter in the tumultuous history of North Carolina's rogue state of Franklin.

Chapter 8

Rocked to Death in the Cradle of Secession

The Antebellum Evolution of Franklin, 1783–1861

In September 1804, Ingram Weirs sued former Franklin diplomat William Cocke over disputed land grants issued by the Spencer County Court [Hawkins County under North Carolina and Tennessee] in the defunct state of Franklin. During the course of the proceedings, attorneys for both litigants debated the circumstances surrounding the creation and governance of Franklin. The legality of Cocke's land claims rested on the legitimacy of the state of Franklin and her court system. The case *Weirs v. Cocke* is emblematic of the divergent historical and popular interpretations of the Tennessee Valley separatist movement. Rhea and Williams, lawyers for the plaintiff, argued, "Surely it will not be contended that the sale by the Sheriff, under the pretended authority of the Franklin Government, can give any legal right to the defendant." They characterized the Franklin statehood movement as "an insurrection, as much so as the opposition to the excise [Whiskey Rebellion], which took place a few years ago in the back parts of Pennsylvania." Rhea and Williams maintained that "None of the acts of such a government can be good, or founded on such principles, as to obtain a moment's consideration in a court of competent authority," therefore, the "proceedings of the [Franklin] court of Spencer cannot be records; if they are, a writ of error would lie in this court, but no lawyer entertains an idea of such a thing."[1] The attorneys for Cocke, G. W. Campbell, and Jenkings Whitesides challenged the plaintiff's comparison of the Franklin movement to the 1794 Whiskey Rebellion, retorting that "The Franklin Government is not to every purpose, to be considered as an usurped one. It is not similar to the insurrection in the western part of Pennsylvania; that was an absolute opposition to a law of the United States essential to its existence; one for raising a revenue."[2] According to the Campbell and Whitesides account, "Franklin arose from necessity; from the situation in which

162

the people of North Carolina, west of the Mountains were placed; detached from anterior settlements in the eastern part of the State, exposed to the incursions and merciless barbarities of the neighboring savages." They believed that the state of North Carolina's unwillingness to "afford the people of this country . . . [the] prompt assistance which was indispensable to their happiness . . . [and] existence" compelled the Franklinites to form "a government of their own." Ignoring the actual historical events surrounding the state of Franklin, Campbell and Whitesides asserted that the Tennessee Valley separatist leaders launched their movement "in a peaceable manner" and that the actions of the Franklin government "were not attended with violence, civil war, or bloodshed."[3] Newly appointed judge to Tennessee's Superior Court of Law and Equity and Middle Tennessee land speculator John Overton apparently agreed with the defense's argument that the state of Franklin served as a legitimate "de facto government," and thereby validated Cocke's land claims. The trial transcripts from *Weirs v. Cocke* reveal the dynamic historical evolution of the state of Franklin and the continued importance of the statehood movement in the political and economic competition for the Tennessee Valley.[4]

Following the collapse of the state of Franklin and the Spanish Intrigue, the residents of the Tennessee Valley continued to struggle with the political uncertainty surrounding their rapidly developing communities. Amid the formation of the state of Tennessee, the socioeconomic development of East Tennessee, and the antebellum turmoil surrounding the divisive political issues of slavery and secession, the descendents of the Franklinites and Tiptonites continued to grapple over the region's political and economic future. Throughout the first half of the nineteenth century, the historical legacy and meaning of the Franklin separatist movement became intertwined with this transmontane hegemonic contest. Through the blending of patriotic rhetoric, nationalistic language, and revolutionary symbolism, contemporary Franklinites forged a history of their separatist movement that inspired local and regional pride, historical interest, and most importantly political loyalty. Building upon these efforts, the descendents of the Franklinites and Tiptonites redefined the movement in an effort to reshape the past, defend the actions of their kinfolk, and advance their families' political and financial fortunes. During the first half of the nineteenth century, the continued evolution of the meaning of Franklin allowed several prominent American figures to recast the movement for their own political purposes. Tracing the contemporary invention of Franklin through its political manipulation by abolitionist Ezekiel Birdseye and North Carolina senator Andrew Johnson reveals the state of Franklin's continued influence on the Tennessee Valley's political and economic maturation.

From the beginning, Tennessee Valley Franklinites doggedly promoted the connections between their separatist movement and the American Revolution. By associating Franklin with America's struggle for independence, the Franklinites hoped to win widespread political and public support for statehood. If America's political leaders could be convinced that Franklin's independence flowed from the same patriotic river giving birth to America's separation from Britain, then the state of Franklin's chances of survival dramatically improved. Public support for Franklin, both inside and outside of the Tennessee Valley, depended heavily upon the region's historical ties to the Battle of King's Mountain and the famed revolutionary sacrifices of the region's Overmountain Men. Through the efforts of skilled orators and savvy diplomats, the Franklinites cemented the link between Tennessee Valley separatism and America's glorious rebellion.[5]

Virginia's Colonel Arthur Campbell made the first connections between backcountry separatism and the American Revolution.[6] In the summer of 1785, Campbell defended his earlier efforts to ignite a Washington County, Virginia, independence movement. In a letter to a Washington County neighbor, Colonel John Edmiston, Campbell responded to his critics, lamenting, "It is extremely unfortunate that many well-meaning and valuable men in America, who remained unshaken during the severest trials, at the end of the [Revolutionary] war, lost sight of the object they were contending for or perhaps they had no object in view at all."[7] Campbell argued that Americans "were provoked and justly angry with England" for attempting to deny America's sons "a republican or free government." He then outlined "three kinds of government," of which Campbell held "Democracy or [a] republican government" to be the ideal. Campbell's analysis supported his Anti-Federalist argument that successful republics only flourished in "small societies or States."[8] Campbell's assertion that backcountry separatism emanated from the same political vein as revolutionary republicanism became one of the earliest rhetorical arguments for Franklin's independence. During the convening of the first Franklin Assembly in March 1785, a member of the convention "arose and made some remarks on the variety of opinions offered, for and against a separation." Drawing upon the revolutionary precedent established by the Declaration of Independence, the unnamed Franklinite compared "the reasons which induced their separation from England, on account of their local situation, etc., and attempted to show that a number of the reasons they had for declaring independence, applied to the counties here represented by their deputies."[9]

The connections between the political and economic leadership of the Tennessee Valley and the American Revolution are well established. Western soldiers like John Sevier, Landon Carter, and John Tipton led hundreds of Tennessee Valley settlers in bloody backcountry battles against British forces and their Indian and southern loyalists. The political leadership of Franklin never allowed either North Carolina or the United States' government to forget their sacrifice during the Revolutionary War and often drew upon this legacy to defend their independence movement and gain the political loyalty of their Tennessee Valley neighbors. In one of John Sevier's few direct addresses to the North Carolina Assembly, he reminded the representatives that "we were all employed and deeply engaged [recently] to keep off the British yoke of slavery and tyranny, and in the days of your greatest extremity, the people who are now suffering for differing in political sentiments, were those who gave you the first relief, at the expense of their blood and the loss of their dearest relations."[10] Sevier challenged the assembled delegates, asking, "Has North Carolina forgot that for such acts America took up arms against the British nation? Has she also forgot that the man and party that now suffers, was her zealous defenders in the days of her greatest extremity?" In a letter read before the Georgia Assembly in the summer of 1787, Sevier accused North Carolinians of forgetting that many Franklinites "fought, bled, and toiled" alongside their citizens for "the common cause of American Independence." To Sevier and his fellow Franklinites, their devotion to America's sovereignty justified their effort to establish their own independent state and obligated the U.S. government and North Carolina to support their independence movement.[11]

Supporters of Franklin pointed out perceived similarities between America's separatist movement and their own on the Tennessee frontier. Through the use of painstakingly chosen language and symbolism, Franklin became an extension of the revolution and the Franklinites stood as its "rear-guard."[12] The blurring of the lines between revolution and separatism became one of the primary strategies used by Franklin's propagandists to defend their state's political sovereignty. The most obvious manifestation of this tactic was the naming of their new state after Benjamin Franklin. Originally, the political leadership of the Tennessee Valley intended upon designating their new state Frankland (meaning "Freeland"), but the Frank-linites eventually abandoned the esoteric reference to the European Franks who dominated the Province of Gaul after the disintegration of the Western Roman Empire.[13] It is unclear as to why they replaced Frankland with Franklin, but amid the postrevolutionary wave of nationalism celebrating the political, ideological, and military leaders of the American Revolution, the name change served to highlight the region's devotion, loyalty, and necessity to the fragile new republic. The Franklinites undoubtedly understood the political and diplomatic benefits of identifying their state with one of America's most celebrated patriot leaders, and as opposition to their statehood movement mounted, the Franklinites increasingly wrapped themselves in the blanket of American nationalism and the rhetoric of revolution.[14]

The Franklinites persistently evoked the language used by America's revolutionaries in their effort to secure support for their own statehood movement. A letter composed by an anonymous Washington County, Virginia, resident on June 1, 1785, reflected the melding of the rhetoric of America's rebellion with the Franklin separatist movement. The recent Franklin visitor proclaimed that "The New Society or state called Franklin, has already put off its infant habit, and seems to step forward with a florid, healthy constitution" and the Franklinites need "only the paternal guardianship of Congress for a short period, to entitle it to be admitted with [illegible], as a member of the Federal Government." The author thundered, "Here the genuine Republican! Here the real Whig will find a safe asylum, a comfortable retreat among the Modern Franks, the hardy mountain men!"[15] The Franklinites interlaced their correspondence and legislation with the powerful prose and mythology of the American Revolution, and words like republican, liberty, independence, and patriot grounded the principles of Franklin separatism in the ideological foundations of America's independence. The Franklinites argued that their efforts to defend their political "independence" and "pursue their own happiness" developed from the identical reasons, rights, and dreams that fostered the political radicalism of the American Revolution. The Tennessee Franklinites asserted that their separation from North Carolina occurred only out of necessity and that unreasonable taxes, political neglect, and eastern tyranny forced them into their fateful decision.[16] To the Franklinites, their statehood movement truly stood as Tennessee senator Andrew Johnson described seventy years later, "The War of Rebellion in Epitome."[17]

In conjunction with the Franklinites' efforts to craft a positive image of their state, opponents of Franklin created a vastly different account of the Tennessee Valley separatist movement. From the first machinations of independence, North Carolina's political leadership conspired to undermine Franklin's sovereignty and dissociate the movement from the sacred revolution. As the Franklinites cast themselves as defenders of the principles of the revolution, North Carolina governor Alexander Martin openly condemned their "revolt" and decried the economic motivations behind Franklin. Martin understood the potential effectiveness of drawing upon the victory of the Overmountain Men, and he warned the Franklinites not to "tarnish . . . the laurels you have so gloriously won at King's Mountain and elsewhere, in supporting the freedom and independence of the United States." To Governor Martin, the "black and traitorous [Franklin] revolt" threatened the stability of the new American government, and during the final months of his governorship, he made every effort to destroy the state.[18]

Governor Martin's attack on the Franklinite propaganda effort fueled the growing Anti-Franklin movement within the region. The Tiptonites emerged victorious at the Battle of Franklin, but ultimately lost the long war of popular opinion in the Tennessee Valley. The Tiptonites struggled to cast the southern separatist movement in a negative light and to undercut the Franklinites' vainglorious efforts to anoint their movement with a sense of honor and patriotism. The Anti-Franklinites attacked the carefully crafted image of the Franklin independence movement. To the opponents of Franklin, the Tennessee Franklinites did not represent a revolutionary vanguard, but instead were "the off scourings of the Earth," "outlaws and vagrants," and "fugitives from Justice."[19] Franklin's independence did not emerge out of necessity, nor did it reflect any of the principles of the American Revolution. For the Tennessee Valley Tiptonites, the Franklin movement disrupted their communities, escalated Indian violence, and retarded the growth of their region. Neither the propaganda war characterizing the political and public debate over the state of Franklin nor the intensity of backcountry partisanship ended with the dissolution of the separatist movement.[20]

The decades following the abandonment of the Franklin movement witnessed a remarkable political and economic transformation of the Tennessee Valley and the reemergence of former Franklinites into positions of political influence. Subsequent to their November 1789 ratification of the U.S. Constitution, the North Carolina legislature once again ceded the state's western territory to the U.S. government. In an effort to avoid the political chaos that followed the passage of the 1784 Cession Act, the U.S. government designated North Carolina's ceded lands the Southwest Territory. President George Washington and Congress immediately laid out a plan for the administration of the new territory and its eventual admission into the union as an independent state. Washington selected North Carolina congressman and wealthy land speculator William Blount to serve as territorial governor, and Congress decreed that the residents of the Southwest Territory be governed under the provisions established by the Northwest Ordinance. Once again, the inhabitants of the Tennessee Valley became embroiled in an effort to fashion a new state out of their communities and in the scramble among the region's leading men to claim positions of back-country authority within the shifting political landscape.[21]

With the designation of the Southwest Territory, several of the former partisan opponents during the Franklin affair managed to recover their positions of political leadership. As Governor Blount began the process of forming a territorial government, he turned to several prominent Franklin-ites to fill important governmental posts. Blount traveled to the former Franklin counties of Greene, Hawkins, Sullivan, and Washington in October 1790 and began reorganizing the local governments, now under the auspices of the U.S. Congress. In a remarkable example of a political resurrection, Blount appointed former Franklin governor John Sevier, now serving as a U.S. congressman representing North Carolina, brigadier general of the Washington District's militia (one of three districts created out of the Southwest Territory, the other two being the Mero and Hamilton districts). Sevier's political appointment became the first in a series of decisions made by Governor Blount that restored former Franklinites to positions of political, judicial, and military influence. In November 1790, Blount selected the former chief judge of the state of Franklin, David Campbell, to be one of the Southwest Territory's three territorial judges, and the following year, Franklin diplomat William Cocke became the attorney general of the Washington District. In December 1793, Southwest Territory residents voted in elections to determine their county representatives in the lower house of the newly created territorial government. When the first session of the territorial government convened in February 1794, former Franklinites and Tip-tonites filled the ranks of the territorial representatives, including John Tipton (Washington County), William Cocke (Hawkins County), and Spanish conspirator Dr. James White (Davidson County). A few months later, President Washington selected John Sevier and Franklin's surveyor general, Stockley Donelson, to the territorial council, which served as an "upper house" within the full territorial legislature. Clearly, John Sevier and his fellow Franklinites managed to escape the political fallout caused by the Franklin debacle, but their families' continued political hegemony rested on defending their political past.[22]

In the years separating the fall of Franklin and the 1796 admission of the state of Tennessee into the union, the population and economy of the Southwest Territory continued to expand at an extraordinary pace. Initially, the communities of the Tennessee Valley (located primarily in the Washington District) experienced the most rapid population growth. In a July 1791 survey of the Southwest Territory conducted at the request of Governor Blount, the census revealed approximately 36,000 inhabitants of the entire western territory. The Washington District's population had swollen to nearly 29,000 residents, and Middle Tennessee's Mero District contained nearly 7,000 inhabitants.[23] In a census conducted four years later to determine if the Southwest Territory's population satisfied the demographic requirements laid out by the Northwest Ordinance for a territory's successful transition to statehood, census takers identified a total territorial population of 77,300. The population of the Washington District had more than doubled, reaching 65,300 inhabitants. In addition to the rapid population growth, the Tennessee Valley's regional economy experienced a dramatic period of expansion. Tennessee Valley farmers expanded their commercial agricultural enterprises, purchased thousands of slaves, and became increasingly connected to regional and national markets. The new wave of Tennessee Valley immigration and the improvement of regional transportation arteries also opened new markets for Tennessee Valley merchants and manufacturers.[24]

By the end of 1795, the majority of the inhabitants of the Southwest Territory began to openly express support for the final phase of the statehood process. In January 1796, fifty-five delegates convened in Knoxville to draft a constitution for the new state. Once again, several former Franklinites and Tiptonites sat among the delegates to the constitutional convention, including Landon Carter, William Cocke, and John Tipton. In less than a month, the delegates crafted the state of Tennessee's first constitution. Despite John Sevier's being absent from the proceedings, a few weeks later the newly elected state representatives elected him to be Tennessee's first governor. On June 1, 1796, President Washington signed the Tennessee statehood bill, thus concluding the two-decade effort to forge a new state out of North Carolina's western frontier.[25]

The creation of the state of Tennessee and the conclusion of the trans-Appalachian Indian wars removed the final barriers to the full realization of the economic potential of the Tennessee frontier. Over the course of the next three decades, East Tennessee continued to experience significant population and economic growth, but this expansion was eclipsed by the profound transformation taking place in Middle Tennessee. By 1820, Middle Tennessee's population dramatically outpaced East Tennessee; the area now contained nearly 68 percent of the state's population. Over the next thirty years, East Tennessee's economy lagged behind the tremendous profits generated by slave labor and commercial agricultural in Middle Tennessee, and by 1830 the Tennessee Valley communities no longer occupied the economic and political center of the state.[26]

Despite the loss of political and economic influence within the state, East Tennessee's leading families continued to compete for control of their own communities. The descendents of the participants in the Franklin affair redefined the significance of the frontier statehood movement in an effort to promote their own political and economic hegemony within a rapidly changing Tennessee Valley. Within their correspondences with early frontier historians like Lyman Draper and Judge John Haywood, the children of the Franklinites and Tiptonites reshaped the history of Franklin in an attempt to secure their own families' claims to regional preeminence. Beginning in the early nineteenth century, American historian Lyman Copeland Draper began collecting materials relating to the state of Franklin and the Tennessee frontier. The loss of most of the official papers relating to the state of Franklin during the last years of its existence made Draper's job exceedingly challenging. In order to enhance his understanding of the complex events surrounding Franklin, Draper contacted several children of leading Franklinites and Tiptonites. Within these exchanges, the sons of separatism continued the partisan struggle to control East Tennessee by reshaping the legacy of Franklin and their ancestors.[27]

On February 9, 1839, Overton County resident Colonel George Washington Sevier sent a short letter and brief biographical sketch of his father, John Sevier, to Lyman Draper. Draper, who originally wrote to George Sevier's "relative," Arkansas senator Ambrose Hundley Sevier, inquired about John Sevier and "the thrilling scenes of those [frontier] days." George

Sevier used his correspondence with Draper to criticize Nashville resident Judge John Haywood's *Civil and Political History of Tennessee,* published in 1823. Although not present for the Franklin debacle, Haywood became one of Tennessee's first Supreme Court judges and also one of the state's earliest historians. Haywood's history of Tennessee offered a remarkably astute analysis of the Franklin statehood movement and painted a strikingly realistic and historically balanced portrait of the actions of both factions during the affair. Haywood's revealing account of frontier Tennessee and the state of Franklin, and specifically the gubernatorial activities of John Sevier, angered George Sevier. He lashed out at Haywood, stating, "Haywood's history of Tennessee is very imperfect & written altogether from the statements of a few old men some of whom have strong prejudices against my father the late Genl John Sevier." Sevier defended his father, arguing, "He was not only a Genl but a Statesman & politician" who fought for "internal improvements" for his constituents. George Sevier's biography of his father is more remarkable for what is not in the account than what he included. In the entire four-page account of his father's life, George Sevier never mentioned the state of Franklin, only acknowledging his father's involvement in the scheme in a short sentence in the accompanying letter to Draper, stating, "My father was the Governor of the small State of Franklin." George Sevier's effort to downplay his family's role in the Franklin debacle through selective biographical omissions only added to Draper's curiosity regarding the failed statehood effort.[28]

Over the next fifty years, Lyman Draper continued to delve deeper into the Franklin affair. He questioned North Carolina congressman and U.S. Indian agent Joseph Martin's son and the grandson of Franklin militia captain Andrew Caruthers, but as participants "of the strong events" surrounding Franklin passed away, the history of Franklin took on a life of its own. In 1851, lawyer, businessman, historian, and John Sevier enthusiast Albigence Waldo Putnam sent Lyman Draper a remarkable "sketch of the life of Gen. John Sevier" recently submitted to the Nashville newspaper the *True Whig.* Putnam's thirteen-page biography romanticized the events of Sevier's exceptional life, and is one of the earliest examples of the historical mythmaking related to the state of Franklin. To Putnam, the "personal, civil, legislative, judicial, executive, and military . . . contention and strife" accompanying Franklin was "aimed at the very man who had done, was doing, and continued to do more to defend the people and promote their peace and prosperity than any other man in all the country." Putnam recounted John Sevier's tormented acquiescence to statehood and his noble rejection of North Carolina's 1784 commission as brigadier general. He then compared Sevier to "Moses," who "chose rather to suffer affliction with his people—than be flattered with the writing on sheep-skin!" Putnam portrayed Sevier as a man courted by the state of North Carolina, but who managed to "keep Old Rip Van Winkle at arms length." According to Putnam, Sevier held the "coon skin money" of the State of Franklin "in more esteem than the parchment roll with the Great Seal of North Carolina attached." He became the embodiment of a frontier patriot, fighting his "political opponents" and savage Indians "hip and thigh and from tree to tree." John Sevier "feared not, faltered not, and failed not!" Regarding the catastrophic Indian wars largely initiated by the Franklinites, Putnam cast the southeastern Indian tribes as the aggressors who "disregarded the treaties" carefully negotiated by Sevier and forced him to "pursue their marauding parties." Putnam paternalistically described "Nolachucky Jack" as the "father, friend, and protector" of the "people living south of [the] Tennessee & Holston River [Sevier, Caswell, and Blount counties]," and did not mention the violence, bloodshed, and suffering he brought upon these settlements. Regarding the end of Franklin, Putnam argued that the Franklinites abandoned their efforts only after forcing North Carolina to concede to a number of "measures proposed and adopted to satisfy the people of Franklin." Putnam excluded accounts of the Battle of Franklin, Sevier's arrest, and the Franklinite's involvement with the Spanish government. Despite the movement's failure to achieve statehood, Putnam's biography depicts it as John Sevier's successful campaign to improve the lives of Tennessee Valley families. A. W. Putnam eventually rewarded Sevier's commitment to the inhabitants of Tennessee by erecting the first monument to Sevier "on Tennessee soil."[29]

Lyman Draper also contacted the descendents of the Tiptonites, who predictably offered him a very different version of the history of the state of Franklin. John Tipton, the grandson of Anti-Franklinite leader Colonel John Tipton, recounted the Franklin affair in a brief biographical sketch of his grandfather sent to Draper on January 22, 1839. Tipton portrayed his grandfather as a frontier warrior "frequently in command and engaged in a number of battles and skirmishes with the Indians." He described "Col. John's" rise to political prominence in East Tennessee and his grandfather's involvement in the violence in Washington County. According to Tipton's account, his grandfather "opposed" the state of Franklin, and "most of his neighbors [meaning Greene and Sullivan counties] sided with him." Tipton attempted to downplay his grandfather's complicity in the backcountry bloodshed, offhandedly commenting, "some men on each side determined to take up arms and in the year [left blank] the fighting men met at the residence of Col. Tipton." Tipton boasted that "a skirmish took place in which the Sevier party was routed with the loss of 6 or 7 killed and wounded." John Tipton's biography of Colonel Tipton defended his grandfather's actions during the Franklin movement while obscuring his direct involvement in the most unsavory aspects.[30]

Dr. Abraham Jobe, the maternal great-grandson of Colonel John Tipton, offered one of the most interesting accounts of the Battle of Franklin. Dr. Jobe, born in Carter County, Tennessee, on October 9, 1817, briefly chronicled his great-grandfather's participation in the defeat of the Franklin separatist movement. The Jobe-Tipton family preserved the stories of their forebears through oral traditions, and Jobe "gathered [his account] from old men and women who distinctly remembered all the facts they detailed." Jobe's sensationalized account of the Battle of Franklin predictably casts John Sevier as the aggressor in the backcountry skirmish. According to Jobe, his great-grandfather's unwavering loyalty to the state of North Carolina and refusal to submit to the authority of Franklin incited Sevier to raise an army and march "on Tipton to coerce him into obedience." As Sevier's forces surrounded "the brave little band in the [Tipton] house," "the first gun fired was at a woman who had been sent out of the house to the spring after water." In Jobe's version of the battle, the Tiptonites' counterattack came as a chivalrous response to the Franklinite assault on an innocent woman. Jobe concluded his tale with his great-grandfather gallantly leading "his men" in a successful assault on Sevier's forces that left several Franklinites wounded or dead. Jobe's account of the history of Franklin mirrored the version offered by the Franklinite descendents. To Dr. Jobe, his great-grandfather's loyalty to North Carolina and the new American republic compelled him to defend the Tennessee Valley communities from political and social anarchy.[31]

It comes as little surprise that the descendents of the participants in the Franklin movement attempted to protect the historical reputations of their families. Their historical revisionism blurred the reality of the frontier separatist movement and projected the backcountry partisanship of the eighteenth century onto the political canvas of the nineteenth century. The complex and dichotomous legacy of Franklin proved extraordinarily malleable. Historical factualism often gave way to political expediency, as Franklin's legacy became intertwined with the two dominant political issues of the nineteenth century: slavery and secession. As Ezekiel Birdseye and Andrew Johnson resurrected backcountry separatism in an effort to defeat Middle Tennessee's slaveholding political aristocracy, and Johnson desperately attempted to forestall Tennessee's secession from the union, the state of Franklin emerged anew in America's political consciousness.

During the first half of the nineteenth century, the state of Tennessee experienced two parallel socioeconomic developments: the expansion and increasing importance of slave labor in Middle Tennessee's thriving commercial agrarian economy and the emergence of a determined antislavery movement in East Tennessee's increasingly economically isolated and politically marginalized communities. Since the earliest settlement of the Tennessee frontier, slave labor remained a fixture in the backcountry agrarian economy. During the decades that followed the Franklin statehood movement, Tennessee's slave population increased exponentially in response to western expansion and the growth of commercial agriculture in both eastern and central Tennessee. The 1791 Southwest Territory census recorded 3,400 slaves (2,300 in the Washington District and 1,100 in the Mero [Cumberland] District), and less than five years later, the 1795 territorial census recorded 10,600 slaves across the territory (with 8,150 slaves residing in the Washington District). The tripling of the Southwest Territory's slave population resulted from the dramatic expansion of the region's market economy and trans-Appalachian population. By the opening of the nineteenth century, the enormous demographic and economic growth in Middle Tennessee and the availability and affordability of suitable farmland led to a significant increase in the state's slave population. By 1810, Tennessee commercial planters expanded the slave population in their state to more than 35,000 slaves, with nearly 80 percent of all slaves working on the cotton and tobacco plantations of Middle Tennessee. East Tennessee's slave population rose only slightly, to 9,300 slaves, but as new antebellum industries developed and improvements to the region's increasingly inadequate transportation and trade arteries failed to materialize, the importance and utilization of slave labor in the region declined. By 1830, the farmers, stockraisers, manufacturers, merchants, and political leaders of eastern Tennessee stood on the periphery of their state's dynamic economic and political transformation, but unexpectedly found themselves at the epicenter of America's growing antislavery movement.[32]

Ezekiel Birdseye moved into the Tennessee Valley at the height of the resurgence of the southern mountain abolitionist movement. Decades prior to Birdseye's 1838 arrival, antislavery forces thrived in East Tennessee. As early as 1815, Quaker leaders like prominent iron manufacturer Elihu Embree, Benjamin Lundy, and Charles Osborne founded emancipation societies and published antislavery newspapers in the Tennessee Valley to "effect the abolition of slavery by political means."[33] Over the next twenty years, prominent Presbyterian ministers joined with Quakers to establish dozens of manumission societies across the region. According to Birdseye biographer Durwood Dunn, "As late as 1827, East Tennessee alone contained nearly one-fifth of all antislavery societies in the United States." In one of the few direct links between Tennessee Valley abolitionism and the Franklin statehood movement, the Reverend Samuel Doak taught many of the Presbyterian leaders of the early Tennessee abolitionist movement at Washington College. "Doak's Log College" became the training ground for prominent antislavery leaders such as John Rankin and David Nelson. By 1841, every county comprising the former political boundary of the state of Franklin contained at least one abolitionist or antislavery organization.[34]

The Tennessee Valley manumission societies waged a highly effective antislavery campaign on the fringes of increasingly politically dominant and proslavery Middle Tennessee. Through the use of rousing political petitions and the publication of antislavery newspapers and pamphlets, Tennessee Valley abolitionists pressured local, state, and federal leaders to confront the moral indignities and economic consequences of the institution of slavery. In an amazing testament to their determination, East Tennessee abolitionists from sixteen counties convinced the delegates to the 1834 Tennessee constitutional convention to debate amending the state's 1796 constitution to end slavery.[35] From 1834 to 1835, a special committee, chaired by Hawkins County native John A. McKinney, considered the gradual emancipation of all slaves in East Tennessee and five additional counties in Middle Tennessee. Despite ultimately being defeated by the proslavery leadership of West and Middle Tennessee, East Tennessee abolitionists continued to promote their antislavery agenda. Members of the Tennessee Valley Manumission Society even backed the African colonization efforts of the 1820s and 1830s, and formed the Tennessee Colonization Society to lend their support to the growing effort to resettle freed slaves in Liberia.[36]

The Tennessee Valley's twenty-five-year history of antislavery activity attracted Ezekiel Birdseye to the former state of Franklin. Birdseye moved from his home near Stratford, Connecticut, to Newport, Tennessee (present-day Cocke County), to join in the flourishing Tennessee Valley antislavery movement. He collaborated with prominent Tennessee abolitionists such as Reverend H. Lea, Robert Bogle, John Caldwell, Reverend Boswell Rogers, Reverend Spencer Henry, and Maryville College president Dr. Isaac Anderson.[37] As the Tennessee Valley antislavery forces strengthened, Ezekiel Birdseye dreamed of establishing an independent "free state" comprising "the mountain areas of Tennessee, North Carolina, and Virginia."[38] Between 1839 and 1840, Birdseye and Newport judge Jacob Peck met to discuss the creation of a free state of "Frankland." In a letter to Gerrit Smith, a wealthy philanthropist and abolitionist from Peterboro, New York, Birdseye described his dream "that East Tennessee might be detached from other parts of the state and made a separate and free state." Despite his effort to "convince those with whom I have been acquainted . . . that such a division would contribute to the well being of East Tennessee," Birdseye found himself "despaired to seeing it accomplished soon if ever."[39]

Ezekiel Birdseye's public advocacy for the creation of an abolitionist state in the heart of the slave south threatened to alienate potential Tennessee Valley slaveholding supporters of East Tennessee statehood.[40] The savvy "Connecticut Yankee" responded by masking his abolitionist motivations for statehood behind a persuasive argument for East Tennessee's economic independence. Birdseye switched his rhetoric promoting Tennessee Valley separatism from controversial moral arguments against the indignities of the "peculiar institution" to more socially palatable appeals involving internal improvements and regional economic growth.[41] Birdseye joined a swelling chorus of East Tennessee's economic and political leaders demanding that the state government in Nashville promote the development of the region's transportation arteries (roads, turnpikes, canals, and railroads) and increasingly isolated market economy.[42] Birdseye echoed regional economic boosters in another letter to Gerrit Smith, stating that "the natural resources of the country were its mineral, agriculture, and manufacturing resources." If East Tennesseans could be convinced to embrace "free labor," "directed industry," "a home market for the farmer," and "such legislation as would encourage improvements," Birdseye believed that the region would experience a renaissance of "wealth and prosperity."[43] Birdseye justified his decision to submerge the abolitionist roots of his support for statehood, confiding to Smith, "Those who hope by this means [creating a new state] to exterminate slavery in East Tennessee think it will be prudent to say little on that subject or publickly [*sic*] on it until the act of separation is determined then to make an effort to carry that measure." Birdseye expressed confidence that "a very large majority of our people would vote for the termination of slavery without delay," but feared that the "surrounding slave states would take the alarm and no doubt make strenuous efforts to counteract a policy which they deem destructive to their interests."[44] After the creation of a new state of Frankland, Birdseye believed that "The friends of the slave would have an open field and opportunity to meet the advocates of slavery in debate."[45]

Birdseye's new fiscal appeals for Tennessee Valley independence drew the northern abolitionist into an unlikely alliance with one of the South's leading political figures, Andrew Johnson. Johnson served as the Tennessee state senator for Greene and Hawkins counties and tenaciously promoted the economic development of East Tennessee.[46] Since 1836, the Tennessee legislature had passed two separate pieces of legislation aimed at improving the region's transportation system. Both efforts proved to be ineffectual, resulting in only "one turnpike and false starts on two railroads."[47] To an ambitious politician and businessman like Andrew Johnson, the development of the Tennessee Valley's economy became a salient political issue. In the winter of 1841, representatives from across the Tennessee Valley convened in Knoxville to promote the construction of a transmontane railroad, turnpikes, and the "improvement of navigation of the Tennessee River." Both Andrew Johnson and Ezekiel Birdseye attended the "internal improvement conventions." Birdseye, representing Cocke County, described the meetings to Gerrit Smith: "On Monday and Tuesday of this week [November 22–23] I attended the internal improvement convention of East Tennessee at Knoxville." Over the span of two separate conventions, the East Tennesseans drafted a memorial to the Tennessee legislature requesting that they release approximately $650,000 dollars to complete the Hiawassee Railroad, to construct a turnpike from Abingdon, Virginia, to Knoxville, and to improve navigation on the Tennessee River.[48] Amid the debate over how to improve the region's economy, the delegates considered a plan for forming an independent state out of the counties of East Tennessee. According to Birdseye, "This was discussed in the convention on both days" and "Not a single opponent appeared."[49] Both Johnson and Birdseye left the internal improvement conventions optimistic about the economic and moral future of their Tennessee Valley communities.[50]

At the next legislative session, representatives from Middle and West

Tennessee de facto rejected the Tennessee Valley memorial by agreeing to sue the Louisville, Cincinnati, and Charleston Railroad Company, owners of the Hiawassee Railroad, for an earlier breach of contract. The lawsuit all but ensured the failure of the trans-Appalachian rail line through the Tennessee Valley and outraged regional politicians. In response to the defeat of the internal improvement memorial, Andrew Johnson introduced a resolution in the Tennessee Senate to organize an independent state of Frankland out of East Tennessee and the mountainous portions of Georgia, North Carolina, and Virginia. Johnson's resolution called for the creation of "a joint select committee appointed to . . . take into consideration the expediency and constitutionality of ceding one of the grand divisions of the state (commonly called East Tennessee) to the General Government, for the purposes of being formed into a sovereign and independent state to be called 'the State of Frankland.'"[51]

Throughout 1841 and 1842, the East Tennessee press enthusiastically promoted Birdseye and Johnson's statehood ideas. In the *Jonesboro Whig*, newspaper editor William G. "Parson" Brownlow applauded the resolution and harshly criticized the political leadership of Middle Tennessee for politically and economically neglecting the eastern part of their state. Ezekiel Birdseye informed Judge Peck, "There are three political newspapers in Knoxville all of which now advocate the policy of separating East from West Tennessee. The other papers in East Tennessee will so far as I am informed give their support of the measure."[52] An anonymous congressman and contributor to the *Knoxville Argus* defended the separatist resolution, stating his East Tennessee constituents did "not [have] a single interest in common with the people west of the mountains." E. G. Eastman, editor of the *Knoxville Argus,* described his utopian version of an independent Frankland. Eastman believed that once the "chains which render East Tennessee subservient to the more powerful division of the State shall be severed," the state of Franklin "will, like a bird thrown free from its cage, rise with buoyant and vigorous wing, and soar high above the clouds of adversity which now hang heavy upon her."[53]

In January 1842, the Tennessee Senate finally voted on Andrew Johnson's Frankland resolution. Led by the determined senators from East Tennessee, the statehood proposal passed by a vote of seventeen to six. The senate appointed Johnson and John R. Nelson, the representative from Knox and Roane counties, to the Frankland statehood committee and passed the resolution on to the state's House of Representatives for their consideration. Samuel Milligan, the representative from Greene and Washington counties, led the effort in the Tennessee House of Representatives to secure passage of the Frankland resolution. The contentious debate surrounding the statehood proposal revealed the bitter factionalism that continued to define East Tennessee politics. The members of the House of Representatives rejected the separatist resolution twenty-nine to forty-one, with the East Tennessee representatives splitting their votes.[54] The defeat of the "Johnson-Milligan resolution" derailed the plan to create an independent state of Frankland.[55] Despite continued support from within the communities of East Tennessee, the second Frankland statehood movement succumbed to entrenched internal regional divisions and vicious partisan attacks from the political leadership west of the Tennessee Valley.[56]

The similarities between Arthur Campbell and John Sevier's state of Franklin and Ezekiel Birdseye and Andrew Johnson's state of Frankland are striking. Both movements generated support within East Tennessee by capitalizing on the perception of political and economic marginalization by the distant centers of state government and the struggle for regional internal improvements. In the first manifestation of backcountry separatism, frontier defense and the development of the Tennessee Valley's land-based economy factored as two of the primary motivations for independence.[57] During the first half of the nineteenth century, the expansion of the region's trade and transportation infrastructure inspired the rebirth of East Tennessee separatism. The moral and religious leadership of the Tennessee Valley played critical roles in both statehood movements, and the efforts to inject the radical principles of republicanism and abolitionism met with identical political rebuke. Andrew Johnson and Ezekiel Birdseye never directly acknowledged that their movement built upon the legacy of the first state of Franklin, but by the middle of the nineteenth century, the memory of Franklin and the heroic defenders of frontier independence increasingly defined the identity of the politically marginalized and perpetually polarized East Tennesseans.

For nearly two decades following the defeat of the second Franklin statehood movement, East Tennessee separatist sentiment lay dormant, but the antebellum secession debates in the U.S. Congress, the Tennessee legislature, and within the communities of the Tennessee Valley rekindled the ideological flames of eastern separatism. In the two decades preceding the Civil War, the Tennessee Valley economy experienced "its own small-scale industrial revolution." The completion of the East Tennessee and Virginia

Railroad across the region and the potential financial windfalls offered by the extraction of the region's coal, iron, and copper deposits threatened to transform the communities of East Tennessee. Rural industrialization and its reliance upon free labor seemed incompatible with Tennessee's entrenched slave labor–based agrarian economy. Across the United States, antislavery industrial boosters and manufacturers attacked the institution as archaic and detrimental to the growth of America's advancing industrial economy.[58] Despite their reputation as rabid southern abolitionists, a significant number of East Tennesseans clearly owned slaves, and the majority of the region's inhabitants supported the preservation of the institution.[59] The development of early mineral extraction and manufacturing industries, the entrenchment of slave labor, and the growth of abolitionism created an explosive situation in the Tennessee Valley.[60]

In February 1860, Tennessee senator and Unconditional Unionist Andrew Johnson stood before a bitterly divided U.S. Senate and harshly denounced the most recent threats made by the political leadership of South Carolina to secede from the union. Over a two-day period, the Greeneville native castigated "run-mad Abolitionists" and "red-hot [southern] disunionists" for being "engaged in [the] unholy and nefarious work of breaking up the Union." During his fiery speech, Johnson laid the blame for the mounting sectional disharmony at the feet of both southerners and northerners. The Tennessean accused "the Abolitionists proper of the North" of "shaking the right hand of fellowship with the disunionists of the South in this work of breaking up the Union" by promoting their radical antislavery agenda. Johnson, who "emerged as the most visible and controversial southern Unionist in Congress," defended himself against personal attacks launched by pro-secessionist southern politicians branding him a "Black Republican" and an "ally" of abolitionism.[61] Mississippi senator Jefferson Davis labeled Johnson a political hypocrite for opposing secession, stating that "Tennessee was born of secession" and "rocked in the cradle of revolution." In a clear reference to the first Franklin statehood movement, Davis revealed to the senators that "Tennessee . . . matured, and claimed to be a State because she had violently severed her connection with North Carolina, and through an act of secession and revolution claimed then to be a State." Davis questioned Johnson's "position" as a "great objector against the exercise of the right of secession" when the state the senator represented "was born of secession."[62] Jefferson Davis transformed the Franklin separatist movement into a patriotic precedent for southern secession, and in the process struck an effective blow against one of the few southern politicians open-ly opposing the dissolution of the union.

Andrew Johnson countered Senator Davis's misrepresentation of early Tennessee history by using the chaos and violence surrounding the Franklin separatist movement to warn of the dangers posed by secession. Johnson challenged Davis's implication that his state owed its existence to secession, and offered his own set of political lessons to be drawn from the Franklin fiasco. Reading from John H. Wheeler's 1851 *Historical Sketches of North Carolina from 1584–1851,* Johnson recounted Wheeler's version of the rise and fall of the state of Franklin and its "brave and patriotic" leader John Sevier. After concluding his reading of Wheeler, Johnson opined that Se-vier "had fallen into this error of secession or separation from the State of North Carolina," and the "doctrine of secession could not even be sustained by him, with his great popularity and with the attachment the people had for him." According to Johnson, "Instead of Tennessee having her origin or birth in secession, the precise reverse [was] true." "The State of Franklin had its birth in an attempt at disunion and was rocked to death in the cradle of secession," leaving its "great defender and founder [John Sevier] lodged in irons." The senator from Tennessee argued that the Franklin statehood movement demonstrated the "nefarious" consequences of the "blighting," and the "withering doctrine of secession." Even the "great" John Sevier, who "even now [is] venerated" in Tennessee, could not escape the "infamous," "diabolical," "hell-born and hell-bound doctrine of secession." Johnson as-sured the senators that Tennessee "has many fond recollections of the Revo-lution, but with all her revolutionary character, her people have never attempted secession." In a remarkable effort at historical revisionism, An-drew Johnson recast the Franklinites as helpless pawns controlled by the irresistible and maddening disease of secession.[63]

Andrew Johnson's contested effort in the U.S. Congress to stall the disintegration of the union reflected the partisan tensions resulting from the secession crisis across the state of Tennessee. After the secession of seven southern states, Tennesseans confronted the difficult decision of whether to join South Carolina, Mississippi, Georgia, Florida, Alabama, Louisiana, and Texas in abandoning the union. In a February 1861 referendum, Ten-nesseans voted "four to one" against convening a secession convention to decide their state's political fate. After the April 1861 Confederate assault on Fort Sumter in Charleston Harbor, residents of Tennessee considered a second secession referendum. The swirling uncertainties of civil war and

President Abraham Lincoln's call for troops to suppress the rebellion convinced Tennessee voters to reverse their state's political course. On June 8, 1861, Tennesseans voted overwhelmingly to "leave the Union," and on June 24, Tennessee governor Isham G. Harris pronounced that "all connection by the state of Tennessee with the Federal Union [is] dissolved." Of the 47,238 votes cast against secession, nearly 18,000 came from East Tennessee, all but ensuring that "East Tennessee would become a Unionist stronghold" throughout the Civil War.[64] The failure of Andrew Johnson and his fellow East Tennesseans to stop their state from abandoning the union ushered in one of the most divisive and violent periods in the Tennessee Valley's history.[65]

The secession of their state from the union bitterly divided the residents of East Tennessee. Despite overwhelming opposition to secession from East Tennesseans, there remained a vocal and determined pro-secession contingent within the region. An examination of East Tennessee's Confederate leadership reveals that regional supporters of secession were primarily drawn "from a rising commercial-professional class that was emerging as the region became even more firmly integrated into the [national] market economy." These young Tennessee Valley entrepreneurs, residing mostly in urban areas and towns, established close commercial ties to the lower South. As a result of these market connections, these new economic elites positioned themselves to compete with the region's entrenched families, mostly Unionists, for economic and political control of the Tennessee Valley.[66] Over the course of the Civil War, East Tennesseans witnessed vicious partisan violence within their region and a destructive "bushwhacker war" that terrorized their communities. East Tennessee remained a political stronghold for southern unionism throughout the conflict and a direct threat to the Confederate military effort. For much of the war, either Union or Confederate troops occupied the former communities of the state of Franklin.[67]

Amid the anarchy and violence gripping East Tennessee, several of the region's leading political figures reintroduced East Tennessee separatism, and on June 17, 1861, East Tennesseans met in Greeneville to consider their next course of action.[68] Over the four-day session, the delegates passed "resolutions expressing their desire not to be involved in civil war," and rejecting their state government's passage of the "ordinance of separation."[69] The attendees also appointed a committee to draft legislation to be presented to the Tennessee legislature "seeking consent" to form an independent state out of East Tennessee and the unionist counties of Middle

Tennessee. On June 29, 1861, the Tennessee legislature rejected the "State of Frankland" petition, defeating Tennessee Valley separatism for a third time in seventy-seven years.[70]

From the original statehood movement through the multiple nineteenth-century manifestations of East Tennessee separatism, the state of Franklin remained inexorably linked to the fierce competition to control the political and economic direction of the Tennessee Valley. By utilizing rhetorical flourishes, patriotic symbolism, and appeals for infrastructural improvement, advocates for East Tennessee independence drew upon the legacy and mythology of John Sevier's state of Franklin to promote their political, economic, and moral agendas.[71] The historical sparring between the descendents of the Franklinites and Tiptonites, Ezekiel Birdseye's free state of Frankland, and Andrew Johnson's desperate efforts to defuse the secession crisis in the U.S. Senate fit onto a historical continuum of redefining the Franklin statehood movement. Franklin's historical, political, and cultural transformation did not end with the Civil War. Over the next 150 years, East Tennessee historians, business leaders, and politicians continued to reshape Franklin's historical legacy and recast the movement's significance to Tennessee and America's history.

Epilogue

Finding Frankland

The Legacy of Separatism in the Twentieth Century

> While no man has the right to object to or to protest the facts of history, neither has any man the right to pervert those facts, nor unjustly to characterize them according to his own whim or fancy, and thereby detract from the good name and fame of men, who in their day and generation served the State and its people faithfully and well, with singular disinterestedness, sacrifice, and devotion.
>
> —Mathews, "The Spanish 'Conspiracy' in Tennessee"

The "facts of history" are rarely unambiguous, and more often than not, they are highly subjective and open to an infinite number of interpretations. The events of and the participants in the Franklin separatist movement present a striking reminder of this historical truism. The state of Franklin stood briefly as America's unrecognized fourteenth state, and the defenders of statehood naturally tried to cast their movement in the most favorable political and historical light possible. Throughout the twentieth century, the historical legacy of the state of Franklin continued to be a source of state and local pride and an effective symbol for the promotion of economic improvements and political interests within East Tennessee. On April 19, 1931, Nashville sculptors Belle Kinney and Leopold F. Scholz unveiled their eight-foot-tall bronze statue of John Sevier at the Statuary Hall in Washington, D.C.[1] The monument, donated by the state of Tennessee, depicts Sevier standing heroically with his arms crossed and a sword draped on his side. The short biographical sketch of Sevier included with the unveiling's "program of exercises" only mentioned the state of Franklin in passing. The program read: "When because of inability of North Carolina to afford governmental protection to the 'over-mountain' people, the independent State of Franklin was established, Sevier became its first and only governor. When the government fell he was arrested for treason, but was never tried, and his disabilities were removed."[2] Less than ten years later, the Tennessee state legislature passed an act to preserve the Knox County home of John Sevier. The 1941 bill provided $4,500 dollars in state funds to purchase Sevier's home and forty adjoining acres of farmland, and allocated $3,500 dollars to restore the property "to as near its original condition as possible." The legislature also set aside $600 dollars annually to maintain what eventually became the Marble Springs Historic Site. John Sevier's prestige as a "commonwealth builder and Revolutionary hero" continued to ascend to new heights.[3]

On June 1, 1946, the Library of Congress included "a display on the state of Franklin" in their sesquicentennial celebration of the founding of the state of Tennessee. The Jefferson and Sevier county chapters of the Association for the Preservation of Tennessee Antiquities even "commemorated the signing of the Treaty of Dumplin Creek." In an "impressive ceremony" held on June 10, 1954, attendees were treated to a lecture by Dr. Robert H. White on the "historical consequences of the signing of the treaty," and "a pageant . . . which reenacted the negotiations which took place between the Commissioners of the State of Franklin and representatives of the Cherokee Indian nation on June 10, 1785." The chairman of the Dumplin Creek Historical Commission, Dr. Dan M. Robison, dedicated a plaque "commemorating the signing of the treaty." The plaque read, "The only treaty made by the State of Franklin was signed here after some negotiation. Commissioners were John Sevier, Joseph Outlaw, and Daniel Kennedy. Signatory Cherokee chiefs were the King of the Cherokee Ancoo of Chota, Abraham of Chilhowee, The Sturgeon of Tallassee, The Bard of the Valley Towns, and some thirty others." The celebration is remarkable in light of the Dumplin Creek Treaty's controversial territorial cessions and disastrous repercussions for the Overhill Cherokee.[4]

During the middle of the twentieth century, the state of Franklin became the subject of two historical romance novels. The novelists cast the turmoil surrounding the state of Franklin as their literary backdrop and many participants in the statehood movement as characters in their love stories. Helen Topping Miller set her 1947 novel, *The Sound of Chariots*, in the early months of the state of Franklin, but only loosely followed the actual historical events of the statehood movement. The novel traces the frontier exploits of Giles Hanna, an impoverished soldier and Sevier loyalist, and Raleigh Bevan, a villainous, foulmouthed land speculator. Most of Miller's story unfolds before the birth of Franklin, but she did include a brief allusion to the future of the doomed state. Miller described Franklin as a "new little state that had been born in the fierce morning of independence, in the minds of the proudly independent men who had fathered it. . . . A valiant little state!" She mournfully repined, "It was to live in a tumult of argument and dissension. It was to fight valorously for its life for four brief years. And then it was no more, and the people who trod its hills and valleys a century after might not know even that it had lived."[5]

In 1952, Chicago native Noel B. Gerson published *The Cumberland Rifles,* which he described as a "Novel about the Lost State of Franklin and Spain's abortive attempt to conquer young America." Gerson's tale included numerous "historical figures," such as John Sevier, George Elholm, John Tipton, Don Diego de Gardoqui, and Don Esteban Miro, as well as several characters that were "the products of [Gerson's] imagination." The novel revolved around the efforts of Boston schoolteacher Rosalind Walker to open a female seminary in the Tennessee Valley and a secretive plot carried out by Spanish undercover agents Janus Elholm and Harold Jordan "to overthrow the stripling government of Franklin." Despite being a work of historical fiction, Gerson capitalized on the immense popularity of John Sevier by making him one of the heroes of his story. In the novel's climactic ending, Sevier and Nashville-founder James Robertson lead the "army of Franklin" in an epic defeat of the treacherous "Castilians." Sales of both novels undoubtedly benefited from the burgeoning Franklin mythology and the romanticization of the Tennessee Valley separatists.[6]

One of the most publicized expressions of the romanticization of John Sevier and the state of Franklin occurred with the 1956 and 1958 productions of Kermit Hunter's outdoor drama *Chucky Jack: The Story of Tennessee.* Hunter, best known for his plays *Unto These Hills* and *Horn in the West,* crafted a moving account of the postrevolutionary life of John Sevier and the founding of the state of Tennessee. With the backing of the Great Smoky Mountains Historical Association, *Chucky Jack* played to large audiences in Gatlinburg's 2,501-seat Hunter Hills Theatre. A 1956 ticket order form described the drama:

> Hero of King's Mountain—one of the first settlers to push down the green valleys to the west—member of the Continental Congress—founder of the Lost State of Franklin—first governor of Tennes-

see—one of the truly great American patriots . . . JOHN SEVIER!
. . . called by the Indians CHUCKY JACK from his pioneer home
on the Nolichucky River. Now this giant figure comes to life in a
vivid and stirring outdoor drama, set in the breathtaking Hunter
Hills Theatre at Gatlinburg in the cool shadows of the Great
Smokies. Sixteen memorable scenes trace the career of this eminent
statesman whose character and leadership at a crucial moment
molded the very foundations of American democracy. Authentic
Colonial costumes, exciting incidents, colorful dances, a magnificent musical score composed by Jack Frederick Kilpatrick
. . . CHUCKY JACK is an experience you will always remember.

For the cost of the $1.50 ticket, one could ride the trackless sightseeing train,
called the "Chucky Jack Special," up to the outdoor amphitheater and witness
the story of "a man who braved the wilderness of long ago to establish a new
social order, to give opportunity and scope to the people around him, to
produce in the western wilderness a better way of life." *Chucky Jack* stood as
the theatrical embodiment of the mythology of John Sevier and the state of
Franklin.[7]

In 1965, the staff of East Tennessee State University's B. Carroll Reece
Memorial Museum began preparations for a Lost State of Franklin exhibition. The yearlong exhibition sought to highlight Franklin's role in the development of East Tennessee. As Reece Museum curator Robert S. Moore
and his staff began to collect documents, paintings, and memorabilia relating to the statehood movement, they unintentionally endorsed the romanticized version of Franklin's history. The organizers of the exhibit failed to
include any meaningful reference to Franklin's turbulent relations with the
southeastern Indians or conspiratorial connections to the Spanish government in their display. Despite the perpetual Indian violence and territorial
disputes plaguing the state, the Franklin exhibitors chose only to feature a
copy of a 1772 "Watauga Treaty with the Indians" and a child's toy "replica
of an Indian bark canoe." There is not a single allusion to the Spanish Intrigue or the clandestine relationship between Franklin governor John Sevier and Dr. James White in the exhibition catalog. By excluding these two
fundamental elements, the staff of the B. Carroll Reece Memorial Museum
purged the most bothersome aspects of the statehood movement from their
exhibition and distorted Franklin's checkered past.[8]

Buried deep within the voluminous papers of Kingsport native and Tennessee state congressman James H. Quillen, preserved in the East Tennessee State University archives, are several copies of a very unusual piece of legislation. Quillen's "Franklin Bill" aimed "to establish and create the territory of Franklin, and to authorize said territory to petition for admittance as the 51st sovereign State of the United States." The largely symbolic act read:

> Whereas; the great traditions and the peerless heritage of the former State of Franklin have been obscured and lost for future generations, and it is deemed beneficial and desirable to the future welfare of our Country that the former State of Franklin be re-created, and that section of our present sovereign State of Tennessee lying to the East of the Cumberland Mountains and comprising the Eastern Grand Division of the State of Tennessee is composed of the descendents of those great men who originally carved out of a wilderness the State of Franklin, and which said section of the State is indigenous to the stalwart characteristics and qualities of leadership which contributed so greatly to the establishment and preservation of our nation.[9]

Amazingly, Quillen penned his State of Franklin Bill in the spring of 1961 to serve as a political gimmick aimed at increasing support for his Republican Party in East Tennessee. A few days after reading his Franklin Bill before the Tennessee House of Representatives, Congressman Quillen received a Western Union telegram from Kentucky state senator H. Nick Johnson expressing his desire for "the State of Franklin to include Southeastern Kentucky." The Republican Congressmen informed Senator Johnson that "I have been having a 'good time' on my bill to recreate the Grand Old State of Franklin." He joked to Johnson, "I really appreciate your joining with me on this to include Southeastern Kentucky. Perhaps we can make Republicans out of them."[10] Of course, the State of Franklin Bill failed to pass in the Tennessee legislature, but James H. Quillen's personal crusade to "publicize" the "colorful history" of the state of Franklin continued for thirty more years.[11]

In 1962, Tennesseans elected James H. Quillen to the U.S. House of Representatives from the First Congressional District. Over the Sullivan County native's thirty-four-year stay in Congress, he managed to procure significant federal funding to improve East Tennessee's economy and transportation network. In 1982, Quillen used his considerable political influence to convince Tennessee's political leaders to build the James H. Quillen

College of Medicine at East Tennessee State University. In December of that same year, Quillen joined with other congressional Republicans to pass the Surface Transportation Assistance Act of 1982. The bill, eventually signed into law by President Ronald Reagan, provided federal funds to complete two important highways in East Tennessee, "Johnson City's State of Franklin Road and the Great Smoky Mountains' Foothills Parkway."[12] The city of Johnson City and Washington County started construction of the State of Franklin Road at the end of the 1970s, but budget shortfalls and logistical problems led to delays in completing the first two sections of the thoroughfare. By 1982, only a small critical stretch of the road remained unfinished, and Congressman Quillen's unwavering support for the "priority" project ensured its eventual completion. Johnson City residents finally witnessed the realization of the State of Franklin Road in 1995, and the roadway remains one of the central arteries in Washington County. By naming one of East Tennessee's most traveled roadways after the state of Franklin, Congressman Quillen and the political leadership of East Tennessee cemented the state's legacy in the minds of the thousands of drivers daily navigating the Johnson City street and once again fused John Sevier's statehood movement to internal improvement efforts within the Tennessee Valley.[13]

In 1968, East Tennessee banker W. E. Newell delivered a remarkable address to the business leaders of East Tennessee, entitled "The Tri-City Area and the State of Franklin." Newell's speech connected the state of Franklin to the "industrial development" and economic "growth" of the Tri-City Area (encompassing Bristol, Kingsport, and Johnson City). He argued, "In order to understand the present economic and industrial situation here in Bristol and the Tri-city area, we must first look at the . . . 'Lost State of Franklin.'" In what assuredly must have seemed like a strange topic for a lecture on regional fiscal promotion, Newell related the history of Franklin to his audience. His familiar romanticized version of Franklin masked the true purpose of his lecture. Newell pointed out that "throughout the entire history of the United States, there has been little in common between the North Carolina country this side of the mountains and the state capital in Raleigh." Similarly, he believed that "There has been little in common between the Tennessee section east of the Cumberlands and the state capital, Nashville," and in truth "economically, agriculturally, politically, and socially, the areas comprising the 'Lost State of Franklin' are [still] more closely bound to each other than they are to the Bluegrass sections of Nashville and Frankfort, the aristocratic Tidewater section of Virginia, or the wealthy Piedmont section of North Carolina."[14] Newell drew upon the "common bond," cemented during the trying days of Franklin, to implore East Tennessee's economic leaders to "seek new industry" and "keep atuned [sic] to the needs of the industry that we already have." He encouraged attendees to "work together toward keeping the milk stool balanced and the legs growing stronger through a cooperative effort for our mutual benefit." In light of the significant relationship between the Franklin statehood movement and the expansion of the Tennessee Valley's frontier economy, Quillen's and Newell's use of the statehood movement for the promotion of regional economic development seems exceedingly appropriate. Newell concluded his speech with these final rousing words: "Yes, beginning with the Lost State of Franklin in the 1700s and running to this day of the so-called Great Society in the 20th Century, we in this area are bound together by strong social, political, geographical, and industrial ties. We are on the march industrially."[15]

The economic boosterism of James H. Quillen and W. E. Newell represented only a small part of the role the state of Franklin continued to play in the fiscal development of East Tennessee during the second half of the twentieth century. Today, a brief scan of the Tri-City Area yellow pages reveals numerous businesses that adopted the state of Franklin into their corporate identities. In February 1996, the first office of the recently chartered State of Franklin Savings Bank opened its doors for business on 612 West Walnut Street in Johnson City. Over the next five years, the bank expanded to include four additional branches and became one of the most successful businesses in the Tennessee Valley. In addition to local banking, East Tennessee entrepreneurs also incorporated Franklin's name into several other businesses, including: State of Franklin Real Estate Company, State of Franklin Chiropractic, State of Franklin Healthcare, and State of Franklin Insurance Company. These business owners hope to profit from the region's pride in the statehood movement that occurred in their communities more than two hundred years earlier.[16]

The history and memory of the state of Franklin continue to evolve, as critics and supporters of the Franklinites defend their positions in the pages of history books, in the words of patriotic oratories, and on the bronzed plaques of marbled monuments. As historian Michael Toomey points out, "it is perhaps fitting that the historical interpretation of the State of Franklin should be as complex as the circumstances under which the government functioned." From the carefully crafted popular images of Franklin contemporaries to the historiographical wars waged in print, Franklin has never been and will never be a "lost" state.[17]

Notes

Introduction

1. Susie Gentry, "The Volunteer State (Tennessee) as a Seceder," *North Carolina Booklet* 3 (July 1903): 5; Abram J. Ryan, *Poems: Patriotic, Religious, Miscellaneous* (New York: P. J. Kennedy and Sons, 1880). In this study, the term Tennessee Valley refers to the upper portion of the Tennessee River Valley, primarily located in eastern Tennessee.

2. Historical Society of Washington County, Virginia, *Washington County Historical Society of Abingdon, Virginia: Addresses Delivered before the Historical Society of Washington County, Virginia* (Abingdon, Va.: Publications of the Washington County Historical Society, 1945), 54–57.

3. Gary J. Kornblith and Carol Lasser, "More Than Great White Men: A Century of Scholarship on American Social History," *Organization of American Historians Magazine of History*, April 2007, 8–9.

4. Thomas Perkins Abernethy depicted the statehood movement as "a game played between two rival groups of land speculators," and he proclaimed that the "whole history of the State of Franklin grew out of the miscarriage of the plans of land dealers" (Thomas Perkins Abernethy, *From Frontier to Plantation in Tennessee: A Study in Frontier Democracy* [Chapel Hill: Univ. of North Carolina Press, 1932], 56–58, 64–90).

5. John Haywood served as attorney general for the state of North Carolina following the collapse of Franklin, and undoubtedly became intimately acquainted with the participants in the statehood affair during his short term. Haywood eventually moved to Tennessee and served as a member of the state Supreme Court from 1812 to 1826. Haywood's book drew extensively from the oral histories maintained by East Tennesseans, and these accounts often contained historical biases, factual errors, or fanciful exaggerations. Perhaps the best example of Haywood's historical inaccuracy is his description of John Sevier's sensational escape from his captors in Morganton. Haywood recounts an escape that never happened, and this account was eventually taken as historical fact until some time later. Haywood's description of the Franklin statehood movement suffered from these scholarly obstacles, but he managed to offer a remarkably objective narrative of the state's tumultuous existence. Haywood neither criticized nor celebrated the exploits of the Franklinites, and his historical approach influenced many of the earli-

est studies of the state of Franklin (John Haywood, *The Civil and Political History of Tennessee from Its Earliest Settlement up to the Year 1796, Including the Boundaries of the State* [Nashville: Publishing House of the Methodist Episcopal Church, South, 1891; reprint, Johnson City, Tenn.: Overmountain Press, 1999], 146–212).

6. Dr. Ramsey's father, Francis A. Ramsey, moved to Washington County in 1783 and worked as a land surveyor until the start of the Franklin movement. F. A. Ramsey emerged as a leading Franklinite and served as Washington County court clerk, secretary to the Franklin constitutional convention, and a Franklin commissioner to the 1787 North Carolina Assembly (David Lawson Eubanks, "Dr. J. G. M. Ramsey of East Tennessee: A Career of Public Service" [Ph.D. diss., University of Tennessee, 1965]).

7. J. G. M. Ramsey, *The Annals of Tennessee to the End of the Eighteenth Century* (Charleston, S.C.: J. Russell, 1853; reprint, Baltimore, Md.: Clearfield Company, 2003), preface, 437–440. Ramsey's *The Annals of Tennessee* followed Haywood's narrative historical format for recounting the statehood effort.

8. For more information regarding the Civil War and Reconstruction in East Tennessee, see: Noel C. Fisher, *War at Every Door: Partisan Politics and Guerrilla Violence in East Tennessee, 1860–1869* (Chapel Hill: Univ. of North Carolina Press, 1997); Kenneth W. Noe and Shannon H. Wilson, eds., *The Civil War in Appalachia: Collected Essays* (Knoxville: Univ. of Tennessee Press, 1997); and W. Todd Groce, *Mountain Rebels: East Tennessee Confederates and the Civil War, 1860–1870* (Knoxville: Univ. of Tennessee Press, 1999).

9. David W. Blight, *Race and Reunion: The Civil War in American Memory* (Cambridge: Belknap Press of Harvard Univ. Press, 2001), 1–5; Gaines M. Foster, *Ghosts of the Confederacy: Defeat, the Lost Cause, and the Emergence of the New South* (New York: Oxford Univ. Press, 1987), 1–8.

10. William A. Henderson, "Nolachucky Jack (Gov. John Sevier)," January 7, 1873, King's Mountain Papers (DD), Draper Manuscript Collection.

11. Walter Faw Cannon, "Four Interpretations of the History of the State of Franklin," *East Tennessee Historical Society's Publications* 22 (1950): 8–9; Stan Klos, "Famous Americans," 2001, http://www.famousamericans.net /jamesrobertsgilmore/ (accessed July 10, 2005).

12. Gilmore also states that John Tipton "was one of those restless spirits who seem never entirely happy unless they are in the midst of strife and discord. Profane, foulmouthed, turbulent, and an irascible, domineering temper, he lacked every quality of a gentleman except personal courage, and that nameless something which comes down in a man's veins from an honorable ancestry. He had ambition but not the ability to lead, and he could not understand why he should give to Sevier such unquestioning allegiance. He was greedy for office, and a born demagogue, and he had the natural jealousy of Sevier that men of low and yet ambitious minds feel for their moral and intellectual superiors" (James R. Gilmore, *John Se-*

vier as a Commonwealth-Builder [New York: D. Appleton and Company, 1887], viii–ix, 10–11, 18, 29–30, 72).

13. Cannon, "Four Interpretations of the History of the State of Franklin," 8–9.

14. Sevier defeated the "evangelical constitution" because "he questioned the expediency of bringing religious tenets into a civil constitution." Gilmore argued, "The union of church and state existed in some of the older countries, but it was clearly contrary to the teachings of the Bible and the example of Christ." Gilmore does not mention the extraordinary expansion of yeoman political power or the democratic principles tantalizingly offered by the Houston-Graham Constitution (Gilmore, *John Sevier as a Commonwealth-Builder,* 18–24, 46–47, 65–71, 74–76, 117–129).

15. Kornblith and Lasser, "More Than Great White Men," 8–9; Ernst Breisach, *Historiography: Ancient, Medieval, and Modern* (Chicago: Univ. of Chicago Press, 1983; reprint, Chicago: Univ. of Chicago Press, 1994), 315–317, 363–365.

16. Theodore Roosevelt, *The Winning of the West* (New York: Current Literature Publishing Company, 1905), 176–178, 190, 199–202; Peter Novick, *That Noble Dream: The "Objectivity Question" and the American Historical Profession* (Cambridge: Cambridge Univ. Press, 1988; reprint, Cambridge: Cambridge Univ. Press, 1997), 92–94.

17. George Henry Alden, "The State of Franklin," *American Historical Review* 8 (January 1903): 271–289.

18. William Edward Fitch, *The Origin, Rise and Downfall of the State of Franklin, Under Her First and Only Governor John Sevier* (New York: New York Society of the Order of the Founders and Patriots of America, 1910), 12–23.

19. Ibid.

20. S. J. Kirkpatrick to O. P. Temple, August 7, 1903, O. P. Temple Papers, Special Collections and Archives, University of Tennessee.

21. Louise Wilson Reynolds, "The Commonwealth of Franklin," *Daughters of the American Revolution Magazine* 52 (January 1918): 23–28. According to Reynolds's account of the Franklin ceremony, "A great cheer arose from the audience as little Miss Hoss drew aside the flags draping the monument" (Louise Wilson Reynolds, "Memorial to State of Franklin Dedicated," *Daughters of the American Revolution Magazine* 52 [September 1918]: 518–519).

22. John H. DeWitt, "History of the Lost State of Franklin," *Tennessee Historical Magazine* 9 (April 1924): 167–170. Williams relied heavily on the previous Franklin scholarship, but also utilized published records of the states of North Carolina, Virginia, and Georgia and private manuscript collections to reconstruct a detailed account of Franklin.

23. Williams's book does not fit neatly into either the orthodox (Democratic) or revisionist schools of Franklin's historiography. Williams also sought to demon-

strate the national importance of the Franklin movement, which he called the "most profound and significant manifestation of the spirit of separation," by connecting the backcountry rebellion to "the movement for separation that was at that time rife on all frontiers, eastern as well as western" (Samuel Cole Williams, *History of the Lost State of Franklin* [Johnson City, Tenn.: Watauga Press, 1924; reprint, Johnson City, Tenn.: Overmountain Press, 1993], vii–viii).

24. Breisach, *Historiography,* 385–386; Novick, *That Noble Dream,* 417–419.

25. Stanley J. Folmsbee, Robert E. Corlew, and Enoch L. Mitchell, *History of Tennessee,* vol. 1 (New York: Lewis Historical Publishing Company, 1960), 154–160.

26. Wilma Dykeman, *Tennessee: A History* (Newport, Tenn.: Wakestone Books, 1975), 65–76.

27. Paul H. Bergeron, Stephen V. Ash, and Jeanette Keith, *Tennesseans and Their History* (Knoxville: Univ. of Tennessee Press, 1999), 39–45; John R. Finger, *Tennessee Frontiers: Three Regions in Transition* (Bloomington: Indiana Univ. Press, 2001), 112–123; Dave Foster, *Franklin: The Stillborn State and the Sevier/Tipton Political Feud* (Pigeon Forge, Tenn.: Top Ten Press, 1994), 1–22; Peter J. Kastor, "'Equitable Rights and Privileges': The Divided Loyalties in Washington County, Virginia, during the Franklin Separatist Crisis," *Virginia Magazine of History and Biography* 105 (spring 1997): 194.

28. Paul M. Fink, "Some Phases of the History of the State of Franklin," *Tennessee Historical Quarterly* 16 (March 1957): 213.

29. Noel B. Gerson, *Franklin: America's Lost State* (New York: Crowell-Collier Press, 1968), 159–160.

30. Edmund S. Morgan, *The Birth of the Republic, 1763–89* (Chicago: Univ. of Chicago Press, 1956), 115–128; Reginald Horsman, *The Diplomacy of the New Republic, 1776–1815* (Arlington Heights, Ill.: Harland Davidson, 1985), 28–41.

31. Thomas P. Slaughter, *The Whiskey Rebellion: Frontier Epilogue to the American Revolution* (New York: Oxford Univ. Press, 1986), 29–45; Morgan, *The Birth of the Republic,* 116–118; Horsman, *The Diplomacy of the New Republic,* 33–35; William S. Powell, *North Carolina: Through Four Centuries* (Chapel Hill: Univ. of North Carolina Press, 1989), 220–221.

32. The primary causes of America's postrevolutionary financial crisis include: America's continued reliance on British trade relations, British restrictions on American trade, the failure of the U.S. government to secure additional foreign trade agreements, and the destruction of America's merchant shipping fleet and urban centers of manufacturing and commerce (Horsman, *The Diplomacy of the New Republic,* 28–41).

33. Gerson, *Franklin: America's Lost State,* 159.

1. Land of the Franks

1. Pat Alderman, *The Overmountain Men* (Johnson City, Tenn.: Overmoun-

tain Press, 1970), 13–14; Brenda C. Calloway, *America's First Western Frontier: East Tennessee* (Johnson City, Tenn.: Overmountain Press, 1989), 71; LaReine Warden Clayton, *Stories of Early Inns and Taverns of the East Tennessee Country* (Nashville: National Society of Colonial Dames of America in the State of Tennessee, 1995), 38–39; Max Dixon, *The Wataugans: Tennessee in the Eighteenth Century* (Johnson City, Tenn.: Overmountain Press, 1989), 5–6, 13; East Tennessee Historical Society, *First Families of Tennessee: A Register of Early Settlers and Their Present-Day Descendants* (Knoxville, Tenn.: East Tennessee Historical Society, 2000), 83; David C. Hsiung, "How Isolated Was Appalachia? Upper East Tennessee, 1780–1835," *Appalachian Journal* 16 (summer 1989): 342–343; Ramsey, *The Annals of Tennessee,* 94–95.

2. Calloway, *America's First Western Frontier,* 71.

3. Alderman, *The Overmountain Men,* 13.

4. Clayton, *Stories of Early Inns and Taverns of the East Tennessee Country,* 38–39.

5. Historian Max Dixon states that Bean was "a man of parts," meaning that he was a substantial landholder in Pittsylvania County, Virginia (Dixon, *The Wataugans,* 5–6).

6. Alderman, *The Overmountain Men,* 15–18.

7. Ibid., 17; Calloway, *America's First Western Frontier,* 74; Ramsey, *The Annals of Tennessee,* 107.

8. Calloway, *America's First Western Frontier,* 74.

9. Dixon, *The Wataugans,* 10–11; Calloway, *America's First Western Frontier,* 74; Rueben Gold Thwaites, ed., *Documentary History of Dunmore's War, 1774* (Madison: Wisconsin Historical Society, 1905), 48–49.

10. Calloway, *America's First Western Frontier,* 74–75; Williams, *History of the Lost State of Franklin,* 330–331.

11. Ibid., 76. For a description of the North and South Carolina Regulator movements, see chapter 3.

12. Ibid., 76–77; Alderman, *The Overmountain Men,* 18; Paul Fink, "Jacob Brown of Nolichucky," *Tennessee Historical Quarterly* 21, no. 3 (September 1962): 237–238; David C. Hsiung, *Two Worlds in the Tennessee Mountains: Exploring the Origins of Appalachian Stereotypes* (Lexington: Univ. Press of Kentucky, 1997), 56.

13. Calloway, *America's First Western Frontier,* 71–72; Alderman, *The Overmountain Men,* 15.

14. Calloway, *America's First Western Frontier,* 71–72; James Robertson Papers, 1742–1814, Tennessee State Library and Archives.

15. Historian John Inscoe described the development of frontier mountain communities around backcountry stores east of the Allegheny Mountains (John C. Inscoe, *Mountain Masters: Slavery and the Sectional Crisis in Western North Carolina* [Knoxville, Tenn.: Univ. of Tennessee Press, 1989], 27).

16. Bergeron, Ash, and Keith, *Tennesseans and Their History,* 21–25.

17. Mary Hardin McCown, *The Wataugah Purchase, March 19, 1775, at Syca-more Shoals of Wataugah River: the Cherokee Indians to Charles Robertson, trustee for the Wataugah Settlers: an Index of the Wataugah purchase, the North Carolina Land Grants, and Deeds Through 1782: a Bicentennial Contribution* (Johnson City, Tenn.: Overmountain Press, 1976), 5–7; Frederick Jackson Turner, "Western State-Making in the Revolutionary Era," *American Historical Review* 1 (October 1895): 75–77.

18. Dixon, *The Wataugans,* 16.

19. Joyce Cox and W. Eugene Cox, comps., *History of Washington County, Tennessee* (Johnson City, Tenn.: Overmountain Press, 2001), 53–55; Dixon, *The Wataugans,* 16–17; Watauga Association of Genealogists, comps., *History of Washington County, Tennessee, 1988* (Marceline, Mo.: Walsworth Publishing Company, 1988), 14–15.

20. East Tennessee Historical Society, *First Families of Tennessee,* 66; Haywood, *The Civil and Political History of Tennessee,* 68–69; Hsiung, *Two Worlds in the Tennessee Mountains,* 25–26.

21. Emma Deane Smith Trent, *East Tennessee's Lore of Yesteryear* (Whitesburg, Tenn.: privately published, 1987), 118–121. According to a survey recorded in the *Senate Journal of 1788,* Greene County "is in its greatest Length about Ninety Miles long; in its greatest Breadth about forty-five Miles Wide, growing narrower by degrees until it comes to a point at the western part of the same, where the French Broad and Holston Rivers make a junction" (Walter Clark, ed., *The State Records of North Carolina,* vol. 20 [Goldsboro, N.C.: Nash Brothers, 1903], 513).

22. Pollyanna Creekmore, comp., *Early East Tennessee Taxpayers* (Easley, S.C.: Southern Historical Press, 1980), 187–190; Hsiung, *Two Worlds in the Tennessee Mountains,* 59.

23. Albert C. Holt, "The Economic and Social Beginnings of Tennessee" (Ph.D. diss., George Peabody College, 1923), 163; Stephen B. Weeks, "Tennessee: A Discussion of the Sources of Its Population and the Lines of Immigration," *Tennessee Historical Quarterly* 2 (June 1916): 246–249. After the state of Franklin completely collapsed in 1789, North Carolina ceded the region to the federal government, adding to the creation of the Southwest Territory. In May 1790, the U.S. government created the Southwestern Territory out of the land ceded by the state of North Carolina (Walter T. Durham, *Before Tennessee: The Southwest Territory, 1790–1796* [Rocky Mount, N.C.: Rocky Mount Historical Association, 1990], 1, 7).

24. Hsiung, "How Isolated Was Appalachia?" 340.

25. Environmental historian Donald Davis states, "By 1788 more than twenty-five thousand individuals . . . had settled the upper reaches of the Tennessee Valley" (Donald Edward Davis, *Where There Are Mountains: An Environmental History of the Southern Appalachians* [Athens: Univ. of Georgia Press, 2000], 97).

26. Elmer T. Clark, ed., *The Journal and Letters of Francis Asbury* (London: Epworth Press and Nashville: Abingdon Press, 1958), 568–569.

27. Ibid.

28. Samuel Cole Williams, *Early Travels in the Tennessee Country, 1540–1800* (Johnson City, Tenn.: Watauga Press, 1928), 291–292.

29. Durwood Dunn, *Cades Cove: The Life and Death of a Southern Appalachian Community, 1818–1937* (Knoxville: Univ. of Tennessee Press, 1988), 63–99.

30. Dwight B. Billings and Kathleen M. Blee, *The Road to Poverty: The Making of Wealth and Hardship in Appalachia* (Cambridge: Cambridge Univ. Press, 2000), 25–51.

31. Daniel Vickers, "Competency and Competition: Economic Culture in Early America," *William and Mary Quarterly* 47 (January 1990): 3–29.

32. Robert D. Mitchell, *Commercialism and Frontier: Perspectives on the Early Shenandoah Valley* (Charlottesville, Va.: Univ. Press of Virginia, 1977).

33. Wilma A. Dunaway, *The First American Frontier: Transition to Capitalism in Southern Appalachia, 1700–1860* (Chapel Hill: Univ. of North Carolina Press, 1996), 1–13.

34. Inscoe, *Mountain Masters*, 1–10; Mitchell, *Commercialism and Frontier;* Robert Weise, *Grasping at Independence: Debt, Male Authority, and Mineral Rights in Appalachian Kentucky, 1850–1915* (Knoxville: Univ. of Tennessee Press, 2001).

35. Hsiung, *Two Worlds in the Tennessee Mountains,* 79.

36. Maxine Mathews, "Old Inns of East Tennessee," *East Tennessee Historical Society's Publications* 2 (1930): 22–25; Clayton, *Stories of Early Inns and Taverns of the East Tennessee Country,* 17–22, 30–37.

37. Mathews, "Old Inns of East Tennessee," 23–25.

38. Hsiung, *Two Worlds in the Tennessee Mountains,* 76–77.

39. WPA Historical Records Survey, *Records of Washington County: Inventories of Estates, 1779–1821* (Nashville: U.S. Works Progress Administration, 1938), 9–11, 14, 20.

40. Lucy K. Gump, "Interpretive Transcription of an East Tennessee Business Record Book, Ledger B," Special Collections, James D. Hoskins Library, University of Tennessee, Knoxville.

41. Clark, ed., *The Journal and Letters of Francis Asbury,* 568–569.

42. Kevin T. Barksdale, "Whiskey Distillation in Antebellum Western North Carolina," *Tuckasegee Valley Historical Review* 5 (1999): 1–5; Paul M. Fink, "Jonesboro's Chester Inn," *East Tennessee Historical Society's Publications* 27 (1955): 19–21; Holt, "The Economic and Social Beginnings of Tennessee," 50–51; Clayton, *Stories of Early Inns and Taverns of the East Tennessee Country,* 17–23, 28–37, 50–53. Greeneville served as the capital of the state of Franklin.

43. Clayton, *Stories of Early Inns and Taverns of the East Tennessee Country,* 50–52; Gump, "Interpretive Transcription of an East Tennessee Business Record

Book"; Alan N. Miller, *East Tennessee's Forgotten Children: Apprentices from 1778–1911* (Baltimore: Clearfield Company, 2001), 147.

44. Holt, "The Economic and Social Beginnings of Tennessee," 163.

45. Emilou McDorman, "A Revised Sketch of the Moses Embree III Family and the Quaker Migration South," Embree Family Papers, Archives of Appalachia, East Tennessee State University; Hsiung, *Two Worlds in the Tennessee Mountains,* 84–85.

46. Finger, *Tennessee Frontiers,* 191–193; Hsiung, *Two Worlds in the Tennessee Mountains,* 84–85.

47. *A Descriptive Review of the Industries and Resources of Upper East Tennessee Embracing the Vicinity of Johnson City, Jonesboro, Greeneville, Rogersville, and Morristown Together with Brief Notices of the Leading Members of those Communities* (New York: Enterprise Publishing, 1885), 15–16; Alderman, *The Overmountain Men,* 42; Hsiung, "How Isolated Was Appalachia?" 343–345.

48. Watauga Association of Genealogists, *History of Washington County,* 6–11.

49. *A Descriptive Review of the Industries and Resources of Upper East Tennessee,* 9, 14–16; J. Reuben Sheeler, "Background Factors of East Tennessee," *Journal of Negro History* 29 (April 1944): 167.

50. Davis, *Where There Are Mountains,* 97–111; Finger, *Tennessee Frontiers,* 186–187; Holt, "The Economic and Social Beginnings of Tennessee," 200–204; Hsiung, "How Isolated Was Appalachia?" 344–345; Inscoe, *Mountain Masters,* 48–49; Ramsey, *The Annals of Tennessee,* 142.

51. Watauga Association of Genealogists, *History of Washington County,* 6–11.

52. Hsiung, *Two Worlds in the Tennessee Mountains,* 75–76.

53. Finger, *Tennessee Frontiers,* 180–182; Holt, "The Economic and Social Beginnings of Tennessee," 24–25; Hsiung, *Two Worlds in the Tennessee Mountains,* 79.

54. Hsiung, *Two Worlds in the Tennessee Mountains,* 75–77. In his study of North Carolina's antebellum mountain economy, John Inscoe argues that the "commercial character of mountain agriculture did not develop only after years of a basic subsistence economy. From its earliest development on, Southern Appalachia attracted both farmers and tradesmen who recognized the market potential of the region" (Inscoe, *Mountain Masters,* 1–9, 39–40, 59–61).

55. Edward Michael McCormack, *Slavery on the Tennessee Frontier* (Nashville: Tennessee American Revolution Bicentennial Commission, 1977), 2–6, 11–15.

56. Creekmore, *Early East Tennessee Taxpayers,* 187–214; Pollyanna Creekmore, "Early East Tennessee Taxpayers XIV, Greene County, 1783," *Journal of East Tennessee History* 39 (1967), 118–130.

57. Goldene Fillers Burgner, *Washington County Tennessee Wills, 1777–1872* (Easley, S.C.: Southern Historical Press, 1983), 1–3.

58. Creekmore, *Early East Tennessee Taxpayers,* 187–214.

59. McCormack, *Slavery on the Tennessee Frontier,* 2–6, 11–15.

60. Bergeron, Ash, and Keith, *Tennesseans and Their History,* 38; Alvaretta Kenan Register, transcr., *State Census of North Carolina, 1784–1787: From the Records in the North Carolina Department of Archives and History,* 2nd ed. (Baltimore, Md.: Genealogical Publishing Company, 1987), 142; Sheeler, "Background Factors of East Tennessee," 167–168.

61. WPA Historical Records Survey, *Records of Greene County: County Court Minutes, 1783–1796* (Nashville: U.S. Works Progress Administration, 1940), 1–8.

62. WPA Historical Records Survey, *Records of Washington County: Inventories of Estates,* 2–3.

63. Hsiung, *Two Worlds in the Tennessee Mountains,* 78.

64. Finger, *Tennessee Frontiers,* 187–189.

65. Inscoe, *Mountain Masters,* 45–46; Hsiung, *Two Worlds in the Tennessee Mountains,* 78. Donald Davis asserts that "between 1771 and 1796, hogs dominated the inventories of farm estates in Washington County, Tennessee," and that "pork was probably the most frequently eaten meat of the frontier period" (Davis, *Where There Are Mountains,* 110–111).

66. Rachel N. Klein, *Unification of a Slave State: The Rise of the Planter Class in the South Carolina Backcountry, 1760–1808* (Chapel Hill: Univ. of North Carolina Press, 1990), 36.

67. Hsiung, *Two Worlds in the Tennessee Mountains,* 58–59.

68. East Tennessee Historical Society, *First Families of Tennessee,* 19–23; Inscoe, *Mountain Masters,* 41–43; Hsiung, "How Isolated Was Appalachia?" 241–343. Historian A. V. Goodpasture states, "The open valley was like the mouth of a funnel" that "became avenues that channeled early migration" into the region (quoted in Holt, "The Economic and Social Beginnings of Tennessee," 195–196).

69. Historian David C. Hsiung argues that "East Tennessee's road system and economic ties should dispel any notions that the region has been like a fly trapped in amber, isolated and untouched for generations" (Hsiung, "How Isolated Was Appalachia?" 339–344).

70. According to Wilma Dykeman, the early travelers into the "Tennessee country led a harsh, lonely, tenacious life" (Dykeman, *Tennessee: A History,* 32–37).

71. Callaway, *America's First Western Frontier,* 21–23; Davis, *Where There Are Mountains,* 95–96; Finger, *Tennessee Frontiers,* 40–44; Robert L. Kincaid, "The Wilderness Road in Tennessee," *East Tennessee Historical Society's Publications* 20 (1948): 37–39; Carroll Van West, ed., *Tennessee History: The Land, the People, and the Culture* (Knoxville: Univ. of Tennessee Press, 1998), 9.

72. Finger, *Tennessee Frontiers,* 32–35.

73. Callaway, *America's First Western Frontier,* 25–26; Kincaid, "The Wilderness Road in Tennessee," 38–39.

74. Kincaid, "The Wilderness Road in Tennessee," 37–39, 42–44.

75. Ibid.

76. Callaway, *America's First Western Frontier*, 25–27; East Tennessee Historical Society, *First Families of Tennessee*, 22–23; Hsiung, "How Isolated Was Appalachia?" 341–343.

77. Hsiung, *Two Worlds in the Tennessee Mountains*, 69–70.

78. Hsiung, "How Isolated Was Appalachia?" 344; Hsiung, *Two Worlds in the Tennessee Mountains*, 63.

79. Slaughter, *The Whiskey Rebellion*, 29–45; Morgan, *The Birth of the Republic*, 116–118; Horsman, *The Diplomacy of the New Republic*, 33–35.

80. Fink, "Some Phases of the History of the State of Franklin," 200–203; William A. Henderson lecture entitled "Nolachucky Jack," January 7, 1873, King's Mountain Papers, Draper Manuscript Collection, State Historical Society of Wisconsin (microfilm, Chicago: University of Chicago).

81. William K. Boyd, *History of North Carolina*, vol. 2, *The Federal Period, 1783–1860* (Chicago: Lewis Publishing Company, 1919), 3–5; Archibald Henderson, *North Carolina: The Old North State and the New* (Chicago: Lewis Publishing Company, 1941), 378–380; Gerald R. Lee, ed., *The Tales and Notes of Henry E. Lee* (Lynwood, Australia: privately published, 1985), 388–389; Morgan, *The Birth of the Republic*, 120–122; Gordon S. Wood, *The Radicalism of the American Revolution* (New York: Vintage Books, 1991), 64–66. Regarding the state of Franklin's payment of her officials in animal skins, historian John Haywood states that many early North Carolinians "preferred peltry to paper bills of credit" due to currency devaluation and uncertainty of the exchange rates (Haywood, *The Civil and Political History of Tennessee*, 120–121, 163–164).

82. Boyd, *History of North Carolina*, 3–4; Oliver Taylor, *Historic Sullivan: A History of Sullivan County, Tennessee, with Brief Biographies of the Makers of History* (Johnson City, Tenn.: Overmountain Press, 1988), 109–110.

83. Dixon, *The Wataugans*, 6; Daniel Jansen, "A Case of Fraud and Deception: The Revolutionary War Military Land Bounty Policy in Tennessee," *Journal of East Tennessee History* 64 (1992): 41–42.

84. Klein, *Unification of a Slave State*, 34.

85. McCown, *The Wataugah Purchase*, 5–6; James Mooney, *History, Myths, and Sacred Formulas of the Cherokees* (Asheville, N.C.: Bright Mountain Books, 1992), 45–47; William G. McLoughlin, *Cherokee Renaissance in the New Republic* (Princeton: Princeton Univ. Press, 1986), 28–29. The treaty negotiated at Lochaber, South Carolina, also attempted to halt white encroachment on Cherokee lands, but "misunderstandings about the treaty" had the unintended consequence of encouraging white settlement in the region (Bergeron, Ash, and Keith, *Tennesseans and Their History*, 18–19, 22–23). A 1770 survey that accompanied the Treaty of Lochaber threatened the Watauga settlements when it was revealed that all of the East Tennessee settlements were actually in violation of the treaty. In

response, the leaders of the Watauga settlements entered into the 1773 lease negotiations with the Cherokee and formed the frontier government they called the
Watauga Association (Dixon, *The Wataugans,* 11–15, 22–23).

86. McLoughlin, *Cherokee Renaissance,* 19. British King George III decreed the
Proclamation Line of 1763 in October of that year. According to Donald Davis, the
proclamation prohibited white settlement west of the crest of the Appalachian
Mountain chain in order to "keep the population confined" to the east coast, so as
to maximize the collection of taxes, promote regional trade, and curtail Indian violence against white squatters (Davis, *Where There Are Mountains,* 94–95).

87. Bergeron, Ash, and Keith, *Tennesseans and Their History,* 18–19, 22–23;
Finger, *Tennessee Frontiers,* 39–40; East Tennessee Historical Society, *First Families of Tennessee,* 34–35; Phillip M. Hamer, "The Wataugans and the Cherokee
Indians in 1776," *East Tennessee Historical Society's Publications* 3 (January 1931):
108–109.

88. Robert J. Conley, *The Cherokee Nation: A History* (Albuquerque: Univ. of
New Mexico Press, 2005), 57–58; Dixon, *The Wataugans,* 27–31: Grace Steele
Woodward, *The Cherokees* (Norman: Univ. of Oklahoma Press, 1963), 88–89.

89. Alderman, *The Overmountain Men,* 22–23; McCown, *The Wataugah Purchase,* 6–7; Ramsey, *The Annals of Tennessee,* 109–111, 121.

90. Dixon, *The Wataugans,* 31–33; McCown, *The Wataugah Purchase,* 7.
Ramsey offers a complete list of the patentees of the Watauga Purchase (Ramsey,
The Annals of Tennessee, 119–120).

91. Klein, *The Unification of a Slave State,* 36–37.

92. Ramsey includes a copy of the "petition of the inhabitants of the Washington District" in his work (Ramsey, *The Annals of Tennessee,* 134–139). The majority of male Watauga settlers signed the 1776 petition. Many historians believe that
this petition was the first instance of George Washington's name being used to
designate a geographical area (Dixon, *The Wataugans,* 47–51).

93. L. Scott Philyaw, *Virginia's Western Visions: Political and Cultural Expansion on an Early American Frontier* (Knoxville: Univ. of Tennessee Press, 2004),
96–99.

94. Jansen, "A Case of Fraud and Deception," 41–67.

95. Albert Bruce Pruitt, *Glasgow Land Fraud Papers,* vol. 2, *North Carolina
Revolutionary War Bounty Land in Tennessee* (Cary, N.C.: privately published,
1993), 1–4; Ramsey, *The Annals of Tennessee,* 274–275; Watauga Association of
Genealogists, *History of Washington County,* 20.

96. Dykeman, *Tennessee: A History,* 66–67.

97. Ibid.

98. Abernethy, *From Frontier to Plantation in Tennessee,* 44–59; Bergeron, Ash,
and Keith, *Tennesseans and Their History,* 39; Henderson, *North Carolina,* 384–
385; Ramsey, *The Annals of Tennessee,* 279–281; Muriel M. C. Spoden, *Kingsport*

Heritage: The Early Years, 1700 to 1900 (Johnson City, Tenn.: Overmountain Press, 1991), 129.

2. Acts of Designing Men

1. Philyaw, *Virginia's Western Visions,* 96–100.

2. Passage of the Cession Act of 1784 did not occur without considerable debate in the North Carolina Assembly. The act was eventually passed with a vote of fifty-two for and forty-three against, with Washington, Greene, and Sullivan counties equally divided over the issue (Alderman, *The Overmountain Men,* 188).

3. Abernethy, *From Frontier to Plantation,* 54–59; Clark, *The State Records of North Carolina,* vol. 24, 561–563; Hugh Talmage Lefler, *North Carolina History: Told by Contemporaries* (Chapel Hill: Univ. of North Carolina Press, 1934), 120–121; Watauga Association of Genealogists, *History of Washington County,* 20–21.

4. Klein, *Unification of a Slave State,* 28–41, 78–82, 107–108. In her masterful study of the formation of South Carolina's backcountry planter aristocracy, Rachel N. Klein draws very similar conclusions about the ties that bound yeoman farmers and emerging planters.

5. Despite the prevalence of Virginia natives, historian James K. Huhta argues that "the greatest numbers [of East Tennesseans] came from North Carolina" (James K. Huhta, "Tennessee and the American Revolution," *Tennessee Historical Quarterly* 31 [winter 1972]: 309).

6. Franklin historian Samuel Cole Williams agreed that "the population of Franklin was composed almost wholly of emigrants from Virginia and North Carolina" (Williams, *History of the Lost State of Franklin,* 275–276). John Tipton arrived in the Tennessee Valley in October 1782 and purchased a farm a few miles from Sinking Creek in Washington County (Selden Nelson, "The Tipton Family of Tennessee," *East Tennessee Historical Society's Publications* 1 [1929]: 68–69).

7. Weeks, "Tennessee: A Discussion of the Sources of Its Population," 249.

8. H. Tyler Blethen and Curtis Wood Jr., *Leave-Taking: The Scotch-Irish Come to Western North Carolina* (Cullowhee, N.C.: Mountain Heritage Center, 1986), 1–6; Williams, *History of the Lost State of Franklin,* 275–277; Sheeler, "Background Factors of East Tennessee," 168; Arthur Herman, *How the Scots Invented the Modern World: The True Story of How Western Europe's Poorest Nation Created Our World and Everything in It* (New York: Three Rivers, Press, 2001), 229–266.

9. Weeks, "Tennessee: A Discussion of the Sources of Its Population," 249.

10. Williams, *History of the Lost State of Franklin,* 275–277.

11. East Tennessee Historical Society, *First Families of Tennessee,* 25–27; Williams, *History of the Lost State of Franklin,* 275–277, 289–338. Weeks's 1790 ethnic survey offers these figures: Dutch 0.2%, French 0.3%, German 2.8%, and all others combined 0.1% (Weeks, "Tennessee: A Discussion of the Sources of Its Population," 249).

12. Charles W. Crawford, ed., *Governors of Tennessee, I: 1790–1835* (Memphis: Memphis State Univ. Press, 1979), 32–33; George W. Sevier to Lyman Draper, February 9, 1839, King's Mountain Papers (DD), Draper Manuscript Collection; Williams, *History of the Lost State of Franklin*, 288–338.

13. Paul P. Hoffman, ed., *The Carter Family Papers, 1659–1797, in the Sabine Hall Collection* (Charlottesville, Va.: University of Virginia Library Microfilm Publications, 1967), 1–10; "Sketch of the Life of General William Cocke, One of the Pioneers of East Tennessee, by his Grandson, Col. William M. Cocke," William Johnston Cocke Papers, Southern Historical Collection, Manuscripts Department, Wilson Library, University of North Carolina at Chapel Hill.

14. Williams, *History of the Lost State of Franklin*, 288–338.

15. Neal O'Steen, "Pioneer Education in the Tennessee Country," *Tennessee Historical Quarterly* 35 (summer 1976): 201–203.

16. Williams, *History of the Lost State of Franklin*, 288–338; Dennis T. Lawson, "The Tipton-Hayes Place: A Landmark of East Tennessee," *Tennessee Historical Quarterly* 29 (summer 1970): 105–107; Nelson, "The Tipton Family of Tennessee," 67–68.

17. Calloway, *America's First Western Frontier*, 113–114.

18. Ibid.; Glenn A. Toomey, *Bicentennial Holston: Tennessee's First Baptist Association and Its Affiliated Churches, 1786–1985* (Morristown, Tenn.: privately published, 1985), 25–29, 49–51.

19. Herman A. Norton, *Religion in Tennessee, 1777–1945* (Knoxville: Univ. of Tennessee Press, 1981), 9–10; Toomey, *Bicentennial Holston*, 25–26, 49–51.

20. WPA Historical Records Survey, *Records of Carter County: Sketch of Sinking Creek Baptist Church* (Morristown, Tenn.: U.S. Works Progress Administration, 1938), 1; WPA Historical Records Survey, *Records of Carter County: Papers Relating to Sinking Creek Baptist Church, 1783–1875* (Morristown, Tenn.: U.S. Works Progress Administration, 1938), 1–2.

21. Calloway, *America's First Western Frontier*, 113–114; Williams, *History of the Lost State of Franklin*, 270–272; Toomey, *Bicentennial Holston*, 25–26, 49–51; Albert W. Wardin, *Tennessee Baptists: A Comprehensive History, 1779–1999* (Brentwood, Tenn.: Executive Board of the Tennessee Baptist Convention, 1999), 17–23. According to Herman Norton, the establishment of Buffalo Ridge Baptist Church "conformed to a pattern" for founding churches in the Tennessee backcountry. "Baptists often would come in a body from Virginia and North Carolina congregations and constitute the nucleus for a Tennessee church." The Buffalo Ridge Baptist Church stood "eight miles north of present-day Jonesboro, Tennessee." The number of Baptists congregations in the Tennessee Valley rose so dramatically that they "had sufficient strength to establish the Holston Association" in 1786, "the first such [religious] organization west of the Allegheny Mountains" (Norton, *Religion in Tennessee*, 9–10).

22. Outline of life of Samuel Witherspoon Doak, Samuel Witherspoon Doak Papers, 1768–1925, Tennessee State Library and Archives; Norton, *Religion in Tennessee*, 3–7.

23. Calloway, *America's First Western Frontier*, 113–115; Williams, *History of the Lost State of Franklin*, 270–271.

24. O'Steen, "Pioneer Education in the Tennessee Country," 205–207.

25. Calloway, *America's First Western Frontier*, 115–117; Norton, *Religion in Tennessee*, 3–7.

26. Ramsay, *The Annals of Tennessee*, 330.

27. O'Steen, "Pioneer Education in the Tennessee Country," 207–208; Ramsay, *The Annals of Tennessee*, 330.

28. Williams, *History of the Lost State of Franklin*, 346–347.

29. O'Steen, "Pioneer Education in the Tennessee Country," 207–209; Williams, *History of the Lost State of Franklin*, 346–347.

30. Klein, *Unification of a Slave State*, 239–240.

31. O'Steen, "Pioneer Education in the Tennessee Country," 205–206; Richard J. Hooker, ed., *The Carolina Backcountry on the Eve of the Revolution: The Journal and Other Writings of Charles Woodmason, Anglican Itinerant*, 2nd ed. (Chapel Hill: Univ. of North Carolina Press, 1969), 69–81.

32. Holt, *The Economic and Social Beginnings of Tennessee*, 257–259.

33. Mary Hardin McCown, Nancy E. Jones Stickley, and Inez E. Burns, comps., *Washington County Tennessee Records* (Johnson City, Tenn.: privately published, 1964), vi–4.

34. Hsiung, *Two Worlds in the Tennessee Mountains*, 27; Klein, *Unification of a Slave State*, 28–37, 45–46.

35. Washington County Court Records, Receipts 1780–1965, Archives of Appalachia, East Tennessee State University; Washington County Court Records, North Carolina State Archives.

36. Hsiung, *Two Worlds in the Tennessee Mountains*, 27–41; Klein, *Unification of a Slave State*, 107–108.

37. Hsiung, *Two Worlds in the Tennessee Mountains*, 41–47. In his study of the development of Appalachian stereotypes in Tennessee, David C. Hsiung disagrees with my assertions that the Franklin statehood movement led to divisions within the Tennessee Valley. Hsiung argues that the internal divisions in the region were "transient" and "brief," and that the bonds created by shared economic and political interests and postrevolutionary backcountry threats (Native Americans and Spain) remained intact.

38. Klein, *Unification of a Slave State*, 47–48, 51.

39. Alderman, *The Overmountain Men*, 20; Finger, *Tennessee Frontiers*, 45–49; Klein, *Unification of a Slave State*, 64–68; Haywood, *History of Tennessee*, 50–52; Sheeler, "Background Factors of East Tennessee," 168.

40. Abernethy, *From Frontier to Plantation in Tennessee*, 346–348.

41. James R. Gilmore, *The Rear-Guard of the Revolution* (New York: D. Appleton and Co., 1886; reprint, Spartanburg, S.C.: Reprint Company, 1974), 1.

42. Woodward, *The Cherokees*, 90–96; Hsiung, *Two Worlds in the Tennessee Mountains*, 27–28.

43. Alderman, *The Overmountain Men*, 70–80; Calloway, *America's First Western Frontier*, 105–113; Finger, *Tennessee Frontiers*, 56–60; Hsiung, *Two Worlds in the Tennessee Mountains*, 27–28; Ramsey, *The Annals of Tennessee*, 175–180.

44. According to John Finger, "Like Patriots in other areas, Tennessee settlers took decisive steps to stifle dissent in their midst" (Finger, *Tennessee Frontiers*, 56, 61, 63, 83–88).

45. Callaway, *America's First Western Frontier*, 96, 99, 107, 109.

46. Cox and Cox, comps., *History of Washington County, Tennessee*, 54–56; A. W. Pruitt to Lyman C. Draper, September 4, 1851, King's Mountain Papers (DD), Draper Manuscript Collection.

47. Ramsey, *The Annals of Tennessee*, 178–182, 209–211; Cox and Cox, comps., *History of Washington County, Tennessee*, 54–55.

48. Ramsey, *The Annals of Tennessee*, 181.

49. Hsiung, *Two Worlds in the Tennessee Mountains*, 26–27. According to David Hsiung, nearly half of the Tennessee Valley loyalists tried in Washington County court were found innocent of the charges. Hsiung believes that backcountry Toryism was not as divisive and threatening to Tennessee Valley communities as I argue.

50. Governor David Campbell to Lyman C. Draper, March 30, 1842, King's Mountain Papers (DD), Draper Manuscript Collection.

51. Hsiung, *Two Worlds in the Tennessee Mountains*, 30.

52. Robert Middlekauff, *The Glorious Cause: The American Revolution, 1763–1789* (New York: Oxford Univ. Press, 1982; reprint, New York: Oxford Univ. Press, 1985), 380–384; Tom Wicker, "Turning Point in the Wilderness," *Military History Quarterly: The Quarterly Journal of Military History* 11, no. 1 (autumn 1998): 62–63.

53. Ramsey, *The Annals of Tennessee*, 210–217; Williams, *History of the Lost State of Franklin*, 334–335. Jonathan Tipton was the brother of Anti-Franklin leader John Tipton.

54. Alderman, *The Overmountain Men*, 70–75; Cox and Cox, *The History of Washington County, Tennessee*, 57–59; Ramsey, *The Annals of Tennessee*, 210–217; Wicker, "Turning Point in the Wilderness," 63–66.

55. Alderman, *The Overmountain Men*, 80–83; Ramsey, *The Annals of Tennessee*, 219–224.

56. Cox and Cox, *The History of Washington County*, 57–60; John S. Pancake, *This Destructive War: The British Campaign in the Carolinas, 1780–1782* (Tuscaloosa: Univ. of Alabama Press, 1985), 108–116. At the time of the Battle of King's

Mountain, Major Ferguson was thirty-six years old and had been in the British military since the age of fifteen (Wicker, "Turning Point in the Wilderness," 63–64).

57. Ramsey, *The Annals of Tennessee*, 219–224; Watauga Association of Genealogists, comps., *History of Washington County*, 18–19; Wicker, "Turning Point in the Wilderness," 64–66.

58. Alderman, *The Overmountain Men*, 82–83; Archibald Henderson, *Conquest of the Old Southwest: The Romantic Story of the Early Pioneers into Virginia, the Carolinas, Tennessee, and Kentucky, 1740–1790* (New York: Century Company, 1920), 289–291; Kastor, "'Equitable Rights and Privileges,'" 198–199; Ramsey, *The Annals of Tennessee*, 223–226; Wicker, "Turning Point in the Wilderness," 65–68; Pancake, *This Destructive War*, 117.

59. Alderman, *The Overmountain Men*, 90–104; Cox and Cox, comps., *History of Washington County, Tennessee*, 60–63; Henderson, *Conquest of the Old Southwest*, 295–304; Ramsey, *The Annals of Tennessee*, 230–240; Middlekauff, *The Glorious Cause*, 461–462; Wicker, "Turning Point in the Wilderness," 67–71; Pancake, *This Destructive War*, 118–121.

60. Klein, *Unification of a Slave State*, 107–108; Wicker, "Turning Point in the Wilderness," 71–72.

61. Irene M. Griffey, *Earliest Tennessee Land Records and Earliest Tennessee Land History* (Baltimore: Clearfield Company, 2000), 131–133, 141–142, 313, 361–362; Williams, *History of the Lost State of Franklin*, 289–325.

62. Griffey, *Earliest Tennessee Land Records*, 242, 364, 394; Williams, *History of the Lost State of Franklin*, 330–338.

63. Klein, *Unification of a Slave State*, 25–41.

3. Agreeable to a Republican Government

1. In 1783, the North Carolina Assembly divided Washington County and formed Greene County out of the western section (Alderman, *The Overmountain Men*, 185–186).

2. Watauga Association of Genealogists, *History of Washington County*, 20; Alderman, *The Overmountain Men*, 19; Williams, *History of the Lost State of Franklin*, 30.

3. Haywood, *The Civil and Political History of Tennessee*, 149–151; Williams, *History of the Lost State of Franklin*, 28–34.

4. Historian Peter J. Kastor argues that "the catalyst" for the separatist sentiments in Washington County, Virginia, "was the Franklin movement in the south," but the evidence clearly shows that Arthur Campbell began agitating for western independence prior to the formation of the state of Franklin (Kastor, "'Equitable Rights and Privileges,'" 206).

5. Thwaites, *Documentary History of Dunmore's War*, 39–40, 48, 107, 160, 215, 221, 252; Kastor, "'Equitable Rights and Privileges,'" 199–206.

6. James Hagy, "Arthur Campbell and the West, 1743–1811," *Virginia Magazine of History and Biography* 90 (October 1982): 461–465; Hartwell L. Quinn, *Arthur Campbell: Pioneer and Patriot of the "Old Southwest"* (Jefferson, N.C.: McFarland, 1990), 57–75; Governor David Campbell to Lyman C. Draper, March 30, 1842, King's Mountain Papers (DD), Draper Manuscript Collection; Middlekauff, *The Glorious Cause,* 495; Kastor, "'Equitable Rights and Privileges,'" 208.

7. Williams, *History of the Lost State of Franklin,* 28, 291–294; Laura E. Luttrell, "Some Founders of Campbell's Station, Tennessee: A Genealogy of Alexander, David, and James Campbell," *East Tennessee Historical Society's Publications* 26 (1954): 107–109; Kastor, "'Equitable Rights and Privileges,'" 208.

8. Griffey, *Earliest Tennessee Land Records,* 127. Arthur Campbell also owned nearly fifty-five hundred acres of land in Washington County, Virginia, making him one of the wealthiest men in the region (Kastor, "'Equitable Rights and Privileges,'" 198).

9. James W. Hagy and Stanley J. Folmsbee, "Arthur Campbell and the Separate State Movements in Virginia and North Carolina," *Journal of East Tennessee History* 42 (1970): 20–21; Philyaw, *Virginia's Western Visions,* 111–112; Kastor, "'Equitable Rights and Privileges,'" 207.

10. Hagy, "Arthur Campbell and the West," 463–465; Kastor, "'Equitable Rights and Privileges,'" 206–207.

11. Lewis Preston Summers, *History of Southwest Virginia, 1746–1786, Washington County, 1777–1870* (Richmond: J. L. Hill Printing Company, 1903; reprint, Baltimore: Regional Publishing Company, 1979), 391–392; Kastor, "'Equitable Rights and Privileges,'" 208.

12. Historian Samuel Cole Williams called Arthur Campbell's Washington County statehood effort the "genesis of the State of Franklin movement" (Williams, *History of the Lost State of Franklin,* 5).

13. William P. Palmer, ed., *Calendar of Virginia State Papers and Other Manuscripts from January 1, 1785, to July 2, 1789, Preserved at the Capital at Richmond,* vol. 4 (Richmond: R. U. Derr, Superintendent of Public Printing, 1884), 73, 93; Thwaites, *Documentary History of Dunmore's War,* 40. At the behest of Virginia governor Patrick Henry, Arthur Campbell was investigated and eventually charged with three crimes: "advising residents not to pay their taxes, counseling them not to vote for representatives to the General Assembly, and 'seducing the Inhabitants of Washington County, to separate from this Commonwealth.'" The commission charged with investigating Campbell eventually uncovered enough evidence to "support the charges against him," and Governor Henry removed Campbell as justice of the peace (Kastor, "'Equitable Rights and Privileges,'" 220–222).

14. Summers, *History of Southwest Virginia,* 390–395; Governor David Campbell to Lyman C. Draper, March 30, 1842, King's Mountain Papers (DD), Draper Manuscript Collection. Historian James William Hagy argues that

"Campbell appears to have had little influence in Franklin," but the level of correspondence, military and familial connections, and obvious similarities between the two movements belies this assertion. Despite claims that Campbell "could not have directed the [Franklin] movement from his home sixty or seventy miles away," and the unwillingness of Franklin's leadership to allow him to "manipulate them," Campbell's immediate influence is pervasive throughout the movement (Hagy, "Arthur Campbell and the West," 405–407). The residents of Virginia's District of Kentucky also felt Campbell's influence. In December 1784, the residents of the Kentucky District assembled in Danville to consider creating a separate state out of the western fringes of Virginia. In a situation remarkably similar to the Franklin movement, a small group of thirty land speculators, military officials, and civic leaders voted twenty to ten to create the independent state of Kentucky. According to Thomas Abernethy, the fact that the "preponderance" of the twenty supporters of statehood were land speculators "is obvious" (Thomas P. Abernethy, "Journal of the First Kentucky Convention, Dec. 27, 1784–Jan. 5, 1785," *Journal of Southern History* 1 [February 1935]: 67–68).

15. Williams, *History of the Lost State of Franklin,* 19–21.

16. Folmsbee, Corlew, and Mitchell, *History of Tennessee,* 149–151; Haywood, *The Civil and Political History of Tennessee,* 147–148.

17. Abernethy, *From Frontier to Plantation in Tennessee,* 54–62.

18. Franklin historian Samuel Cole Williams argued that "In all probability a large majority [of residents of the Tennessee Valley] would have favored it [Cession Act]." Williams believed that the "Virginian element," comprising the majority of the residents, "never felt a warm attachment to North Carolina" and considered themselves "alienated from the mother state" (Williams, *History of the Lost State of Franklin,* 22–26). Historian Thomas Perkins Abernethy challenged Williams's assertions, arguing that cession was "opposed by the men who lived beyond the mountain," and that the "vote on the question of cession was a very clear-cut matter between the east and the west, and the east, with the help of [western land] speculators [specifically Richard Caswell and William Blount], won" (Abernethy, *From Frontier to Plantation in Tennessee,* 54–62).

19. Williams, *History of the Lost State of Franklin,* 28; Alderman, *The Overmountain Men,* 188; Folmsbee, Corlew, and Mitchell, *History of Tennessee,* 149–151; Haywood, *The Civil and Political History of Tennessee,* 148–150; Henderson, *North Carolina,* 384–385.

20. Abernethy, *From Frontier to Plantation in Tennessee,* 58.

21. G. Melvin Herndon, *William Tatham, 1752–1819: American Versatile* (Johnson City: Research Advisory Council, East Tennessee State University, 1973), 50–51; Williams, *History of the Lost State of Franklin,* 24–25.

22. Alderman, *The Overmountain Men,* 189. In his study of the "web of influences" that "pushed Virginia into" the American Revolution, Woody Holton ar-

gues that obstacles to land speculation and western settlement created by British colonial Indian policies served as one of the motivating factors for prominent Virginia political figures (mostly land speculators) to support the American independence movement. The Proclamation of 1763 (and the resulting boundary line) and the Treaty of Hard Labor with the Cherokee prevented Virginia land speculators from purchasing millions of acres of land and selling it for a handsome profit. In this respect, the Franklin statehood movement did share in the economic underpinnings that sparked the American Revolution (Woody Holton, *Forced Founders: Indians, Debtors, Slaves, and the Making of the American Revolution in Virginia* [Chapel Hill: Univ. of North Carolina Press, 1999], xviii, 3–38).

23. William Alexander Provine Papers, Tennessee State Library and Archives.

24. Alderman, *The Overmountain Men,* 188–190; Haywood, *The Civil and Political History of Tennessee,* 149–151; Williams, *History of the Lost State of Franklin,* 26–29.

25. Henderson, *North Carolina,* 384–385.

26. Abernethy, *From Frontier to Plantation in Tennessee,* 69–71; Alderman, *The Overmountain Men,* 190–191; Williams, *History of the Lost State of Franklin,* 35–37. Historian Archibald Henderson states that North Carolina repealed the Cession Act because "it did not properly safeguard North Carolina's interests." Led by William R. Davie and Hugh Williamson, powerful eastern state political leaders argued that North Carolina "needed to consider the welfare of the people at home." Regarding opposition to the repeal of the Cession Act, twenty members of the North Carolina House of Commons dissented from the majority vote, calling the repeal "disgraceful." Opposition leaders argued that those who voted to repeal the act did so out of financial considerations and failed to support the new republic (Henderson, *North Carolina,* 384–385).

27. Haywood, *The Civil and Political History of Tennessee,* 152–155. According to Haywood, the scheduled September 1784 meeting was delayed until November, and that meeting "broke up in confusion."

28. Plan of Association presented by William Cooke and Joseph Hardin, September 16, 1784, William Alexander Provine Papers, Tennessee State Library and Archives.

29. Alderman, *The Overmountain Men,* 191–193; Haywood, *The Civil and Political History of Tennessee,* 152–155.

30. Ramsey, *The Annals of Tennessee,* 287–288.

31. Haywood, *The Civil and Political History of Tennessee,* 154–155.

32. Ramsey, *The Annals of Tennessee,* 287–288; Alderman, *The Overmountain Men,* 189–190.

33. Williams, *History of the Lost State of Franklin,* 41–43.

34. Ramsey, *The Annals of Tennessee,* 291–292.

35. Mary French Caldwell, *Tennessee: The Dangerous Example, Watauga to*

1849 (Nashville: Aurora Publishers, 1974), 156; Haywood, *The Civil and Political History of Tennessee,* 154–155. During the 1789 congressional debate over extending a pardon to John Sevier for his actions as Franklin's governor, the North Carolina Assembly acknowledged that he originally attempted to delay separatist efforts to hold a vote on statehood among the Tennessee Valley residents.

36. Williams, *History of the Lost State of Franklin,* 57–63; Alderman, *The Overmountain Men,* 194.

37. Griffey, *Earliest Tennessee Land Records,* 80–81, 126–128, 131–133, 136, 200, 385.

38. Alderman, *The Overmountain Men,* 194; Ramsey, *The Annals of Tennessee,* 292–293.

39. Isaac C. Anderson to Governor David Campbell, April 11, 1846, King's Mountain Papers (DD), Draper Manuscript Collection; Griffey, *Earliest Tennessee Land Records,* 477–478; Haywood, *The Civil and Political History of Tennessee,* 155–156. Wayne County was carved out of Washington County. Caswell and Spencer counties were carved out of Hawkins County. Sevier County was carved out of Greene County and a portion of land reserved for the Cherokee (East Tennessee Historical Society, *First Families of Tennessee,* 66–67).

40. Griffey, *Earliest Tennessee Land Records,* 126, 131–134, 141–142, 165–174, 213–214, 227, 253, 339–340, 408; Ramsey, *The Annals of Tennessee,* 295–296.

41. Alexander Martin to Samuel Henderson, February 27, 1785, Newspaper Abstracts (JJ), Draper Manuscript Collection; Williams, *History of the Lost State of Franklin,* 61–63; Finger, *Tennessee Frontiers,* 49–50. Richard Henderson and his fellow Transylvania Company associates purchased 20 million acres of land in the Kentucky territory and Middle Tennessee from the Cherokee, pulling off one of the largest private land deals in North American history.

42. Fink, "Some Phases of the History of the State of Franklin," 197–199; Henderson, *North Carolina,* 388; Ramsey, *The Annals of Tennessee,* 292–294. Judge Richard Henderson controlled the successful land-speculating organization known as the Transylvania Company.

43. Clark, ed., *The State Records of North Carolina,* vol. 22, 637–642; Landon Carter and William Cage to Alexander Martin, March 22, 1785, Newspaper Abstracts (JJ), Draper Manuscript Collection. A copy of Carter and Cage's letter to Martin is also contained in Alexander Martin's Governor Letter Book in the North Carolina State Archives in Raleigh.

44. John Sevier to Alexander Martin, March 22, 1785, Alexander Martin's Governor Letter Book, North Carolina State Archives.

45. Clark, ed., *The State Records of North Carolina,* vol. 22, 642–647; Alexander Martin to John Tipton, April 25, 1785, King's Mountain Papers (DD), Draper Manuscript Collection.

46. Sevier counter-manifesto, May 14, 1785, Letters concerning the indepen-

dence of the State of Franklin, North Carolina State Archives; "State of Franklin: A Proclamation," May 15, 1785, Newspaper Abstracts (JJ), Draper Manuscript Collection; Williams, *History of the Lost State of Franklin,* 72–73; Clark, ed., *The State Records of North Carolina,* vol. 22, 648. John Sevier was the sole name on the counter-manifesto.

47. Alexander Martin enclosed a copy of his manifesto in the April 25 letter he sent to John Tipton. Tipton's expression of loyalty convinced Governor Martin that it was "proper to send you the enclosed manifesto," and he requested that Tipton "make the same [manifesto] public thru your county" (Alexander Martin to John Tipton, April 25, 1785, King's Mountain Papers [DD], Draper Manuscript Collection).

48. Foster, *Franklin: The Stillborn State,* 7.

49. Williams, *History of the Lost State of Franklin,* 73–76. The Muscle Shoals project lasted from 1783 to 1789 and eventually became intertwined with the state of Franklin (A.P. Whitaker, "The Muscle Shoals Speculation," *Mississippi Valley Historical Review* 12 [December 1926]: 365–367). Sevier biographer Carl Driver argues that Sevier's discouragement of the independence movement in 1784 and early 1785 among his fellow Tennessee Valley residents was economically motivated. "Sevier actually began to discourage the creation of a new state because he was afraid it would interfere with the Muscle Shoals speculating project he was involved in" (Carl Driver, *John Sevier: Pioneer of the Old Southwest* [Chapel Hill: Univ. of North Carolina Press, 1932], 72–87).

50. Griffey, *Earliest Tennessee Land Records,* 134, 361.

51. John Sevier to Richard Caswell, May 14, 1785, Letters concerning the independence of the State of Franklin, North Carolina State Archives.

52. Clark, ed., *The State Records of North Carolina,* vol. 22, 648.

53. John Sevier to Richard Caswell, May 14, 1785, Letters concerning the independence of the State of Franklin, North Carolina State Archives.

54. "Letter from a gentlemen in Franklin to his friend in Virginia," August 17, 1785, Newspaper Abstracts (JJ), Draper Manuscript Collection; Alice Barnwell Keith, *The John Gray Blount Papers,* vol. 1, *1764–1789* (Raleigh: State Department of Archives and History, 1952), 191.

55. Cannon, "Four Interpretations of the History of the State of Franklin," 3–5; Quinn, *Arthur Campbell,* 81; Ramsey, *The Annals of Tennessee,* 313–318.

56. Conley, *The Cherokee Nation,* 73–74. Only a small contingent of younger Cherokee chiefs, including Ancoo, Chief of Chota; Abraham, Chief of Chilhowe; the Bard, the Sturgeon, the Leach, the Big Man Killer, and the translator Cherokee Murphy, agreed to the Treaty of Dumplin Creek (Clark, ed., *The State Records of North Carolina,* vol. 22, 649–650).

57. Williams, *History of the Lost State of Franklin,* 77; Holton, *Forced Founders,* 3–37.

58. Landon Carter and William Cage to the Continental Congress, May 16, 1785, Letters concerning the independence of the State of Franklin, North Carolina State Archives.

59. Williams, *History of the Lost State of Franklin*, 85–88.

60. Paul H. Smith, ed., *Letters of Delegates to Congress*, vol. 22 (Washington, D.C.: Library of Congress, 1976), 434–435.

61. Williams, *History of the Lost State of Franklin*, 83–88; Alderman, *The Overmountain Men*, 203–204.

62. Julian P. Boyd, ed., *The Papers of Thomas Jefferson*, vol. 8, *25 February to 31 October 1785* (Princeton: Princeton Univ. Press, 1953), 508.

63. Sketch of the Life of General William Cocke, William Johnston Cocke Papers, Southern Historical Collection, Manuscripts Department, Wilson Library, University of North Carolina at Chapel Hill.

64. No records exist regarding the August assembly at Jonesboro, but Williams states that the Franklinites hoped to expand their state's boundaries by passing an act "for the encouragement of an expedition down the Tennessee river to take possession of the Bent [present-day Muscle Shoals, Alabama]" (Williams, *History of the Lost State of Franklin*, 90–93).

65. Richard Alan Humphrey, "The State of Franklin: Clergy, Controversy, and Constitution," *Appalachian Heritage: A Magazine of Southern Appalachian Life and Culture* 7 (fall 1979): 35–36.

66. Clark, ed., *The State Records of North Carolina*, vol. 22, 637–640.

67. James William Hagy, "Democracy Defeated: The Franklin Constitution of 1785," *Tennessee Historical Quarterly* 40 (fall 1981): 240. According to Richard Alan Humphrey, the Tennessee Valley's Presbyterian leadership wielded more political influence than the region's Methodist and Baptist leaders because they "outnumbered" the other denominations, had more "educated clergy," established more churches (twenty-three) and academies (two), and "took an active interest in the political establishment of the State of Franklin" (Humphrey, "The State of Franklin," 35–36).

68. William Graham also taught Samuel Doak, Hezekiah Balch, Samuel Newell, and David Campbell at Liberty Hall (Hagy, "Democracy Defeated," 244–246).

69. Joshua W. Caldwell, *Constitutional History of Tennessee* (Cincinnati: Robert Clarke Company, 1895), 58–61; Fink, "Some Phases of the History of the State of Franklin," 204; J. T. McGill, "Franklin and Frankland: Names and Boundaries," *Tennessee Historical Magazine* 8 (1924): 248–250; Quinn, *Arthur Campbell*, 82–88; Ramsey, *The Annals of Tennessee*, 323–334; Williams, *History of the Lost State of Franklin*, 94–97; Philyaw, *Virginia's Western Visions*, 112. The use of the name Frankland by Campbell and Houston symbolized the democratic principles espoused in the document. The rejection of the name Frankland, or "land of free-

men," and the adoption of Franklin, named for Benjamin Franklin, by the assembly signaled the end of radicalism within the statehood movement.

70. Ramsey, *The Annals of Tennessee,* 323–324.

71. Hagy, "Democracy Defeated," 249–251.

72. Ibid., 246–252.

73. Humphrey, "The State of Franklin," 37.

74. Fink, "Some Phases of the History of the State of Franklin," 206–207; Ramsey, *The Annals of Tennessee,* 323–324; Williams, *History of the Lost State of Franklin,* 95–98.

75. In his work on the constitutional debate, James Hagy establishes two competing constitutional camps and downplays the influence economic considerations and future land dealings played in the constitutional debate. He argues that "the records [of the constitutional convention] do not support [the] interpretation" that the democratic frame of government presented by Houston and Graham "was killed by the desire for land." Instead Hagy believes that the defeat of the radical Franklin Constitution occurred because "men like John Sevier . . . did not want to lose their status by a constitution which would limit the control of the governor or other officials." Additionally, Hagy believes that the Franklinites' believed that the acceptance of the North Carolina Constitution "would drive less of a wedge between" the parent state of North Carolina and the Franklinites and further the efforts of William Cocke to secure acceptance of Franklin (Hagy, "Democracy Defeated," 250–256).

76. According to Thomas Perkins Abernethy, "if this influence [Sevier and his land speculation financiers William Blount and Richard Caswell] could be overthrown by adopting a really democratic form of government, anyone who had power and influence might acquire property in the new country" (Abernethy, *From Frontier to Plantation,* 78–79). Rachel N. Klein describes a similar dynamic that occurred in the South Carolina backcountry during the French Revolution. South Carolina backcountry slaveholders were concerned that the "democratic-republican political ideas" inspired by the French Revolution could potentially lead "in dangerously radical [political] directions" (Klein, *Unification of a Slave State,* 203).

77. Caldwell, *Tennessee: The Dangerous Example,* 166–167; Williams, *History of the Lost State of Franklin,* 96.

78. Clark, ed., *The State Records of North Carolina,* vol. 21, 43.

4. Strange Spectacle of Two Empires

1. Bergeron, Ash, and Keith, *Tennesseans and Their History,* 44; Ramsey, *The Annals of Tennessee,* 339; Foster, *Franklin: The Stillborn State,* 10; Haywood, *The Civil and Political History of Tennessee,* 173.

2. Richard Caswell to John Sevier, July 12, 1786, Tennessee Papers (XX),

Draper Manuscript Collection. As historian Thomas Abernethy succinctly states, "there could have existed, under the circumstances, no real hostilities between Caswell and Sevier, although legally Sevier was governor of a state in rebellion against the state of which Caswell was governor" (Abernethy, *From Frontier to Plantation in Tennessee*, 80–81).

3. Bergeron, Ash, and Keith, *Tennesseans and Their History*, 44; Finger, *Tennessee Frontiers*, 114.

4. Cox and Cox, comps., *History of Washington County, Tennessee*, 85.

5. Foster, *Franklin: The Stillborn State*, 10–11.

6. Cox and Cox, comps., *History of Washington County, Tennessee*, 85.

7. Haywood, *The Civil and Political History of Tennessee*, 173; Ramsey, *The Annals of Tennessee*, 337–339.

8. Clark, ed., *The State Records of North Carolina*, vol. 18, 243–245; Haywood, *The Civil and Political History of Tennessee*, 172–173.

9. Franklin historian Samuel Cole Williams characterized these parallel elections as "a fatal error" (Williams, *History of the Lost State of Franklin*, 107–109).

10. John Allison, *Dropped Stitches in Tennessee History* (Nashville: Marshall and Bruce, 1897), 32; Caldwell, *Tennessee: The Dangerous Example*, 173–175; Foster, *Franklin: The Stillborn State*, 10. In his study of the expansion of Virginia's western frontier following Lord Dunmore's War, Scott Philyaw also describes the emergence of two competing court systems established in the District of Augusta by the states of Virginia and Pennsylvania. In a series of events that mirrored the Franklin debacle, Philyaw argues, "Within this chaotic cauldron of competing claims and loyalties, some western settlers took the inevitable next step" of promoting the formation of a fourteenth colony (Philyaw, *Virginia's Western Visions*, 71–72).

11. Lawson, "The Tipton-Hayes Place," 108–109.

12. Haywood, *The Civil and Political History of Tennessee*, 175; Ramsey, *The Annals of Tennessee*, 338–339; Watauga Association of Genealogists, *History of Washington County*, 21. It does not appear as though the Franklinites elected a representative to the North Carolina Senate, and the North Carolina House of Commons did not qualify the elections of either Carter or Chapman. None of the Franklinites attended the November convening of the North Carolina Assembly. Samuel Cole Williams points out that a number of old state supporters accused Franklin's militia of threatening violence if they did not vote in Jonesboro (Williams, *History of the Lost State of Franklin*, 107–109).

13. In a report read before the North Carolina House of Commons on November 23, 1786, John Tipton and Thomas Hutchings state that "Inhabitants [of Washington County] were warned to meet at the last mentioned Election [elections held by Franklinites in August 1786] by the acting Military officer of said county at General Muster under certain penalty." The report goes on to accuse

Franklinites of "deterring" residents from "attending the [North Carolina–inspected] elections" with "the above mentioned threats" (Clark, ed., *The State Records of North Carolina,* vol. 18, 243–245).

14. Klein, *Unification of a Slave State,* 107–108.

15. Bergeron, Ash, and Keith, *Tennesseans and Their History,* 44; Clark, ed., *The State Records of North Carolina,* vol. 18, 243–245. Both sides appointed their own poll inspectors. Joseph Tipton (John Tipton's son), Robert English, and William Hughes served as election inspectors for the Tiptonite-backed elections in Washington County, and Robert Rogers, Samuel William, and Anderson Smith oversaw the Franklin elections (Ramsey, *The Annals of Tennessee,* 238–239; Williams, *History of the Lost State of Franklin,* 108–109).

16. Haywood, *The Civil and Political History of Tennessee,* 173–174; Ramsey, *The Annals of Tennessee,* 339.

17. Henderson, "Nolachucky Jack," King's Mountain Papers (DD), Draper Manuscript Collection.

18. Judge John Haywood's account of the courtroom raids serves as the only contemporary account of these incidents. Haywood also states that the court records of both judicial systems "were retaken" by each side several more times and eventually most of the important legal records (including marriage and estate records) were lost. These courthouse raids also resulted in the loss of the majority of the state of Franklin's historical records (Haywood, *The Civil and Political History of Tennessee,* 173–174).

19. Fink, "Some Phases of the History of the State of Franklin," 207–208.

20. Haywood, *The Civil and Political History of Tennessee,* 173–174.

21. Caldwell, *Tennessee: The Dangerous Example,* 175.

22. Henderson, "Nolachucky Jack," King's Mountain Papers (DD), Draper Manuscript Collection.

23. Haywood, *The Civil and Political History of Tennessee,* 173–174.

24. Clark, ed., *The State Records of North Carolina,* vol. 20, 396; John Sevier to Benjamin Franklin, April 9, 1787, in *The Works of Benjamin Franklin,* vol. 10, ed. Jared Sparks (Boston: Whitemore, Niles, and Hall, 1856), 290–291.

25. Alderman, *The Overmountain Men,* 215; Ramsey, *The Annals of Tennessee,* 347.

26. Clark, ed., *The State Records of North Carolina,* vol. 22, 659–661, 672–673.

27. Ibid.

28. Haywood, *The Civil and Political History of Tennessee,* 177–179; Alderman, *The Overmountain Men,* 215. A sudden illness costing David Campbell the use of his eye prevented the Franklin judge from attending the session, but he dispatched a letter, carried by William Cocke, to Governor Caswell presenting his case for separation (Clark, ed., *The State Records of North Carolina,* vol. 22, 659–661,

672–673). In all probability, the Franklinites formulated these new political arguments for independence at the October 1786 Franklin convention.

29. Clark, ed., *The State Records of North Carolina*, vol. 22, 660–661.

30. Clark, ed., *The State Records of North Carolina*, vol. 18, 790–791.

31. Mary French Caldwell described William Cocke as a "magnificent" man, a "tall, handsome, well-proportioned man, with dark skin, black hair, and flashing black eyes," and whose appearance could "capture the attention of his audience even before his masterful appeal was heard" (Caldwell, *Tennessee: A Dangerous Example*, 171–172).

32. Clark, ed., *The State Records of North Carolina*, vol. 22, 651–652. The November session of the North Carolina General Assembly commenced on November 20, 1786. In a response penned on February 23, 1787, Governor Caswell assured John Sevier that "nature never designed the settlers there [Franklin] to be longer under the same Government [North Carolina] with the people here, than their numbers and opulence would enable them to support a Government of their own" (Clark, ed., *The State Records of North Carolina*, vol. 20, 617–618).

33. Clark, ed., *The State Records of North Carolina*, vol. 18, 85–86; vol. 22, 653–654.

34. Clark, ed., *The State Records of North Carolina*, vol. 22, 653–654.

35. Clark, ed., *The State Records of North Carolina*, vol. 18, 85–87, 89, 96, 112, 130, 324, 354, 355. The North Carolina Assembly actually passed the bill of pardon a few days later.

36. Clark, ed., *The State Records of North Carolina*, vol. 18, 117, 133, 158, 171, 183, 358; Williams, *History of the Lost State of Franklin*, 119–120.

37. John Sevier to Benjamin Franklin, April 9, 1787, in Sparks, ed., *The Works of Benjamin Franklin*, vol. 10, 290–291.

38. Kastor, "Equitable Rights and Privileges," 209.

39. Boyd, ed., *The Papers of Thomas Jefferson*, vol. 8, 215–261, 279–280, 286–288, 508; Kastor, "Equitable Rights and Privileges," 214–215.

40. According to Scott Philyaw, Thomas Jefferson "stood almost alone in his belief that the West—not the East—should direct western destiny, even to the point of political independence." Jefferson's western ideology eventually found political expression in his work on the "Confederation's congressional Committee on Western Lands" and the drafting of the Ordinance of 1784 (Philyaw, *Virginia's Western Visions*, 97–100, 111–112).

41. Harold C. Syrett, ed., *The Papers of Alexander Hamilton*, vol. 4, *January 1787–May 1788* (New York: Columbia Univ. Press, 1962), 316–317.

42. Caldwell, *Tennessee: A Dangerous Example*, 169–171.

43. Historian John Finger appropriately described this coalition as "a marriage of convenience between Georgia and Franklin, arranged by speculators." William

Blount "served as paymaster" for North Carolina troops in the Revolutionary War and was elected to the North Carolina Assembly in 1781 and as a state delegate to Continental Congress in 1782. Finger argues that "From the outset his [Blount's] politics and business were inseparable" (Finger, *Tennessee Frontiers,* 99–100, 107, 113).

44. Whitaker, "The Muscle Shoals Speculation," 365–366, 369–370.

45. *Cherokee and Creek Indians,* Ethnographic Report on Royce, Area 79: Chickasaw, Cherokee, Creek [by] Charles Fairbanks; Cherokee Treaties [by] John H. Goff, Commission Findings [by] Indian Claims Commission (New York: Garland Publishing, 1974), 102–105; Ramsey, *The Annals of Tennessee,* 376–377; Cora Bales Sevier and Nancy S. Madden, *Sevier Family History with the Collected Letters of Gen. John Sevier, First Governor of Tennessee* (Washington, D.C.: privately published, 1961), 59.

46. Abernethy, *From Frontier to Plantation in Tennessee,* 64–67, 75–76, 80.

47. Whitaker, "The Muscle Shoals Speculation," 366–371; Ramsey, *The Annals of Tennessee,* 377–378. The 1782 survey also proved that South Carolina held a claim to some of the Muscle Shoals district, and the Muscle Shoals land company also invited a number of prominent Palmetto State figures, including Wade Hampton, to join the business commission (Finger, *Tennessee Frontiers,* 107; Abernethy, *From Frontier to Plantation in Tennessee,* 64–67, 75–76, 80).

48. *Cherokee and Creek Indians,* 104–106; Kenneth Coleman, general ed., *A History of Georgia* (Athens: Univ. of Georgia Press, 1977), 91. The state of Georgia suffered under financial strains similar to those of North Carolina and the state of Franklin. The loss of British markets, a shortage of specie, mounting debt, and the enormous expense of combating the Native American groups threatened the financial stability of Georgia.

49. Kathryn E. Holland Braund, *Deerskins and Duffels: The Creek Indian Trade with Anglo-America, 1685–1815* (Lincoln: Univ. of Nebraska Press, 1993), 172–173.

50. Palmer, ed., *Calendar of Virginia State Papers,* vol. 4, 333–334.

51. Braund, *Deerskins and Duffels,* 172–173.

52. Abernethy, *From Frontier to Plantation in Tennessee,* 80; *Cherokee and Creek Indians,* 6–8, 108–109; Coleman, *A History of Georgia,* 92–93; Robbie Ethridge, *Creek Country: The Creek Indians and Their World* (Chapel Hill: Univ. of North Carolina Press, 2003), 11; Michael D. Green, *The Politics of Indian Removal: Creek Government and Society in Crisis* (Lincoln: Univ. of Nebraska Press, 1982), 33–34. Alexander McGillivray served as an outspoken and skilled leader of the Upper Creeks. McGillivray was the son of Scottish trader Lachlan McGillivray and a "woman of the Wind Clan" from the Creek town of Octiapofa (Hickory Ground). McGillivray emerged as one of the most influential leaders of the Creeks after the American Revolution. Before the revolution, McGillivray's father sent

him to Charleston, South Carolina, for "schooling," and he was given a "position in the British Indian Department" by British Superintendent of Indian Affairs John Stuart (Braund, *Deerskins and Duffels*, 45, 168, 261). He opposed any land cession to white settlers and managed to utilize diplomatic relations with the Spanish, British, and American governments to benefit his Creek followers. It remains unclear whether the Franklinites understood the similarities between their political agenda and that of the Creek Nation. The Creek Nation was divided into two groups, the Lower Creeks and Upper Creeks. The Upper Creeks inhabited the upper Chattahoochee River Valley in present-day Georgia and the Coosa, Tallapoosa, and upper Alabama rivers in present-day Alabama (John Walton Caughey, *McGillivray of the Creeks* [Norman: Univ. of Oklahoma Press, 1938], 3–6).

53. Whitaker, "The Muscle Shoals Speculation," 371.

54. Ibid., 374.

55. Clark, ed., *The State Records of North Carolina*, vol. 20, 619–620.

56. Clark, ed., *The State Records of North Carolina*, vol. 22, 676–678.

57. Richard Caswell to John Sevier, July 12, 1786, Tennessee Papers (XX), Draper Manuscript Collection.

58. Clark, ed., *The State Records of North Carolina*, vol. 18, 607–608, 756–758; Finger, *Tennessee Frontiers*, 113–114. In February 1787, Governor Caswell made several attempts to have Franklin and Georgia force the removal of their citizens from the Creek lands near the Muscle Shoals district. In an April 1, 1787, response to Governor Caswell's demands for the removal of Franklin citizens from the disputed territory, Colonel Thomas Hutchins informed the governor that "The People on the Indian Hunting Grounds I learn are very Obstinate & suppose will pay little or no respect to your Excellency's Proclamation for their Removal" (Clark, ed., *The State Records of North Carolina*, vol. 22, 678–679).

59. Ramsey, *The Annals of Tennessee*, 376–382.

60. Williams, *History of the Lost State of Franklin*, 140, 309–310.

61. William Bacon Stevens, *A History of Georgia, From Its First Discovery by Europeans to the Adoption of the Present Constitution in MDCCXCVIII*, vol. 2 (Savannah: Beehive Press, 1972), 380–382.

62. *New York Gazette*, September 29, 1787, Draper's Notes (S), Draper Manuscript Collection; Haywood, *The Civil and Political History of Tennessee*, 172. At the March 1787 assemblage of the Franklin legislature, the Franklinites honored Elholm by naming one of the two newly created districts the Elholm District. The representatives of Franklin named the other district the Washington District, thus elevating Elholm to the level of one of America's most celebrated citizens (Williams, *History of the Lost State of Franklin*, 140). In a letter addressed to Joseph Martin a few weeks after the Battle of Franklin, an angry Tiptonite offered a far less glowing account of George Elholm's emigration from Europe. According to the author, "As to Major Elholm, there needs to be no more said of him, than that

the cause of his Coming to America was his wanting to dispose of the King of Poland and his granting a free toleration in religion to his subjects. That he sacrificed his native country, his fortune, and his friends to his ambition" (Member of the Tipton Party to Joseph Martin, August 20, 1788, King's Mountain Papers [DD], Draper Manuscript Collection). After the eventual abandonment of the military invasion of the Creek lands in 1788, Elholm remained in the region and served as the Franklin militia's "adjunct and drill-master" (Williams, *History of the Lost State of Franklin*, 309–310).

63. Stevens, *A History of Georgia*, vol. 2, 380–382.

64. Ramsey, *The Annals of Tennessee*, 378–383.

65. Clark, ed., *The State Records of North Carolina*, vol. 18, 758; Ramsey, *The Annals of Tennessee*, 378–383.

66. George Elholm to Edward Telfair, September 30, 1786, John Sevier Papers, Tennessee State Library and Archives.

67. Ramsey, *The Annals of Tennessee*, 378–383.

68. J. Meriweather, July 20, 1787, King's Mountain Papers (DD), Draper Manuscript Collection.

69. John Sevier to George Mathews, June 25, 1787, William Alexander Provine Papers, Tennessee State Library and Archives.

70. John Sevier to Gilbert Christian, November 28, 1787, John Sevier Papers, Tennessee State Library and Archives; Ramsey, *The Annals of Tennessee*, 399.

71. Ramsey, *The Annals of Tennessee*, 383–387.

72. Ibid.

73. Ibid. According to Pat Alderman, Elijah Clark "had been a guest in [Sevier's] home" (Alderman, *The Overmountain Men*, 219).

74. Ramsey, *The Annals of Tennessee*, 397.

75. Palmer, ed., *Calendar of Virginia State Papers*, vol. 4, 353–354.

76. Whitaker, "The Muscle Shoals Speculation," 374–376. Whitaker described Georgia's Governor Hadley as "more pacific" than former Governor Mathews.

77. Stevens, *A History of Georgia*, 382–383.

78. In a September 19, 1787, letter, Landon Carter informed John Sevier of the ongoing survey of "six hundred and forty [acres] each which will be the size of the warrants when made out." Carter does not mention the location of the surveys, but the historical context of the letter points toward the Muscle Shoals property (Sevier and Madden, *Sevier Family History*, 81, 86–87, 92).

79. Stevens, *A History of Georgia*, 382–383; Whitaker, "The Muscle Shoals Speculation," 374–376.

80. Abernethy, *From Frontier to Plantation in Tennessee*, 84–85; *Cherokee and Creek Indians*, 105; Clark, ed., *The State Records of North Carolina*, vol. 21, 527–528; Foster, *Franklin: The Stillborn State*, 15–16; Ramsey, *The Annals of Tennessee*, 383–400; Williams, *History of the Lost State of Franklin*, 189–193.

5. Where the Fire of Peace Is Always Kept Burning

1. King Fisher "Talk" to Joseph Martin, June 8, 1787, Cherokee Collection, Tennessee State Library and Archives. Joseph Martin is considered by many scholars to have been the Cherokee's closest ally. Martin lived among the Cherokee for several years and eventually married Betsy, the daughter of the Cherokee's "beloved woman" Nancy Ward. Martin's familial connections with the tribe and long tenure as a North Carolina, Virginia, and U.S. Indian Agent often placed him in precarious positions during the decades of frontier conflict (Williams, *History of the Lost State of Franklin,* 217).

2. Holton, *Forced Founders,* 3–37.

3. David J. Weber, *The Spanish Frontier in North America* (New Haven, Conn.: Yale Univ. Press, 1992), 52–53; Conley, *The Cherokee Nation,* 17–20.

4. Weber, *The Spanish Frontier in North America,* 71; Conley, *The Cherokee Nation,* 19.

5. Finger argues that epidemic diseases brought by the Spanish, such as smallpox, measles, and influenza, and internal tensions led to the dissolution of the Mississippian chiefdoms (Van West, ed., *Tennessee History,* 7–8). For more information on the prehistoric ancestors of the Cherokee, see Roy S. Dickens Jr., "The Origin and Development of Cherokee Culture," in *The Cherokee Indian Nation: A Troubled History,* ed. Duane H. King (Knoxville: Univ. of Tennessee Press, 1979), 3–32.

6. Dunaway, *The First American Frontier,* 31–32; McLoughlin, *Cherokee Renaissance,* 4–5.

7. McLoughlin, *Cherokee Renaissance,* 12–13. Other tribal groups also occupied the Tennessee River Valley, including Creeks and Choctaws. The Cherokee tribe was divided into three general groupings, Overhill (Upper), Middle, and Lower (Valley) Cherokee. The Overhill Cherokee occupied East Tennessee and western North Carolina. The Middle Cherokee resided in South Carolina, and the Lower Cherokee lived in North Georgia (Mooney, *History, Myths, and Sacred Formulas of the Cherokees,* 14–16; Conley, *The Cherokee Nation,* 25).

8. Davis, *Where There Are Mountains,* 59–70; East Tennessee Historical Society, *First Families of Tennessee,* 33; Van West, *Tennessee History,* 8–9.

9. Finger, *Tennessee Frontier,* 24–25.

10. Van West, *Tennessee History,* 9–10; King, *The Cherokee Indian Nation,* 34–43. James Needham eventually organized a small party, comprising Overhill Cherokee, Oconeechee, and a Native American translator named Indian John, to return to Fort Henry and formally establish trade relations. Indian John murdered Needham before they could reach the Appomattox River, and nineteen-year-old Gabriel Arthur spent the next year living with the Cherokee at Chota (Conley, *The Cherokee Nation,* 21–22).

11. Davis, *Where There Are Mountains,* 59–70; Dunaway, *The First American Frontier,* 31–35; Finger, *Tennessee Frontiers,* 22–26; McLoughlin, *Cherokee Renaissance,* 6–7.

12. McLoughlin, *Cherokee Renaissance,* 6–7.

13. According to John Finger, "Trade . . . was usually the dominant consideration in relations with Britain, France, Spain, and later the United States" (Finger, *Tennessee Frontiers,* 24–27).

14. William G. McLoughlin states that the Cherokee actually "honored their alliance with England" until 1760, but then "some Cherokee switched sides" (McLoughlin, *Cherokee Renaissance,* 17–18).

15. The Cherokee initially agreed to ally with the English during the French and Indian War. The Cherokee demanded that the English construct forts near their principal towns in order to provide protection from the French and their Indian allies. The English responded by constructing Fort Loudon near the Cherokee town of Tellico on the Little Tennessee River. Eventually the Cherokee sided with the French during the conflict, and on August 8, 1760, Fort Loudon fell to a sizeable force of warriors led by Oconostota, chief of the Overhill Cherokee. The Cherokee destroyed the fort and, after allowing the women and children to escape, eventually executed the fort's commander, Raymond Demere, and twenty-nine English soldiers. The fort's second in command, Captain John Stuart, escaped execution with the help of Cherokee chief Atakullakulla (Little Carpenter), and the Englishman eventually became Superintendent of the Southern Tribes under the victorious British regime. Captain Stuart also became one of the most sympathetic British officials to the Cherokee tribe (Mooney, *History, Myths, and Sacred Formulas of the Cherokee,* 39–45; Conley, *The Cherokee Nation,* 45–55).

16. Alderman, *The Overmountain Men,* 4–5; John Preston Arthur, *Western North Carolina: A History from 1730 to 1913* (Johnson City, Tenn.: Overmountain Press, 1996), 68–69; Ramsey, *The Annals of Tennessee,* 56–60; Van West, *Tennessee History,* 10–12; McLoughlin, *Cherokee Renaissance,* 18.

17. Mooney, *History, Myths, and Sacred Formulas of the Cherokee,* 45–46; Conley, *The Cherokee Nation,* 54.

18. Holton, *Forced Founders,* 6–7.

19. Davis, *Where There Are Mountains,* 94–95; Conley, *The Cherokee Nation,* 54–55. According to Woody Holton, the Proclamation Line of 1763 had its greatest impact on Virginia's land speculators, many of whom were members of Virginia's leading colonial families (Arthur Lee, George Washington, Patrick Henry, and Thomas Jefferson). Holton very convincingly argues that Britain's own Native American policies (including the Proclamation of 1763 and the Treaty of Hard Labor [1768]) fostered revolutionary discontent among Virginia's gentry and ultimately played a significant role in initiating America's independence movement (Holton, *Forced Founders,* 3–37).

20. Alderman, *The Overmountain Men*, 12; Dixon, *The Wataugans*, 4; Ramsey, *The Annals of Tennessee*, 68–71. King George III forbade English colonists from trespassing on Native American lands. King George clearly wanted to avoid another round of expensive Indian warfare and also hoped to prevent the loss of tax revenue from settlers venturing into the American backcountry.

21. Callaway, *America's First Western Frontier*, 70–72. The Cherokee ceded 850 square miles with the Treaty of Hard Labor, 9,050 square miles (544,000 acres) with the Treaty of Lochaber, 10,917 square miles (6,986,800 acres) with an unnamed 1772 treaty with Virginia, and 1,050 square miles (672,000 acres) with another unnamed treaty with Georgia (McLoughlin, *Cherokee Renaissance*, 26–29; Conley, *The Cherokee Nation*, 249).

22. The Cherokee signed the Treaty of Hard Labor on October 14, 1768. The treaty extended the boundaries of Virginia and North Carolina but did not include the Watauga settlements. The Treaty of Lochaber, signed on October 18, 1770, further extended the boundaries established by the Treaty of Hard Labor. Despite these land treaties, most of the Watauga settlers remained squatters on Cherokee land (Mooney, *History, Myths, and Sacred Formulas of the Cherokee*, 45–46).

23. Davis, *Where There Are Mountains*, 94–95; Dixon, *The Wataugans*, 5–7, 10.

24. Arthur, *Western North Carolina*, 66–67; McLoughlin, *Cherokee Renaissance*, 19.

25. Unknown European diseases, such as smallpox, typhus, whooping cough, and measles, decimated the Cherokee population (McLoughlin, *Cherokee Renaissance*, 19).

26. Haywood, *The Civil and Political History of Tennessee*, 53–56; Van West, *Tennessee History*, 13–15.

27. Dixon, *The Wataugans*, 6–12, 16–18.

28. Conley, *The Cherokee Nation*, 58–60. In addition to Dragging Canoe, Cherokee chiefs such as The Glass, Bloody Fellow, Tolluntuskee, Fool Charles, The Badger, Will Weber, Will Elders, Doublehead, Pumpkin Boy, Unacata, and John Watts all protested land cessions (McLoughlin, *Cherokee Renaissance*, 20).

29. Hamer, "The Wataugans and the Cherokee Indians in 1776," 114–115.

30. Atakullakulla (also spelled Attakullakulla, Attacullaculla, and Adagal'kala) is described as a man who "was remarkably small, and of slender and delicate frame; but he was endowed with superior abilities." The Cherokee chief was best known for his diplomatic skill and became the primary advocate among the Cherokee for appeasement (Van West, *Tennessee History*, 14–15; Conley, *The Cherokee Nation*, 243–244). Oconostota (Agan'stat') and Atakullakulla both agreed to the Henderson Purchase (McLoughlin, *Cherokee Renaissance*, 19).

31. John Ehle, *Trail of Tears: The Rise and Fall of the Cherokee Nation* (New

York: Anchor Books, Doubleday, 1988), 14–17; Albert V. Goodpasture, "Indian Wars and Warriors of the Old Southwest, 1730–1807," *Tennessee Historical Magazine* 4 (March 1918): 4–5.

32. Randolph C. Downes, "Cherokee-American Relations in the Upper Tennessee Valley, 1776–1791," *East Tennessee Historical Society's Publications* 8 (1936): 35–36; McLoughlin, *Cherokee Renaissance,* 19.

33. Hamer, "The Wataugans and the Cherokee Indians in 1776," 108–109.

34. Ramsey, *The Annals of Tennessee,* 149–165.

35. After learning of Dragging Canoe's plans for a Second Cherokee War, the Watauga settlers appealed to North Carolina and Virginia for help with the impending attack. In response, North Carolina created the Washington District out of the southernmost settlements and Virginia created the Pendleton District out of the northern settlements (thought to be in Virginia). The Washington District became Washington County, North Carolina, and the Pendleton District became Sullivan County, North Carolina (Alderman, *The Overmountain Men,* 29–34).

36. The actions of Nancy Ward during the American Revolution made the Cherokee councilwoman a frontier legend. She is given credit with saving the life of William Bean's wife, Lydia, after she was captured during the attack on Fort Watauga (Callaway, *America's First Western Frontier,* 97–105). The white traders Ward contacted were named Thomas, Williams, and Fawlings (Conley, *The Cherokee Nation,* 60). According to Conley, Nancy Ward was either Dragging Canoe's sister or first cousin (Conley, *The Cherokee Nation,* 68).

37. Conley, *The Cherokee Nation,* 64.

38. Many of the leaders of the state of Franklin movement participated in repelling the Cherokee invasion and in Colonel Christian's counterinvasion, including John Sevier, Gilbert Christian, William Cocke, John Campbell, John Carter, Evan Shelby, and Joseph Rhea (Ramsey, *The Annals of Tennessee,* 149–165).

39. The July 20 parlay was with the states of North Carolina and Virginia, and was preceded by another treaty, held on May 20, conducted with negotiators representing South Carolina and Georgia. The Cherokee ceded 2,051 square miles with the May treaty and 6,174 square miles with the July treaty (McLoughlin, *Cherokee Renaissance,* 26).

40. Mooney, *History, Myths, and Sacred Formulas of the Cherokee,* 52–54; Van West, *Tennessee History,* 16. The Treaty of Great Island is also called the Treaty of Long Island but should not be confused with the Treaty of Long Island conducted in 1781. The Cherokee ceded all of the Watauga settlements with the Treaty of Great Island.

41. Conley, *The Cherokee Nation,* 65, 250; McLoughlin, *Cherokee Renaissance,* 20; Williams, *History of the Lost State of Franklin,* 303. Historian John Finger argues that the Chickamauga Cherokee "were complex in composition." "Besides an undeniable core of Overhill Cherokee, they incorporated an exotic mix of peoples

whose common denominator was opposition to white settlement." This mixture included Creeks, Shawnees, Delaware, a few African Americans, and "whites ranging from prominent traders to French-speaking boatmen" (Van West, *Tennessee History,* 16).

42. Callaway, *America's First Western Frontier,* 107; McLoughlin, *Cherokee Renaissance,* 20. By 1780, there were roughly five hundred Chickamauga Cherokee (Van West, *Tennessee History,* 16).

43. Conley, *The Cherokee Nation,* 66. British agents and British loyalists lived among the Chickamauga Cherokee throughout the American Revolution. Many of these men married into Cherokee families and participated in Dragging Canoe's guerilla war against the Tennessee Valley settlers (McLoughlin, *Cherokee Renaissance,* 20).

44. Alderman, *The Overmountain Men,* 49; Mooney, *History, Myths, and Sacred Formulas of the Cherokee,* 55.

45. Major James Sevier to Lyman C. Draper, August 19, 1839, John Sevier Papers, Tennessee State Library and Archives.

46. Downes, "Cherokee-American Relations in the Upper Tennessee Valley," 35–39.

47. Palmer, ed., *Calendar of Virginia State Papers,* vol. 4, 56.

48. Old Tassel to Joseph Martin, September 19, 1785, Cherokee Collection, Tennessee State Library and Archives.

49. Callaway, *America's First Western Frontier,* 115–119; Mooney, *History, Myths, and Sacred Formulas of the Cherokee,* 59–60; Ramsey, *The Annals of Tennessee,* 271–273. In September 1782, John Sevier commanded two hundred militiamen in another raid on Dragging Canoe's Chickamauga Cherokee (Downes, "Cherokee-American Relations in the Upper Tennessee Valley," 37–41).

50. Downes, "Cherokee-American Relations in the Upper Tennessee Valley," 40–41.

51. Joseph Martin to Patrick Henry, April 16, 1785, King's Mountain Papers (DD), Draper Manuscript Collection. Chota (also known as Echota) was one of the oldest and most important Overhill towns (King, *The Cherokee Indian Nation,* 56–57).

52. Palmer, ed., *Calendar of Virginia State Papers,* vol. 4, 25.

53. Downes, "Cherokee-American Relations in the Upper Tennessee Valley," 40–41.

54. Chilhowe (also spelled Chilhoe, Chilhowie, or Chilhowee) was an Overhill town located on a small creek that flowed into the Little Tennessee River (Holton, *Forced Founders,* 21; King, *The Cherokee Indian Nation,* 56; Conley, *The Cherokee Nation,* 61). The towns of Tallassee and Settico are both Overhill towns (King, *The Cherokee Indian Nation,* 56).

55. Alderman, *The Overmountain Men,* 204–205; Clark, ed., *The State Records*

of North Carolina, vol. 22, 649–650. Old Tassel and Hanging Maw (war chief) replaced Atakullakulla and Oconostota, both deceased, as the two primary chiefs of the Overhill Cherokee. According to Robert Conley, the Franklinites "negotiated a treaty with an inexperienced delegation of young chiefs led by 'Ancoo' in May of 1785" (Conley, *The Cherokee Nation,* 73–74).

56. Downes, "Cherokee-American Relations in the Upper Tennessee Valley," 42–43; Williams, *History of the Lost State of Franklin,* 289–325.

57. Letter from Caswell County resident to a gentleman in Washington County, Virginia, May 26, 1785, Newspaper Extracts (JJ), Draper Manuscript Collection.

58. Clark, ed., *The State Records of North Carolina,* vol. 22, 651–652.

59. Downes, "Cherokee-American Indian Relations in the Upper Tennessee Valley," 42–43; Clark, ed., *The State Records of North Carolina,* vol. 22, 651–652.

60. Conley, *The Cherokee Nation,* 74; Ramsey, *The Annals of Tennessee,* 319. Old Tassel's complete letter is reprinted in Ramsey's *The Annals of Tennessee.*

61. Samuel Cole Williams states that the Treaty of Dumplin Creek resulted in a large number of settlers occupying Cherokee lands, including members of Reverend Samuel Houston's family, Samuel Wear, and Samuel Newell (Williams, *History of the Lost State of Franklin,* 78–80).

62. Downes, "Cherokee-American Indian Relations in the Upper Tennessee Valley," 42–43; McLoughlin, *Cherokee Renaissance,* 21; Morgan, *The Birth of the Republic,* 113–114.

63. Alderman, *The Overmountain Men,* 205–207.

64. Conley, *The Cherokee Nation,* 74.

65. Alderman, *The Overmountain Men,* 207; Mooney, *History, Myths, and Sacred Formulas of the Cherokee,* 61–62.

66. Conley, *The Cherokee Nation,* 74.

67. Downes, "Cherokee-American Indian Relations in the Upper Tennessee Valley," 43; McLoughlin, *Cherokee Renaissance,* 21; Alderman, *The Overmountain Men,* 207.

68. Mooney, *History, Myths, and Sacred Formulas of the Cherokee,* 61–62.

69. Ramsey, *The Annals of Tennessee,* 334–335; McLoughlin, *Cherokee Renaissance,* 21. According to Pat Alderman, "the final boundaries agreed on at Hopewell started at the Cumberland River 40 miles North of Nashville and ran to a point six miles South of the Nolichucky and southward of Oconee River" (Alderman, *The Overmountain Men,* 207).

70. Both North Carolina and the U.S. government were either unwilling or unable to enforce the provisions of the Treaty of Hopewell (McLoughlin, *Cherokee Renaissance,* 22–23).

71. Clark, ed., *State Records of North Carolina,* vol. 22, 651–652.

72. Clark, ed., *State Records of North Carolina,* vol. 18, 595–596.

73. McLoughlin, *Cherokee Renaissance,* 22–23.

74. Ramsey, *The Annals of Tennessee,* 341–344.

75. Downes, "Cherokee-American Indian Relations in the Upper Tennessee Valley," 43–44; Mooney, *History, Myths, and Sacred Formulas of the Cherokee,* 62–63; Haywood, *The Civil and Political History of Tennessee,* 175–176; King, *The Cherokee Indian Nation,* 56.

76. Clark, ed., *The State Records of North Carolina,* vol. 18, 603–604. During this period, Spanish-American Indian agents secretly encouraged the regional tribes to attack the Tennessee settlements. The Spanish provided weapons and supplies to the southeastern tribes in their effort to expand their territorial holdings in North America.

77. Clark, ed., *The State Records of North Carolina,* vol. 18, 604–606.

78. McLoughlin, *Cherokee Renaissance,* 23.

79. Ibid., 607–608.

80. The list of persons provided by Colonel Bledsoe killed by the Cherokee included the names Joseph Thomas, William Gubbins, Pear Planting, William Miller, David Lucas, William Shannon, Thomas Frigit, and Samuel Buckhannon. The Cherokee wounded Squire Grant, John Patton, Thomas Patton, John Frazier, William McGee, and Andrew Barber during the spring of 1786 (Clark, ed., *The State Records of North Carolina,* vol. 18, 607–608).

81. Downes, "Cherokee-American Indian Relations in the Upper Tennessee Valley," 44; Mooney, *History, Myths, and Sacred Formulas of the Cherokee,* 63–64; Ramsey, *The Annals of Tennessee,* 342–343; Conley, *The Cherokee Nation,* 74. Samuel Cole Williams states that Colonel Logan and the Kentuckians destroyed the Cherokee town known as Crow Town (Williams, *History of the Lost State of Franklin,* 140–141).

82. Clark, ed., *The State Records of North Carolina,* vol. 22, 656–658.

83. Ibid.; Ramsey, *The Annals of Tennessee,* 342–343; Alderman, *The Overmountain Men,* 213. The Treaty of Coyatee required that the Overhill Cherokee cede all "remaining land north of the Little Tennessee River" (Conley, *The Cherokee Nation,* 74).

84. Joseph Martin to Alexander McGillivray, April 15, 1788, Cherokee Collection, Tennessee State Library and Archives.

85. "The party of Indians proves [*sic*] to be hunters from the friendly Towns, to the number of 17, and was returned with their skins. The Chief that was killed belonged to Chota. On the news reaching the Towns, the Indians assembled in a rage, blamed the Virginians [the Kentucky territory still being part of Virginia], and threatened to take satisfaction" (Palmer, ed., *Calendar of Virginia State Papers,* vol. 4, 254–256).

86. Clark, ed., *The State Records of North Carolina,* vol. 21, 500–501.

87. Palmer, ed., *Calendar of Virginia State Papers,* vol. 4, 262.

88. Williams, *History of the Lost State of Franklin*, 166–167; Downes, "Cherokee-American Indian Relations in the Upper Tennessee Valley," 46–47; Ramsey, *The Annals of Tennessee*, 402–403.

89. Clark, ed., *The State Records of North Carolina*, vol. 22, 675–676.

90. Clark, ed., *The State Records of North Carolina*, vol. 20, 653–654.

91. Sparks, ed., *The Works of Benjamin Franklin*, vol. 10, 260–261, 266–267, 290–291.

92. Clark, ed., *The State Records of North Carolina*, vol. 22, 683.

93. Palmer, ed., *Calendar of Virginia State Papers*, vol. 4, 256–257; Robert A. Rutland et al., eds., *The Papers of James Madison*, vol. 10, *27 May 1787–3 March 1788* (Chicago: Univ. of Chicago Press, 1977), 271–272; Conley, *The Cherokee Nation*, 74–75.

94. Downes, "Cherokee-American Indian Relations in the Upper Tennessee Valley," 45.

95. Clark, ed., *The State Records of North Carolina*, vol. 22, 693–694.

96. "The letters enclosed are from his friends [Powell] residing on the extreme frontiers. Joseph Hind's house had been attacked, and his son killed and scalped. On their retreat the Indians had carried of [*sic*] many horses and had killed the cattle, taking off the meat" (Palmer, ed., *Calendar of Virginia State Papers*, vol. 4, 428–429). Williams, *History of the Lost State of Franklin*, 210–213. In a September 19, 1787, talk addressed to the state governments of North Carolina, Cherokee Chief Old Tassel pleaded with the two governments to "take pity on us and not take our ground from us because he is stronger than we" (Clark, ed., *The State Records of North Carolina*, vol. 20, 779–780).

97. Clark, ed., *The State Records of North Carolina*, vol. 21, 462–464.

98. Arthur, *Western North Carolina*, 117; Mooney, *History, Myths, and Sacred Formulas of the Cherokee*, 64–65; Ramsey, *The Annals of Tennessee*, 413–415.

99. Williams, *History of the Lost State of Franklin*, 212–214.

100. General Sevier—1st Campaign of 88, Draper's Notes (S), Draper Manuscript Collection.

101. Clark, ed., *The State Records of North Carolina*, vol. 22, 695–696.

102. Downes, "Cherokee-American Indian Relations in the Upper Tennessee Valley," 46–47; Palmer, ed., *Calendar of Virginia State Papers*, vol. 4, 452; Conley, *The Cherokee Nation*, 74. Contemporaries used the name Citico, after Citico Creek (a small tributary of Chickamauga Creek), interchangeably with Chickamauga to describe Dragging Canoe's small breakaway group of Cherokee resisters.

103. Alderman, *The Overmountain Men*, 227; Arthur, *Western North Carolina*, 117; Downes, "Cherokee-American Indian Relations in the Upper Tennessee Valley," 47–49; Dykeman, *Tennessee: A History*, 68–69; Clark, ed., *The State Records of North Carolina*, vol. 22, 695–696.

104. Clark, ed., *The State Records of North Carolina*, vol. 22, 695–696; Conley, *The Cherokee Nation*, 74.

105. In sworn depositions to the North Carolina Assembly, two Sevier loyalists declared Sevier to be innocent of the charges being leveled against him regarding the murder of the two Indian chiefs. According to Hubbard and Evans, the executions were "contrary to John Sevier's Orders and that it was done by a [illegible] John Cirk [Kirk] who had his mother and two brothers and sisters killed a few days before" (Nathaniel Evans and James Hubbard [Hubbart], October 22, 1788, Depositions from Greene County in defense of John Sevier, General Assembly Record Group, North Carolina State Archives).

106. Foster, *Franklin: The Stillborn State*, 18.

107. Clark, ed., *The State Records of North Carolina*, vol. 22, 695–696.

108. Clark, ed., *The State Records of North Carolina*, vol. 21, 495–497.

109. In a proclamation issued on July 29, 1788, Governor Johnston characterized the murder of Old Abraham and Old Tassel as being "cruel & unjustifiable." Joseph Martin also accused James Hubbard of the murder of an innocent Cherokee named Butler in the spring of 1785 (Clark, ed., *The State Records of North Carolina*, vol. 21, 487–488).

110. Alderman, *The Overmountain Men*, 227; Arthur, *Western North Carolina*, 117; Downes, "Cherokee-American Indian Relations in the Upper Tennessee Valley," 47–49; Palmer, ed., *Calendar of Virginia State Papers*, vol. 4, 18–19; Roosevelt, *The Winning of the West*, 216–217; Spoden, *Kingsport Heritage*, 142–143; Williams, *History of the Lost State of Franklin*, 211–213. North Carolina historian John Preston Arthur argues that Sevier "knew well the fierce bloodlust of his followers, and was criminally negligent to leave to their mercy the friendly Indians who had trusted to his good faith; and moreover, he made no effort to punish the murderer" (Arthur, *Western North Carolina*, 117). Wilma Dykeman states that James Hubbard, "an avid Indian hater," lured Old Tassel and Old Abraham with "a flag of truce." Once inside the white encampment, "Hubbard closed the door, posted guards at the windows, handed a tomahawk to John Kirk Jr., and invited him to take vengeance for his loved ones" (Dykeman, *Tennessee: A History*, 68–69).

111. Clark, ed., *The State Records of North Carolina*, vol. 21, 487.

112. Clark, ed., *The State Records of North Carolina*, vol. 22, 718.

113. Clark, ed., *The State Records of North Carolina*, vol. 21, 495–498.

114. Clark, ed., *The State Records of North Carolina*, vol. 21, 490.

115. McLoughlin, *Cherokee Renaissance*, 23.

116. Major James Sevier to Lyman C. Draper, August 19, 1839, John Sevier Papers, Tennessee State Library and Archives.

117. Clark, ed., *The State Records of North Carolina*, vol. 21, 490, 497–498, 506–507.

118. Alderman, *The Overmountain Men*, 227–228; Cox and Cox, comps., *History of Washington County, Tennessee*, 88–89; Downes, "Cherokee-American Indian Relations in the Upper Tennessee Valley," 48–53; Mooney, *History, Myths, and Sacred Formulas of the Cherokee*, 68–69. According to John Finger, the continued violence in the Tennessee Valley forced the Overhill Cherokee to abandon several of their Overhill towns, including Chota, and settle in Georgia. These valley refugees joined with Dragging Canoe's Chickamauga Cherokee to fight against the former Franklinites. North Carolina congressman Hugh Williamson believed that "the conduct of Mr. Sevier was not only fatal [to treaty negotiations]," but also threatened the southern states with "a general Indian War" (Van West, *Tennessee History*, 16–17).

6. Death in All Its Various and Frightful Shapes

1. Clark, ed., *The State Records of North Carolina*, vol. 20, 707–709.

2. In keeping with their divide-and-conquer strategy, the state of North Carolina created Hawkins County in 1786 out of the Franklin-created county of Spencer. The North Carolina Assembly named the new western county after Benjamin Hawkins, member of both the North Carolina Assembly and the Continental Congress (Alderman, *The Overmountain Men*, 215–216). Over the two centuries of historical examination that followed the collapse of the state of Franklin, many scholars have contended that the statehood movement quietly disappeared with little fanfare. A group of Tennessee textbook authors asserted, "The State of Franklin had gone out with a whimper and not a bang," and North Carolina historian Captain Samuel A. Ashe concluded that "the last vestige of the State of Franklin was, by conciliation and moderation, buried out of sight." Even noted Cherokee and Tennessee frontier historian John R. Finger described the final breath of Franklin "not [as] a burst of glory," but as a quiet "whimper" (Bergeron, Ash, and Keith, *Tennesseans and Their History*, 44; Samuel A. Ashe, "The State of Franklin," *North Carolina Booklet* 14 [1914]: 48–49; Finger, *Tennessee Frontiers*, 122).

3. Clark, ed., *The State Records of North Carolina*, vol. 20, 616–619.

4. Ibid. Governor Richard Caswell never settled in the Tennessee Valley and he died on November 10, 1789, in Fayetteville, North Carolina, from a stroke (Jan Barwick, "Richard Caswell: North Carolina's Forgotten Governor," *Olde Kinston Gazette*, June 1998, http://www.kinstonpress.com/kinston_gaz/caswell_forgotten.htm [accessed June 25, 2008]).

5. Williams, *History of the Lost State of Franklin*, 137.

6. Hutchings also pleaded with Governor Caswell to further intervene in the region and argued that "Unless these people are entitled to Exclusive and Separate emoluments from the Rest of the Community, they Ought Certainly to be Quelled." Essentially, Hutchings's correspondence attempted to induce Caswell to commit the North Carolina militia to war against the Franklinites. This of

course never came to fruition (Clark, ed., *The State Records of North Carolina*, vol. 22, 678–679).

7. Ibid.

8. Clark, ed., *The State Records of North Carolina*, vol. 20, 646–647; Foster, *Franklin: The Stillborn State*, 10.

9. Clark, ed., *The State Records of North Carolina*, vol. 22, 678–679.

10. Alderman, *The Overmountain Men*, 216–217; Foster, *Franklin: The Stillborn State*, 10. Samuel Cole Williams describes Evan Shelby as "a blunt, stern man, sixty-seven years of age," and J. G. M. Ramsey states that Shelby was "high in confidence of his countrymen everywhere, remarkable for his probity, candour [*sic*], good sense, and patriotism." During his meeting with Sevier, Shelby served as Brigadier General for North Carolina's Washington District (Williams, *History of the Lost State of Franklin*, 142–143; Ramsey, *The Annals of Tennessee*, 357–358).

11. Clark, ed., *The State Records of North Carolina*, vol. 20, 646–648; Evan Shelby Jr., biography of his father, Evan Shelby Sr., Shelby Family Papers, Archives of Appalachia, East Tennessee State University.

12. Ramsey, *The Annals of Tennessee*, 357–358; Williams, *History of the Lost State of Franklin*, 142–143.

13. Williams, *History of the Lost State of Franklin*, 143–144.

14. Clark, ed., *The State Records of North Carolina*, vol. 20, 690.

15. Clark, ed., *The State Records of North Carolina*, vol. 20, 654–657.

16. Clark, ed., *The State Records of North Carolina*, vol. 20, 643. The state of North Carolina appointed Thomas Hutchings colonel of the Hawkins County militia in 1787 (Williams, *History of the Lost State of Franklin*, 144).

17. Clark, ed., *The State Records of North Carolina*, vol. 20, 641–643.

18. Ibid.

19. Clark, ed., *The State Records of North Carolina*, vol. 22, 679–680.

20. Clark, ed., *The State Records of North Carolina*, vol. 20, 681–682.

21. Ibid., 646–647.

22. Ibid., 689–691.

23. In a letter dated May 4, 1787, Anthony Bledsoe informed Governor Caswell, "I have myself heard the Franklin party wish the period of the commencement of hostilities. To me it is a dread thought. Might I be permitted to request your Excellency's addressing these people and advising them the necessity and advantage of returning to their duty once more and the danger and evil consequences of their persisting in the attempt of supporting an independence." There is no evidence that the Franklinites wanted war to break out between themselves and North Carolina, but it is apparent that many opponents of Franklin believed this to be true (Clark, ed., *The State Records of North Carolina*, vol. 22, 683–684).

24. Alderman, *The Overmountain Men*, 220–221; Williams, *History of the Lost State of Franklin*, 149–150.

25. Alderman, *The Overmountain Men*, 220–222; Williams, *History of the Lost State of Franklin*, 149–160. As with the bulk of the state of Franklin's legislative records, copies of the debate over the 1787 elections are missing from the historical record. Samuel Cole Williams and Pat Alderman include accounts gleaned from the July 14 and 28, 1787, issues of the *Georgia State Gazette*.

26. Alderman, *The Overmountain Men*, 220–222; Williams, *History of the Lost State of Franklin*, 149–160.

27. Clark, ed., *The State Records of North Carolina*, vol. 22, 685–686.

28. Ramsey, *The Annals of Tennessee*, 391. The only extant copy of the Sevier letter to Kennedy is reprinted in J. G. M. Ramsey's seminal work on Tennessee history, *The Annals of Tennessee*, 391.

29. Caldwell, *Tennessee: The Dangerous Example*, 174.

30. Haywood, *The Civil and Political History of Tennessee*, 187–188; Ramsey, *The Annals of Tennessee*, 339, 389, 401.

31. Clark, ed., *The State Records of North Carolina*, vol. 20, 616–617. David Campbell ultimately accepted the appointment as Superior Court judge of the Washington District, representing North Carolina at the 1787 meeting of the North Carolina Assembly. The decision sparked the ire of the Franklinites, who accused the former Franklin supporter of "the desertion of his friends in very undisguised terms of reprobation" (Haywood, *The Civil and Political History of Tennessee*, 187–188).

32. Ramsey, *The Annals of Tennessee*, 339, 401.

33. Williams, *History of the Lost State of Franklin*, 161–164.

34. Caldwell, *Tennessee: The Dangerous Example*, 174–175; Fink, "Some Phases of the History of the State of Franklin," 206–209.

35. Caldwell, *Tennessee: The Dangerous Example*, 174–175.

36. Clark, ed., *The State Records of North Carolina*, vol. 20, 322–326.

37. Joseph Martin to Richard Caswell, March 16, 1787, Draper's Notes (S), Draper Manuscript Collection.

38. Caldwell, *Tennessee: The Dangerous Example*, 174–175; Williams, *History of the Lost State of Franklin*, 161–164.

39. The North Carolina Assembly initially refused to certify the election of either man, but after careful deliberation, representatives determined "that John Tipton, esq., is duly Elected" and "ought to be permitted to qualify & take his seat accordingly" (Clark, ed., *The State Records of North Carolina*, vol. 20, 322–326).

40. Fink, "Some Phases of the History of the State of Franklin," 206–207; Evan Shelby Jr., biography of his father, Evan Shelby Sr., Shelby Family Papers, Archives of Appalachia, East Tennessee State University. In Washington County, residents elected both John Tipton and Landon Carter for the same North Carolina Senate seat. According to Samuel Cole Williams, both Landon Carter and John Sevier fought to deny Tipton his senate seat. Both Sevier and Carter blamed

Tipton for the 1786 defeat of the Franklin petition for statehood delivered by William Cocke and David Campbell. Williams also states that Greene County residents elected David Campbell to the North Carolina Senate. In a letter recorded by Lyman Draper, Joseph Martin informed Governor Caswell that "Sullivan and Hawkins County are unanimously in favor of the Old State," but conceded that "Washington [County is] much divided between Tipton & Sevier." During the same August legislative session calling for competing elections, the Franklinites also selected a gubernatorial replacement for John Sevier, whose term expired on March 1, 1788. The Franklinites chose Evan Shelby as Sevier's successor, and Governor Sevier sent the general a letter urging him to accept the position. Shelby ultimately rejected the governorship (Williams, *History of the Lost State of Franklin,* 161–164); Joseph Martin to Richard Caswell, March 16, 1787, Draper's Notes (S), Draper Manuscript Collection).

41. Clark, ed., *The State Records of North Carolina,* vol. 22, 689–691.

42. Caldwell, *Tennessee: The Dangerous Example,* 174–175; Ramsey, *The Annals of Tennessee,* 391–392; Williams, *History of the Lost State of Franklin,* 163–164. Paul M. Fink states that "the North Carolina Grand Jury brought an indictment against Caldwell because he 'with force of arms an assault did make on him Jonathan Pugh, Esquire, then & there did Beat, Wound and Evil Intreat [*sic*] & then & there other enormous things did'" to Pugh (Fink, "Some Phases of the History of the State of Franklin," 208–209).

43. Ramsey, *The Annals of Tennessee,* 391–392.

44. Ibid.; Williams, *History of the Lost State of Franklin,* 163–164.

45. Caldwell, *Tennessee: The Dangerous Example,* 174–175; Fink, "Some Phases of the History of the State of Franklin," 208–209; Foster, *Franklin: The Stillborn State,* 12–13. In a letter reprinted in the *Columbian Magazine* in November 1787, William Cocke informed George Elholm that "a body of about fifteen hundred veterans, embodied to rescue their governor (as they thought) out of the hands of the North Carolinians, and bring him back to the mountains" (Ramsey, *The Annals of Tennessee,* 391–392).

46. Ramsey, *The Annals of Tennessee,* 401–403.

47. Haywood, *The Civil and Political History of Tennessee,* 187; Williams, *History of the Lost State of Franklin,* 189–193.

48. Clark, ed., *The State Records of North Carolina,* vol. 20, 775–777.

49. U.S. House of Representatives, "The United States Constitution," http://www.archives.gov/exhibits/charters/constitution.html (accessed June 1, 2007).

50. Cox and Cox, comps., *History of Washington County, Tennessee,* 87.

51. Alderman, *The Overmountain Men,* 222; Bergeron, Ash, and Keith, *Tennesseans and Their History,* 44; Fink, "Some Phases of the History of the State of Franklin," 206–207; Williams, *History of the Lost State of Franklin,* 189–190.

52. Haywood, *The Civil and Political History of Tennessee,* 187; Ramsey, *The*

Annals of Tennessee, 404–405; Williams, *History of the Lost State of Franklin,* 193–197.

53. Clark, ed., *The State Records of North Carolina,* vol. 20, 119–120, 202, 218, 223, 247–248, 261–262, 270, 273, 276, 284, 293, 300–302, 326. Governor John Sevier also sent Francis A. Ramsey, the father of Tennessee historian J. G. M. Ramsey, to the November session with Landon Carter and David Campbell. The act to cede their western lands to the federal government, originally passed in 1785 and repealed shortly after, failed to pass (Ramsey, *The Annals of Tennessee,* 404–405).

54. Clark, ed., *The State Records of North Carolina,* vol. 20, 119–120, 202, 218, 223, 247–248, 261–262, 270, 273, 276, 284, 293, 300–302, 326.

55. Clark, ed., *The State Records of North Carolina,* vol. 22, 705–714.

56. Clark, ed., *The State Records of North Carolina,* vol. 20, 119–120, 202, 218, 223, 247–248, 261–262, 270, 273, 276, 284, 293, 300–302, 326.

57. Ramsey, *The Annals of Tennessee,* 403–405.

58. Clark, ed., *The State Records of North Carolina,* vol. 22, 693–694.

59. Cox and Cox, comps., *History of Washington County, Tennessee,* 87. During the buildup to the Battle of Franklin, the enemies of John Sevier reported several incidents of the Franklin governor and groups of armed men threatening Tiptonites. In a letter to Robert Love, John Tipton described such an occurrence: "Sevier and his Gang persist in opposition to the Laws of North Carolina they have been at my house in a hostile Manner" (John Tipton to Robert Love, January 21, 1788, Henry Toole Clark Papers, North Carolina State Archives).

60. Clark, ed., *The State Records of North Carolina,* vol. 20, 456.

61. Haywood, *The Civil and Political History of Tennessee,* 190–191.

62. The author is speculating regarding John Tipton's ordering Sheriff Pugh's collection of back taxes from Governor Sevier, but as Washington County's clerk of court, the execution unquestionably originated from the mind of John Tipton.

63. Alderman, *The Overmountain Men,* 223–224; Cox and Cox, comps., *History of Washington County, Tennessee,* 87–88; Foster, *Franklin: The Stillborn State,* 12–13; Ramsey, *The Annals of Tennessee,* 406–407. Williams and Haywood state that the Franklin troops under Sevier's command mostly mustered from Greene, Sevier, and Caswell counties in southern Franklin. Inhabitants of these three counties remained the most rabid supporters of Sevier and the state of Franklin (Williams, *History of the Lost State of Franklin,* 198–200; Haywood, *The Civil and Political History of Tennessee,* 190–191). There remains considerable debate over the details of the so-called Battle of Franklin.

64. Deposition from John Tipton and others, August 20, 1788, Miscellaneous Folder, North Carolina State Archives. There are a number of reasons that the residents of the southernmost Franklin counties retained their loyalty to John Se-

vier and the Franklin movement long after the northern Tennessee Valley counties abandoned their allegiance. First, the southern Franklin counties were created out of contested Cherokee land secured by the treaties of Dumplin Creek and Coyatee. Neither the state of North Carolina nor the U.S. government acknowledged these Indian land cessions. Additionally, the inhabitants of these southern counties remained vulnerable to Cherokee attacks, and these residents believed John Sevier's Franklin government stood as their best line of defense. The residents of "lesser Franklin," the name given to these southern counties by historian Samuel Cole Williams, clearly had the most to gain by supporting Sevier and the Franklin statehood movement, and the most to lose if the movement failed.

65. Alderman, *The Overmountain Men,* 223–224; Cox and Cox, comps., *History of Washington County, Tennessee,* 87–88; Franklin Government, Lyman Draper, Draper's Notes (S), Draper Manuscript Collection; Ramsey, *The Annals of Tennessee,* 406–407. Williams states that forty-five men protected John Tipton at the beginning of the siege, but Haywood argues that only fifteen men held up at the Tipton home (other sources put the number of men guarding the Tipton home at seventy-five and seventy) (Williams, *History of the Lost State of Franklin,* 198–200).

66. Williams, *History of the Lost State of Franklin,* 201.

67. Clark, ed., *The State Records of North Carolina,* vol. 22, 691–693.

68. Ibid., 714.

69. Deposition from John Tipton and others, August 20, 1788, Miscellaneous Folder, North Carolina State Archives.

70. Alderman, *The Overmountain Men,* 223–226; *Winchester Advertiser,* "Extract of a letter from a gentleman in the new State of Franklin," March 1788, Newspaper Extracts (JJ), Draper Manuscript Collection. The facts surrounding the so-called Battle of Franklin are at best cloudy. Many of the details regarding troop totals, the chronology of events, numbers of participants killed or wounded, and even the specific occurrences vary widely, depending upon conflicting accounts. The author attempted to draw upon as many of these sources as possible to recreate the events of the Battle of Franklin, but even participants in the conflict did not agree on what actually occurred over those frigid winter days. John Sevier commanded the Franklin troops alongside county militia captains Colonel Charles Robertson, Colonel Henry Conway, and Major General George Elholm. An account by an unnamed source, reprinted in the *Winchester Advertiser,* stated that Sevier "intended to burn the [Tipton] house," but there is no corroborative evidence proving this statement (*Winchester Advertiser,* "Extract of a letter from a gentleman in the new State of Franklin," March 1788, Newspaper Extracts [JJ], Draper Manuscript Collection). There is also confusion over the possible existence of a cannon at the Battle of Franklin. Although there is no reference to a Franklinite cannon in any of the contemporary accounts, J. G. M. Ramsey, Samuel Cole Williams, and several others believed in the presence of the military ordnance. In

one account, copied in Lyman Draper's notes, Major James Sevier stated that "there was no cannon there, but [he] designed on getting one from Holston" (Franklin Government, Lyman Draper, Draper's Notes [S], Draper Manuscript Collection).

71. Deposition from John Tipton and others, August 20, 1788, Miscellaneous Folder, North Carolina State Archives.

72. Clark, ed., *The State Records of North Carolina,* vol. 22, 691–693; *Winchester Advertiser,* "Extract of a letter from a gentleman in the new State of Franklin," March 1788, Newspaper Extracts (JJ), Draper Manuscript Collection; Franklin Government, Lyman Draper, Draper's Notes (S), Draper Manuscript Collection. Lyman Draper includes this account of the wounding of Rachel Devinsly in his notes: "Erwing Ellison & [illegible] Houston fired, & shot a woman in the shoulder, she was a young woman of the name Rachel Devinsly [author's best approximation of the nearly illegible surname], who had been sent out thinking they [Franklinites] would not fire at a female, but it was dusk they could not distinguish" (Franklin Government, Lyman Draper, Draper's Notes [S], Draper Manuscript Collection). J. G. M. Ramsey also believed that the shooting of Devinsly "was purely accidental" (Ramsey, *The Annals of Tennessee,* 407–409).

73. Williams, *History of the Lost State of Franklin,* 201.

74. Alderman, *The Overmountain Men,* 224–225. The expedition led by John Sevier Jr. and Joseph Hardin never located the Sullivan County troops, and after marching "within half a mile from the ford . . . wearily, doubtless, and cold, refused to go any further, seeing no signs of meeting a foe & believing that Cox had deceived them—returned to camp that night" (Williams, *History of the Lost State of Franklin,* 201–202; Alderman, *The Overmountain Men,* 224).

75. Clark, ed., *The State Records of North Carolina,* vol. 22, 691–693; George Maxwell and John Tipton to Arthur Campbell, March 12, 1788, King's Mountain Papers (DD), Draper Manuscript Collection; deposition from John Tipton and others, August 20, 1788, Miscellaneous Folder, North Carolina State Archives.

76. *Winchester Advertiser,* "Extract of a letter from a gentleman in the new State of Franklin," March 1788, Newspaper Extracts (JJ), Draper Manuscript Collection. According to Lyman Draper, on the evening of February 28, William Cox "came in & gave intelligence that the people of Sullivan were embodying to reinforce Tipton & would that night cross the Watauga [River] at Dungan's Mill ford." The Franklinites did not believe Cox, thinking his communication to be a "double pact," and "many gave no heed to the information" (Franklin Government, Lyman Draper, Draper's Notes [S], Draper Manuscript Collection).

77. Samuel Cole Williams speculated that the Franklinites believed that "Tipton referred to Parkinson's company which, they knew, had been turned back" (Williams, *History of the Lost State of Franklin,* 201).

78. Clark, ed., *The State Records of North Carolina,* vol. 22, 691–693; deposi-

tion from John Tipton and others, August 20, 1788, Miscellaneous Folder, North Carolina State Archives.

79. Franklin Government, Lyman Draper, Draper's Notes (S), Draper Manuscript Collection.

80. Clark, ed., *The State Records of North Carolina,* vol. 22, 691–693; Haywood, *The Civil and Political History of Tennessee,* 193; deposition from John Tipton and others, August 20, 1788, Miscellaneous Folder, North Carolina State Archives.

81. Clark, ed., *The State Records of North Carolina,* vol. 22, 691–693.

82. "Intelligence from the State of Franklin" reprinted in *Virginia Independent Chronicle,* April 8, 1788, Newspaper Extracts (JJ), Draper Manuscript Collection.

83. Franklin Government, Lyman Draper, Draper's Notes (S), Draper Manuscript Collection.

84. *Winchester Advertiser,* "Extract of a letter from a gentleman in the new State of Franklin," March 1788, Newspaper Extracts (JJ), Draper Manuscript Collection; deposition from John Tipton and others, August 20, 1788, Miscellaneous Folder, North Carolina State Archives. In November 1788, William Delancy applied to the North Carolina government for compensation for the wound he sustained "in an action under the command of Colo. Tipton." The state eventually rewarded Delancy the "Sum of Thirty pounds, five Shillings and Six pence" for his injuries (Clark, ed., *The State Records of North Carolina,* vol. 21, 176).

85. Franklin Government, Lyman Draper, Draper's Notes (S), Draper Manuscript Collection.

86. George Maxwell and John Tipton to Arthur Campbell, March 12, 1788, King's Mountain Papers (DD), Draper Manuscript Collection.

87. Haywood, *The Civil and Political History of Tennessee,* 192–194.

88. Bond of Andrew Hains (Haynes), John Sevier Jr., and James Sevier, March 1, 1788, Paul Fink Collection, W. L. Eury Collection, Appalachian State University; Clark, ed., *The State Records of North Carolina,* vol. 22, 691–693. The Sevier brothers previously appealed to Thomas Love for permission "to return to visit John Smith [wounded that day]" at his home, and "returned the next day, after giving their bonds for their appearance at court." The two brothers never stood trial for the assault on the Sullivan County forces (Haywood, *The Civil and Political History of Tennessee,* 192–194). Copies of the bonds securing the release of several captured Franklin soldiers are contained in the Paul Fink Collection in the W. L. Eury Collection at Appalachian State University in Boone, North Carolina. The collection, compiled by Franklin historian Paul Fink, also contains a claim by John Sevier Jr. for a gun taken from him by John Tipton during his arrest.

89. Clark, ed., *The State Records of North Carolina,* vol. 22, 715–716.

90. Haywood, *The Civil and Political History of Tennessee,* 194–195.

91. Clark, ed., *The State Records of North Carolina,* vol. 22, 693, 715–716.

92. George Maxwell and John Tipton to Arthur Campbell, March 12, 1788, King's Mountain Papers (DD), Draper Manuscript Collection.

93. Clark, ed., *The State Records of North Carolina,* vol. 22, 693.

94. Cox and Cox, comps., *The History of Washington County, Tennessee,* 87–89.

95. Joseph Martin believed that the Chickamauga party [led by Dragging Canoe] posed the only real threat to the Tennessee Valley, and that they "could easily be drove out of that country" (Clark, ed., *The State Records of North Carolina,* vol. 22, 716–717).

96. Ibid.

97. Haywood, *The Civil and Political History of Tennessee,* 200–202. Details of Sevier's spring Cherokee campaign are included in chapter 4.

98. Clark, ed., *The State Records of North Carolina,* vol. 21, 462–463.

99. Ibid.

100. Haywood, *The Civil and Political History of Tennessee,* 200–201.

101. Clark, ed., *The State Records of North Carolina,* vol. 21, 487, 496. Governor Johnston informed Secretary Thomson of the arrest warrant he issued against John Sevier in a letter dated September 29, 1788. Haywood, *The Civil and Political History of Tennessee,* 200–201. In an April 30, 1788, response to Joseph Martin, Sevier informed the brigadier general that "I am ready to suspend all kinds of hostilities and prosecutions on our part, and bury in total oblivion all past conduct" (John Sevier to Joseph Martin, March 27, 1788, and John Sevier to Joseph Martin, April 30, 1788, Draper's Notes [S], Draper Manuscript Collection).

102. Clark, ed., *The State Records of North Carolina,* vol. 21, 484–485.

103. In a May 8, 1788, letter to Dr. James White, Governor Johnston blamed John Sevier for the violence occurring on the Tennessee frontier. He argued that Sevier "duped" the supporters of Franklin, and that the former Franklin governor's "folly and presumption has reduced his affairs to so desperate a situation that it is not convenient for him to live under any wholesome and Regulated Government" (Clark, ed., *The State Records of North Carolina,* vol. 21, 469–470). On July 29, Governor Johnston ordered General Joseph Martin to organize "a sufficient number of the Militia of the District of Washington to aid and assist the Sheriff of any County in the said District in the Execution of any Warrant or Warrants for the apprehending any person or persons who have been guilty of Treasonable practices against the State and furnish such Sheriff with a sufficient Guard or Escort to enable him to convey such prisoners to the place of their Destination" (Clark, ed., *The State Records of North Carolina,* vol. 21, 485).

104. Haywood, *Civil and Judicial History of Tennessee,* 200–203; Williams, *History of the Lost State of Franklin,* 231–232.

105. Ibid.

106. Clark, ed., *The State Records of North Carolina,* vol. 22, 699–701.

107. Ibid.

108. Haywood, *Civil and Judicial History of Tennessee*, 200–203; Williams, *History of the Lost State of Franklin*, 231–232. Although David Campbell refused to carry out the arrest of John Sevier, another North Carolina judge, Samuel Spencer, did agree to issue "the bench warrant" for Sevier's apprehension. Thomas Gourley, Washington County clerk of court, and Andrew Caldwell, justice of the peace for Washington County, concurred with David Deaderick's deposition (Andrew Caldwell Examination, no date given, Paul Fink Collection, W. L. Eury Collection, Appalachian State University).

109. Clark, ed., *The State Records of North Carolina*, vol. 22, 699–701.

110. Caldwell, *Tennessee: The Dangerous Example*, 180–181; Cox and Cox, comps., *History of Washington County, Tennessee*, 90–91; Haywood, *Civil and Judicial History of Tennessee*, 203–205; Ramsey, *The Annals of Tennessee*, 424–425; Williams, *History of the Lost State of Franklin*, 230–233. There are several descriptions of the arrest of John Sevier, but few contemporary accounts exist of what transpired during those October days. The bulk of this account is taken from John Haywood, J. G. M. Ramsey, and Samuel Cole Williams. William Morrison, sheriff of Burke County, took possession of the prisoner after his arrival in Morganton.

111. Franklin Government, Lyman Draper, Draper's Notes (S), Draper Manuscript Collection.

112. Alderman, *The Overmountain Men*, 231–232; Haywood, *Civil and Judicial History of Tennessee*, 203–205; Williams, *History of the Lost State of Franklin*, 232–234; Fink, "Some Phases of the History of the State of Franklin," 212–213.

113. Franklin Government, Lyman Draper, Draper's Notes (S), Draper Manuscript Collection; "Sevier Taken by Tipton," Lyman Draper, Draper's Notes (S), Draper Manuscript Collection.

114. Franklin Government, Lyman Draper, Draper's Notes (S), Draper Manuscript Collection. Burke County sheriff William Morrison also served with Sevier at King's Mountain. After Sevier posted bail, Morrison simply allowed him to ride out of town. Samuel Cole Williams lists the names of the family members and friend who traveled to Morganton to secure Sevier's release. These participants included: John Sevier Jr., Nathaniel Evans, George North, James Cosby, Jesse Green, and William Matlock (Williams, *History of the Lost State of Franklin*, 232–234).

115. Clark, ed., *The State Records of North Carolina*, vol. 22, 697–699.

116. Ibid.

117. The senate voted twenty-four to nineteen not to exclude John Sevier from the act of pardon, and the House of Commons voted fifty-two to thirty-three for pardoning all of the former Franklinites. John Sevier and the Franklinites benefited greatly from the high percentage of former Franklin supporters representing the western counties in the North Carolina Assembly ("Bill to Repeal Part of Act Once More to Extend Act of Pardon Offenses of Certain Persons, Etc.," General

Assembly Record Group, North Carolina State Archives; Clark, ed., *The State Records of North Carolina*, vol. 21, 43, 56, 64, 73, 77, 110, 114, 218, 221, 222, 230, 232, 239, 256, 285–286).

118. The committee determined that John Sevier's actions during the Franklin affair "was not as highly reprehensible as many others" (Clark, ed., *The State Records of North Carolina*, vol. 22, 728–729).

119. Alderman, *The Overmountain Men*, 234–235. Several Franklin loyalists, including Thomas Amis, William Cocke, and Willie Jones, held seats in the November session (Williams, *History of the Lost State of Franklin*, 245–247). There is some confusion surrounding the year in which North Carolina actually pardoned Sevier. It is the author's best estimation that the assembly pardoned all but Sevier in 1788 and eventually agreed to pardon Sevier in 1789.

120. Clark, ed., *The State Records of North Carolina*, vol. 21, 547; Clark, ed., *The State Records of North Carolina*, vol. 22, 729.

121. Alderman, *The Overmountain Men*, 238.

7. Vassals del Rey de España

1. John Sevier's home at Plum Grove was located approximately six to ten miles from the town of Jonesboro.

2. Finger, *Tennessee Frontiers*, 123–124.

3. Samuel Cole Williams utilized the term "Lesser Franklin" to describe the efforts of the southern counties of the Tennessee Valley to maintain their independence from North Carolina following the collapse of support in the northern counties of Washington and Sullivan. Williams derived the terms from Arthur Campbell's use of the term "Greater Franklin" to convey his desire to affix his home of Washington County, Virginia, to the statehood movement (Williams, *History of the Lost State of Franklin*, 218–220).

4. Folmsbee, Corlew, and Mitchell, *History of Tennessee*, 168–169; Russell Dean Parker, "Historical Interpretations of the Spanish Intrigue in Tennessee: A Study," *East Tennessee Historical Society's Publications* 58–59 (1986–1987): 44; Whitaker, "The Muscle Shoals Speculation," 377; A. P. Whitaker, "Spanish Intrigue in the Old Southwest: An Episode, 1788–89," *Mississippi Valley Historical Review* 12 (September 1925): 159.

5. See chapter 4 for details regarding the original Muscle Shoals Company and the failed Franklin-Georgia alliance.

6. Holton, *Forced Founders*, 6–9.

7. Whitaker, "The Muscle Shoals Speculation," 365–376.

8. Braund, *Deerskins and Duffels*, 172–173.

9. Following the conclusion of the Revolutionary War, the American government found itself confronting a litany of foreign and domestic challenges that threatened to reverse the political, economic, and diplomatic gains of the revolu-

tionary decade. One of the most alarming threats to the sovereignty of the United States during the "Confederation period" resulted from territorial challenges posed by Britain and Spain to America's amorphous borders and the inability of the politically impotent Confederation Congress to confront these foreign empires. The weakness of the national government under the Articles of Confederation enabled the British to remain firmly ensconced in a series of forts that stretched from Canada into America's northwestern frontier, while the Spanish continued to exert control over Florida and much of the Mississippi River Valley. These foreign governments stood determined to retain possession of their North American land holdings and presented formidable diplomatic obstacles to America's postrevolutionary effort to secure its national boundaries and revitalize American commerce. Both British and Spanish colonial officials utilized secretive negotiations and discreet backcountry contacts in their attempts to protect their North American territories and possibly to topple the vulnerable American government (Horsman, *The Diplomacy of the New Republic,* 23–37; Alexander DeConde, *Entangled Alliance: Politics and Diplomacy under George Washington* [Durham, N.C.: Duke Univ. Press, 1958; reprint, Westport, Conn.: Greenwood Press, 1974], 82–85).

10. Caughey, *McGillivray of the Creeks,* 22–26, 28–33; *Cherokee and Creek Indians,* 121–124; Alexander McGillivray to Estevan Miro (governor of New Orleans), March 28, 1784, in D. C. Corbitt and Roberta Corbitt, eds., "Papers from the Spanish Archive Relating to Tennessee and the Old Southwest, 1783–1800," *East Tennessee Historical Society's Publications* 9 (1937): 117–118. The Corbitt and Corbitt-edited "Papers from the Spanish Archive Relating to Tennessee and the Old Southwest, 1783–1800" henceforth will be referred to as "Spanish Papers." The Spanish government in Pensacola agreed to allow Panton, Leslie, and Company, founded after the American Revolution by Scottish entrepreneurs (and British loyalists) William Panton, John Leslie, and William Alexander, an exclusive trade deal with the Creek Nation. Through the intermediation of a "silent partner," Alexander McGillivray, the company flourished and eventually was "operating stores in virtually every Creek village." Panton, Leslie, and Company also "served as a quiet conduit for the presents of arms and ammunition that the Spanish sent to McGillivray for his war against illegal American settlements" (Braund, *Deerskins and Duffels,* 173–174).

11. Abernethy, *From Frontier to Plantation,* 91–102. Parker describes Abernethy's economic interpretation as "The Muscle Shoals Connection" to the Spanish Intrigue. Details of the connection between William Blount and both the Spanish Intrigue and the post-1784 Muscle Shoals land deal remain obscured (Parker, "Historical Interpretations of the Spanish Intrigue," 56–59). Blount biographer William Masterson points out several links between William Blount and the conspiracy. Both William Blount and James White worked in Philadelphia during the earliest phases of the scheme, and Masterson speculated that Blount

"probably knew of it." Masterson also associated Blount with the Spanish Intrigue in Cumberland, but ultimately concluded that "he saw earlier than some of his Western associates that, while the intrigue could be well used as a threat to extort a cession from North Carolina, yet the essential incompatibility of the aims of the Westerners and of Spain precluded carrying separatist ideas to any radical conclusion" (William H. Masterson, *William Blount* [Baton Rouge: Louisiana State Univ. Press, 1954], 151).

12. Archibald Henderson, "The Spanish Conspiracy in Tennessee," *Tennessee Historical Magazine* 3 (December 1917): 229–231.

13. Griffey, *Earliest Tennessee Land Records*, 410–411; William D. Reeves, *Paths to Distinction: Dr. James White, Governor E. D. White, and Chief Justice Edward Douglass White of Louisiana* (Thibodaux, La.: Friends of the Edward Douglass White Historic Site, 1999), 1–16.

14. One of the most compelling motives provoking Franklinite negotiations with Spanish colonial officials was the inability and unwillingness of the U.S. government to apply diplomatic pressure on Spain to force them to accept America's right to navigate the Mississippi River. Eastern political leaders opposed to opening the Mississippi River to American commercial traffic argued that it would further escalate the tremendously expensive Indian wars, that it would result in the loss of tax revenue, and that it could sever the United States into two competing sections (Slaughter, *The Whiskey Rebellion*, 30, 37, 40–42, 52–60).

15. Summary of a conversation between James White and Gardoqui, August 26, 1786, "Spanish Papers," *East Tennessee Historical Society's Publications* 16 (1944): 83–84. Gardoqui included a summary of his secret meeting with White in his October 28 communiqué with Conde de Floridablanca. In the same letter, Gardoqui commented on the fortuitous change of events affecting the future navigation of the Mississippi River. Gardoqui stated that "18 months ago nobody would have dared to propose to [the U.S.] Congress giving up the Navigation of the Mississippi, nor did I have any hope whatever of achieving, what has been accomplished, but we have had for a while a group of able, tractable, and respectable persons from the Northern States, who have been very noble, and to them I have been able to explain the importance and generosity of His Majesty, and it is to them that we are indebted for the working of this miracle." Gardoqui also comments on his ongoing negotiations over the details and language of the Mississippi River deal with the "intractable" and "insupportable" secretary of foreign affairs, John Jay (Gardoqui to Conde de Floridablanca [Spain's secretary of state], October 28, 1786, "Spanish Papers," *East Tennessee Historical Society's Publications* 16 [1944]: 85–86).

16. Gardoqui to Conde de Floridablanca (Spain's secretary of state), October 28, 1786, "Spanish Papers," *East Tennessee Historical Society's Publications* 16 (1944): 86–87.

17. Ibid.

18. Parker, "Historical Interpretations of the Spanish Intrigue," 43–44; Whitaker, "The Muscle Shoals Speculation," 377.

19. Henderson, "The Spanish Conspiracy in Tennessee," 230–233; Parker, "Historical Interpretations of the Spanish Intrigue," 45.

20. Clark, ed., *The State Records of North Carolina,* vol. 21, 437–438.

21. Ibid., 464–467.

22. In a June 1, 1787, exchange between the governor of New Orleans and the Marquis de Sonora, Governor Miro stated, "John [James] White tried to seduce the Indians [Creeks] by proposing to them to make common cause against a Power [the United States] that aimed to subject them" (Miro to Sonora, June 1, 1787, "Spanish Papers," *East Tennessee Historical Society's Publications* 11 [1939]: 78–79). There is ample evidence proving that Spain provided McGillivray's Creeks military aid throughout 1784–1789 (McGillivray to Miro, February 1, 1789, "Spanish Papers," *East Tennessee Historical Society's Publications* 19 [1947]: 82–83). McGillivray "claimed" he dispatched "between five hundred and six hundred warriors" into the Cumberland District (Braund, *Deerskins and Duffels,* 173).

23. Clark, ed., *The State Records of North Carolina,* vol. 21, 468–470.

24. Gardoqui to Ezpeleta, November 12, 1787, "Spanish Papers," *East Tennessee Historical Society's Publications* 13 (1941): 102–105.

25. Gardoqui to Conde de Floridablanca, April 18, 1788, "Spanish Papers," *East Tennessee Historical Society's Publications* 17 (1945): 105–111.

26. Ibid.

27. Whitaker, "Spanish Intrigue in the Old Southwest," 157–158. Following the April 18, 1788, meeting between White and Gardoqui, the Spanish minister sent three letters denying Spain's involvement in aiding McGillivray's Upper Creeks in the war against the Tennessee Valley squatters. Gardoqui addressed these letters to Samuel Johnston, John Sevier, and Colonel Elijah Robertson of Cumberland (brother of James Robertson) (Whitaker, "The Muscle Shoals Speculation," 377).

28. Whitaker, "The Muscle Shoals Speculation," 378–380.

29. Whitaker, "Spanish Intrigue in the Old Southwest," 160.

30. Sevier to Gardoqui, September 12, 1788, "Spanish Papers," *East Tennessee Historical Society's Publications* 15 (1943): 103. In his excellent analysis of the historiography of the Spanish Intrigue, Russell Dean Parker offers his analysis of James Gilmore's account of the September 12 meeting between Sevier and White. Purportedly recorded directly from John Sevier by J. G. M. Ramsey, Gilmore asserts, in his flattering biography of Sevier entitled *Advanced Guard of Western Civilization,* that White divulged the details of the Spanish scheme on the Kentucky frontier. According to Gilmore, Sevier sent a letter to Isaac Shelby describing the James Wilkinson–led Kentucky intrigue and warning Shelby to prevent the

plot from occurring (Parker, "Historical Interpretations of the Spanish Intrigue," 45–46).

31. Sevier to Gardoqui, September 12, 1788, Letters in the North Carolina Archives in Foreign Documents, North Carolina State Archives.

32. Henderson, "The Spanish Conspiracy in Tennessee," 233–235; Parker, "Historical Interpretations of the Spanish Intrigue," 45–47; Whitaker, "The Muscle Shoals Speculation," 379; Whitaker, "Spanish Intrigue in the Old Southwest," 160–161.

33. Williams, *History of the Lost State of Franklin,* 219–220.

34. Gardoqui to Miro, October 3, 1788, and October 10, 1788, "Spanish Papers," *East Tennessee Historical Society's Publications* 18 (1946): 132–133. Gardoqui attempted to calm Miro's suspicions of James White by offering a brief background of the American conspirator. Gardoqui informed Miro, "I have known him as a Member of this Congress from North Carolina for a period of three years, and he was commissioned by it for the settlement of treaties with the Indians; in view of his general knowledge, and especially of the Boundaries, and his understanding of the secret views of this government, nobody can inform you more accurately." In a "list of passports to New Orleans," Gardoqui included this entry, "October 11, To Mr. John Sevier for himself and several Associates" (Gardoqui to Miro, October 3, 1788, and October 10, 1788, "Spanish Papers," *East Tennessee Historical Society's Publications* 18 [1946]: 132–133).

35. Henderson, "The Spanish Conspiracy in Tennessee," 236–237, 137–139; Parker, "Historical Interpretations of the Spanish Intrigue," 49–50; Whitaker, "Spanish Intrigue in the Old Southwest," 160–161. According to several sources, the General Assembly of Franklin met at an undisclosed location on October 15, 1788, and addressed the shortage of specie in the region and the growing concern among the political leadership regarding the payment of their salaries. There is considerable debate over the actual occurrence of this legislative session, but there is little doubt that many Tennessee Valley residents retained their support for the dying statehood movement (Williams, *History of the Lost State of Franklin,* 219–220).

36. Clark, ed., *The State Records of North Carolina,* vol. 21, 500–501. Johnston believed that "the Treaty of Hopewell will probably ever be reprobated by every good Citizen of this State" (Clark, ed., *The State Records of North Carolina,* vol. 21, 500–501).

37. Ibid.

38. Clark, ed., *The State Records of North Carolina,* vol. 21, 497–498, 500–501. In his September 6, 1788, letter to Governor Johnston, Hugh Williamson, delegate to the North Carolina Assembly, informed the North Carolina governor of the open hostility toward the Treaty of Hopewell. Williamson stated, "The Treaty of Hopewell had given much offense to many good Citizens in our State because it was supposed to have surrendered Lands to the Indians which they had formerly

sold or exceeded to the State." Williamson goes on to give Johnston the details of a proposed amendment to the Treaty of Hopewell that stated, "Whenever the present Settlements shall have acquired sufficient strength and the State shall be desirous to extend her Settlements she has only to buy a farther claim of Soil from the Indians" (Clark, ed., *The State Records of North Carolina*, vol. 21, 497–498, 500–501). Williamson may have been referring to the land sales transacted by John Armstrong in 1783 and 1784 or the territorial cessions secured from the Indians by Franklin's highly controversial Treaty of Dumplin Creek (see chapter 4). John Sevier and the Dumplin Creek claimants continued to petition the North Carolina Assembly to recognize the Treaty of Dumplin Creek. The inhabitants of the southern Tennessee Valley communities defended their land claims on the basis of the treaty, which established the state of Franklin's southern and western boundaries at "the dividing ridge between Little [Tennessee] River and the Great Tennessee, and south of the Great Rivers Holston and French Broad" (Memorial of John Sevier, November 20, 1789, State Records, North Carolina State Archives).

39. The petitioners included proposed boundaries for the new county in their November petition. "Beginning at the main Dividing Ridge or Appalachian Mountains Where the waters of the Little Pigeon and Little [Tennessee] Rivers interlock from there along the divide between the two rivers to the waters of Boyd Creek Thence along the Divide between Boyd Creek and the Little Pigeon to the [illegible] point of a large island in the French Broad Known by the name of Sevier Island Thence a West course to the Hawkins [County] line" (Report on petitions of inhabitants of Greene Co. and south of French Broad River, November 20, 1788, State Records, North Carolina State Archives). The proposed county encompassed huge tracts of land in Sevier and Caswell counties (neither yet formally recognized by the North Carolina government).

40. William R. Shepherd, "Wilkinson and the Beginnings of the Spanish Conspiracy," *American Historical Review* 9 (April 1904): 490–493.

41. The Supreme Council of Spain rendered their decision as to which of Wilkinson's propositions to adopt on November 20, 1788. After careful consideration, the Spanish government chose the emigration strategy, "until the Kentuckians attain their independence from the United States" ("Papers Bearing on James Wilkinson's Relations with Spain," *American Historical Review* 9 [July 1904]: 748–749).

42. Abernethy, "Journal of the First Kentucky Convention," 67–78; Allison, *Dropped Stitches in Tennessee History,* 86–89; Henderson, "The Spanish Conspiracy in Tennessee," 235.

43. Miro and Navarro to Valdes, September 25, 1787, "Spanish Papers," *East Tennessee Historical Society's Publications* 12 (1940): 102–109.

44. Gardoqui to Conde de Floridablanca, October 28, 1786, "Spanish Papers," *East Tennessee Historical Society's Publications* 16 (1944): 85–90.

45. Miro and Navarro to Valdes, September 25, 1787, "Spanish Papers," *East Tennessee Historical Society's Publications* 12 (1940): 102–109.

46. Ibid.

47. Ibid.

48. Ezpeleta to Valdes, December 29, 1788, "Spanish Papers," *East Tennessee Historical Society's Publications* 18 (1946): 139–143.

49. Ibid.

50. Ibid.

51. White to Ezpeleta, December 24, 1788, "Spanish Papers," *East Tennessee Historical Society's Publications* 18 (1946): 143–144.

52. Clark, ed., *The State Records of North Carolina,* vol. 22, 698.

53. Miro and Navarro to Valdes, September 25, 1787, "Spanish Papers," *East Tennessee Historical Society's Publications* 12 (1940): 102–109.

54. White to Ezpeleta, December 24, 1788, "Spanish Papers," *East Tennessee Historical Society's Publications* 18 (1946): 143–144.

55. Ibid.

56. Alderman, *The Overmountain Men,* 236–237; Williams, *History of the Lost State of Franklin,* 223–225.

57. Patrick Henry called Sevier's loyalists "Mr. Martins decided foes," and defended the Indian agent by arguing, "I believe the complaints against Mr. Martin but will come from the new govern't [*sic*] party, I mean Franklinites either in No. Carolina or Virg'a [*sic*]" ("Patrick Henry to William Grayson, March 31, 1789," *Virginia Magazine of History and Biography* 14 [June 1907]: 202–204).

58. Clark, ed., *The State Records of North Carolina,* vol. 22, 723–725.

59. Alderman, *The Overmountain Men,* 236–237.

60. White to Miro, April 18, 1789, "Spanish Papers," *East Tennessee Historical Society's Publications* 20 (1948): 103–105.

61. Miro's Memorandum of Concessions to Westerners, April 20, 1789, "Spanish Papers," *East Tennessee Historical Society's Publications* 20 (1948): 103–105. In March 1789, Dr. Hugh Williamson wrote, "There is a Report in Town that the King of Spain is dead. One of his sons and that son's wife certainly are dead of Small Pox." Spain's King Carlos III died on December 14, 1788 (Clark, ed., *The State Records of North Carolina,* vol. 21, 539).

62. Miro to Valdez, April 30, 1789, "Spanish Papers," *East Tennessee Historical Society's Publications* 20 (1948): 108–110.

63. Parker, "Historical Interpretations of the Spanish Intrigue," 49, 50; Whitaker, "The Spanish Intrigue in the Old Southwest," 162–163; Whitaker, "The Muscle Shoals Speculation," 382–384; Reeves, *Paths to Distinction,* 17–46. In 1788, the political leadership of the Cumberland communities renamed their communities the Mero District (misspelled) to honor Estevan Miro.

64. Whitaker, "Spanish Intrigue in the Old Southwest," 156–157; Williams,

History of the Lost State of Franklin, 235–244. Historians continue to debate John Sevier and his fellow Franklinites' complicity and motives during the Spanish Intrigue. The scarcity of information relating to the backcountry episode led early intrigue scholars to either misrepresent the incident or omit the conspiracy all together. The translation and publication of an extensive collection of papers pertaining to Spanish-American frontier relations enhanced historical understanding of what actually occurred on the southwestern frontier. The appearance of the "Spanish Papers" definitively proved Sevier and company's duplicity in the frontier conspiracy, and the historiography surrounding the enigmatic event blossomed following their revelation. Sevier apologists defended his role in the treasonous scheme by attaching venerable ulterior motives to his actions. Russell Dean Parker offers several of these interpretations in his historiographical study of the intrigue (Parker, "Historical Interpretations of the Spanish Intrigue," 39–40, 42–44, 46–48). Sevier biographers James R. Gilmore and Francis M. Turner assert that Sevier utilized the threat of an alliance with Spain to either force the United States to take a harder line with the Spanish government over the navigation of the Mississippi River or to pressure North Carolina to cede their western land. To these authors, North Carolina's unwillingness to adequately fund the Tennessee Valley's frontier drove John Sevier to open negotiations with Gardoqui and White (Gilmore, *John Sevier as a Commonwealth-Builder,* 117–118; Francis Marion Turner, *Life of General John Sevier* [New York: Neal Publishing Company, 1910], 1–99). As Sevier defender Thomas E. Mathews pointed out, "North Carolina had never shown any but the slightest interest in the welfare of these western settlers who had crossed the mountains to make homes for themselves in the wilderness" (Thomas E. Mathews, "The Spanish 'Conspiracy' in Tennessee," *Tennessee Historical Magazine* 4 [March 1918]: 69–72). Another group of historians simply contended that the "defiance of North Carolina" served as Sevier's true motivation for opening talks with Spain. Clearly the timing of the Franklinites' involvement in the conspiracy makes this a compelling argument. Whatever excuse is offered for Sevier's willingness to parley with Gardoqui and White, Nolachucky Jack always emerges as a pragmatic leader who retained his loyalty to the American Republic. Franklin historian Noel B. Gerson described the entire affair as "an Elaborate Hoax," and proclaimed that "at no time, to be sure, were Sevier and his associates actually planning to make an alliance with Spain" (Gerson, *Franklin: America's Lost State,* 136). Thomas Mathews castigated critics of John Sevier, insisting, "Such men ought not to be lightly, much less unjustly and wantonly, accused of crimes, for if their reputations may be thus assailed, then no man's reputation is safe" (Mathews, "The Spanish 'Conspiracy' in Tennessee," 69–72).

65. There is another group of historians offering a much harsher critique of Sevier and the Tennessee Valley's political leadership. Although still maintaining that the Franklin conspirators never actually planned to swear their allegiance to

Spain, these scholars associate financial motives with the Franklinites' actions. Historian Thomas Perkins Abernethy pioneered the "economic interpretation" of the Spanish Intrigue. Abernethy contended that the Spanish conspiracy had little to do with frontier defense or preserving the Franklin statehood movement. Instead, Abernethy argued that support for the scheme stemmed from the insatiable desire to secure control of the Muscle Shoals territory. Abernethy accused influential land speculators, such as William Blount, Richard Caswell, and John Sevier, of secretly promoting the scheme in the Tennessee Valley for personal financial gain. According to Abernethy, the failure of the Muscle Shoals land speculators to secure "the cession of western land to Congress" in 1784 and the United States' inability to secure rights to "the navigation of the Mississippi" convinced Blount and company to turn to Spain. A Spanish alliance offered "the only way in which the [Mississippi] river could be opened to trade," the termination of the Indians' "war against the settlements," and "the hope of enticing new settlers to the West to increase the value of lands" (Abernethy, *From Frontier to Plantation,* 91–102). Details of the connection between William Blount and both the Spanish Intrigue and the post-1784 Muscle Shoals land deal remain obscured (Parker, "Historical Interpretations of the Spanish Intrigue," 56–59). Blount biographer William Masterson points out several links between Blount and the conspiracy. Both William Blount and James White worked in Philadelphia during the earliest phases of the scheme, and Masterson speculates that Blount "probably knew of it." Masterson also associates Blount with the Spanish Intrigue in Cumberland, but ultimately concludes that "he saw earlier than some of his Western associates that, while the intrigue could be well used as a threat to extort a cession from North Carolina, yet the essential incompatibility of the aims of the Westerners and of Spain precluded carrying separatist ideas to any radical conclusion" (Masterson, *William Blount,* 151).

8. Rocked to Death in the Cradle of Secession

1. *Ingram Weirs v. William Cocke,* September 1804, William Alexander Provine Papers, Tennessee State Library and Archives; John Overton, *Tennessee Reports, or Cases Ruled and Adjudged in the Superior Courts of Law and Equity, and Federal Courts for the State of Tennessee* (Knoxville: privately published, 1813).

2. Ibid.

3. Ibid.

4. Ibid.

5. Noel C. Fisher, "Definitions of Victory: East Tennessee Unionists in the Civil War and Reconstruction," in *Guerrillas, Unionists, and Violence on the Confederate Home Front,* ed. Daniel E. Sutherland (Fayetteville: Univ. of Arkansas Press, 1999), 90–91.

6. Kastor, "Equitable Rights and Privileges," 210–212.

7. Palmer, ed., *Calendar of Virginia State Papers,* vol. 4, 100–101.

8. Ibid.

9. Watauga Association of Genealogists, *History of Washington County,* 20.

10. Clark, ed., *The State Records of North Carolina,* vol. 22, 697–699.

11. John Sevier to Georgia Assembly, June 25, 1787, William Alexander Provine Papers, Tennessee State Library and Archives.

12. Gilmore, *The Rear-Guard of the Revolution.*

13. McGill, "Franklin and Frankland: Names and Boundaries," 248–250. The debate surrounding the original name for Franklin continued for years after the collapse of the state. In 1843, frontier historian and archivist Lyman Draper initiated an inquiry into the origin of the name Franklin. General Stephen Cocke, son of Colonel William Cocke, relayed to Draper that "his father had informed him that as friends of the new government aimed to form a sovereign state, free of North Carolina, they hit upon the name 'Frankland' as particularly appropriate—for 'Frankland' is equivalent to 'Freeland.'" The name Frankland only appeared on a handful of official documents and within contemporary correspondences (L. C. Draper on the Name of Franklin, William Alexander Provine Papers, Tennessee State Library and Archives).

14. Dykeman, *Tennessee: A History,* 66; Fisher, "Definitions of Victory," 90–91.

15. Unknown author, June 1, 1785, Newspaper Abstracts (JJ), Draper Manuscript Collection.

16. Clark, ed., *The State Records of North Carolina,* vol. 22, 697–699; Abraham Jobe, "Autobiography, or Memoirs of Doctor A. Jobe," Archives of Appalachia, East Tennessee State University.

17. Frank Moore, *Speeches of Andrew Johnson, President of the United States. With a Biographical Introduction* (Boston: Little, Brown, 1866), 263–276.

18. Clark, ed., *The State Records of North Carolina,* vol. 22, 642–647; Fisher, "Definitions of Victory," 90–91.

19. Clark, ed., *The State Records of North Carolina,* vol. 22, 637.

20. Clark, ed., *The State Records of North Carolina,* vol. 21, 462–463, 487, 496. These two dramatically divergent contemporary views of the state of Franklin persist to this very day and define the two broadest historiographical schools interpreting the statehood movement.

21. Bergeron, Ash, and Keith, *Tennesseans and Their History,* 47–49; Morgan, *The Birth of the Republic,* 113–114. The Northwest Ordinance created a "three-stage" process that allowed a territory to achieve statehood. Stage one required the president of the United States to appoint a territorial governor, secretary, and three territorial judges. After five thousand adult males resided in the territory, stage two called for the popular election of representatives to the lower house of the territorial legislature (the governor appointed the members of the upper house). After the

territory's population reached sixty thousand, the final stage called for the drafting of a constitution (approved by Congress) and finally the admission of the territory to the union as a state (Finger, *Tennessee Frontiers,* 127–128).

22. Bergeron, Ash, and Keith, *Tennesseans and Their History,* 50–51, 57–62; Finger, *Tennessee Frontiers,* 127–129.

23. Finger, *Tennessee Frontiers,* 131; Bergeron, Ash, and Keith, *Tennesseans and Their History,* 59–65; Holt, "The Economic and Social Beginnings of Tennessee," 163.

24. Bergeron, Ash, and Keith, *Tennesseans and Their History,* 59–65; Finger, *Tennessee Frontiers,* 149, 179–201.

25. Bergeron, Ash, and Keith, *Tennesseans and Their History,* 63–69.

26. Ibid., 70–73, 79–82; Finger, *Tennessee Frontiers,* 179–201; Fisher, "Definitions of Victory," 91–92.

27. Ned Irwin, "The Lost Papers of the 'Lost State of Franklin,'" *Journal of East Tennessee History* 69 (1997): 84–96.

28. George W. Sevier to Lyman C. Draper, February 9, 1839, June 17, 1840, King's Mountain Papers (DD), Draper Manuscript Collection; James Sevier to Lyman C. Draper, August 19, 1839, John Sevier Papers, Tennessee State Library and Archives; Haywood, *The Civil and Political History of Tennessee,* 5–14.

29. A. W. Putnam to Lyman C. Draper, September 4, 1851, King's Mountain Papers (DD), Draper Manuscript Collection; William B. Robinson to Lyman C. Draper, September 23, 1880, King's Mountain Papers (DD), Draper Manuscript Collection; Jeanette Tillotson Acklen, comp., *Tennessee Records: Tombstone Inscriptions and Manuscripts* (Nashville: privately published, 1933; reprint, Baltimore: Clearfield Company, 1998), 10. "Rip Van Winkle State" was one of the state of North Carolina's earliest nicknames. A. W. Putnam also founded the Tennessee Historical Society (Albigence Waldo Putnam Papers, 1775–1869, Tennessee State Library and Archives, Nashville).

30. John Tipton to Lyman C. Draper, January 22, 1839, King's Mountain Papers (DD), Draper Manuscript Collection.

31. Abraham Jobe, "Autobiography, or Memoirs of Doctor A. Jobe," Archives of Appalachia, East Tennessee State University; Dunn, *Cades Cove,* 11–16. The fact that most of Jobe's "informants" came from the Tipton and Jobe families, including "old Aunt Sally Tipton" and "Uncle Abraham Jobe," explains Dr. Jobe's pro-Tipton bias.

32. Bergeron, Ash, and Keith, *Tennesseans and Their History,* 63–64, 70–73, 80, 111–113; Hsiung, *Two Worlds in the Tennessee Mountains,* 75–92; Finger, *Tennessee Frontier,* 184–194; Fisher, "Definitions of Victory," 91–92.

33. Durwood Dunn, *An Abolitionist in the Appalachian South: Ezekiel Birdseye on Slavery, Capitalism, and Separate Statehood in East Tennessee, 1841–1846* (Knoxville: Univ. of Tennessee Press, 1997), 4–7, 17; Bergeron, Ash, and Keith, *Tennes-*

seans and Their History, 126. Historian Caitlin Fitz argues that the Tennessee antislavery movement occurred in two distinct phases. The first emerged following the War of 1812, with the formation of the Tennessee Manumission Society (1815). Led by Tennessee's religious leadership, the first phase of the movement advocated the end of slavery and the gradual emancipation of Tennessee slaves based on "Christian ideals" and "republican egalitarianism." The second phase of the Tennessee antislavery movement emerged in the 1830s, and utilized a "strong class appeal" to end the use of slave labor because of its impact on free white laborers and yeoman farmers (Caitlin A. Fitz, "The Tennessee Antislavery Movement and the Market Revolution, 1815–1835," *Civil War History* 52 [March 2006]: 6–9).

34. Henry Lee Swint, "Ezekiel Birdseye and the Free State of Frankland," *Tennessee Historical Quarterly* 3 (March 1944): 226–228; Jeff Biggers, *The United States of Appalachia: How Southern Mountaineers Brought Independence, Culture, and Enlightenment to America* (Emeryville, Calif.: Shoemaker and Hoard, 2005), 83–96.

35. Bergeron, Ash, and Keith, *Tennesseans and Their History,* 94; Fitz, "The Tennessee Antislavery Movement," 8–11, 16–18.

36. Dunn, *An Abolitionist in the Appalachian South,* 4–7, 10–14; Sheeler, "Background Factors of East Tennessee," 167–168; Bergeron, Ash, and Keith, *Tennesseans and Their History,* 126–127; Biggers, *The United States of Appalachia,* 96–98; Fisher, *War at Every Door,* 16; Fitz, "The Tennessee Antislavery Movement," 16.

37. Dunn, *Cades Cove,* 124–125; Fitz, "The Tennessee Antislavery Movement," 18–20, 38–39.

38. Swint, "Ezekiel Birdseye and the Free State of Frankland," 226–229.

39. Dunn, *An Abolitionist in the Appalachian South,* 25, 197–198.

40. Many Tennessee Valley slaveholders "grudgingly" purchased slaves out of economic necessity. In order to contend with the South's competitive commercial agricultural markets, antislavery slaveholders were forced to invest in slave labor and were unable to emancipate their slaves (Fitz, "The Tennessee Antislavery Movement," 28–29).

41. Fisher, "Definitions of Victory," 91–92. Birdseye's use of the widely held argument among East Tennesseans that slave labor discouraged internal improvements and industrial development built upon similar appeals offered during the 1830s by antislavery proponents among regional manufacturers and Whig Party members (Fitz, "The Tennessee Antislavery Movement," 32–34).

42. Swint, "Ezekiel Birdseye and the Free State of Frankland," 226–227, 230–233; Bergeron, Ash, and Keith, *Tennesseans and Their History,* 114–115; Hsiung, *Two Worlds in the Tennessee Mountains,* 92–98; Fitz, "The Tennessee Antislavery Movement," 38–39.

43. Dunn, *An Abolitionist in the Appalachian South,* 197–198.

44. Ibid.

45. Eric Russell Lacy, "The Persistent State of Franklin," *Tennessee Historical Quarterly* 23 (December 1964): 322–323.

46. Fitz, "The Tennessee Antislavery Movement," 39–40.

47. The state of Tennessee poured a tremendous amount of money into the defunct Louisville, Cincinnati, and Charleston Railroad. The economic depression of the 1830s derailed the East Tennessee portion of the railroad, and regional politicians pressured the state to mark the $650,000 dollars that remained for the project for the much-needed Tennessee Valley internal improvements (Swint, "Ezekiel Birdseye and the Free State of Frankland," 226–227, 230–233).

48. Hsiung, *Two Worlds in the Tennessee Mountains,* 135.

49. Dunn, *An Abolitionist in the Appalachian South,* 18–19, 197–198; Fisher, *War at Every Door,* 18–19.

50. According to Eric Russell Lacy, representative Joseph L. Williams (a Knoxville Whig) first proposed statehood for East Tennessee during the November internal improvement convention (Lacy, "The Persistent State of Franklin," 322–324).

51. Johnson proposed that the state of Franklin committee "consist of two members on the part of the Senate, and three on the part of the House of Representatives to be chosen from the eastern portion of the State" (Swint, "Ezekiel Birdseye and the Free State of Frankland," 233–235; Lacy, "The Persistent State of Franklin," 324–325).

52. Dunn, *An Abolitionist in the Appalachian South,* 18–19, 197.

53. Swint, "Ezekiel Birdseye and the Free State of Frankland," 233–235.

54. Lacy, "The Persistent State of Franklin," 325–327.

55. Swint, "Ezekiel Birdseye and the Free State of Frankland," 235–236.

56. Dunn, *An Abolitionist in the Appalachian South,* 18–19.

57. Kastor, "Equitable Rights and Privileges," 208–212.

58. Fisher, "Definitions of Victory," 91–92; Fitz, "The Tennessee Antislavery Movement," 17–18, 30–32. In 1847, Washington College (Lexington, Virginia) president Henry Ruffner published a pamphlet that called for gradual emancipation of western Virginia's slaves in order to encourage the growth of industry (salt, iron, oil, and coal) and the improvement of trans-Allegheny education (Otis K. Rice and Stephen W. Brown, *West Virginia: A History,* 2nd. ed. [Lexington: Univ. Press of Kentucky, 1993], 103).

59. Daniel W. Crofts, *Reluctant Confederates: Upper South Unionists in the Secession Crisis* (Chapel Hill: Univ. of North Carolina Press, 1989), 43–44.

60. Fisher, "Definitions of Victory," 92; Hsiung, *Two Worlds in the Tennessee Mountains,* 135–138; Bergeron, Ash, and Keith, *Tennesseans and Their History,* 116–117; Fisher, *War at Every Door,* 6–8, 16–18. According to Lacy, antebellum East Tennessee "had acquired half of the state's chartered railroads and three-fourths of its mileage." Out of all the former Franklin counties, Hawkins County

maintained the highest percentage of slaveholders (Lacy, "The Persistent State of Franklin," 325–327, 330).

61. Crofts, *Reluctant Confederates*, 21–22.

62. Moore, *Speeches of Andrew Johnson*, 263–266.

63. Ibid., 265–275; John H. Wheeler, *Historical Sketches of North Carolina from 1584 to 1851* (Philadelphia: Lippincott, Grambo, and Co., 1851).

64. Lacy, "The Persistent State of Franklin," 330; Bergeron, Ash, and Keith, *Tennesseans and Their History*, 133–136; William W. Freehling, *The South vs. the South: How Anti-Confederate Southerners Shaped the Course of the Civil War* (Oxford: Oxford Univ. Press, 2001), 40–42; Fisher, *War at Every Door*, 24–25, 35–36.

65. Dunn, *An Abolitionist in the Appalachian South*, 21; Fisher, *War at Every Door*, 28–29; Fisher, "Definitions of Victory," 92–93. East Tennessee was also politically divided over secession. The counties of upper East Tennessee "were about two to one against secession," and all of the "middle" East Tennessee counties voted against "separation." Only in the "lower" East Tennessee counties did residents cast their votes for secession (John Alexander Williams, *Appalachia: A History* [Chapel Hill: Univ. of North Carolina Press, 2002], 159).

66. Fisher, "Definitions of Victory," 92–93; W. Todd Groce, "The Social Origins of East Tennessee's Confederate Leadership," in *The Civil War in Appalachia: Collected Essays*, ed. Kenneth W. Noe and Shannon H. Wilson (Knoxville: Univ. of Tennessee Press, 1997), 31–48.

67. In his book *The South vs. the South*, William W. Freehling argues that regions within the South that retained string unionist sentiment (western Virginia, eastern Tennessee, and western North Carolina) contributed to the Confederacy's defeat during the Civil War.

68. Williams, *Appalachia: A History*, 164–167. For a detailed account of partisan violence in East Tennessee during the Civil War, consult Noel C. Fisher's *War at Every Door: Partisan Politics and Guerrilla Violence in East Tennessee, 1860–1869*.

69. Lacy, "The Persistent State of Franklin," 331–332; Fisher, *War at Every Door*, 37–38.

70. Dunn, *An Abolitionist in the Appalachian South*, 21; Fisher, *War at Every Door*, 39–40; Fisher, "Definitions of Victory," 93–96.

71. Historian Noel C. Fisher argues that a "fervent sense of patriotism," aroused by their region's actions during the American Revolution, served as one of the motivating factors inspiring strong unionist sentiment in eastern Tennessee (Fisher, "Definitions of Victory," 95–95).

Epilogue

1. The Nashville-born Belle Kinney and her Austrian husband, Leopold Shultz, sculpted numerous Tennessee monuments, including statues at the Tennessee War Memorial and at the reconstructed Parthenon and busts of Presidents

Andrew Jackson and James K. Polk (Carroll Van West, "The Tennessee Encyclopedia of History and Culture," 2002, http://tennesseeencyclopedia.net/imagegallery.php?EntryID=K014 [accessed April 7, 2007]).

2. John H. DeWitt, "Biographical Sketch," John Sevier Papers, Tennessee State Library and Archives.

3. John Sevier Memorial Association, "The Marble Springs Historic Site," 2003, http://www.korrnet.org/jsma/index.htm (accessed July 14, 2005); Public Act of Tennessee 1941, February 10, 1941, John Sevier Papers, Tennessee State Library and Archives.

4. "The Lost State of Franklin," B. Carroll Reece Museum Records, Archives of Appalachia, East Tennessee State University. The Treaty of Dumplin Creek plaque stands in Kodak in Sevier County, Tennessee.

5. Helen Topping Miller, *The Sound of Chariots* (Chicago: People's Book Club, 1957), 283–288.

6. Noel B. Gerson, *The Cumberland Rifles* (New York: Doubleday, 1952), 37–39, 92–95, 298–314.

7. Brochures, programs, and playbills for productions of *Chucky Jack* in the Hunter Hills Theatre, Gatlinburg, Tennessee, 1956 and 1958, Wilber White Stout Papers, McCain Library and Archives, University of Southern Mississippi.

8. John J. Baratte, Lost State of Franklin, 1965–1966, B. Carroll Reece Museum Records, Archives of Appalachia, East Tennessee State University. John J. Baratte served as the B. Carroll Reece Museum's director at the time of the Lost State of Franklin exhibition.

9. State of Franklin Bill, March 7, 1961, James H. Quillen Papers, Archives of Appalachia, East Tennessee State University.

10. Hendrick L. Smith to James H. Quillen, March 25, 1961; H. Nick Johnson to James H. Quillen, March 10, 1961; James H. Quillen to H. Nick Johnson, March 16, 1961, all in James H. Quillen Papers, Archives of Appalachia, East Tennessee State University.

11. Ibid.

12. Charles B. Tyson to James Quillen, September 20, 1982; News from Congressman James H. Quillen, January 5, 1983; *Kingsport Times* (Kingsport, Tennessee), September 8, 1982, all in James H. Quillen Papers, Archives of Appalachia, East Tennessee State University.

13. Ron McCarley and Alan Bridwell, "Historical Timeline for Key Events for Johnson City, Tennessee Area Transportation and Economic Development," n.d., http://www.jcedb.org/history/time/time2.htm (accessed July 16, 2005).

14. W. E. Newell, *The Tri-City Area and the State of Franklin* (Bristol, Tenn.: privately published, 1968), 1–5.

15. Ibid.

16. "State of Franklin Savings Bank," 2003, http://www.stateoffranklin.com/ (accessed July 16, 2005).

17. Cox and Cox, comps., *History of Washington County, Tennessee,* 91–93. Dr. Michael Toomey, staff historian for the East Tennessee Historical Society, published an excellent concise account of the history of Franklin, entitled "'Our Present Confused Situation': The State of Franklin, 1784–1789," in Joyce and Eugene Cox's *History of Washington County, Tennessee.*

Bibliography

Unpublished Manuscript Collections

Brewer, Carson, Collection. Special Collections and Archives, University of Tennessee, Knoxville.

Broadside Television Collection, 1970–1978. Archives of Appalachia, East Tennessee State University, Johnson City.

Brownlow, William G., Papers, 1848–1902. Special Collections and Archives, University of Tennessee, Knoxville.

Caldwell Family Papers. Archives of Appalachia, East Tennessee State University, Johnson City.

Carriger, Sarah, Collection. Special Collections and Archives, University of Tennessee, Knoxville.

Carter Family Papers, 1659–1797. Tennessee State Library and Archives, Nashville.

Cherokee Baptist Church Records, Jonesboro, 1787–1923. Tennessee State Library and Archives, Nashville.

Cherokee Collection, 1775–1878. Tennessee State Library and Archives, Nashville.

Cherokee Documents in Foreign Archives. Special Collections, Western Carolina University, Cullowhee.

Claiborne, John Francis Hamtramck, Papers. Southern Historical Collection, University of North Carolina, Chapel Hill.

Clark, Henry Toole, Papers. North Carolina State Archives, Raleigh.

Cocke, William Johnston, Papers. Southern Historical Collection, University of North Carolina, Chapel Hill.

Dickson, William, Papers. North Carolina State Archives, Raleigh.

Doak, Samuel Witherspoon, Papers, 1768–1925. Tennessee State Library and Archives, Nashville.

Draper Manuscript Collection. State Historical Society of Wisconsin, Madison.

Embree Family Papers. Archives of Appalachia, East Tennessee State University, Johnson City.

Fink, Paul, Collection. William Leonard Eury Collection, Special Collections, Belk Library, Appalachian State University, Boone.

Fox Family Papers. Special Collections and Archives, University of Tennessee, Knoxville.

Haywood, John, Papers, 1768–1796. Tennessee State Library and Archives, Nashville.

Jobe, Abraham, Autobiography. Archives of Appalachia, East Tennessee State University, Johnson City.

Letters in the North Carolina Archives in Foreign Documents. North Carolina State Archives, Raleigh.

McIver, John, Diary, 1780–1805. Tennessee State Library and Archives, Nashville.

Martin, Alexander, Governor Letter Book. North Carolina State Archives, Raleigh.

Provine, William Alexander, Papers. Tennessee State Library and Archives, Nashville.

Putnam, Albigence Waldo, Papers, 1775–1869. Tennessee State Library and Archives, Nashville.

Quillen, James H., Papers. Archives of Appalachia, East Tennessee State University, Johnson City.

Ramsey Family Papers. Special Collections and Archives, University of Tennessee, Knoxville.

Range Family Papers. Archives of Appalachia, East Tennessee State University, Johnson City.

Records of the Cumberland District, Davidson and Washington counties. Tennessee State Library and Archives, Nashville.

Reece, B. Carroll, Museum Records. Archives of Appalachia, East Tennessee State University, Johnson City.

Robertson, James, Papers, 1742–1814. Tennessee State Library and Archives, Nashville.

Sevier, John, Collection. Special Collections and Archives, University of Tennessee, Knoxville.

Sevier, John, Papers. Tennessee State Library and Archives, Nashville.

Shelby Family Papers. Archives of Appalachia, East Tennessee State University, Johnson City.

Shelby and Hart Family Papers, 1775–1814. Southern Historical Collection, University of North Carolina, Chapel Hill.

Stout, Wilber White, Papers. McCain Library and Archives, University of Southern Mississippi, Hattiesburg.

Temple, O. P., Papers. Special Collections and Archives, University of Tennessee, Knoxville.

Washington College Records. Tennessee State Library and Archives, Nashville.

Washington County Court Records, Receipts, 1780–1965. Archives of Appalachia, East Tennessee State University, Johnson City.

Washington County Court Records. North Carolina State Archives, Raleigh.
Williams, Samuel Cole, Papers. Tennessee State Library and Archives, Nashville.

Published Manuscript Collections

Ballagh, James Curtis, ed. *The Letters of Richard Henry Lee.* New York: De Capo Press, 1970.

Boyd, Julian P., ed. *The Papers of Thomas Jefferson.* 35 vols. Princeton: Princeton Univ. Press, 1953.

Clark, Elmer T., ed. *The Journal and Letters of Francis Asbury.* London: Epworth Press and Nashville: Abingdon Press, 1958.

Corbitt, D. C., and Roberta Corbitt, eds. "Papers from the Spanish Archive Relating to Tennessee and the Old Southwest, 1783–1800." *East Tennessee Historical Society's Publications* 9–49 (1937–1977).

Fries, Adelaide L., ed. *Records of the Moravians in North Carolina.* Raleigh: North Carolina Historical Commission, 1941.

Griffey, Irene M. *Earliest Tennessee Land Records and Earliest Tennessee Land History.* Baltimore: Clearfield Company, 2000.

Gump, Lucy K. "Interpretive Transcription of an East Tennessee Business Record Book, Ledger B." Special Collections, James D. Hoskins Library, University of Tennessee, Knoxville.

Hamilton, Stanislaus Murray. *The Writings of James Monroe.* New York: G. P. Putnam's Sons, 1898.

"Henry, Patrick, to William Grayson, March 31, 1789." *Virginia Magazine of History and Biography* 14 (1907): 202–204.

Henry, William Wirt. *Patrick Henry: Life, Correspondence, and Speeches.* New York: Burt Franklin, 1969.

Keith, Alice Barnwell. *The John Gray Blount Papers.* 4 vols. Raleigh: State Department of Archives and History, 1952.

Madison, James. *The Papers of James Madison: Congressional Series.* Ed. Robert A. Rutland, Charles F. Hobson, William M. E. Rachal, and Fredrika J. Teute. Vol. 10, *27 May 1787–3 March 1788.* Chicago: Univ. of Chicago Press, 1977.

Moore, Frank. *Speeches of Andrew Johnson, President of the United States. With a Biographical Introduction.* Boston: Little, Brown, 1866.

Sevier, Cora Bales, and Nancy S. Madden. *Sevier Family History with the Collected Letters of Gen. John Sevier, First Governor of Tennessee.* Washington, D.C.: privately published, 1961.

Smith, Ethel Wheeler, ed. *Washington County, Tennessee, Marriages and Wills.* Johnson City: Parrish Printing, 1961.

Smith, Paul H., ed. *Letters of Delegates to Congress.* 25 vols. Washington, D.C.: Library of Congress, 1976.

Sparks, Jared, ed. *The Works of Benjamin Franklin.* Boston: Whitemore, Niles, and Hall, 1856.

Syrett, Harold C., ed. *The Papers of Alexander Hamilton.* 27 vols. New York: Columbia Univ. Press, 1962.

WPA Historical Records Survey. *Records of Carter County: Papers Relating to Sinking Creek Baptist Church, 1783–1875.* Morristown, Tenn.: U.S. Works Progress Administration, 1938.

————. *Records of Carter County: Sketch of Sinking Creek Baptist Church.* Morristown, Tenn.: U.S. Works Progress Administration, 1938.

————. *Records of Greene County: County Court Minutes, 1783–1796.* Nashville: U.S. Works Progress Administration, 1940.

————. *Records of Sullivan County, Tennessee: Deed Book, 1775–1790.* Nashville: U.S. Works Progress Administration, 1936.

————. *Records of Washington County: General Index to Deeds and Mortgages, 1779–1865.* U.S. Works Progress Administration, 1940.

————. *Records of Washington County: Inventories of Estates, 1779–1821.* Nashville: U.S. Works Progress Administration, 1938.

————. *Records of Washington County: Superior Court Minutes, 1791–1804.* Nashville: U.S. Works Progress Administration, 1938.

Government Documents

Burnett, Edmund C. *Letters of Members of the Continental Congress.* Washington, D.C.: Carnegie Institute of Washington, 1936.

Carter, Clarence Edwin, ed. *The Territorial Papers of the United States.* Washington, D.C.: GPO, 1936.

Clark, Walter, ed. *The State Records of North Carolina.* Goldsboro, N.C.: Nash Brothers, 1903.

Farrand, Max, ed. *The Records of the Federal Convention of 1787.* New Haven, Conn.: Yale Univ. Press, 1911.

Hall, Wilmer L. *Journals of the Council of the State of Virginia.* Richmond: Virginia State Library, 1969.

Journals of the Continental Congress. Washington, D.C.: GPO, 1907–1937.

Palmer, William P., ed. *Calendar of Virginia State Papers and Other Manuscripts from January 1, 1785, to July 2, 1789, Preserved at the Capital at Richmond,* vol. 4. Richmond: R. U. Derr, Superintendent of Public Printing, 1884.

Papers of the Continental Congress. Washington, D.C.: GPO, 1971.

Secondary Sources

Abernethy, Thomas Perkins. *From Frontier to Plantation in Tennessee: A Study in Frontier Democracy.* Chapel Hill: Univ. of North Carolina Press, 1932.

———. "Journal of the First Kentucky Convention, Dec. 27, 1784–Jan. 5, 1785." *Journal of Southern History* 1 (February 1935): 67–78.

Acklen, Jeanette Tillotson, comp. *Tennessee Records: Tombstone Inscriptions and Manuscripts.* Nashville: privately published, 1933. Reprint, Baltimore: Clearfield Company, 1998.

Alden, George Henry. "The State of Franklin." *American Historical Review* 8 (January 1903): 271–289.

Alderman, Pat. *The Overmountain Men.* Johnson City, Tenn.: Overmountain Press, 1970.

Allen, Penelope Johnson, comp. *Tennessee Soldiers in the Revolution.* Nashville: Tennessee Daughters of the American Revolution, 1935.

Allison, John. *Dropped Stitches in Tennessee History.* Nashville: Marshall and Bruce, 1897.

Anderson, William T., and Robert M. McBride, eds. *Landmarks of Tennessee History.* Nashville: Tennessee Historical Society, 1965.

Arthur, John Preston. *Western North Carolina: A History from 1730 to 1913.* 1914. Reprint, Johnson City, Tenn.: Overmountain Press, 1996.

Ashe, Samuel A. *Biographical History of North Carolina from Colonial Times to the Present.* Greensboro: Charles L. Van Noppen, 1905.

———. "The State of Franklin." *North Carolina Booklet* 14 (1914): 28–49.

Barksdale, Kevin T. "Whiskey Distillation in Antebellum Western North Carolina." *Tuckasegee Valley Historical Review* 5 (1999): 1–14.

Barnhart, John D. *Valley of Democracy: The Frontier versus the Plantation in the Ohio Valley, 1775–1818.* Bloomington: Indiana Univ. Press, 1953.

Barwick, Jan. "Richard Caswell: North Carolina's Forgotten Governor." *Olde Kinston Gazette,* June 1998, http://www.kinstonpress.com/kinston_gaz/caswell_forgotten.htm (accessed June 25, 2008).

Beeman, Richard, Stephen Brotein, and Edward C. Carter II. *Beyond Confederation: Origins of the Constitution and American National Identity.* Chapel Hill: Univ. of North Carolina Press, 1987.

Bergeron, Paul H., Stephen V. Ash, and Jeanette Keith. *Tennesseans and Their History.* Knoxville: Univ. of Tennessee Press, 1999.

Biggers, Jeff. *The United States of Appalachia: How Southern Mountaineers Brought Independence, Culture, and Enlightenment to America.* Emeryville, Calif.: Shoemaker and Hoard, 2005.

Billings, Dwight B., and Kathleen M. Blee. *The Road to Poverty: The Making of Wealth and Hardship in Appalachia.* Cambridge: Cambridge Univ. Press, 2000.

Black, Henry C. "Some Forgotten Constitutions: Franklin." *Constitutional Review* 10 (April 1926): 115–119.

Blethen, H. Tyler, and Curtis Wood Jr. *Leave-Taking: The Scotch-Irish Come to Western North Carolina.* Cullowhee, N.C.: Mountain Heritage Center, 1986.

Blight, David W. *Race and Reunion: The Civil War in American Memory.* Cambridge: Belknap Press of Harvard Univ. Press, 2001.

Boyd, William K. "Early Relation of North Carolina and the West." *North Carolina Booklet* 7 (1907): 193–209.

———. *History of North Carolina,* vol. 2, *The Federal Period, 1783–1860.* Chicago: Lewis Publishing Company, 1919.

Braund, Kathryn E. Holland. *Deerskins and Duffels: The Creek Indian Trade with Anglo-America, 1685–1815.* Lincoln: Univ. of Nebraska Press, 1993.

Breazeale, J. W. M. *Life as It Is; or Matters and Things in General.* Knoxville: James Williams, 1842.

Breisach, Ernst. *Historiography: Ancient, Medieval, and Modern.* Chicago: Univ. of Chicago Press, 1983. Reprint, Chicago: Univ. of Chicago Press, 1994.

Brewster, William. *The Fourteenth Commonwealths: Vermont and the States that Failed.* Philadelphia: George S. MacManus Company, 1960.

Burgner, Goldene Fillers. *Washington County Tennessee Wills, 1777–1872.* Easley, S.C.: Southern Historical Press, 1983.

Caldwell, Joshua W. *Constitutional History of Tennessee.* Cincinnati: Robert Clarke Company, 1895.

Caldwell, Mary French. *Tennessee: The Dangerous Example, Watauga to 1849.* Nashville: Aurora Publishers, 1974.

Calloway, Brenda C. *America's First Western Frontier: East Tennessee.* Johnson City, Tenn.: Overmountain Press, 1989.

Cannon, Walter Faw. "Four Interpretations of the History of the State of Franklin." *East Tennessee Historical Society's Publications* 22 (1950): 3–18.

Caughey, John Walton. *McGillivray of the Creeks.* Norman: Univ. of Oklahoma Press, 1938.

Cheney, John L., ed. *North Carolina, 1585–1979: A Narrative and Statistical History.* Raleigh: North Carolina Department of the Secretary of State, 1979.

Cherokee and Creek Indians. Ethnographic Report on Royce. Area 79: Chickasaw, Cherokee, Creek [by] Charles Fairbanks; Cherokee Treaties [by] John H. Goff, Commission Findings [by] Indian Claims Commission. New York: Garland Publishing, 1974.

Clayton, LaReine Warden. *Stories of Early Inns and Taverns of the East Tennessee Country.* Nashville: National Society of Colonial Dames of America in the State of Tennessee, 1995.

Coleman, Kenneth, general ed. *A History of Georgia.* Athens: Univ. of Georgia Press, 1977.

Conley, Robert J. *The Cherokee Nation: A History.* Albuquerque: Univ. of New Mexico Press, 2005.

Connelly, Thomas Lawrence. "Indian Warfare on the Tennessee Frontier, 1776–1794: Strategy and Tactics." *Journal of East Tennessee History* 36 (1964): 3–22.

"Constitution of the State of Franklin." *American Historical Magazine* 9 (1904): 399–408.

Corlew, Robert E. *Statehood for Tennessee*. Nashville: Tennessee American Revolution Bicentennial Commission, 1976.

Cox, Joyce, and W. Eugene Cox, comps. *History of Washington County, Tennessee*. Johnson City, Tenn.: Overmountain Press, 2001.

Crawford, Charles W., ed. *Governors of Tennessee, I: 1790–1835*. Memphis: Memphis State Univ. Press, 1979.

Creekmore, Pollyanna. "Early East Tennessee Taxpayers XIV, Greene County, 1783." *Journal of East Tennessee History* 39 (1967): 118–130.

————, comp. *Early East Tennessee Taxpayers*. Easley, S.C.: Southern Historical Press, 1980.

Crofts, Daniel W. *Reluctant Confederates: Upper South Unionists in the Secession Crisis*. Chapel Hill: Univ. of North Carolina Press, 1989.

Davis, Donald Edward. *Where There Are Mountains: An Environmental History of the Southern Appalachians*. Athens: Univ. of Georgia Press, 2000.

DeConde, Alexander. *Entangled Alliance: Politics and Diplomacy under George Washington*. Durham, N.C.: Duke Univ. Press, 1958. Reprint, Westport, Conn.: Greenwood Press, 1974.

Descriptive Review of the Industries and Resources of Upper East Tennessee Embracing the Vicinity of Johnson City, Jonesboro, Greeneville, Rogersville, and Morristown Together with Brief Notices of the Leading Members of those Communities, A. New York: Enterprise Publishing, 1885.

DeWitt, John H. "History of the Lost State of Franklin." *Tennessee Historical Magazine* 9 (April 1924): 167–170.

Dickens, Roy S., Jr. "The Origin and Development of Cherokee Culture." In *The Cherokee Indian Nation: A Troubled History*, ed. Duane H. King, 3–32. Knoxville: Univ. of Tennessee Press, 1979.

Dixon, Max. *The Wataugans: Tennessee in the Eighteenth Century*. Johnson City, Tenn.: Overmountain Press, 1989.

Downes, Randolph C. "Cherokee-American Relations in the Upper Tennessee Valley, 1776–1791." *East Tennessee Historical Society's Publications* 8 (1936): 35–53.

Driver, Carl. *John Sevier: Pioneer of the Old Southwest*. Chapel Hill: Univ. of North Carolina Press, 1932.

Dunaway, Wilma A. *The First American Frontier: Transition to Capitalism in Southern Appalachia, 1700–1860*. Chapel Hill: Univ. of North Carolina Press, 1996.

Dunn, Durwood. *An Abolitionist in the Appalachian South: Ezekiel Birdseye on Slavery, Capitalism, and Separate Statehood in East Tennessee, 1841–1846*. Knoxville: Univ. of Tennessee Press, 1997.

————. *Cades Cove: The Life and Death of a Southern Appalachian Community, 1818–1937.* Knoxville: Univ. of Tennessee Press, 1988.

Durham, Walter T. *Before Tennessee: The Southwest Territory, 1790–1796.* Rocky Mount, N.C.: Rocky Mount Historical Association, 1990.

————. "The Southwest Territory: Progress to Statehood." *Journal of East Tennessee History* 62 (1990): 3–17.

Dyer, Bill. *Chucky Jack's A-Comin': The Thrilling Life and Times of John Sevier, Founder of Tennessee.* Gatlinburg: Great Smoky Mountain Historical Association, 1956.

Dykeman, Wilma. *The First American Frontier: Transition to Capitalism in Southern Appalachia, 1700–1860.* Chapel Hill: Univ. of North Carolina Press, 1996.

————. *Tennessee: A History.* Newport, Tenn.: Wakestone Books, 1975.

East Tennessee Historical Society. *First Families of Tennessee: A Register of Early Settlers and Their Present-Day Descendants.* Knoxville, Tenn.: East Tennessee Historical Society, 2000.

Ehle, John. *Trail of Tears: The Rise and Fall of the Cherokee Nation.* New York: Anchor Books, Doubleday, 1988.

Ethridge, Robbie. *Creek Country: The Creek Indians and Their World.* Chapel Hill: Univ. of North Carolina Press, 2003.

Eubanks, David Lawson. "Dr. J. G. M. Ramsey of East Tennessee: A Career of Public Service." Ph.D. diss., University of Tennessee, 1965.

Finger, John R. *Tennessee Frontiers: Three Regions in Transition.* Bloomington: Indiana Univ. Press, 2001.

Fink, Paul M. "Early Explorers in the Great Smokies." *East Tennessee Historical Society's Publications* 51 (1979): 40–53.

————. "Jacob Brown of Nolichucky." *Tennessee Historical Quarterly* 21, no. 3 (September 1962): 235–250.

————. *Jonesborough: The First Century of Tennessee's First Town.* Springfield, Va.: National Technical Information Service, 1972.

————. "Jonesboro's Chester Inn." *East Tennessee Historical Society's Publications* 27 (1955): 19–38.

————. "Some Phases of the History of the State of Franklin." *Tennessee Historical Quarterly* 16 (March 1957): 195–213.

Fisher, Noel C. "Definitions of Victory: East Tennessee Unionists in the Civil War and Reconstruction." In *Guerrillas, Unionists, and Violence on the Confederate Home Front,* ed. Daniel E. Sutherland, 89–112. Fayetteville: Univ. of Arkansas Press, 1999.

————. *War at Every Door: Partisan Politics and Guerrilla Violence in East Tennessee, 1860–1869.* Chapel Hill: Univ. of North Carolina Press, 1997.

Fitch, William Edward. *The Origin, Rise and Downfall of the State of Franklin,*

Under Her First and Only Governor John Sevier. New York: New York Society of the Order of the Founders and Patriots of America, 1910.

Fitz, Caitlin A. "The Tennessee Antislavery Movement and the Market Revolution, 1815–1835." *Civil War History* 52 (March 2006): 5–40.

Folmsbee, Stanley J., Robert E. Corlew, and Enoch L. Mitchell. *History of Tennessee,* vol. 1. New York: Lewis Historical Publishing Company, 1960.

Foster, Dave. *Franklin: The Stillborn State and the Sevier/Tipton Political Feud.* Pigeon Forge, Tenn.: Top Ten Press, 1994.

Foster, Gaines M. *Ghosts of the Confederacy: Defeat, the Lost Cause, and the Emergence of the New South.* New York: Oxford Univ. Press, 1987.

Freehling, William W. *The South vs. the South: How Anti-Confederate Southerners Shaped the Course of the Civil War.* Oxford: Oxford Univ. Press, 2001.

Garrett, William R. "The Provisional Constitution of Frankland." *American Historical Magazine* 1 (January 1896): 48–63.

Gentry, Susie. "The Volunteer State (Tennessee) as a Seceder." *North Carolina Booklet* 3 (July 1903): 5–14.

Gerson, Noel B. *The Cumberland Rifles.* New York: Doubleday, 1952.

———. *Franklin: America's Lost State.* New York: Crowell-Collier Press, 1968.

Gilmore, James R. *John Sevier as a Commonwealth-Builder.* New York: D. Appleton and Company, 1887.

———. *The Rear-Guard of the Revolution.* New York: D. Appleton and Co., 1886. Reprint, Spartanburg, S.C.: Reprint Company, 1974.

Goodpasture, Albert V. "Indian Wars and Warriors of the Old Southwest, 1730–1807." *Tennessee Historical Magazine* 4 (March 1918): 3–15.

Green, Michael D. *The Politics of Indian Removal: Creek Government and Society in Crisis.* Lincoln: Univ. of Nebraska Press, 1982.

Groce, W. Todd. *Mountain Rebels: East Tennessee Confederates and the Civil War, 1860–1870.* Knoxville: Univ. of Tennessee Press, 1999.

———. "The Social Origins of East Tennessee's Confederate Leadership." In *The Civil War in Appalachia: Collected Essays,* ed. Kenneth W. Noe and Shannon H. Wilson, 31–48. Knoxville: Univ. of Tennessee Press, 1997.

Hagy, James. "Arthur Campbell and the West, 1743–1811." *Virginia Magazine of History and Biography* 90 (October 1982): 456–471.

———. "Democracy Defeated: The Franklin Constitution of 1785." *Tennessee Historical Quarterly* 40 (fall 1981): 239–256.

Hagy, James W., and Stanley J. Folmsbee. "Arthur Campbell and the Separate State Movements in Virginia and North Carolina." *Journal of East Tennessee History* 42 (1970): 20–46.

Hamer, Phillip M. "The Wataugans and the Cherokee Indians in 1776." *East Tennessee Historical Society's Publications* 3 (January 1931): 108–126.

Haywood, John. *The Civil and Political History of Tennessee from Its Earliest Settle-*

ment up to the Year 1796, Including the Boundaries of the State. Nashville: Publishing House of the Methodist Episcopal Church, South, 1891. Reprint, Johnson City, Tenn.: Overmountain Press, 1999.

Henderson, Archibald. *Conquest of the Old Southwest: The Romantic Story of the Early Pioneers into Virginia, the Carolinas, Tennessee, and Kentucky, 1740–1790.* New York: Century Company, 1920.

————. *North Carolina: The Old North State and the New.* Chicago: Lewis Publishing Company, 1941.

————. "The Spanish Conspiracy in Tennessee." *Tennessee Historical Magazine* 3 (December 1917): 229–249.

Herman, Arthur. *How the Scots Invented the Modern World: The True Story of How Western Europe's Poorest Nation Created Our World and Everything in It.* New York: Three Rivers Press, 2001.

Herndon, G. Melvin. *William Tatham, 1752–1819: American Versatile.* Johnson City: Research Advisory Council, East Tennessee State University, 1973.

Historical Society of Washington County, Virginia. *Washington County Historical Society of Abingdon, Virginia: Addresses Delivered before the Historical Society of Washington County, Virginia.* Abingdon, Va.: Publications of the Washington County Historical Society, 1945.

Hoffman, Paul P., ed. *The Carter Family Papers, 1659–1797, in the Sabine Hall Collection.* Charlottesville, Va.: University of Virginia Library Microfilm Publications, 1967.

Holmes, Jack D. L. "Spanish-American Rivalry over the Chickasaw Bluffs, 1780–1795." *Journal of East Tennessee History* 34 (1962): 26–57.

Holston Territory Genealogical Society, comp. *Families and History of Sullivan County, Tennessee,* vol. 1, *1779–1992.* Waynesville, N.C.: Walsworth, 1992.

Holt, Albert C. "The Economic and Social Beginnings of Tennessee." Ph.D. diss., George Peabody College, 1923.

Holton, Woody. *Forced Founders: Indians, Debtors, Slaves, and the Making of the American Revolution in Virginia.* Chapel Hill: Univ. of North Carolina Press, 1999.

Hooker, Richard J., ed. *The Carolina Backcountry on the Eve of the Revolution: The Journal and Other Writings of Charles Woodmason, Anglican Itinerant,* 2nd ed. Chapel Hill: Univ. of North Carolina Press, 1969.

Horsman, Reginald. *The Diplomacy of the New Republic, 1776–1815.* Arlington Heights, Ill.: Harland Davidson, 1985.

Hosen, Frederick E. *Unfolding Westward in Treaty and Law: Land Documents in United States History from the Appalachians to the Pacific, 1783–1934.* Jefferson, N.C.: McFarland, 1988.

Hsiung, David C. "How Isolated Was Appalachia: Upper East Tennessee, 1780–1835." *Appalachian Journal* 16 (summer 1989): 336–349.

————. *Two Worlds in the Tennessee Mountains: Exploring the Origins of Appalachian Stereotypes*. Lexington: Univ. Press of Kentucky, 1997.

Huhta, James K. "Tennessee and the American Revolution." *Tennessee Historical Quarterly* 31 (winter 1972): 303–315.

Humphrey, Richard Alan. "The State of Franklin: Clergy, Controversy, and Constitution." *Appalachian Heritage: A Magazine of Southern Appalachian Life and Culture* 7 (fall 1979): 35–41.

Hunter, Kermit. *Chucky Jack: The Story of Tennessee*. 1956.

————. *Horn in the West*. 1951.

Inscoe, John C. *Mountain Masters: Slavery and the Sectional Crisis in Western North Carolina*. Knoxville, Tenn.: Univ. of Tennessee Press, 1989.

Irwin, Ned. "The Lost Papers of the 'Lost State of Franklin.'" *Journal of East Tennessee History* 69 (1997): 84–96.

————. "'The Lost State of Franklin': Sources for Research and Study." *Bulletin of Biography* 55 (1998): 35–41.

Jansen, Daniel. "A Case of Fraud and Deception: The Revolutionary War Military Land Bounty Policy in Tennessee." *Journal of East Tennessee History* 64 (1992): 41–67.

Jenson, Merrill. "The Creation of the National Domain, 1781–1784." *Mississippi Valley Historical Review* 26 (December 1939): 323–342.

Kastor, Peter J. "'Equitable Rights and Privileges': The Divided Loyalties in Washington County, Virginia, during the Franklin Separatist Crisis." *Virginia Magazine of History and Biography* 105 (spring 1997): 193–226.

Keedy, Edwin R. "The Constitution of the State of Franklin, the Indian Stream Republic and the State of Deseret." *University of Pennsylvania Law Review* 101 (January 1953): 516–527.

Kincaid, Robert L. "The Wilderness Road in Tennessee." *East Tennessee Historical Society's Publications* 20 (1948): 37–48.

King, Duane H., ed. *The Cherokee Indian Nation: A Troubled History*. Knoxville: Univ. of Tennessee Press, 1979.

Klein, Rachel N. *Unification of a Slave State: The Rise of the Planter Class in the South Carolina Backcountry, 1760–1808*. Chapel Hill: Univ. of North Carolina Press, 1990.

Kornblith, Gary J., and Carol Lasser. "More Than Great White Men: A Century of Scholarship on American Social History." *Organization of American Historians Magazine of History*, April 2007, 8–13.

Lacy, Eric Russell. "The Persistent State of Franklin." *Tennessee Historical Quarterly* 23 (December 1964): 321–332.

Lawson, Dennis T. "The Tipton-Hayes Place: A Landmark of East Tennessee." *Tennessee Historical Quarterly* 29 (summer 1970): 105–124.

Lee, Gerald R., ed. *The Tales and Notes of Henry E. Lee.* Lynwood, Australia: privately published, 1985.

Lefler, Hugh Talmage. *North Carolina History: Told by Contemporaries.* Chapel Hill: Univ. of North Carolina Press, 1934.

Lester, Anne J. "Settlement Patterns in the Upper Counties of East Tennessee to 1796." Master's thesis, North Carolina State University, 1981.

Luttrell, Laura E. "Some Founders of Campbell's Station, Tennessee: A Genealogy of Alexander, David, and James Campbell." *East Tennessee Historical Society's Publications* 26 (1954): 107–119.

Magrath, C. Peter. *Yazoo: Law and Politics in the New Republic: The Case of Fletcher v. Peck.* Providence: Brown Univ. Press, 1966.

Masterson, William H. "The Land Speculator and the West: The Role of William Blount." *East Tennessee Historical Society's Publications* 27 (1955): 3–8.

———. *William Blount.* Baton Rouge: Louisiana State Univ. Press, 1954.

Mathews, Maxine. "Old Inns of East Tennessee." *East Tennessee Historical Society's Publications* 2 (1930): 22–33.

Mathews, Thomas E. "The Spanish 'Conspiracy' in Tennessee." *Tennessee Historical Magazine* 4 (March 1918): 69–72.

McCormack, Edward Michael. *Slavery on the Tennessee Frontier.* Nashville: Tennessee American Revolution Bicentennial Commission, 1977.

McCown, Mary Hardin. *The Wataugah Purchase, March 19, 1775, at Sycamore Shoals of Wataugah River: the Cherokee Indians to Charles Robertson, trustee for the Wataugah Settlers: an Index of the Wataugah purchase, the North Carolina Land Grants, and Deeds Through 1782: a Bicentennial Contribution.* Johnson City, Tenn.: Overmountain Press, 1976.

McCown, Mary Hardin, Nancy E. Jones Stickley, and Inez E. Burns, comps. *Washington County Tennessee Records.* Johnson City, Tenn.: privately published, 1964.

McGill, J. T. "Franklin and Frankland: Names and Boundaries." *Tennessee Historical Magazine* 8 (1924): 248–257.

McLaughlin, Andrew Cunningham. *The Confederation and the Constitution, 1783–1789.* New York: Harper and Brothers, 1905.

McLoughlin, William G. *Cherokee Renaissance in the New Republic.* Princeton: Princeton Univ. Press, 1986.

Middlekauff, Robert. *The Glorious Cause: The American Revolution, 1763–1789.* New York: Oxford Univ. Press, 1982. Reprint, New York: Oxford Univ. Press, 1985.

Miller, Alan N. *East Tennessee's Forgotten Children: Apprentices from 1778–1911.* Baltimore: Clearfield Company, 2001.

Miller, Helen Topping. *The Sound of Chariots.* Chicago: People's Book Club, 1957.

Mitchell, Robert D. *Commercialism and Frontier: Perspectives on the Early Shenandoah Valley*. Charlottesville, Va.: Univ. Press of Virginia, 1977.

Mooney, James. *History, Myths, and Sacred Formulas of the Cherokees*. Asheville, N.C.: Bright Mountain Books, 1992.

Moore, John Wheeler. *History of North Carolina: From the Earliest Discoveries to the Present Time*. Raleigh, N.C.: Alfred Williams and Company, 1880.

Morgan, Edmund S. *The Birth of the Republic, 1763–89*. Chicago: Univ. of Chicago Press, 1956.

Myer, William E. *Indian Trails of the Southeast*. Nashville: Blue and Gray Press, 1971.

Nelson, Selden. "The Tipton Family of Tennessee." *East Tennessee Historical Society's Publications* 1 (1929): 67–76.

Newell, W. E. *The Tri-City Area and the State of Franklin*. Bristol, Tenn.: privately published, 1968.

Newsome, Albert Ray. "North Carolina's Ratification of the Federal Constitution." *North Carolina Historical Review* 17 (October 1940): 287–301.

Noe, Kenneth W., and Shannon H. Wilson, eds. *The Civil War in Appalachia: Collected Essays*. Knoxville: Univ. of Tennessee Press, 1997.

Norton, Herman A. *Religion in Tennessee, 1777–1945*. Knoxville: Univ. of Tennessee Press, 1981.

Novick, Peter. *That Noble Dream: The "Objectivity Question" and the American Historical Profession*. Cambridge: Cambridge Univ. Press, 1988. Reprint, Cambridge: Cambridge Univ. Press, 1997.

Onuf, Peter S. *American Culture, 1776–1815*. New York: Garland Publishing, 1991.

———. "From Colony to Territory: Changing Concepts of Statehood in Revolutionary America." *Political Science Quarterly* 97 (autumn 1982): 447–459.

———. "State-Making in Revolutionary America: Independent Vermont as a Case Study." *Journal of American History* 67 (March 1981): 797–815.

———. "Toward Federalism: Virginia, Congress, and the Western Lands." *William and Mary Quarterly* 34 (July 1977): 353–374.

O'Steen, Neal. "Pioneer Education in the Tennessee Country." *Tennessee Historical Quarterly* 35 (summer 1976): 199–219.

Overton, John. *Tennessee Reports, or Cases Ruled and Adjudged in the Superior Courts of Law and Equity, and Federal Courts for the State of Tennessee*. Knoxville: privately published, 1813.

Pancake, John S. *This Destructive War: The British Campaign in the Carolinas, 1780–1782*. Tuscaloosa: Univ. of Alabama Press, 1985.

"Papers Bearing on James Wilkinson's Relations with Spain." *American Historical Review* 9 (July 1904): 746–766.

Parker, Russell Dean. "Historical Interpretations of the Spanish Intrigue in Tennessee: A Study." *East Tennessee Historical Society's Publications* 58–59 (1986–1987): 39–62.

Phelan, James. *History of Tennessee: The Making of a State.* Boston: Houghton, Mifflin, 1888.

Philyaw, L. Scott. *Virginia's Western Visions: Political and Cultural Expansion on an Early American Frontier.* Knoxville: Univ. of Tennessee Press, 2004.

Potts, Louis W. "Hugh Williamson: The Poor Man's Franklin and the National Domain." *North Carolina Historical Review* 64 (October 1987): 371–393.

Powell, William S. *North Carolina: Through Four Centuries.* Chapel Hill: Univ. of North Carolina Press, 1989.

Pruitt, Albert Bruce. *Glasgow Land Fraud Papers,* vol. 2, *North Carolina Revolutionary War Bounty Land in Tennessee.* Cary, N.C.: privately published, 1993.

Quinn, Hartwell L. *Arthur Campbell: Pioneer and Patriot of the "Old Southwest."* Jefferson, N.C.: McFarland, 1990.

Ramsey, J. G. M. *The Annals of Tennessee to the End of the Eighteenth Century.* Charleston, S.C.: J. Russell, 1853. Reprint, Baltimore, Md.: Clearfield Company, 2003.

Redd, John. "Reminiscences of Western Virginia." *Virginia Magazine of History and Biography* 7 (July 1899): 1–17.

Reeves, William D. *Paths to Distinction: Dr. James White, Governor E. D. White, and Chief Justice Edward Douglass White of Louisiana.* Thibodaux, La.: Friends of the Edward Douglass White Historic Site, 1999.

Register, Alvaretta Kenan, transcr. *State Census of North Carolina, 1784–1787: From the Records in the North Carolina Department of Archives and History.* Baltimore, Md.: Genealogical Publishing Company, 1987.

Reynolds, Louise Wilson. "The Commonwealth of Franklin." *Daughters of the American Revolution Magazine* 52 (January 1918): 23–28.

———. "Memorial to State of Franklin Dedicated." *Daughters of the American Revolution Magazine* 52 (September 1918): 518–519.

Rice, Otis K., and Stephen W. Brown. *West Virginia: A History,* 2nd ed. Lexington: Univ. Press of Kentucky, 1993.

Rogan, James W. *Historical Sketches of Hawkins County: From Its Earliest Settlement to 1891.* Rogersville, Tenn.: Hawkins County Genealogical and Historical Society, 1989.

Roosevelt, Theodore. *The Winning of the West.* New York: Current Literature Publishing Company, 1905.

Ryan, Abram J. *Poems: Patriotic, Religious, Miscellaneous.* New York: P. J. Kennedy and Sons, 1880.

Sayers, Jerry Alan. "Disunited States: The Lost State of Franklin and Frontier

State Movements at the Dawn of the American Republic." Master's thesis, University of Virginia, 2002.

Sheeler, J. Reuben. "Background Factors of East Tennessee." *Journal of Negro History* 29 (April 1944): 166–175.

Shepherd, William R. "Wilkinson and the Beginnings of the Spanish Conspiracy." *American Historical Review* 9 (April 1904): 490–506.

Simonds, Katharine. "Vinland to Franklin: Eight Centuries of the American Dream." *William and Mary Quarterly* 10 (April 1953): 343–347.

Slaughter, Thomas P. *The Whiskey Rebellion: Frontier Epilogue to the American Revolution.* New York: Oxford Univ. Press, 1986.

Spoden, Muriel M. C. *Kingsport Heritage: The Early Years, 1700 to 1900.* Johnson City, Tenn.: Overmountain Press, 1991.

Stevens, William Bacon. *A History of Georgia, From Its First Discovery by Europeans to the Adoption of the Present Constitution in MDCCXCVIII.* 2 vols. Savannah, Ga.: Beehive Press, 1972.

Summers, Lewis Preston. *History of Southwest Virginia, 1746–1786, Washington County, 1777–1870.* Richmond: J. L. Hill Printing Company, 1903. Reprint, Baltimore: Regional Publishing Company, 1979.

Swint, Henry Lee. "Ezekiel Birdseye and the Free State of Frankland." *Tennessee Historical Quarterly* 3 (March 1944): 226–236.

Taylor, Oliver. *Historic Sullivan: A History of Sullivan County, Tennessee, with Brief Biographies of the Makers of History.* Johnson City, Tenn.: Overmountain Press, 1988.

Tennessee Daughters of the American Revolution. *Two Famous Tennesseans: John Sevier and Andrew Jackson.* Nashville: privately published, 1923.

Tennessee Historical Commission. *Tennessee Old and New.* Kingsport, Tenn.: Kingsport Press, 1946.

Thwaites, Rueben Gold, ed. *Documentary History of Dunmore's War, 1774.* Madison: Wisconsin Historical Society, 1905.

Toomey, Glenn A. *Bicentennial Holston: Tennessee's First Baptist Association and Its Affiliated Churches, 1786–1985.* Morristown, Tenn.: privately published, 1985.

Toomey, Michael. "Our Present Confused Situation: The State of Franklin, 1784–1789." In *History of Washington County, Tennessee,* comps. Joyce Cox and W. Eugene Cox. 71–96. Johnson City, Tenn.: The Overmountain Press, 2001.

Trent, Emma Deane Smith. *East Tennessee's Lore of Yesteryear.* Whitesburg, Tenn.: privately published, 1987.

Turner, Francis Marion. *Life of General John Sevier.* New York: Neal Publishing Company, 1910.

Turner, Frederick Jackson. "Western State-Making in the Revolutionary Era." *American Historical Review* 1 (October 1895): 70–87.

Van West, Carroll, ed. *Tennessee History: The Land, the People, and the Culture.* Knoxville: Univ. of Tennessee Press, 1998.

Vickers, Daniel. "Competency and Competition: Economic Culture in Early America." *William and Mary Quarterly* 47 (January 1990): 3–29.

Wardin, Albert W. *Tennessee Baptists: A Comprehensive History, 1779–1999.* Brentwood, Tenn.: Executive Board of the Tennessee Baptist Convention, 1999.

Watauga Association of Genealogists, comps. *History of Washington County, Tennessee, 1988.* Marceline, Mo.: Walsworth Publishing Company, 1988.

Weber, David J. *The Spanish Frontier in North America.* New Haven, Conn.: Yale Univ. Press, 1992.

Weeks, Stephen B. "Tennessee: A Discussion of the Sources of Its Population and the Lines of Immigration." *Tennessee Historical Quarterly* 2 (June 1916): 245–253.

Weise, Robert. *Grasping at Independence: Debt, Male Authority, and Mineral Rights in Appalachian Kentucky, 1850–1915.* Knoxville: Univ. of Tennessee Press, 2001.

Wheeler, John H. *Historical Sketches of North Carolina from 1584 to 1851.* Philadelphia: Lippincott, Grambo, and Co., 1851.

Whitaker, A. P. "The Muscle Shoals Speculation, 1783–1789." *Mississippi Valley Historical Review* 12 (December 1926): 365–386.

———. "The South Carolina Yazoo Company." *Mississippi Valley Historical Review* 16 (December 1929): 383–394.

———. "Spanish Intrigue in the Old Southwest: An Episode, 1788–89." *Mississippi Valley Historical Review* 12 (September 1925): 155–176.

White, Katherine Keogh. *The King's Mountain Men: The Story of the Battle, with Sketches of the American Soldiers Who Took Part.* Baltimore: Genealogical Publishing Company, 1970.

Wicker, Tom. "Turning Point in the Wilderness." *Military History Quarterly: The Quarterly Journal of Military History* 11, no. 1 (autumn 1998): 62–71.

Wilkie, Katharine E. *John Sevier: Son of Tennessee.* New York: Julie Messner, 1958.

Williams, John Alexander. *Appalachia: A History.* Chapel Hill: Univ. of North Carolina Press, 2002.

Williams, Samuel Cole. Address entitled "Greeneville College: Its Founders and Early Friends." Greeneville, Tenn. [June 1940]. McClung Collection, Lawson McGhee Library, Knoxville.

———. *Early Travels in the Tennessee Country, 1540–1800.* Johnson City, Tenn.: Watauga Press, 1928.

———. *History of the Lost State of Franklin.* Johnson City: Watauga Press, 1924. Reprint, Johnson City, Tenn.: Overmountain Press, 1993.

Winsor, Justin. *The Westward Movement: The Colonies and the Republic, West of the Alleghenies, 1763–1798.* New York: Burt Franklin, 1897.

Wood, Gordon S. *The Radicalism of the American Revolution.* New York: Vintage Books, 1991.

Wood, Mayme Parrott. *Hitch Hiking along the Holston River from 1792–1962.* Gatlinburg, Tenn.: publisher unknown, 1964.

Woodward, Grace Steele. *The Cherokees.* Norman: Univ. of Oklahoma Press, 1963.

Index